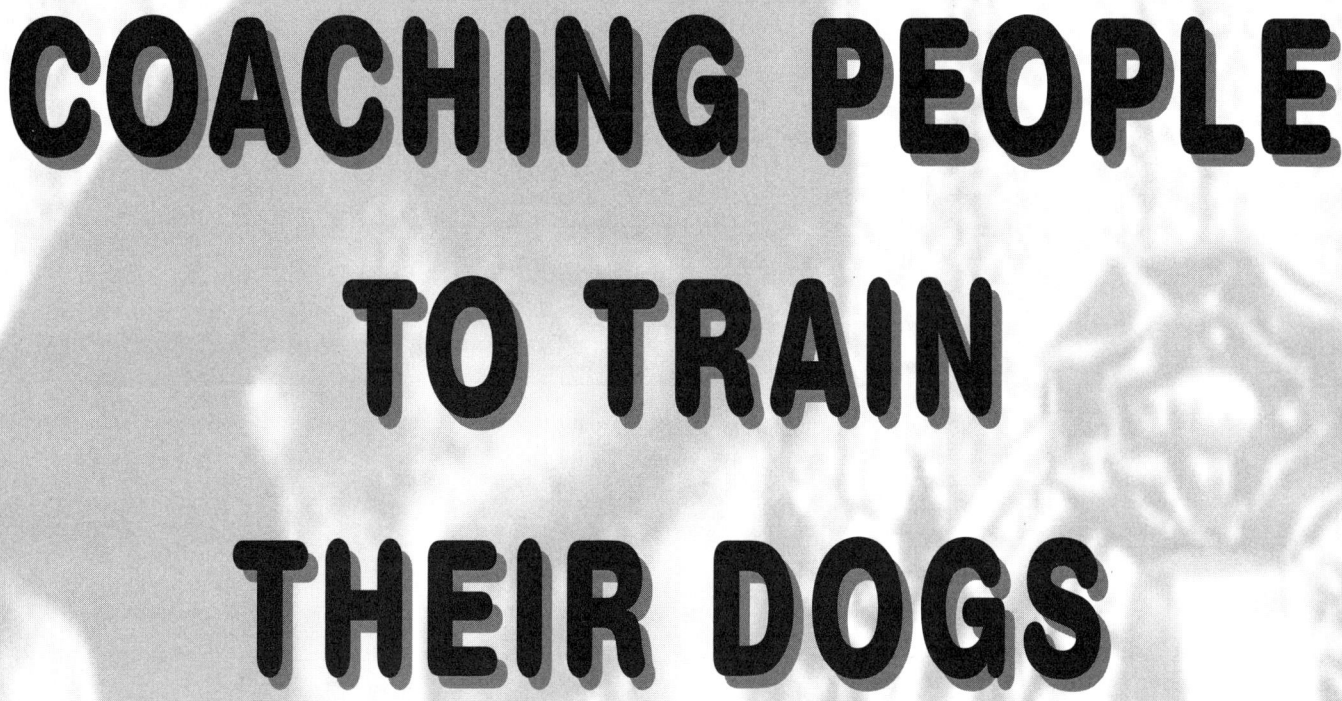

# COACHING PEOPLE TO TRAIN THEIR DOGS

## Terry Ryan

The art in this book was commissioned and is copyrighted by Terry Ryan, Legacy Canine Behavior and Training, Inc. Unless otherwise noted, all illustrations are drawn by Jackie McCowen. Thanks to Carol Byrnes for the drawings on pages 150 through 153, and Elaine Diedrich for the art on page 255. All rights reserved. Limited excerpts of the appendix of this book may only be reproduced with prior written permission.

**Photo Credits:**

Title Page, Bill Ryan; Chapter 1, Bill Ryan; Chapter 2, Tim Dix; Chapter 3, Terry Ryan; Chapter 4, Bill Ryan; Chapter 5, Tim Dix; Chapter 6, Tim Dix; Chapter 7, Bill Ryan; Chapter 8, Jerry Hayes; Appendix, Bill Ryan; Back Cover Photo, Jennifer Ryan Edwards

**Cover Design:** Todd Arbuckle Design

**COACHING PEOPLE TO TRAIN THEIR DOGS**
A Resource Manual for Pet Dog Class Instructors

First Edition Published January 2005
© Terry Ryan, 2005

Second Edition Published January 2008
© Terry Ryan, 2008

ISBN 978-0-9742464-2-0

Printed in the United States of America

# *Dedication*

THIS BOOK IS DEDICATED TO

RUTH E. FOSTER

MENTOR OF MANY CLASS INSTRUCTORS,

PIONEER OF INNOVATIVE TRAINING METHODS AND EQUIPMENT,

A BELIEVER IN THE HUMAN-ANIMAL BOND.

# Acknowledgements

*You can't be an effective instructor if you live in a vacuum. Thanks to my network for the help and support in writing this manual. You know who you are . . . your names are throughout this book.*

*Terry*

*An extra special thanks to Bill Ryan, Legacy's C.E.O. and Jenni Dix, Legacy's Program Coordinator. They patiently listen to all of my wild ideas, and help me make them happen.*

# Contents

Foreword .................................................................................. xv

**CHAPTER 1** **OVERVIEW** ............................................................... 1
    What We've Learned about the Human Animal Bond ........................... 3
    The Human Animal Bond Is an Important Concept for Instructors ............ 3
    The People Pet Partnership ...................................................... 4
    Delta Society—Program Examples and Definitions ............................ 5
    Animal-Assisted Activities, Animal-Assisted Therapy .......................... 5
    Global Interest in the Relationship between People and Animals ............ 6
    The State of Dog Training—Where We've Been, Where We're Going,
        How to Get There ............................................................ 6
    Training Philosophies ........................................................... 7
    Definition of a Successful Training Method .................................... 8
    Cross Overs ..................................................................... 9
    Change .......................................................................... 9
    National Standards for Humane Training .................................... 10
    National Organizations for Trainers and Instructors ......................... 10
    World Developments .......................................................... 10
    *Additional Reading/Resources* ................................................ 11

**CHAPTER 2** **ETHOLOGY** ............................................................. 13
    Comparing Dogs with Humans ................................................ 14
    Our Dog's Ancestors .......................................................... 14
    Early Relationships—Speculations ............................................ 15
    An Example of Purposeful Domestication Using Selective Breeding ........ 16
    Comparing Dogs with Wolves ................................................. 17
    Wolf/Dog Hybrids ............................................................. 18
    Behavior: Why Do Dogs Do That? ............................................ 19
    Phylogenetic Behavior ......................................................... 19
    Fixed Action Patterns ......................................................... 20
    Ontogenetic Behavior ......................................................... 20
    Temperament—Nature and Nurture .......................................... 20
    Instinctive Drift—The Breland Effect ......................................... 21
    The Biology of Learning ...................................................... 22
    Critical Periods ................................................................ 22
    Effects of Puberty, Hormones, Spay, and Neutering on Behavior ........... 23

|   |   |
|---|---|
| Relationship between Brain and Behavior | 24 |
| Engrams | 24 |
| Reticular Activating System | 25 |
| Limbic System and Cerebral Cortex | 25 |
| Opposition Reflex | 26 |
| Social Hierarchy: What It Is, What It Isn't | 26 |
| The Alpha Roll—The Wolf's Point of View | 27 |
| The Language of Dogs | 29 |
| Sound | 29 |
| Smell | 30 |
| Sight | 30 |
| The Dog Are Telling Us What We Need to Know | 31 |
| Critical Zones—Personal Space | 34 |
| Stress Behavior | 35 |
| Fearful Behavior | 37 |
| Reactive, Excitable Behavior | 37 |
| Ambivalence | 38 |
| Displacement Behavior | 38 |
| The Slide of No Return Analogy | 38 |
| Calming Signals | 39 |
| Agonistic Behavior: Conflict Resolution | 41 |
| Avoidance | 41 |
| Appeasement | 41 |
| Submission | 41 |
| Threats of Aggression and Aggression | 42 |
| Offensive Motivation for Threats/Aggression | 43 |
| Defensive Motivation for Threats/Aggression | 43 |
| Conflicted or Mixed Motivation for Threats/Aggression | 44 |
| Triggers, Categories, and Reasons for Threats/Aggression | 44 |
| Predatory Behavior | 46 |
| What's An Instructor To Do? | 46 |
| Biting Is a Natural Option | 47 |
| Classifying Bites | 47 |
| *Chapter 2 Review Questions* | 49 |
| *Additional Reading/Resources* | 50 |

**CHAPTER 3**  **THE SCIENCE OF LEARNING** ........................................ 53

|   |   |
|---|---|
| Learning Theory Basics | 54 |
| Training Is a Science, an Art, and a Mechanical Skill | 54 |
| Classical Conditioning | 55 |
| Classical Conditioning Working Against You | 56 |
| Conditioned Emotional Response | 56 |
| Operant Conditioning | 57 |
| ABC's of Learning | 58 |
| Four Important "Learning" Terms | 58 |

Contents

Application of Behavioral Consequences—An Operant Conditioning Diagram . . . . . . . .59
What Could Be Confusing about *R+*, *P+*, *P–*, and *R–* ? . . . . . . . . . . . . . . . . . . . . . . . . .60
Extinction—Operant and Classical . . . . . . . . . . . . . . . . . . . . . . . . . . . . . . . . . . . . . . . . . .62
Extinction Burst . . . . . . . . . . . . . . . . . . . . . . . . . . . . . . . . . . . . . . . . . . . . . . . . . . . . . . . . .63
Spontaneous Recovery . . . . . . . . . . . . . . . . . . . . . . . . . . . . . . . . . . . . . . . . . . . . . . . . . . .63
Bob Bailey on Extinction . . . . . . . . . . . . . . . . . . . . . . . . . . . . . . . . . . . . . . . . . . . . . . . . . .64
How Extinction Differs from Negative Punishment *P–* . . . . . . . . . . . . . . . . . . . . . . . . . .64
What to Use as a Primary Reinforcer . . . . . . . . . . . . . . . . . . . . . . . . . . . . . . . . . . . . . . . .65
Food as a Reinforcer . . . . . . . . . . . . . . . . . . . . . . . . . . . . . . . . . . . . . . . . . . . . . . . . . . . . .65
Timing of the Reinforcer . . . . . . . . . . . . . . . . . . . . . . . . . . . . . . . . . . . . . . . . . . . . . . . . . .66
Criteria Selection in Reward-based Training . . . . . . . . . . . . . . . . . . . . . . . . . . . . . . . . . .66
Rate of Reinforcement . . . . . . . . . . . . . . . . . . . . . . . . . . . . . . . . . . . . . . . . . . . . . . . . . . .67
Value of Reinforcement . . . . . . . . . . . . . . . . . . . . . . . . . . . . . . . . . . . . . . . . . . . . . . . . . .67
One More Important Point about Reinforcement . . . . . . . . . . . . . . . . . . . . . . . . . . . . . .67
Schedules of Reinforcement . . . . . . . . . . . . . . . . . . . . . . . . . . . . . . . . . . . . . . . . . . . . . . .68
Continuous Schedule of Reinforcement . . . . . . . . . . . . . . . . . . . . . . . . . . . . . . . . . . . . .68
Variable Schedules of Reinforcement . . . . . . . . . . . . . . . . . . . . . . . . . . . . . . . . . . . . . . .68
Secondary Reinforcers: The Clicker and Others . . . . . . . . . . . . . . . . . . . . . . . . . . . . . . .70
More about Clickers and Clicker Training . . . . . . . . . . . . . . . . . . . . . . . . . . . . . . . . . . . .71
A Special Word ("YES!") . . . . . . . . . . . . . . . . . . . . . . . . . . . . . . . . . . . . . . . . . . . . . . . . . .71
Behavior Analysis . . . . . . . . . . . . . . . . . . . . . . . . . . . . . . . . . . . . . . . . . . . . . . . . . . . . . . .72
Getting the Behavior . . . . . . . . . . . . . . . . . . . . . . . . . . . . . . . . . . . . . . . . . . . . . . . . . . . . .73
Methods to Get Behavior . . . . . . . . . . . . . . . . . . . . . . . . . . . . . . . . . . . . . . . . . . . . . . . . .73
Physical Modeling . . . . . . . . . . . . . . . . . . . . . . . . . . . . . . . . . . . . . . . . . . . . . . . . . . . . . . .73
Luring and Fading Lures . . . . . . . . . . . . . . . . . . . . . . . . . . . . . . . . . . . . . . . . . . . . . . . . . .74
Target Training Nose, Paw, and Rear End . . . . . . . . . . . . . . . . . . . . . . . . . . . . . . . . . . . .74
Catching a Behavior . . . . . . . . . . . . . . . . . . . . . . . . . . . . . . . . . . . . . . . . . . . . . . . . . . . . .75
Shaping . . . . . . . . . . . . . . . . . . . . . . . . . . . . . . . . . . . . . . . . . . . . . . . . . . . . . . . . . . . . . . .75
Chaining . . . . . . . . . . . . . . . . . . . . . . . . . . . . . . . . . . . . . . . . . . . . . . . . . . . . . . . . . . . . . .76
Backward Chaining . . . . . . . . . . . . . . . . . . . . . . . . . . . . . . . . . . . . . . . . . . . . . . . . . . . . . .77
Premack Principle . . . . . . . . . . . . . . . . . . . . . . . . . . . . . . . . . . . . . . . . . . . . . . . . . . . . . . .77
Cueing Behaviors . . . . . . . . . . . . . . . . . . . . . . . . . . . . . . . . . . . . . . . . . . . . . . . . . . . . . . .78
When to Introduce a Cue . . . . . . . . . . . . . . . . . . . . . . . . . . . . . . . . . . . . . . . . . . . . . . . . .78
Special Note about Food as a Cue . . . . . . . . . . . . . . . . . . . . . . . . . . . . . . . . . . . . . . . . . .78
Stimuli Packages and Environmental Control . . . . . . . . . . . . . . . . . . . . . . . . . . . . . . . . .79
Cues: Overshadowing, Blocking, and Salience . . . . . . . . . . . . . . . . . . . . . . . . . . . . . . . .79
Stimulus Control: Discrimination, Generalization and Context Learning . . . . . . . . . . . .80
Superstitious Behavior . . . . . . . . . . . . . . . . . . . . . . . . . . . . . . . . . . . . . . . . . . . . . . . . . . .81
*Chapter 3 Review Questions* . . . . . . . . . . . . . . . . . . . . . . . . . . . . . . . . . . . . . . . . . . . . . . . .83
*Additional Reading/Resources* . . . . . . . . . . . . . . . . . . . . . . . . . . . . . . . . . . . . . . . . . . . . . .84

**CHAPTER 4** **HUSBANDRY** . . . . . . . . . . . . . . . . . . . . . . . . . . . . . . . . . . . . . . . . . . . . . . . . . . . . . . . .85
**PART I: Health and Wellness Information** . . . . . . . . . . . . . . . . . . . . . . . . . . . . . . . .87
Puppys . . . . . . . . . . . . . . . . . . . . . . . . . . . . . . . . . . . . . . . . . . . . . . . . . . . . . . . . . . . . . . . .87
Disease Prevention/Wellness . . . . . . . . . . . . . . . . . . . . . . . . . . . . . . . . . . . . . . . . . . . . . .88

Preparing for Emergencies . . . . . . . . . . . . . . . . . . . . . . . . . . . . . . . . . . . . . . . . . .90
Health Maintenance . . . . . . . . . . . . . . . . . . . . . . . . . . . . . . . . . . . . . . . . . . . . . .91
The Role of Spaying and Neutering . . . . . . . . . . . . . . . . . . . . . . . . . . . . . . . . . .91
Factors That Interfere with Learning . . . . . . . . . . . . . . . . . . . . . . . . . . . . . . . .93

**PART II: Training Equipment** . . . . . . . . . . . . . . . . . . . . . . . . . . . . . . . . . . . . .99
What Is Your Equipment Policy? . . . . . . . . . . . . . . . . . . . . . . . . . . . . . . . . . . . .99
Belt-Type Collar . . . . . . . . . . . . . . . . . . . . . . . . . . . . . . . . . . . . . . . . . . . . . . . .100
The Limited-Slip Collar . . . . . . . . . . . . . . . . . . . . . . . . . . . . . . . . . . . . . . . . . .100
Gentle Leader® Head Collar . . . . . . . . . . . . . . . . . . . . . . . . . . . . . . . . . . . . . .101
The Control Harness . . . . . . . . . . . . . . . . . . . . . . . . . . . . . . . . . . . . . . . . . . . .104
Break Away Safety Collar . . . . . . . . . . . . . . . . . . . . . . . . . . . . . . . . . . . . . . . .104
Choke Chain Collar (Slip Collar) . . . . . . . . . . . . . . . . . . . . . . . . . . . . . . . . . . .105
Pinch Collars . . . . . . . . . . . . . . . . . . . . . . . . . . . . . . . . . . . . . . . . . . . . . . . . . .105
Body Harness . . . . . . . . . . . . . . . . . . . . . . . . . . . . . . . . . . . . . . . . . . . . . . . . .105
Leashes . . . . . . . . . . . . . . . . . . . . . . . . . . . . . . . . . . . . . . . . . . . . . . . . . . . . . .105
Training Leash . . . . . . . . . . . . . . . . . . . . . . . . . . . . . . . . . . . . . . . . . . . . . . . .106
Retractable Leash . . . . . . . . . . . . . . . . . . . . . . . . . . . . . . . . . . . . . . . . . . . . . .106
Long Line . . . . . . . . . . . . . . . . . . . . . . . . . . . . . . . . . . . . . . . . . . . . . . . . . . . .106
Selecting Training Rewards . . . . . . . . . . . . . . . . . . . . . . . . . . . . . . . . . . . . . . .106
Remote or Hand-Held Electronic Training Devices . . . . . . . . . . . . . . . . . . . . .107
Citronella Release Devices for Barking . . . . . . . . . . . . . . . . . . . . . . . . . . . . . .107
Crates . . . . . . . . . . . . . . . . . . . . . . . . . . . . . . . . . . . . . . . . . . . . . . . . . . . . . . .107
A Word about Electronic Containment Systems . . . . . . . . . . . . . . . . . . . . . . .108
*Chapter 4 Review Questions* . . . . . . . . . . . . . . . . . . . . . . . . . . . . . . . . . . . . . .109
*Additional Reading/Resources* . . . . . . . . . . . . . . . . . . . . . . . . . . . . . . . . . . . . .110

**CHAPTER 5** **THE BUSINESS** . . . . . . . . . . . . . . . . . . . . . . . . . . . . . . . . . . . . . . . . . . . . .111
Setting Up Your Business . . . . . . . . . . . . . . . . . . . . . . . . . . . . . . . . . . . . . . . .112
Legal Matters in General . . . . . . . . . . . . . . . . . . . . . . . . . . . . . . . . . . . . . . . . .114
The Legalities of Handling Food . . . . . . . . . . . . . . . . . . . . . . . . . . . . . . . . . . .114
Ethics and Professional Limitations . . . . . . . . . . . . . . . . . . . . . . . . . . . . . . . . .115
Insurance . . . . . . . . . . . . . . . . . . . . . . . . . . . . . . . . . . . . . . . . . . . . . . . . . . . . .115
Ongoing Money Matters . . . . . . . . . . . . . . . . . . . . . . . . . . . . . . . . . . . . . . . . .116
Setting a Fee Structure . . . . . . . . . . . . . . . . . . . . . . . . . . . . . . . . . . . . . . . . . .116
Payment . . . . . . . . . . . . . . . . . . . . . . . . . . . . . . . . . . . . . . . . . . . . . . . . . . . . .116
Refunds . . . . . . . . . . . . . . . . . . . . . . . . . . . . . . . . . . . . . . . . . . . . . . . . . . . . . .117
Compensation for Your Staff . . . . . . . . . . . . . . . . . . . . . . . . . . . . . . . . . . . . . .117
Is It a Business Expense? . . . . . . . . . . . . . . . . . . . . . . . . . . . . . . . . . . . . . . . . .227
General Safety . . . . . . . . . . . . . . . . . . . . . . . . . . . . . . . . . . . . . . . . . . . . . . . . .117
Good Samaritan Statute . . . . . . . . . . . . . . . . . . . . . . . . . . . . . . . . . . . . . . . . .118
Advertising . . . . . . . . . . . . . . . . . . . . . . . . . . . . . . . . . . . . . . . . . . . . . . . . . . .188
Registration Procedures . . . . . . . . . . . . . . . . . . . . . . . . . . . . . . . . . . . . . . . . .120
Appropriate First Contact Information . . . . . . . . . . . . . . . . . . . . . . . . . . . . . .120
The Training Site . . . . . . . . . . . . . . . . . . . . . . . . . . . . . . . . . . . . . . . . . . . . . . .121

 Contents

Site Selection ................................................................. 121
Size: Amount of Space Per Dog ............................................... 122
Restrooms .................................................................... 122
Water ........................................................................ 122
Trash Containers ............................................................. 123
Signs ........................................................................ 123
What's Under Foot? ........................................................... 123
Acoustics .................................................................... 124
Public Address System (PA) ................................................... 124
Music ........................................................................ 124
Furnishing for the Training Area ............................................. 124
Supplies for the Training Site ............................................... 125
Where Will Owners Put "Stuff"? ............................................... 126
Where Will You Put Your "Stuff"? ............................................. 126
Records ...................................................................... 127
Conclusion ................................................................... 127
*Additional Reading/Resources* ............................................... 127

**CHAPTER 6** **PEOPLE SKILLS** ...............................................129
Profile of a Great Instructor ................................................ 130
Some Attributes of a Good Instructor ......................................... 130
Learning Styles .............................................................. 133
Tell Me and I'll Forget ...................................................... 134
Roadblocks to Verbal Communication ........................................... 135
It's Not What You Say, It's What They Hear ................................... 136
The Telephone Game ........................................................... 137
Cross-checks for Comprehension—Was Your Message Received Properly? .......... 138
Make the Exercise Valuable to the Student .................................... 139
Common Verbal Communication Problems in Class ................................ 139
This Is New Stuff—From Our Students' Point of View ........................... 140
The LeftBrain/Right Brain Paradigm ........................................... 140
Turning Negative Instructions Into Positive Instructions ..................... 143
Improving Your Listening Skills .............................................. 143
Teacher Effectiveness Training ............................................... 143
Turning "You" Message into "I" Messages ...................................... 145
Dealing with Emotional Students .............................................. 146
The Talkers in Class ......................................................... 146
Late Arrivals ................................................................ 147
Pet Loss ..................................................................... 147
What You Can Do to Help Your Client .......................................... 148
Human Personality Differences ................................................ 149
Edward De Bono's Six Thinking Hats™ Method for Dog People .................... 150
The White Hat Style of Thinking .............................................. 150
The Red Hat Style of Thinking ................................................ 151
The Black Hat Style of Thinking .............................................. 151

The Yellow Hat Style of Thinking . . . . . . . . . . . . . . . . . . . . . . . . . . . . . . . . . . . . . . .152
The Green Hat Style of Thinking . . . . . . . . . . . . . . . . . . . . . . . . . . . . . . . . . . . . . . .152
The Blue Hat Style of Thinking . . . . . . . . . . . . . . . . . . . . . . . . . . . . . . . . . . . . . . . .153
Demonstrations and Other Visual Aids . . . . . . . . . . . . . . . . . . . . . . . . . . . . . . . . . .154
Demonstrations with Dogs . . . . . . . . . . . . . . . . . . . . . . . . . . . . . . . . . . . . . . . . . . . .154
Demonstrations with the Head Instructor's Dog . . . . . . . . . . . . . . . . . . . . . . . . . . .154
Demonstrations with a Dog from Class . . . . . . . . . . . . . . . . . . . . . . . . . . . . . . . . . .155
Demonstrations with an Assistant's Dog . . . . . . . . . . . . . . . . . . . . . . . . . . . . . . . . .155
Puppets and Toys . . . . . . . . . . . . . . . . . . . . . . . . . . . . . . . . . . . . . . . . . . . . . . . . . . .156
More Demonstrations—Without Dogs . . . . . . . . . . . . . . . . . . . . . . . . . . . . . . . . . .156
Demo Dog—Your Hand . . . . . . . . . . . . . . . . . . . . . . . . . . . . . . . . . . . . . . . . . . . . .156
Control the Head, Control the Dog—The 2″ × 4″ Dog . . . . . . . . . . . . . . . . . . . . .156
Control the Head, Control the Dog—What Moves First? . . . . . . . . . . . . . . . . . . .157
Control the Head, Control the Dog—A Client on a Chair as a Dog . . . . . . . . . . . .157
Control the Head, Control the Dog—Client on Hands and Knees as a Dog . . . . . .157
Control the Head, Control the Dog—All Owners Stand . . . . . . . . . . . . . . . . . . . .157
Opposition Reflex . . . . . . . . . . . . . . . . . . . . . . . . . . . . . . . . . . . . . . . . . . . . . . . . . .158
Test and Punish versus Lure and Reward . . . . . . . . . . . . . . . . . . . . . . . . . . . . . . . .158
The Training Game—What This Interactive Exercise Can Teach Students . . . . . . .159
Other Training Aids . . . . . . . . . . . . . . . . . . . . . . . . . . . . . . . . . . . . . . . . . . . . . . . .180
Video . . . . . . . . . . . . . . . . . . . . . . . . . . . . . . . . . . . . . . . . . . . . . . . . . . . . . . . . . . .180
Slides, PowerPoint®, and Overhead Projector (OHP) . . . . . . . . . . . . . . . . . . . . . . .161
Motivational Messages . . . . . . . . . . . . . . . . . . . . . . . . . . . . . . . . . . . . . . . . . . . . . .161
Spontaneous White Board Visuals . . . . . . . . . . . . . . . . . . . . . . . . . . . . . . . . . . . . .161
Bulletin Boards . . . . . . . . . . . . . . . . . . . . . . . . . . . . . . . . . . . . . . . . . . . . . . . . . . . .162
Giant Post-Its® or Plastic Write/Erase Sheets . . . . . . . . . . . . . . . . . . . . . . . . . . . . .162
Handouts . . . . . . . . . . . . . . . . . . . . . . . . . . . . . . . . . . . . . . . . . . . . . . . . . . . . . . . .162
Involve Me and I'll Understand . . . . . . . . . . . . . . . . . . . . . . . . . . . . . . . . . . . . . . .163
Spouses and Friends . . . . . . . . . . . . . . . . . . . . . . . . . . . . . . . . . . . . . . . . . . . . . . . .164
The Children in the Family . . . . . . . . . . . . . . . . . . . . . . . . . . . . . . . . . . . . . . . . . .164
Handlers with Disabilities . . . . . . . . . . . . . . . . . . . . . . . . . . . . . . . . . . . . . . . . . . .166
Using Music as an Aid to Communication . . . . . . . . . . . . . . . . . . . . . . . . . . . . . .168
Remembering Names . . . . . . . . . . . . . . . . . . . . . . . . . . . . . . . . . . . . . . . . . . . . . . .169
Impartiality . . . . . . . . . . . . . . . . . . . . . . . . . . . . . . . . . . . . . . . . . . . . . . . . . . . . . .169
Absent Students . . . . . . . . . . . . . . . . . . . . . . . . . . . . . . . . . . . . . . . . . . . . . . . . . . .170
Evaluations . . . . . . . . . . . . . . . . . . . . . . . . . . . . . . . . . . . . . . . . . . . . . . . . . . . . . . .171
Other Ways to Measure Your Effectiveness . . . . . . . . . . . . . . . . . . . . . . . . . . . . . . .171
Private Lesson—Special Considerations . . . . . . . . . . . . . . . . . . . . . . . . . . . . . . . . .172
Evolution of Change . . . . . . . . . . . . . . . . . . . . . . . . . . . . . . . . . . . . . . . . . . . . . . .173
Using the Chinese Wisdom Puzzle to Practice Teaching Skills . . . . . . . . . . . . . . . .174
The Basic Exercise . . . . . . . . . . . . . . . . . . . . . . . . . . . . . . . . . . . . . . . . . . . . . . . . .175
Cross-Training for Training Trainers! . . . . . . . . . . . . . . . . . . . . . . . . . . . . . . . . . . .177
*Chapter 6 Review Questions* . . . . . . . . . . . . . . . . . . . . . . . . . . . . . . . . . . . . . . . . .179
*Additional Reading/Resources* . . . . . . . . . . . . . . . . . . . . . . . . . . . . . . . . . . . . . . . .180

## CHAPTER 7  CLASS ORGANIZATION ....................................................181

Definitions of a Good Training Class ..........................................................182
The Site and Equipment for Your Class ......................................................183
The People in Class ....................................................................................183
The Dogs in Class ......................................................................................183
Dogs That Act Out Offensively or Defensively ............................................184
Disabled Dogs ............................................................................................184
Deaf or Blind Dogs ....................................................................................185
Females in Estrus ......................................................................................186
Two Handlers and Two Dogs from the Same Household ..........................187
Preventing Dog Fights ..............................................................................187
Associate Instructors for Your Classes ......................................................188
Nurturing New Class Instructors ..............................................................188
Class Associate To Do List ........................................................................189
Jobs for Class Helpers ..............................................................................190
Perks for Associates ..................................................................................190
Orientation ................................................................................................191
Orientation Topics ....................................................................................192
The Orientation Notebook ........................................................................193
Class Time Scheduling—The Entire Course ..............................................193
Considerations When Choosing Training Methods ..................................195
Owner Aptitude ........................................................................................195
Owner Acceptance ....................................................................................195
The Impact on the Dog ............................................................................195
Ethical, Legal, Successful, Safe, and Humane ............................................195
Attitude of the Instructor ..........................................................................195
Entry Level Classes ....................................................................................196
Puppy Classes—In General ......................................................................196
Puppy HeadStart—For Very Young Puppies ............................................197
KinderPuppy Class—For Young Puppies ..................................................198
Pet Dog Manners—Four Months and Older ............................................198
Instructional Format for the Individual Exercises ......................................199
P.R.E.D.I.C.T.O.R. ....................................................................................200
Plan ............................................................................................................200
Revise ........................................................................................................200
Explain ......................................................................................................200
Demonstrate ..............................................................................................200
Instruct ......................................................................................................201
Coach ........................................................................................................201
Train ..........................................................................................................201
Observe ......................................................................................................201
Review ......................................................................................................202
Traffic Control Strategies for Stationary Exercises ....................................202
Individual or Group Exercises in Class? ....................................................202

Positioning the Dogs and People within the Training Area . . . . . . . . . . . . . . . . . .202
Traffic Control Patterns for Moving Exercises . . . . . . . . . . . . . . . . . . . . . . . . . . .203
Instructional Format for Homework Assignments . . . . . . . . . . . . . . . . . . . . . . . .205
Continuing Education Classes . . . . . . . . . . . . . . . . . . . . . . . . . . . . . . . . . . . . . . .206
Pet Dog Manners II . . . . . . . . . . . . . . . . . . . . . . . . . . . . . . . . . . . . . . . . . . . . . . .206
Fun and Games Class 101 . . . . . . . . . . . . . . . . . . . . . . . . . . . . . . . . . . . . . . . . . .206
Fun and Games Class 102 . . . . . . . . . . . . . . . . . . . . . . . . . . . . . . . . . . . . . . . . . .206
Drama Dogs . . . . . . . . . . . . . . . . . . . . . . . . . . . . . . . . . . . . . . . . . . . . . . . . . . . . .206
Run, Jump, and Fetch Classes . . . . . . . . . . . . . . . . . . . . . . . . . . . . . . . . . . . . . . .206
Click-a-Trick Classes . . . . . . . . . . . . . . . . . . . . . . . . . . . . . . . . . . . . . . . . . . . . . .207
Kids and Canines . . . . . . . . . . . . . . . . . . . . . . . . . . . . . . . . . . . . . . . . . . . . . . . .207
Dancing with Dogs . . . . . . . . . . . . . . . . . . . . . . . . . . . . . . . . . . . . . . . . . . . . . . .207
Let's Get Ready To . . . Rally . . . . . . . . . . . . . . . . . . . . . . . . . . . . . . . . . . . . . . . .207
Demonstration Team . . . . . . . . . . . . . . . . . . . . . . . . . . . . . . . . . . . . . . . . . . . . .207
Animal-Assisted Activity Classes . . . . . . . . . . . . . . . . . . . . . . . . . . . . . . . . . . . . .208
Agility Foundation Class . . . . . . . . . . . . . . . . . . . . . . . . . . . . . . . . . . . . . . . . . . .208
Obedience Competition . . . . . . . . . . . . . . . . . . . . . . . . . . . . . . . . . . . . . . . . . . .208
Supervised Floor Time . . . . . . . . . . . . . . . . . . . . . . . . . . . . . . . . . . . . . . . . . . . .208
Game Night . . . . . . . . . . . . . . . . . . . . . . . . . . . . . . . . . . . . . . . . . . . . . . . . . . . . .208
The Nose Knows Class . . . . . . . . . . . . . . . . . . . . . . . . . . . . . . . . . . . . . . . . . . . .209
Feisty Fidos . . . . . . . . . . . . . . . . . . . . . . . . . . . . . . . . . . . . . . . . . . . . . . . . . . . . .209
Good Citizen Prep Class . . . . . . . . . . . . . . . . . . . . . . . . . . . . . . . . . . . . . . . . . . .209
Local or Regional Good Dog Organizations Class . . . . . . . . . . . . . . . . . . . . . . . .209
One-Skill, One-Time Seminars . . . . . . . . . . . . . . . . . . . . . . . . . . . . . . . . . . . . . .209
Leadership Headstart . . . . . . . . . . . . . . . . . . . . . . . . . . . . . . . . . . . . . . . . . . . . .210
Dog Selection . . . . . . . . . . . . . . . . . . . . . . . . . . . . . . . . . . . . . . . . . . . . . . . . . . .210
The Toolbox for Remodeling Your Problem Dog . . . . . . . . . . . . . . . . . . . . . . . .210
The Bark Stops Here . . . . . . . . . . . . . . . . . . . . . . . . . . . . . . . . . . . . . . . . . . . . . .210
Stress Reduction and the Latchkey Dog . . . . . . . . . . . . . . . . . . . . . . . . . . . . . . .210
Come When Called . . . . . . . . . . . . . . . . . . . . . . . . . . . . . . . . . . . . . . . . . . . . . .210
Special Events . . . . . . . . . . . . . . . . . . . . . . . . . . . . . . . . . . . . . . . . . . . . . . . . . . .211
Options for the Last Class . . . . . . . . . . . . . . . . . . . . . . . . . . . . . . . . . . . . . . . . . .213
*Chapter 7 Review Questions* . . . . . . . . . . . . . . . . . . . . . . . . . . . . . . . . . . . . . . . .215
*Additional Reading/Resources* . . . . . . . . . . . . . . . . . . . . . . . . . . . . . . . . . . . . . .216

## CHAPTER 8  A TOOLBOX FOR REMODELING PROBLEM BEHAVIOR . . . . . . . . . . .217
Remodeling Problem Behavior . . . . . . . . . . . . . . . . . . . . . . . . . . . . . . . . . . . . . .218
"First Do No Harm" . . . . . . . . . . . . . . . . . . . . . . . . . . . . . . . . . . . . . . . . . . . . . .218
The Law of Parsimony . . . . . . . . . . . . . . . . . . . . . . . . . . . . . . . . . . . . . . . . . . . .218
Thinking Outside of the Box . . . . . . . . . . . . . . . . . . . . . . . . . . . . . . . . . . . . . . .219
Document the Problem—What's Really Going On? . . . . . . . . . . . . . . . . . . . . . .219
Build a House—A Metaphor for Instructional Formatting . . . . . . . . . . . . . . . . .221
Decide Upon Clear Goals—What Do You Really Want? . . . . . . . . . . . . . . . . . . .222

Delta Society's Flowchart for Selecting Techniques ............................ 223
The Language of Punishment .................................................... 224
The Four-Piece Dog Training Puzzle .............................................. 225
Legacy's "Toolbox" Concept for Changing Behavior ............................... 225
H.E.L.M. ....................................................................... 225
Health ......................................................................... 226
Environment .................................................................... 226
Leadership ..................................................................... 226
Management ..................................................................... 226
Tools For Changing Unwanted Behavior ........................................... 227
Y  Yield ....................................................................... 227
E  Eliminate the Trigger ....................................................... 228
S  Systematic Desensitization .................................................. 228
T  Take Away the Reward ........................................................ 229
R  Reward an Incompatible Behavior ............................................. 230
A  Acclimate ................................................................... 231
I  Improve the Association ..................................................... 231
N  Not Much Nasty Stuff ........................................................ 232
*Chapter 8 Review Questions* ................................................... 233
*Additional Reading/Resources* ................................................. 234
*Answers to Lateral Thinking Questions on Page 219* ............................ 234

# APPENDIX .................................................................... 235

# INDEX ....................................................................... 395

*About the Author* ............................................................. 405

# Foreword

There are many ways of measuring the impact of an individual on a given field of human endeavor. Academicians might use the number of publications; teachers might use the number of classes taught; dog trainers might use the number of dogs trained; historians might use the length or durability of career; book publishers might use readership or the number of copies sold. Any way one measures Terry Ryan, we see that she has made a major and lasting impact in pet dog training and in fostering the human-animal bond. An accomplished trainer, author, teacher, and a promoter of good-feeling animal relationships, Terry has been touching the lives of dog trainers and the public for decades.

Terry's impact on my life was more recent. The words of Terry and Karen Pryor prompted my wife Marian and me to "un-retire" from the world of trainer teaching. One of our earliest modern-day teaching escapades was at a Terry Ryan Training Camp in Wooster, Ohio in the mid 1990s. Terry had been very persuasive in recruiting us, and Marian and I found ourselves in a large barn, facing some 120 students and a flock of very strange looking chickens, some no larger than small pigeons. Together, the three of us pulled off the training. Such were the people skills and animal skills of Terry Ryan.

There is much I do not know about the dog training business, or the challenges of teaching the pet dog owner, so I cannot speak knowledgably about Terry's expertise in these areas. However, as a teacher with some experience, I can make a first-person observation about Terry: she understands the needs of both teachers and students. Terry has trained chickens in my operant conditioning class. It takes a special person to shed the honored mantle of Sensei, or Teacher, which Terry usually wears and to assume the subordinate role of student, duty bound to follow the path illuminated by another. I believe that at least part of Terry's skills as a teacher and "facilitator of learning" is due to her understanding of, and respect for, the student.

A student is more than just a client or customer. A teacher without students has no influence. Students deserve a teacher's respect and concern. A teacher shows respect and concern for the student by being a good teacher who is knowledgeable, skilled, sensitive, and well-prepared. I believe that the information in this book will help teachers to be good teachers, as well as helping already good teachers become great ones.

Bob Bailey
Animal Behavior Enterprises

# CHAPTER 1

# OVERVIEW

“ *Brothers and Sisters, I bid you beware of giving your heart to a dog to tear.* ”

—Rudyard Kipling

My goal for this book is to increase the depth and breadth of knowledge about dogs and people so we can better serve them in a classroom-learning environment.

Some of the text here originated as handouts and booklets for my various dog training and instructor workshops and camps. The appendix in this book contains copies of the materials currently used by Legacy for pet dog classes conducted at our training center in Washington State. Some of the information in this book is also in a book I wrote for the Japanese Animal Hospital Association. Published in the Japanese language in 1995 and revised in 2002, it is the textbook for their national dog training class instructors' program.

This document addresses the five main categories of knowledge deemed important for all good trainers as outlined first by The Association of Pet Dog Trainers and now used by the Certification Council for Pet Dog Trainers: Instructional Skills, Animal Husbandry, Ethology, Learning Theory, and Equipment.

*Coaching People to Train Their Dogs* will, as much as possible, present information based on data. You will find information referenced from ethologists, biologists, behavioral psychologists, veterinarians, and professionals from other fields. Unfortunately, there are many gaps in the knowledge about dog behavior and learning. Even the experts I hold in highest regard don't agree with each other. A lot of this book contains anecdotal information—the theories and opinions of dog trainers and instructors I respect from all over the world and from my 35 years' experience coaching people to train their dogs.

—Terry Ryan

# WHAT WE'VE LEARNED ABOUT THE HUMAN-ANIMAL BOND

Dogs are good for us. Part of our job as training class instructors is to make life with people good for both the dogs and people. Most of us can give examples from our personal experience to illustrate the benefits of living with a dog. Dogs' acceptance of their people is non-judgmental, forgiving, and uncomplicated by the psychological games people often play. Here are some examples:

Studies have shown that when dogs visit a care facility, such as a nursing home or hospital, there is more laughter and interaction among residents and patients than during any other therapy or entertainment time. Mental stimulation occurs because of increased communication with other people and recalled memories. In situations that are depressing or institutional, the presence of animals serves to brighten the atmosphere and may help to decrease people's feelings of isolation and alienation. Feelings of loneliness and helplessness have also been shown to decrease. Animals can facilitate the rapport between people by opening a channel of emotionally safe communication. Research has shown that a dependent animal can create a will to live, or a reason to get up in the morning in otherwise despondent people. Programs involving dogs with children are becoming more common. Dogs are aiding child psychiatric counselors and are serving as facilitators for elementary school reading programs. Recent information suggests that if a child lives in a home in which a pet is considered a member of the family, that child is more empathetic than those living in homes without pets. As children get older, their ability to empathize with animals will carry over into their experiences with people. Research-based information on the effects of human-animal interactions is available from the national and international resources listed at the end of this chapter.

# THE HUMAN-ANIMAL BOND IS AN IMPORTANT CONCEPT FOR INSTRUCTORS

Why is the first chapter of a dog training class instructor's book addressing the human-animal bond? The physical and mental well-being of animals and their people are intertwined. Class instructors are in a position to help this special relationship. We can enhance (sometimes repair!) the bond between dogs and their people and improve life for both. Work in the human-animal bond was an important part of my professional development.

# The People-Pet Partnership

My formal involvement in the human-animal bond began in 1974. The People-Pet Partnership (PPP) was a newly formed public-service activity of the College of Veterinary Medicine at Washington State University (WSU CVM). Dr. Leo K. Bustad, then Dean of WSU CVM, and Linda Hines, a key member of his staff, founded the PPP. The program promoted the human-animal bond and animal-assisted therapy and activities. The People-Pet Partnership trained volunteers and their animals to participate in a variety of innovative programs and served as an early example for others. Dr. Bustad, a pioneer in the study of the human-animal bond, traveled the world to promote the relationship between animals and humans. Early organization of the Delta Society, an international human-animal bond resource organization, was taking place at roughly the same time. Dr. Bustad was the first president of Delta. Linda Hines moved on to become the executive director of Delta. I worked as Dr. Bustad's Program Coordinator for the People-Pet Partnership for the next 13 years. Leo Bustad died in 1998 at the age of 78. We are still reaping the benefits of his work to promote the human-animal bond.

Some of the original PPP programs included:

- **The Pet Education Partnership Program (PEP)** taught responsible pet ownership and stewardship of the environment. We developed an elementary school curriculum published as *Learning and Living Together: Building the Human-Animal Bond.* One of the more popular lessons, "Prevent a Bite," is still being taught today.

- **The Companion Animal Partnership Program (CAP)** provided animal-assisted therapy and activities at health care facilities, hospitals, and mental health centers. "Guidelines, Animals in Nursing Homes" was one of the first documents written on the topic of starting and supervising a visiting pet program. Boof, a dog we placed as a companion for an individual in a care facility, was one of the world's first "prescription pets."

- **The Partnership in Equine Therapy and Education (PETE)** provided recreational and therapeutic horseback riding to people with emotional, mental, and physical disabilities. It was the first therapeutic horseback-riding program based at a university.

- **The Pet Loss Partnership (PLP)** provided support to people living with chronically or terminally ill pets, individuals making decisions about euthanasia, or individuals whose pets had died. This outreach program was administered by a psychologist working part time in the PPP office.

- **The Prison Pet Partnership (PPP)** was established in 1976 at the Washington State Corrections Center for Women, a maximum-security facility. PPP worked with Sister Pauline Quinn to begin the program. Dogs acquired from shelters lived at the prison. They were good rehabilitation for the inmates. In turn the dogs learned skills to make them more adoptable. Some dogs were selected and trained as aids for people with disabilities.

# DELTA SOCIETY—PROGRAM EXAMPLES AND DEFINITIONS

There are numerous human-animal bond programs throughout the United States and the world. The one I am most familiar with is the Delta Society. The Delta Foundation was established in 1977 in Portland, Oregon, under the leadership of Michael McCulloch, Leo Bustad, and Linda Hines. It became the Delta Society in 1981, and its first full-time office opened in 1983. Delta's founders wanted to understand the quality and impact of the relationship between pet owners, pets, and caregivers, hence the "delta" name which is based on this triangle. Delta's early years focused on funding the first credible research on why animals are important to the general population and, specifically, how they affect health and well-being.

Once the importance of animals was established from this research, Delta began to look at how animals can change the lives of people who are ill and disabled. In the late 1980s, Delta began creating educational materials to apply the scientific information to everyday life. Membership expanded to pet owners and a broader general public. I had the privilege of working on some of Delta's first materials and participating in some of their early programs.

## *Animal-Assisted Activities (AAA)*

Animal-Assisted Activities provides opportunities for motivational, educational, recreational, and/or therapeutic activities that enhance quality of life. Trained professionals and/or volunteers, with animals that meet specific criteria, deliver AAA in a variety of environments. Typical animal-assisted activities are casual "meet and greet" visits or dogs performing for entertainment. AAA are valuable programs that brighten the day of everyone concerned.

## *Animal-Assisted Therapy (AAT)*

Animal-Assisted Therapy (AAT) is a more formal process than AAA. Animal-Assisted Therapy is a goal-directed intervention. An animal and handler, meeting specific criteria, are an integral part of the treatment process. AAT is goal directed, planned and supervised by human health care professionals. Progress is measured and documented in the patient's record.

Although animal-assisted activities (AAA) and animal-assisted therapy (AAT) are the commonly preferred terms, and the most widely published, some people refer to similar programs as "pet-facilitated therapy," "animal-facilitated therapy," or "pet therapy." Well-meaning individuals often start AAA programs. As dog training instructors, we are a natural for assuming the leadership role in a visiting pet program. We need to be advocates for everyone concerned. As beneficial as AAA and AAT can be, they are not always appropriate for every situation. Not every loving, responsible pet owner is capable of becoming a competent handler for a visiting program. Not every well-trained dog is temperamentally suited for this situation either. These limitations may not be apparent until an accident happens and harm has been done. The Delta Society and other concerned organizations provide education and certification for those involved with animal visitation.

# GLOBAL INTEREST IN THE RELATIONSHIP BETWEEN PEOPLE AND ANIMALS

The United States is not the only, or even the first, country to become interested in the human-animal bond. People of like-minds around the world now come together under the leadership of The International Association of Human-Animal Interaction Organizations (IAHAIO). IAHAIO was founded in 1990 to gather together national associations and related organizations interested in advancing the understanding and appreciation of the link between animals and humans. A conference is held every three years. IAHAIO's mission is to promote research, education, and sharing of information about human-animal interaction and the unique role that animals play in human well-being and quality of life. IAHAIO's goal is to educate policy makers at local, national, and international levels about the benefits of human-animal interaction. Currently, there are 18 countries associated with IAHAIO with the headquarters located in Washington State.

# THE STATE OF DOG TRAINING: WHERE WE'VE BEEN, WHERE WE'RE GOING, AND HOW TO GET THERE

I've been a dog trainer and class instructor since the 1960s. Wow! That's a long time! My methods have changed over the years and continue to change. I have been influenced by what other dog trainers do to get good results. I have become interested in relevant scientific research and data. I am attracted to information shared by the best experts in canine behavior, the dogs themselves. My classes are designed with the needs of the community in mind. The classes I'm teaching now in Sequim, Washington, a small town between the lush Olympic National Park and the Pacific Ocean, are vastly different from those I taught 30 years ago in the large desert city of Albuquerque, New Mexico. They are different from those I taught 10 years ago in a college town where the average age of the client was 19. Many of Legacy's current hometown students are retirees with a different set of goals! What is important in pet dog classes? **"It depends."** My best reference tool when working on class curriculum is the stack of profiles my students have filled out over the years. They reflect the community's needs. For example, I don't call my classes "obedience classes" anymore. The word *obedience* seems to imply "do it or else." Judging by more than 30 years worth of profiles from my clients, that's not what the typical community needs. And it's not what we at Legacy want to teach. On the other hand, the word *behavior* implies the need to understand dogs, who they are, and how they process information. And the word *training* alludes to showing the dog the correct behavior and then rewarding the dog for it. Our classes are behavior and training classes.

Dog trainers have an impact on more than just one dog or one dog's family and neighbors. We have an impact on society as a whole. One example is the recent interest in and startling evidence of the cycle of violence. Children learn from adult role models and the environment in which they live. A home of violence, abuse, or neglect produces children who may exhibit these same behaviors as children and as adults. (*The Cruelty to Animals and Interpersonal Violence*, 1998, Lockwood/Ascione). A child who observes family dog training lessons taught by reward-based methods might apply this viewpoint to other relationships.

# TRAINING PHILOSOPHIES

How do we train dogs? Trainers have embraced many different philosophies and techniques over the centuries.

> **William Dobson, 1817, England.**
>
> On teaching a puppy to lie down:
>
> *". . . Show him the whip, in order that he may perceive and acknowledge you as master of dominance."*—**Psychological intimidation**

> **Konrad Most, 1906, Germany.**
>
> On teaching a dog to retrieve:
>
> *"With a commanding 'FETCH IT' and a swift thrust forward of the collar with the left hand, the dog's jaws are very quickly brought into snapping range of the dumbbell and the spikes cause pain. The dog tries to defend itself by biting and the trainer then presses the dog's open jaws against the dumbbell."*—**Pain**

> **Robert Bailey and Marian Breland-Bailey, 2000, USA**
>
> On all species training:
>
> *"In slightly over 100 years of combined training experience, with over 10,000 animals from over 145 species, we have used punishment about 12 times. Reward the good behavior."*—**Positive reinforcement**

The quotes above are from three different periods in time, three different parts of the world, and reflect three different attitudes about training: domination, pain, and reward. As in the past, the future will bring many choices to dog trainers. We need to evaluate our options. Consider carefully what is being said when you read a book or attend a workshop. Anyone can write a book. Anyone can give advice. It's up to you to decide for yourself what is good for you and your clients. Dog trainers and instructors need to be versatile and creative. We need to be critical thinkers, asking why? Who said so? Where is the data? People, dogs, and their environment are all different. As a society, we are changing rapidly. We need to be lateral thinkers, always adapting and thinking of a better way. A lateral thinker is willing to go "outside the box" and will look for a different way, and will not be influenced by peer pressure or fads. A lateral thinker will not set limitations when no limitations are needed. We need to develop new ideas for training our dogs in our modern (sometimes unnatural for the dog) conditions.

Dogs already know most of the good behaviors we want to teach them. They know how to sit, lie down, and be quiet. Our task is to communicate a few rules that will govern these activities. There is more than one way to train a dog. This book leans heavily toward reward-based training. The information and training sequences presented in this book reflect how Legacy teaches pet dog classes.

# DEFINITION OF A "SUCCESSFUL" TRAINING METHOD

Trainers and instructors should follow the Hippocratic oath, "First, do no harm." We need to devise a system that appeals to the human clients, is clearly understood, enjoyable, humane, and effective for all concerned. We need to stand ready to adapt lessons to fit the special needs or goals of the individual dog and family. Our lessons should take a relatively short amount of time and effort to reach mutually agreed upon goals. Further, instructors need to consider the long-term well-being and relationship of the client, the dog, and the community by looking to the future and making sure the training plan does not carry unwanted baggage detrimental to continued success.

Since 1990 I have been teaching in Japan. I spend about three months a year there working with several organizations on reward-based dog training and instructor education. One national group that we formed is the Japanese Canine Good Citizen Association. It's a way of training that ends in a "good citizen test" for both dog and owner. It currently has about a 20% pass rate. The bar is high, but the dog and owner receive a leather passport document that allows them into various participating restaurants, hotels, and other public places that restrict access to other dogs. Our training goal is simple and could be used as a model in any country:

---

**JAPAN'S CANINE GOOD CITIZEN ASSOCIATION'S MISSION STATEMENT:**

- To show a good relationship with your dog as a result of motivational training.
- To have good control with minimal handling and maximum enjoyment by both.
- To be non-obtrusive to the public's eye, as dog and owner.

# CROSS-OVERS

Anyone who has been involved in training for more than 15 or 20 years has probably relied somewhat on compulsive methods: physically put the dog into a Sit, tell her she's good if she stays, correct or punish her if she doesn't. I'm in a first-hand position to know what I like and what I don't like about compulsion. I trained some of my own dogs and my students' dogs that way. I was fairly successful at it, if you equate success with high obedience trial scores. People new to dog training, depending on where they learned their skill, may be relying on lure or shaped behavior followed by a reward. The dog has a choice, but the deck is so stacked, she's going to make the "right" choice. People who have a background in compulsion but want to change to reward-based methods are called cross-over trainers. I crossed over to a more balanced method years ago. But I remember. Change is difficult. It's hard to get out of old, comfortable, familiar habits and try new methods. If current methods are working, why change? That's where critical thinking comes in. Just because a method is different from that which you are currently using doesn't make it right or wrong. Look at new information. Be objective and keep this new information on neutral ground until you think it over. When I was young, I learned a motto in 4-H (an international youth group that teaches useful life skills), which is, "Make your best better." Perhaps there is room for improvement in your classes. Could you be doing a better job? Could a different approach help you to improve?

# CHANGE

The turn of the century has seen a worldwide change in dog training. I've participated in a number of exciting programs in the last several years. PETsMART, a major chain of pet shops and dog training centers in North America, has revised their training program and adopted mostly reward-based training methods for their hundreds of stores. In Japan, the Japanese Animal Hospital Association, the Canine Good Citizen Association, and the Animal Fanciers School remain on the forefront of change in Japanese society regarding canine/human interactions, especially dog training. I feel fortunate to have played an active role in these endeavors.

---

**A NATIONAL OBSESSION?**

American Pet Products Manufacturers Association, 2002:

**Forty million households (39 percent!) include at least one dog.**

Other examples of change are:

## National Standards for Humane Training

In 2001, The American Humane Association and the Delta Society both published information that endeavored to define humane dog training. The following is a quote from *Professional Standards for Dog Trainers: Effective, Humane Principles* (Delta Society, 2001):

*"Humane training is that which is performed with kindness, compassion and respect for the animal, and without inflicting unnecessary discomfort or distress. Training choices that are ineffective, inhumane, or both can result in harm to dogs, anxiety for owners, and in some cases, lawsuits and news stories that damage the image of the training profession as a whole."*

## National Organizations for Trainers and Instructors

There are several groups in the United States involved with trainer or instructor education. I have been an active member of three such organizations and recommend them as a resource for all instructors:

- The National Association of Dog Obedience Instructors (NADOI) produces both a newsletter and a professional journal. NADOI encourages continuing education through their website and annual conferences. NADOI has criteria by which they endorse instructors. I am past president and a life member of NADOI.

- The Association of Pet Dog Trainers (APDT) hold annual 4–5 day educational conferences. APDT has several lively Internet lists as well as their informative website and newsletter. I am a charter member of ADPT and am often given the honor of speaking at their events. APDT was instrumental in starting the first national certification for dog trainers.

- The Certification Council for Pet Dog Trainers (CCPDT), created in 2001, is an independent certification program for dog trainers. It meets the testing standards of the Professional Testing Corporation with rigorous testing and recertification procedures. Legacy has CPDT instructors on staff.

## World Developments

Several other countries have developed educational programs and organizations to educate trainers and instructors. The world is not such a big place now that we have the Internet to communicate with each other about dogs. On-line courses, special interest groups, chat lists, and help lines are now available. A new organization that will eventually take a role in the worldwide education of pet dog training instructors is D.I.N.G.O. (Dog Instructors' Network of Great Opportunity). Originating in Japan, the pilot program is slowly and methodically being field-tested in several other countries.

## ADDITIONAL READING/RESOURCES

**The Association of Pet Dog Trainers**
150 Executive Center Drive, Box 35
Greenville, SC 29615
1-800-PET-DOGS
(1-800-738-3647)
*information@apdt.com*

**Certification Council for Pet Dog Trainers**
CCPDT Administrator, Professional
Testing Corporation
1350 Broadway, 17th Floor
New York, NY 10019
(212) 356-0682
*www.ccpdt.org*

**The Delta Society**
875 124th Avenue NE, Suite 101
Bellevue, WA 98005-2531
(425) 679-5500
*info@deltasociety.org*

**D.I.N.G.O.**
Dog Instructors' Network of Great Opportunity
For International Information
9-5-604 Sarugaku-cho
Japan
(81-3-3780-4858)
*www.dingo.gr.jp*

**International Association of Human-Animal Interaction Organizations (IAHAIO)**
c/o The Delta Society
875 124th Avenue NE, Suite 101
Bellevue, WA 98005-2531
(425) 679-5500
*info@iahaio.org*

**The National Association of Dog Obedience Instructors**
PMB 369
720 Grapevine Hwy
Hurst, Texas 76054-2085
*www.nadoi.org*

# CHAPTER 2

# ETHOLOGY: WHAT IS A DOG?

"*Train with your brain, not pain.*"
—Pat Miller

# Evolution and Domestication

There are many different aspects to training dogs. Some helpful information might be outside of our own area of expertise, so it's important to network with others. From **A**nthropology to **Z**oology, there's hardly a discipline that can't help us a little or a lot.

What is a dog anyway? That depends on your point of view. Our students might have an unrealistic idea. For some it might be easier to define what a dog is not.

## Comparing Dogs with Humans

If your clients think of dogs as humans, they might be disappointed. Teach pet owners to appreciate dogs for what they are. Can dogs think? Do dogs have emotions? It all depends on the definition or interpretation of the word *think* or *emotion*. They can process information, but on a different level than humans. Dogs can discriminate, and they are good at reading their environment. Dogs are not abstract thinkers. Humans think about the past and foresee the future differently than dogs. Dogs live more in the moment than do humans. Dogs have a range of "feelings" but they probably don't equate exactly to our own emotions.

Humans and dogs are different. Dogs are not furry little child substitutes, but they are special, important members of the family. We all fall into the trap of anthropomorphism (assigning human traits and motivations to animals). We love our dogs and assume they unconditionally love us back. Your client might believe her dog works to please her. I'd like to think that too, but we objectively could build a case for the idea that dogs are actually opportunists. Perhaps they hang out with us because we have the opposable thumbs that can open dog food cans. We have the car that can take them for rides. We have the great resting places with electric blankets that we are willing to share with them.

## Our Dogs' Ancestors

The simplistic approach to training a dog could be compared to a person's attitude about driving a car. "I just want to get into the driver's seat and drive. I don't want to know all about what's going on under the hood or how to maintain the car." Superficially learning to drive might be okay, until something unusual happens. Something may go wrong that requires knowing more than how to turn the key and step on the gas pedal. I believe it's the same with dogs. It helps to understand the inner workings of our dogs before we get into the driver's seat and try to drive, much less have a hope to maintain a dog successfully. We will benefit from knowing how dogs evolved, what dogs are capable of biologically, and how they operate naturally. A combination of DNA, behavior, chemistry, vocalization, and anatomy studies indicate that the most probable ancestor of our dog is the wolf, *Canis lupus*.

*Coaching People to Train Their Dogs*

When these prehistoric animals became domesticated and turned into a separate species—*Canis familiaris*—is still uncertain. Experts used to put that date about 12,000 years ago. This was determined by radiocarbon dating, collecting data from cave drawings, and studying artifacts from ancient burial sites. In recent years it has become less and less clear. A group of biologists at UCLA calculated the number of diversions in the mitochondrial DNA of dogs, wolves, and coyotes. Their work suggests that dogs branched off from the wolf anywhere between 80,000 to 130,000 years ago. Robert Wayne says, "The domestic dog is an extremely close relative of the gray wolf, differing from it by at most 0.2% of mitochondrial DNA sequence. In comparison, the gray wolf differs from its closest wild relative, the coyote, by about 4% of mitochondrial DNA sequence." (Molecular evolution of the dog family, 1993, *Trends in Genetics*, 9:218–224) In 1993, the Smithsonian Institution and the American Society of Mammalogists taxonomically reclassified the dog from its separate species designation of *Canis familiaris* to *Canis lupus familiaris*. Now, both dog and wolf fall under the genetic umbrella of the gray wolf: *Canis lupus*. Modern dog is now classified as a subspecies of the gray wolf.

## *Early Relationships—Speculations*

What sort of relationship did early dog and human share? How did that relationship first form? How did human intervention in the breeding of dogs affect the development of behavior and form? Following are some popular speculations.

**Early humans adopted and tamed early dog-like creatures.** Nobel-prize winner Konrad Lorenz envisions the relationship between humans and dogs may have begun when a bored cave-child raided the den of a wild dog-like animal and carried a puppy back to the family dwelling. "But Mommy, I couldn't help it, he followed me home!" At first Mom said no, but relented after being barraged by a primal temper tantrum—the puppy stayed and the human-canine bond was born. This is a fanciful idea, but it's exactly the way in which I acquired my first dog! I used pieces of my lunch sandwich to lure home a stray dog that was hanging around the school yard!

...BUT HE FOLLOWED ME HOME!

The definition of a tame animal is one accustomed to human presence. (This animal's threshold for flight is lessened over its' lifetime.)

**Dispersing wolves form a symbiotic relationship with humans.** An interesting hypothesis on domestication circulating among dog fanciers involves dispersed wolves. It's not uncommon for a wolf to leave its pack between its first and third birthday, looking for a mate of its own. Dispersed from its pack, the wolf is destined to live a solitary life if he or she cannot find acceptance from another group. It's hard to make a living alone. What if the dispersing wolf is of Omega status? An Omega wolf is sometimes the scapegoat of the pack. He or she might be picked on, prevented from eating, and barred from participating in rallies (group greetings). A needy, dispersed wolf of lower status might be more inclined toward teaming up with humans. Humans may have tolerated the arrival of dispersed wolves near their camps because they were good for garbage clean up and they were good for alerting the group to dangers. These animals may have proven helpful in scenting and acquiring prey for the group to share. No one knows for sure.

**Early wild adult proto-dogs adopt humans.** Lorna and Ray Coppinger, in the book *Dogs,* report that there is no solid evidence that people purposefully domesticated wolves by artificial selection. Humans provided a niche: the village. Some proto-dogs invaded the new niche and gained access to a new food source, comparative safety, and possibly more opportunities for reproduction. Those "new niche" wolves were genetically predisposed to show less flight distance than regular wolves. "New niche" wolves gained selective advantage for living with humans over regular wolves. In this model, dogs evolved by natural selection. The only thing people had to do with it was to establish the villages. The dogs we see living around dumps throughout the world might be descendents of those ancient village dogs, not our pet dogs that have reverted to a feral state.

## An Example of Purposeful Domestication Using Selective Breeding

Steven Lindsay says, "Many wild animals can be readily 'tamed' by patient handling and socialization, but they cannot be considered domesticated until they have undergone extensive behavioral and biological changes resulting from selective breeding over the course of many generations. Such breeding is designed consciously or unconsciously to enhance various behavioral and physical characteristics conductive to domestic harmony and utility" (*Handbook of Applied Dog Behavior and Training,* Vol. 1, Adaptation and Learning, 2000, Ames, Iowa State Press).

Consider the research conducted by Dr. Dmitry Belyaev: Dr. Belyaev began an experiment with silver foxes from a commercial fur farm in Russia in 1959. The task was to breed foxes tame enough to be handled by farm workers. To accomplish this, only foxes that showed the least amount of flight behavior were selected. These less flighty individuals were bred exclusively. In 18 generations the farm had a population of foxes that allowed humans to handle them. Surprisingly, these animals showed changes in physical appearance as well. Breeding for function also affected the form of the animal. The "new" foxes with reduced flight distance behavior looked different. Some of them developed a piebald (spotted) coat. This was very bad for the fox fur business! Some had drooping ears instead of the normally erect ears of the wild fox. Some had curly tails. Wild foxes do not have curly tails. Their vocalizations changed. Barking increased. They engaged in antics described as play. In plain terms, they retained care-soliciting behavior, acting and looking like babies.

Babies of all species trigger a nurturing, care-giving reaction in humans. I call this the cute factor. Babyish behavior goes along with the babyish looks. Neoteny is the scientific term for the retention of juvenile traits by adults. Neoteny includes morphological traits (looks, form, structure) and behavioral traits (actions, response to stimuli). L. N. Trut (Canid Domestication: The Farm Fox Experiment, *American Scientist,* Vol. 87, No. 2, 1999) suggests that the changes that occurred in Belyaev's foxes might be the same changes that occurred as dogs were domesticated from wolves. Trut hypothesizes that dogs, evolving from self-sufficient pack creatures to ones living with a dependence on humans, may have been selected for function (baby-like tameness), which is linked to form (baby-like looks). Morphological changes, such as skulls that are unusually broad for their length, and behavioral changes, such as whining, barking, and submissiveness, have taken place. These are all characteristics that wolves outgrow but that dogs do not.

The study of the line of Belyaev's foxes continues. Cognition researcher Brian Hare of Harvard University states, "We want to know whether selecting certain animals for tameness, not cognition, did in fact cause cognitive change. . . . What's at stake is our theory on dogs: we think they survived because they're better able to read human cues. It could be that reading human cues wasn't selected at all; what was selected was simply tameness. Cognition was just a byproduct of selection for tameness. This fox study will help us follow up on our dog theories" ("Siberian Study—Brian Hare and the Belyaev Foxes," Chris McNamara, Bark, Summer 2003).

## *Comparing Dogs with Wolves*

Years ago I would use wolf analogies based on what I saw on television or read in books about wolves. I should have done some research and some critical thinking. I should have talked with ethologists. When an ethologist is at work, he or she will study animals by observing and documenting their behaviors in minute detail. This is done objectively, without interpretation and without forming opinions on why the animals are doing what they are doing. Ethological study methods have been refined in Europe for years, but aren't as mainstream in North America. Each summer for several years I have been on the teaching staff for a wolf and dog behavior course at Wolf Park. Wolf Park is a non-profit education and research facility established in 1972 by Dr. Erich Klinghammer. The park, incorporated under the North American Wildlife Park Foundation in Battle Ground, Indiana, is home to several packs of gray wolves. I'm in awe of wolves and believe Leon Whitney's statement in his book *Dog Psychology,* "To understand wolves is to better understand dogs." Instructors should keep in mind, however, that wolves are different from dogs due to influences in their respective evolutionary paths. The staff at Wolf Park has compiled an excellent ethogram of wolf behavior that should be of interest to anyone studying the body language of the dog.

**Selection: Form and Function.** Obvious differences are seen in form and function between wolves and dogs. Many modern dog breeds retain neotenous characteristics. A physical difference in ears is one illustration. Cocker spaniels are extreme examples of floppy ears. The ears of a newborn wolf puppy are folded over, but within a matter of days become erect like those of an adult. Change in behavior goes along with change of type. The natural selection for physical and behavioral characteristics necessary to survive in the wild is different than the artificial selection process in which humans decide which traits are desirable in a dog.

**Definitions: Tame versus Domestic.** A wolf is a wild animal. A person can tame a particular wolf by decreasing flight distance and increasing tolerance to humans over one individual's lifespan. Domestication is very different. Our dogs are the result of generations of selection for traits that make a good companion to humans including reduced distance of the flight response. Cows are domesticated, elk are not. It is possible to tame an elk—reduce an individual's distance of flight response, over the lifetime of that individual.

## Wolf/Dog Hybrids

You may be approached by someone who wants to enroll a wolf/dog mix (hybrid) in your classes. In years past I have allowed alleged hybrids in my classes. I have changed that policy. One of the issues of allowing wolf/dog hybrids in class is that of rabies. The effectiveness of current rabies vaccines on wolves and wolf hybrids is highly controversial and is still under debate. In some cases, local legislation banning wolf hybrids has been based on the lack of a recognized vaccine.

Dr. Klinghammer, professor emeritus of Purdue University and founder of Wolf Park in Indiana says, "While low percentage wolf-dog hybrids may be unlike pure wolves in many respects, and many can and are kept like pure dogs, they all retain, as do many dogs, the motivation for predatory behavior. This means that a person, especially a child who tripped and fell, or who is moaning, crying, or screaming, may be considered wounded prey and attacked. Grave injuries, even death, are all too frequent in such cases."

Monty Sloan, long-time staff member at Wolf Park, is considered a leading expert in wolf hybrid care and behavior. Wolf Park's website *(www.wolfpark@wolfpark.org)* and other educational materials are good resources for instructors. Monty says, "A wolf as a pet is an animal out of context. Owners are faced with a myriad of challenges and obstacles to properly and humanely maintain such an animal, which far exceeds the typical problems faced by owners of dogs. Although wolves crossed with dogs tend to present fewer problems than pure wolves, that is not the perspective of the private owner whose past experience and current management tools are based on dogs. From a dog mixed with wolf, insurmountable obstacles can emerge for those unaware of the potential these animals present."

# Behavior: Why Do Dogs Do That?

A trainer or instructor, in addition to deciphering canine communication, must interpret the human language describing canine behavior. Each field of study that involves dogs seems to have a different vocabulary to describe them. This book attempts to bring together as many terms as necessary for us to learn from each other.

## Phylogenetic Behavior

Phylogeny is the evolutionary history of an organism. Phylogenetic behaviors are behaviors common to the dog as a species in general. They have developed over generations. They have evolutionary significance. The environment has naturally selected them to maximize reproduction. Innate fear of fire or of loud noises is an example of phylogenetic behavior. Biologist Raymond Coppinger and others maintain that all canine behavior can be categorized into one of three motivations:

- Food acquisition
- Hazard avoidance, safety/comfort seeking
- Reproductive behaviors

If we use these motivations as a guide, we can see that a trainer might use hazard avoidance as a means to gain compliance from dogs: "Do that and it will hurt." This approach might come with baggage in terms of freeze, fight, or flight responses from the dog. There is a strong and growing population of trainers who employ the food acquisition rather than hazard avoidance motivation in their training programs: "Do this and I'll feed you."

**Food Acquisition Sequence.** The natural food acquisition chain includes: Hear, see, smell prey → orient, stare, freeze → creep, stalk, run → grab, hold, shake → bring down → kill → dismember → eat → guard.

We see bits of this behavior chain in activities we call play. Catching a frisbee, playing tug of war, chewing on a stick, or burying a bone can all be seen as modern-day expressions of innate food acquisition behavior. We can use this behavior when selecting toys and games as rewards when training. Phylogenetic behavior can be modified.

*Chapter 2  Ethology: What Is a Dog?*

## Fixed Action Patterns

Dr. Konrad Lorenz is one of the forefathers of the scientific field of ethology. He and Niko Tinbergen defined fixed action patterns as specific examples of innate or phylogenetic behavior. A particular trigger is needed to start the behavior. Once the fixed action pattern has begun, it needs to go to completion before the animal stops. It is a stereotypic movement pattern that is relatively constant in form. Nursing is one example of a fixed action pattern and snarling is another. Behavior modification can change a fixed action pattern. In 1954 Dr. Lorenz said, "The motor patterns of urination performed by a male dog show all the phenomena here under discussion. A very strong releasing stimulus situation, such as the smell of a rival's mark in the dog's own territory, will cause him to lift his leg even when the amount of urine at his disposal is, at the moment, negligible. Even under the pressure of a much higher urinating potential, the dog will still look for a releasing stimulus situation, such as upright objects, preferably on exposed corners, at which to lift his leg."

## Ontogenetic Behavior

Ontogenetic behaviors develop over the lifetime of an individual dog. An ontogenetic behavior is a response to environmental influences. It has been learned in the dog's individual lifetime. For example, a dog soon learns to run quickly to her human for a piece of food when she hears her name. The run-to-your-human behavior as a response to that particular stimulus, is learned; it has been rewarded. The dog was not born knowing this. Ontogenetic behavior can be modified.

## Temperament—Nature and Nurture

*Temperament, character, personality,* and *disposition* are words used by dog owners to describe their dogs. A dog's genetic material and experience both affect the dog. The term nature versus nurture is deceiving. It can't be one or the other. Nature/nurture effects are a synergism. They work together and cannot be separated into categories. Dogs are programmed at birth for certain behaviors. Nursing is an innate (automatic) behavior in puppies. The pup can nurse without having been taught. Other behaviors are learned. Running over to the refrigerator when the door is opened is not an innate behavior in puppies. It's not automatic. The pup needs to have lived life and gained experience before performing approach-refrigerator-behavior. In a conversation among three people, you may hear, "Fear of loud noises is genetic." "No, fear of loud noises is a learned behavior," or "No, fear of loud noises is 60% nature and 40% nurture." At this time many experts suggest such answers are guesses because genes consist of DNA. DNA transmits information about traits. Genes are linked together to form chromosomes. Dogs inherit half of their chromosomes, thus half their genes, from each parent. Most traits are affected by more than one gene. Both genetics and environmental factors affect behavior. Clients should understand that they can train their dog to do one thing but nature is sometimes suggesting another. When practical, take advantage of natural behavior patterns and use them in your training program. Dr. Ray Coppinger and Dr. Erich Klinghammer point out that a dog is the result of nature/nurture plus experiences that occur between the onset and offset of critical periods.

Pat Goodmann has spent the last 31 years of her life studying wolves and dogs. By teaching courses together, I have learned a great deal from Pat. She explained nature/nurture, phylogenetic/ontogenetic to me in this way: "Envision a puppy which has hoses leading into it from the environment (nurture) and its phylogenetic (nature) history. The environment would be continually putting things into the puppy but if the other reservoir, the phylogenetic one, did not have its valve open at certain times in its development, the puppy would not be able to make the most of its heritage. If the phylogenetic valve were open but the environment was not currently putting out the 'right stuff,' the puppy would not make the most of its heritage."

## *Instinctive Drift—The Breland Effect*

Our clients should not have unrealistic expectations of their training. This concept was published in the *American Psychologist Journal* in "The Misbehavior of Organisms" written by Marian and Keller Breland in 1961 in rebuttal to B. F. Skinner's earlier work entitled *Behavior of Organisms* in 1938. Marian Breland was one of Skinner's graduate students. B. F. Skinner was credited for popularizing the concept of operant conditioning. We'll discuss more about that in Chapter 3 as we explore learning theory as a powerful tool for instructors and trainers. Canine behavior cannot be adequately understood, predicted, or modified without knowing about the evolutionary history and innate behavior patterns of the dog and the principles of learning. In other words, instincts, drives, and fixed action patterns might come back to haunt us in spite of our training.

Breland and Breland (Misbehavior of Organisms, 1961) say, "It seems obvious that these animals are trapped by strong instinctive behaviors, and clearly we have here a demonstration of the prepotency of such behavior patterns over those which have been conditioned. We have termed this phenomenon 'instinctive drift.'" The general principle seems to be that wherever an animal has strong instinctive behavior, the organism will drift toward the instinctive behavior to the detriment of the conditioned behavior, even to the delay or preclusion of the reinforcement. In a very boiled-down, simplified form, it might be stated that the learned behavior drifts toward instinctive behavior.

The word *instinct* or *drive* is used by dog trainers to describe or categorize the motivation for certain behaviors, mostly those thought to be a compulsive urge directed toward self-preservation, for example, reproduction, food acquisition, or defense. Sheila Booth (*Schutzhund Obedience, Training in Drive,* 1992) and others have developed training programs around drives. For example, chasing a ball might be categorized as the prey drive, the acquisition of food. For your pet dog classes, speaking in terms of breed-specific drives or drives in general might lead owners astray. It might create a feeling of hopelessness: "My dog is a natural _____ (you fill in the blank), therefore . . ."

I asked Dan Estep, Ph.D., a Certified Applied Animal Behaviorist, about drives. Dan is a scientist who has been helping people with their dogs for years through Animal Behavior Associates, Inc. Dr. Estep said: "Scientists don't use drive or instinct any more to explain animal behavior because 1) it oversimplifies all the complex factors that influence and cause behavior, 2) there is no simple mechanism in the brain (or anywhere else in the body) that controls individual instincts or drives—all kinds of different structures are involved, 3) the body doesn't store energy to motivate the instincts or drives. Are the terms instinct or drive describing behavior, or explaining it?

For example:

**Q:** Why does my dog chase a ball?
**A:** Because he has high prey drive.

**Q:** How do I know my dog has high prey drive?
**A:** Because he chases balls.

Nothing has really been explained here."

It's helpful to remind pet owners that a dog does dog-like things, but to think of each dog as an individual. Encourage and help them to work out their individual dog's motivation to perform a learned task.

# THE BIOLOGY OF LEARNING

## Critical Periods

There are times in a pup's life when experience can have a greater influence on development than at other times. Critical periods take place between three and sixteen weeks of age. During this time the pup has the greatest capacity to learn particular skills and responses including the forming of appropriate social relationships with people and dogs. If a pup remains with the litter and receives little human contact during his or her critical socialization period, that pup may not develop appropriate social bonds with people. If the pup is removed from the litter and placed in a people-only environment, the pup may not develop appropriate relationships with other dogs. The onset and closing of the social window differs within a breed, and the average for each breed will differ, but, in general, the social window is beginning to diminish by sixteen weeks of age. It's not just social skills that are influenced in this way: "Each behavioral system—fear, submission, investigation, play—has its own rate of development, and varies among breeds. Each is dependent on glandular development and hormone secretions, as well as motor coordination and sensory perception" (Raymond and Lorna Coppinger, *Dogs*).

We never know exactly when the various windows of maximum opportunity will open or shut. As instructors, we are not apt to see puppies younger than seven weeks; however, breeders, shelters, and others working with very young puppies can influence their behavioral development at that early age. A good overview of the development of behavior in dogs can be found in Steven Lindsay's *Handbook of Applied Dog Behavior and Training,* Vol. I (2000). If your school cannot provide a puppy class immediately, your clients should have a "to do" list of experiences for the puppy to receive at home. Once in class, conduct exercises to minimize fear and maximize pleasant learning experiences.

The Coppingers suggest, "Before the onset of fear responses, animals do not show fear to novel shapes and sounds. For a newborn puppy, everything is novel. But after the onset of fear new novel shapes, and sounds cause avoidance behaviors—call them hazard avoidance behaviors. Gun-dog trainers expose their pups to gunshots before the puppies grow the fear portion of their brains. Shooting guns around puppies for their first six weeks grows a brain that expects those sounds from the environment. Gunshots become normal. But if the gunshots are not introduced until after the onset of fear (which in this case might simply be the threshold where the sound is perceived as loud), the dog will perceive them as hazards to be avoided."

I think of puppy brains as lots of little electrical sockets and lots of electrical plugs floating in space. There are brief periods in which they can be hooked up for the pup to reach maximum potential as a well-adjusted pet. A good puppy class will organize events that will help stimulate the plugs to find the sockets within the time limit.

## *Effects of Puberty, Hormones, Spay, and Neutering on Behavior*

Dogs become capable of breeding as early as six months, but they may not be behaviorally mature until one or two years of age. Anecdotally, the seven-month crazies are reported, and testing the rules often occurs at this age. As dogs reach puberty, chemicals begin to affect behavior. Dogs are also becoming more independent and self-reliant at this age due in part to good socialization! No, your dedication during puppy classes doesn't come back to haunt you. In the long run we want confident, but under-control dogs. Young puppies are natural followers, but as independence increases, the owner becomes less the center of the dogs' attention. The environment becomes more interesting. Encourage owners to work through their dogs' adolescence successfully by setting a bit of time aside each day for ongoing socialization and training.

- *Male*—Testosterone is the principal androgen or male hormone manufactured by the testes. These male hormones influence behaviors such as mounting, mating, searching for females, scent marking, and aggression.

Because the presence of testosterone can make reactions more intense, some class instructors recommend castration as a means of reducing unwanted behavior. Behavioral changes seen after neutering can be gradual and/or minimal. If the dog has a history of being reinforced for such behavior, that behavior now has a conditioned element which doesn't depend on testosterone. Dr. Stefanie Schwartz (*Canine and Feline Behavior Problems*, 1994, AVP, CA) reports that castration "can help minimize the severity and escalation of aggressiveness." The Harts reported the first definitive study of castration effects in 1985 (Hart, B. and Hart, L., *Canine and Feline Behavioral Therapy*, Lea & Fibiger, 1985, p. 239).

- *Female*—Estrogen and progesterone become active near puberty. These female hormones peak twice a year in estrus cycles at which time females become sexually receptive. Approximately 20 days in duration, these periods are referred to as the dog being "in heat" or "in season" at which time females may court males or allow males to breed with them. Spaying does not reduce aggression levels in females. In fact there is evidence to suggest that spaying might raise the level of aggression (Valerie O'Farrell, 1992, *Manual of Canine Behavior*, Sussex, British Small Animal Veterinary Association).

Think through your class goals and decide upon a class policy for intact and/or in season pet dogs. A Legacy client handout prepared by our veterinarian on spaying and neutering appears in the Appendix as INFOSpay&Neuter.doc, "Neutering Your Male Dog, Spaying Your Female Dog."

## *Relationship Between Brain and Behavior*

There are very real limitations to what a dog can and cannot learn. There are times when your expectations cannot be met because of brain chemistry. The science of the relationship between the brain and behavior is called neuropsychology. Trainers and instructors can design better training programs if they understand a few basic facts about the brain and behavior.

## *Engrams*

Much has been said of muscle memory as it relates to the training of people and dogs. In fact, muscles do not have memory. Movement is learned through the development and storage of familiar motor actions called engrams. Sometimes it is referred to as motor memory: Neuromuscular programming is established by repetition. Christine Zink, DVM, says, "Every newborn puppy, when it first begins to move, starts to send messages regarding movement along specific neural pathways in the brain. These neural pathways are called engrams. They are like ruts in the brain along which the messages prefer to travel" (Peak Performance—Coaching the Canine Athlete®, 1997, Canine Sports Productions). Dogs, and their people, are learning new patterns of movement in class. At first a conscious effort is made to put the body in a particular position, or to move it in a certain way. To learn a new movement, the dogs and their owners need to practice that movement over a long enough period of time so that the movement becomes automatic. A conscious action becomes an automatic action.

*A human example:* If you heard the phone ring in a different room, you would not have to think about the process of moving your body to the phone, picking up the receiver, and putting it to your ear. Walking is something we can do without thinking about it. You just decide where you want to go, and your body does the rest. Walking is a mechanical skill you needed to learn at some point in your life. When you were a baby, it took concentration and practice; now you don't think about how to do it.

*A canine example:* You want to teach the dog to sit up—rear on the floor, front paws off the floor. At first the dog might have to struggle to get his body into this position, he might fall over, he might overshoot and get too high. With repetition, working his body into this position becomes a smooth, coordinated action that becomes automatic. An instructor should build lots of repetition into the lessons for both people and dogs.

## Reticular Activating System

The Reticular Activating System (RAS) is the attention center in the brain. It is the key to "turning on the brain." It is the part of the brain where activities in the world outside are perceived, processed, and, ultimately, acted upon. Dogs are capable of tuning out things that are unimportant. It's the same system that human brains use to figure out what is important. For example, if you move to a home near an airport, you will only hear the airplanes for the first few days. After that, you don't pay attention to them. The reason is that your brain knows that noise is unimportant. Dogs are the same way. If the owner says the word, "No" repeatedly, but it has no real meaning, the dog might eventually tune out her owner. The dog hears, but she has learned that "No" is unimportant information. Carefully coach owners how to communicate with their dogs. Important information should be communicated clearly and concisely, in meaningful terms. That is our challenge. That is the benchmark of good training and instructing.

## Limbic System and Cerebral Cortex

James O'Heare (*Canine Neuropsychology,* 2002, Dog Psychology Publishing, Ottawa, Canada) says that the limbic system is a network of cells in the brain that integrates instinct and learning. The conflict between what a dog instinctively wants to do and what we teach her to do takes place in the brain's limbic system. Humans can override this system by giving rewards to the dog for obeying her owners rather than her instincts. The limbic system is involved with emotions such as fear. The cerebral cortex is involved with cognitive functions, such as learning and problem solving. It coordinates movement and receives and processes sensory, visual, and auditory information.

If the limbic system is activated, the cerebral cortex is inhibited. Conversely, if the cerebral cortex is activated, the limbic system is inhibited. If the dog is engaged in a mentally stimulating situation, such as paying attention to a learning sequence, her cerebral cortex is engaged. In this state, she is less likely to experience intense emotional responses such as fear because that part of the brain, the limbic system, is inhibited. A dog that is busy retrieving a ball with her owner is less apt to be afraid of a strange sound.

Conversely, consider a dog that is emotionally involved, such as a dog trying to avoid a frightening or painful situation. This dog is working from the limbic system and is unlikely to be able to process information (learning) at the same time. A dog that is very frightened by the threats of another dog in a training class or the slippery floors of the classroom is not able to learn the lessons.

Fear, stress, and anxiety are at the root of many problems owners have with their dogs. Instructors should help owners learn to predict when a dog is about to enter a fearful state. How? The dog will tell you. Observe the subtle body language that is the precursor of fear. A thoughtful owner will know what triggers the dog's fearful behavior and avoid the situation when possible.

## *Opposition Reflex*

Newton's Third Law of Motion states that "for every action, there is an equal and opposite reaction." That's physics. A tonic reflex involves the dog's body trying to maintain equilibrium. I explain to students that the dog's body will oppose pressure. This reaction is a form of thigmotaxis: If you pull one way with your leash, the dog's natural reflex is to pull the other. If you try to push him away from you, his natural reflex will make him lean into you. If you push his rear toward the floor, his natural reaction is to brace his hind legs and oppose that pressure. We can use this knowledge to our advantage rather than to our disadvantage. When teaching "Sit," "Down," or walking on the leash to your class, demonstrate how thigmotaxis can work against progress.

# SOCIAL HIERARCHY: WHAT IT IS, WHAT IT ISN'T

Even in puppyhood, dogs have the ability to show what people tend to call dominant or subordinate behaviors or postures during play. The same dog can be seen displaying one or the other at different times in a play session. Social hierarchy is flexible. It is affected by variables such as context and physical state of the dog and those around him. One dog might be able to dominate all others when it comes to resting places, but that individual might freely yield food to any other. A dog may dominate food only if hungry. There is more room in the world for subordinate individuals than dominant ones. Therefore, ranking of individuals in a social living group might more accurately be described as a subordinance hierarchy than a dominance hierarchy. Subordinate members show submissive behaviors to the dominant member more than the dominant individual displays his or her superior rank. It's often obvious who is at the bottom of the hierarchy. The animals in the middle are most often the ones who initiate threats and aggression. Dominance is not the same as aggression. A dog can be aggressive, but not dominant, within his social group. A dog can be dominant, but not aggressive, in the same situation.

Erik Zimen, a respected German wolf researcher, states in *Social Dynamics of the Wolf Pack,* "The dominance relationship between two animals is expressed by the degree of social freedom each animal allows itself during an encounter."

Owners and trainers talk about dominant (high ranking) dogs and subordinate (low ranking) dogs; however, dogs cannot be quickly labeled dominant or subordinate. These social relationships are established over time, by numerous interactions. Therefore, to look at a dog in a group of strangers and say it's a dominant dog is incorrect. The dog might be displaying dominant type behaviors and postures at that moment. In my opinion, most dogs labeled as dominant by their owners simply lack manners and training. Or they are resource guarding . . . at the moment. Or a dog with a low reactivity threshold or even a high energy level might be labeled dominant.

## The Alpha Roll—The Wolf's Point of View

Popular dog training literature compares the social structure of wolves with that of pet dogs and their human families. While there may be some similarities, many myths have developed that just aren't true. Following is an excerpt from an article I wrote that was published in the July 2001 newsletter of the Association of Pet Dog Trainers. I quote several experts on dog behavior. My intention was to debunk the alpha roll correction practiced by many dog trainers.

"The alpha roll is an often-mentioned technique in popular canine behavior and training literature. There seems to be no standard definition of the alpha roll; in fact, there are many variations demonstrated by trainers and instructors. One variation starts with a scruff shake, grabbing the dog on either side of the neck, lifting the dog's weight off the front feet and staring into the dog's eyes until the dog submits. However, there is usually no clear definition of the term *submit* or explanation of what to do if a dog doesn't submit. Turning the dog onto his back and pinning him there until he assumes this vague definition of submission is usually how an owner tries to train his dog. Why are dog owners encouraged to do the alpha roll? It is purported to simulate the natural method of establishing leadership, dominating the dog, correcting a dog, punishing an inappropriate behavior.

Definitions and critical thinking are called for. Trainers justify the technique of the alpha roll because they think it's simply the way wolves do it.

If we could successfully interview a wolf (or a dog for that matter), we'd be light years ahead in training. We have to go by careful observation and astute second guessing. I have received quotes from several professional second guessers with a strong background in wolf behavior. They are part of the team that teaches the Wolf and Dog Behavior course with me every summer at Wolf Park, Indiana."

**Ethologist Erich Klinghammer, Ph.D.**
Professor Emeritus Purdue University

*President of the North American Wildlife Federation says:*
"As for myself, the so-called alpha roll-over practiced by some is nonsense. The context in which people do it with dogs does not coincide with the situation in

which a wolf actively submits to a high-ranking wolf. We certainly do not use it with our hand-raised wolves. There is no way we can administer the intensity of a dominance attack on a wolf that they use with each other on very rare occasions. Establishing dominance is usually a drawn out series of encounters that eventually convinces a wolf to submit and run away, a preferred strategy. If I were to go up to a hand-raised wolf that did not know me and attempt to dominate it physically, it would either run away or I would have one helluva fight on my hands, if the wolf could not get away. There is really a big difference between wolves and dogs. To simply extrapolate from wolves to dogs is at best problematical."

**Ken McCort,**

Dog Breeder, Exhibitor, Kennel Owner

*Full time training and behavior consultant says:*

"My point of view has been that I am not a dog and don't want to be thought of as such. I don't eat placentas, roll in feces, sniff butts, lick faces, or demonstrate many other normal dog behaviors. If you only speak a few words of a foreign language, do the locals think you are a native? Mimicking a few behaviors our dogs perform does not make us resemble dogs. The only benefit (?) I can see from some of these techniques is we can develop dogs that will allow people to treat them roughly. My observation of dogs and wolves has shown this type of discipline is very uncommon. In fact, with wolves, the inguinal presentation behavior is usually volunteered by a lower ranking wolf as sort of an appeasement to a dominant animal in the face of some threat or altercation. With my own personal dogs (eight of them), I have rarely, if ever, seen a pinning behavior from any of them. One of the things I often hear is that mothers pin puppies to actively wean them. In wolves and dogs, most of the mothers I see weaning pups use avoidance rather than confrontation. How can a mother dog/wolf pin four, five, six or more puppies at the same time? Leaders in packs control assets (possessions, territory) more often than physically controlling individuals. We need to look in that direction rather than all this silliness regarding pinning, scruffing, and man-handling our dog friends."

**Pat Goodmann, MS**

*Dog Lover and Ethologist, Wolf Park says:*

"I don't know of anything in peer reviewed literature about testing reactions of dogs to the variations of the alpha-roll. I think it would be a bit hard to do safely and ethically. My personal experience in interacting with wolves and watching them interact with each other convinces me that it is an unnecessarily risky move when we have so many other options available. In watching the wolves, I find it is rare for them to forcibly push down and hold down a subordinate, a rival, a youngster. In the overwhelming majority of cases rather than being pushed down, the wolf that ends up on the ground is already going down in response to psychological pressure. They may get frantic and struggle if physical pressure is added. Sometimes they succeed in struggling free. Sometimes it results in the threatened wolf fighting back when it was willing to show some submission and avoidance before being cornered and held down. I have seen the alpha roll 'work' in wolf-wolf and in wolf-human encounters, but I have also seen it backfire in that it escalates very rapidly and the wolf being held down has the experience of struggling intensely and possibly drastically increasing the level of defensive aggression it shows. Any time you contain a terrified animal and close off all chances of escape, there is a chance of provoking this critical reaction—very high arousal and defensive aggression. It can even become offensive aggression—this is how our first alpha female lost her status and her life in a matter of minutes."

**Dr. Raymond Coppinger**
Professor of Biology, Hampshire College
Cofounder, Livestock Guarding Dog Project, Champion sled dog racer

*Coauthor of the thought-provoking book* Dogs *(2001) says:*

"In evolutionary terms, to be descended from a wolf doesn't mean dogs are wolves or behave like wolves. Chimps and humans are descended from a common ancestor that looked more like chimps, and dogs and wolves are descended from a common ancestor that looked more like wolves. But humans have a very different social structure than chimps. If you were told that in order to teach your kid to tie his shoes you should grab him, throw him down and piss on him and dominate him in the primate way, you might treat the information with a jaundiced eye. That is exactly the way I treat the concept of dominating dogs with the alpha roll.

Wolves display dominance to limit their competitors' access to valuable resources such as mates or food. Wolves are not trying to teach other wolves anything. Domination is a threat, which is responded to with fear and a lack of motion. Submission is inhibitory motor patterns limiting the severity of the threat. Learning is play behavior. In social play, individuals give up social rank. Dominant individuals often assume subservient roles, and vice versa. Play is when each individual solicits other individuals to enter into social games of no consequence. What each partner has to do is learn the rules of the game. At the same time, each understands that there is not a consequence for making a mistake. I never want my animals to be thinking social hierarchy. Once they do, they will be spending their time trying to figure out how to move up in the hierarchy. Play behavior is the best way to get around hierarchy. During play the dog will try to learn the rules of the game, and that is what you are trying to teach."

# THE LANGUAGE OF DOGS

We have questions about dogs. The dogs have the answers. We humans try to teach dogs our own language, but it's only fair for us to try to learn theirs as well. Understanding the dog's body language and what he is "saying" is a crucial part of dog training. Dogs send and receive signals via sound, smell, and sight.

## Sound

Barking, growling, whining—humans can guess what these all mean by the quality of the sound. Whines are pathetic, and growling is menacing. A layman's interpretation of what barks might mean is described in the handout "The Bark Stops Here" listed in the Appendix as INFOBarking.doc., "The Bark Stops Here."

## *Smell*

The dog's sense of smell is better than ours. Humans may be able to tell if the lawn was cut within the last hour, but a dog can tell who walked on that lawn the day before. Our students are all familiar with the communicative value of marking. Both female and male dogs can urine mark, but the behavior is more common in males. Dogs can also leave information for each other via feces and even by shedding rafts of old skin. By sending and receiving chemicals called pheromones, dogs can determine if another individual is stressed or if a female is ready for breeding. Pheromones produced by a lactating female are thought to create a sense of well-being in the pups. Synthetically produced and marketed as Dog Appeasing Pheromones, or DAP, they may also help anxieties in adult dogs caused by separation or intra-dog aggression. Anal glands, located on either side of the rectum, are normally expressed during defecation, but can be expressed when the dog is frightened . . . or by dragging his or her rear across the living room carpet!

## *Sight*

**The Story of Clever Hans.** This true story, which took place in the early 1900s in Germany, demonstrates how carefully animals observe body language. Wilhelm von Osten, a retired school teacher, had a horse named Hans. Wilhelm believed he had taught Clever Hans to solve mathematical problems. If Wilhelm wrote a problem on a chalkboard, for example 3 + 2 = ?, Clever Hans would answer by tapping his hoof five times. Hans consistently answered a variety of math problems correctly in this manner. He did make some mistakes, but not many! His fame spread far and wide. Scientists of the time were sure there must be a trick to Hans' mathematical ability, not to mention his ability to read! Led by Oskar Pfungst, they were determined to find the truth. They did a series of experiments. Pfungst asked Wilhelm to blindfold Clever Hans and read the problem to him instead of showing Hans the board. He asked Wilhelm to give Hans the problem on a piece of paper instead of on the board. He bypassed Wilhelm and Pfungst and presented the problem to the horse himself. Hans remained clever throughout all of these tests. They tried changing the position of Hans and then the position Wilhelm. Finally, a clue! Hans failed if he could not see Wilhelm's face. Somehow Wilhelm had been telling Hans the answer, but even Wilhelm didn't know how he was doing that. Wilhelm still thought the horse could do math. After much more testing and observation, Pfungst found that when a problem was presented to Clever Hans, Wilhelm's eyebrows lowered to the ground to watch Hans tap out the answer. He didn't realize that he was doing so. When Clever Hans got to the correct number, Wilhelm would look back up at him. Clever Hans was indeed clever. He was very good at reading subtle body language. Think about that the next time you consult a fortune teller.

**Clever Lacey, Clever Brody.** Our family has had two different dogs, at two different times, in two different houses with the same power to predict their bath time. I'm in the process now of systematically narrowing down the possible cues that signal for disappearing when a bath is imminent. It's not walking to a certain sink, not reaching for shampoo or towels . . . it's got to be, as one of my students suggested, my "shampoo face."

## *The Dogs Are Telling Us What We Need to Know*

Instructors could provide a far better service to clients if we could be half as observant as Hans, Lacey, or Brody. For now, let's settle for reading the body language that can be predictive of behavior about to happen. Dogs are pretty honest about their communication. If a client tells you his dog did something without warning, it's possible there was a warning, but it was missed. A dog's body language can be subtle. There is no single body feature that will be a reliable predictor of what a dog is communicating. One must look at clusters of postures and expressions and the context in which they are shown. Not every body movement is intended as communication. A dog might scratch because he itches or he might scratch as a displacement activity. Dogs seem to use the same communication signals when interacting with people as they do with other dogs.

It is easy to anthropomorphize and use familiar terms like shy, fearful, nervous, anxious, or stressed when talking about dogs. We all do it. To be sure our clients understand what we are talking about, try to describe or demonstrate the behavior. Ask your clients to do the same. First, communicate what is seen without making assumptions or personal interpretations of what is going on.

**Ears.** Ears need to be observed in context and in combination with other body postures. Ears back could signal appeasement and greeting but can also reflect a fearful or defensive state. Ears straining forward reflect a more bold or offensive dog. Coach students to observe their dogs in a neutral state and then take note of ear positions in various social situations in conjunction with other body signals.

**Eyes.** As an instructor, pay attention to the eyes of the dogs in your class. Is a dog staring at you or purposely avoiding looking at you? Is a dog focused on another dog? Direct, prolonged eye contact with hard, cold eyes is usually part of an offensive threat. Reduce this type of eye contact between dogs by standing between them or erecting a low barrier such as a table on its side, a dog crate with a blanket over it, or even an expandable gate with a towel draped over. A dog that looks away and avoids eye contact may be indicating fear or submission. Anxious dogs may also continually scan their environment. Their eyes quickly dart in different directions. Such dogs aren't as apt to be successful at eye contact with their owners as dogs more comfortable in their environment. Dogs that are extremely frightened may try to turn their head away from the problem, but need to watch for danger; therefore the whites of the eyes may be more visible. Trainer Sue Sternberg refers to this as "whale eye." When dogs become fearful or defensive, the pupils of the eyes might dilate. When this happens, the dog's eyes will appear very black and large. But remember, lighting conditions can also affect whether or not a dog's pupils are dilated.

Dogs have yellow-blue-green spectrum cones (rods and cones are the light-sensitive cells inside the eye's retina that detect color), but they do not have red cones. The cones in a dog's eyes are dichromatic, similar to those in a color-blind person.

**Mouth and Muzzle, Teeth and Tongue.** Often the first sign of communication is a hardening of the face. On some dogs, wrinkles or furrows normally not apparent become visible on the forehead or at the corners of the mouth when aroused. While studying at Wolf Park in Indiana, I learned to look at whisker beds. When the face starts to become tense, the whiskers start to move; you can see that movement by watching the position of the whisker beds.

When showing the teeth as an offensive threat, a dog's lips retract vertically, so that the canine teeth are visible. When showing teeth defensively, the lips appear to be more horizontally retracted. A submissive "grin" has the lips drawn back and down at the corners. Some dogs will actually show their teeth during a submissive greeting. Often referred to as a smile, I find it very interesting. Over the years I've made it a point to collect photos of these "smiling" dogs.

Primitive scenting organs are located in the roof of the mouth approximately where the teeth meet the soft palate. Referred to as the vomeronasal organ or Jacobson's organ, dogs extend their tongues and bring them back into their mouth to receive olfactory information from their environment. This Flehmen response is seen in many animals; most notable is the forked tongue of a snake flicking in and out of the mouth. It has been observed that dogs in a conflict situation sometimes stretch their tongues forward and back in a quick, distinct motion.

**Tail.** A wagging tail doesn't always mean a friendly dog; it is simply a sign of excitement or arousal. The dog may be experiencing happiness, anxiety, anger, hunger, or romance. A dominant dog will hold his or her tail high, moving the tip back and forth only slightly. A lower tail carriage and a faster wag indicate a more subordinate dog. Ask owners to observe their dogs and decide what their dog's tail looks like in a neutral position and then pay attention to changes in the baseline in various contexts. Then they can compare that with what they understand about the rest of the dog's communication and get a larger picture of what's going on.

**Baseline Posture.** When a dog is relaxed, his or her entire body shows that relaxation. The muscles are fluid and they move gracefully. When a dog is aroused, his muscles and entire body look and feel hard. The dog's gait is more rigid than flexible. The baseline posture drawing depicts a middle of the road type of dog. Not too bold, not too worried, this dog is probably pretty easy to be around. Compare this baseline position to the following drawings to see how postures and expressions change depending on the mental state of the dog.

**Mutual Curving Nose to Tail.** Curving is a form of greeting behavior. Friendly greetings might include submissive behaviors. A friendly dog usually approaches another dog with a somewhat relaxed body and wagging tail. If the dog is somewhat unsure, the body will be stiff, and the tail will be held up stiff and high, wagging slowly. Friendly dogs may lick each other's faces and may sniff each other's rear end—and may try to do the same with other species, including humans!

**The Bow, What Does It Mean?** The bow, in which the dog places his front legs on the ground and raises his rear high in the air, seems to act as a social facilitator. Most people call it a play bow. It may invite play and some think it may serve to make sure any playful growling or body postures are not taken in the wrong way. However, others consider a bow as evidence of the dog's inward state of confusion. The dog is ready to do something but he is not sure what to do. The most common interpretation of the bow posture is as a meta-communication signal. Meta signals qualify the behavior that follows. The play bow, for example, is a meta cue telling others that what will happen next is not serious; it's just play.

**Hackles.** Dogs can raise the fur along their spines, sometimes all the way to the tail or forehead. This is called piloerection and can occur whenever the dog is aroused. Any type of arousal can produce raised hackles, even a dog that is enjoying seemingly friendly romping with another dog.

*Chapter 2   Ethology: What Is a Dog?*

## Critical Zones—Personal Space

Dogs are concerned about their personal space, also known as critical distance or flight distance. Many confrontations result from space issues. Much of canine communicative behavior is devoted to indicating tolerance at having others approach.

Let's use a human example of how dogs might feel when their personal space is invaded. Imagine sitting on a bus that is very full. There is only one very small space left in the bus, the seat right next to you. If someone boards the bus and sits in the space, it's okay. Next scene: You are on a bus that is totally empty. Someone boards the bus and sits right next to you. In this situation, that might not be okay with you. It's the same with dogs. Critical space is dictated by many variables.

It may help if you think of your dog's critical space as an imaginary line circling your dog. The circle can grow larger or smaller for the individual dog depending on factors such as environment, arousal level, and overall stress threshold.

**Traffic Light Analogy.** For the purposes of this section, we will describe personal space like the three colors of a traffic light. The colors correspond to how dogs feel about their personal space. These feelings change in each dog, depending on where the dog is, who is approaching, and other variables. Remember, your critical space on the bus changed when the conditions were different. Traffic light colors have different meanings: red means stop, yellow means caution, and green means go. A dog with a friendly or neutral reaction to someone approaching is a green light. For other dogs, the signal might be red. Just being within sight of another dog is a violation of personal space, regardless of physical distance. Some dogs are predictable when it comes to comfort distance. With other dogs, a variety of factors besides actual space have an impact on where the line is drawn that day. Watch the dog and he will tell you what you need to know.

Getting into one another's space can be stressful for dogs, especially during the first few class meetings. When dog and owner first come into a Legacy class, they are accompanied by a staff member from the parking lot or from the door and shown to a specific seat in the training area. The seats are located an appropriate distance apart to reduce space problems. During orientation, I talk about traffic lights. For simplicity, I say that dogs fall roughly into one of three categories when it comes to critical space. I then describe what a particular dog might be "thinking" when another dog or person is approaching.

- *Green Light:* "IT'S A GO! MEET ME! EVERYTHING IS OKAY, I HAVE NO SPACE PROBLEMS." Due to adequate socialization, overall personality, environment, and familiarity with the approaching individual, the dog is saying: "I'm not worried. It's okay to approach for a visit." The body language will be relaxed or even excited. The dog may even be straining to make contact. But be watchful: the dog may turn from green to yellow as an individual gets closer.

- *Yellow Light:* "CAUTION, I'M A BIT WORRIED, PLEASE DON'T STRESS ME FURTHER, I MIGHT NOT BE UNDER CONTROL." The owner needs to work with this dog more before anyone enters his space. This dog might show appeasement language or offensive or defensive threatening behavior. In class, this dog needs to feel secure that no one will enter his space uninvited. The dog might need more time or experience and perhaps later the yellow signal may become green.

- *Red Light:* "STOP, I'M VERY AFRAID OR VERY ANGRY—I MIGHT NOT BE UNDER CONTROL." The dog has defined, at this moment in time, a critical personal space. The dog does not want that space violated. The red light dog might make a last-ditch effort to keep people or dogs out of the zone. The defensive dog would rather leave or back up if given the option. Sometimes, due to small facilities or short leashes, this is impossible. The dog might bite (act of aggression) if the approaching individual continues to advance.

Green light dogs are fun to have in class and they make good demo dogs. Yellow light dogs can do well in class also. If I have a yellow light dog in my class, I ask the owner if he or she would like to place one of my yellow bandanas on the dog. That way the other people in class will remember that the dog is cautious and allow that dog plenty of space; however, it is the instructor's ultimate responsibility to keep dogs adequately separated. Red light dogs can be disruptive in beginner's class. It's counterproductive to try to teach them anything, and their behavior is upsetting to the other dogs and people in class. Hopefully you will have identified red light dogs through the registration process and suggested specialized training. The traffic light analogy is not without fault because space issues are constantly changing, depending on the state of the dog and particulars of the environment. There is no set formula for determining critical space other than allowing the dog to define it for you. Hone your skills at reading dogs.

# STRESS BEHAVIOR

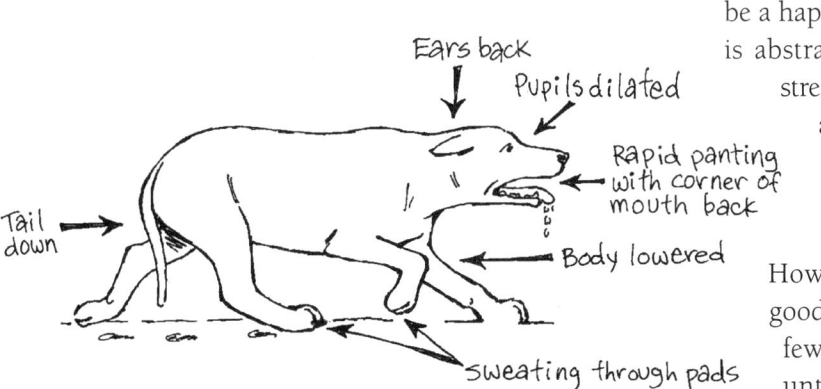

Almost any reactive state can produce stress. Social situations and fearful situations are two examples of reactive states. Stress is an influence on the dog that deviates the dog from homeostasis, the neutral, normal baseline state of one particular dog. It can make the dog more active than normal or less active than normal. It can be a happy state or an unhappy state. Stress is abstract and subjective. What's terribly stressful for one dog could be neutral for another. There's good stress and bad stress. Stress in manageable doses has a positive effect on individuals. It helps us perform to our potential. How I get ready to pack for a trip is a good example. The suitcase comes out a few days in advance. It remains empty, until perhaps the day before the trip when I've thrown one pair of socks into the case. However if it's an hour before I have to meet the van for my flight, my suitcase packing behavior increases in frequency and intensity. One could argue that I become a better, faster, and now more efficient packer of suitcases under stress. Too much stress inhibits the learning process because of chemical influences in the brain. Stressors leading to fear and anxiety behaviors activate the dog's flight or fight responses. These behaviors are essentially out of the dog's control and should be avoided in your classroom. Too much stress can produce illness because stress hormones accumulate in the body. They take a long time to dissipate. This means stress has long-term effects on a dog, some of which may not become apparent until years later.

Inevitably, we stress dogs a little even in the most positive training programs. Withholding a reward to increase behavior is probably stressful for the dog. Called an extinction burst, the dog becomes more active. The dog appears to try harder, giving us more behavior and more opportunity to catch a behavior we want to reinforce. Dog trainers walk a fine line. An overly stressed dog in your classroom needs to be detected and dealt with quickly for the well-being of that individual and for the safety and well-being of others in class. Stress is linked with numerous behavior and training problems. Dogs under stress are more likely to perform an aggressive act as a result of frustration than dogs in a more neutral state. The dogs tell us a great deal about all of this.

Here is a list of some of the common signs of stress. If you see clusters of two or more of these signs, be thinking of how to manipulate the environment to make the dog more comfortable.

- **Panting**—A dog that pants when not hot may be stressed. It's also an indicator of physical problems. Or maybe the dog just went for a run.

- **Drooling**—Look for a deeper cause of stress if drooling cannot be related to anticipation of food, sexual arousal, or an upset stomach.

- **Trembling**—Again, we must look for clusters of signs but shaking can be one indicator of stress. A dog might tremble from the cold, but if it's not cold out, a different stressor could be at work.

- **Sweaty paws**—Why are there wet paw prints on the tile floor? It's not wet out. Consider stress. Dogs perspire through their paw pads.

- **Tense body**—Rigidity is an indication of a dog that is stressed. Sometimes you have to touch the dog to feel the tension. At other times you can see tension just by the way the dog holds or moves his body. Also, look for a clenched mouth and jaws.

- **Shedding and dandruff**—Excessive hair on the veterinary examining table or the training hall floor may be an indicator of stress or other physical problems. The dog's anxiety causes tensing of the body, which in turn helps loose fur work its way out.

- **Change in eyes**—If it's not particularly dark out but your dog is wide eyed and his pupils are dilated, it could be a sign of stress. The eyes of some very frightened dogs will show more white than normal.

## Fearful Behavior

The term fearful dog is too broad; a dog can be afraid of some things and not others. Fearful behavior is also contextual. Fearful behaviors are caused by experiences the dog considers risky. Fear doesn't necessarily have to do with social hierarchy. A dog can be subordinate to, but not fearful of, other individuals. Dogs can be fearful without being threatening or aggressive.

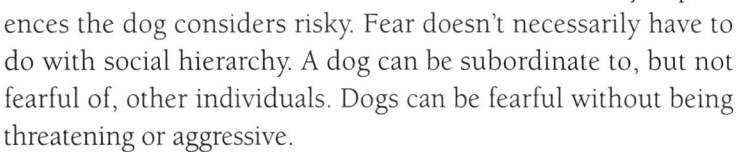

Physiological indicators of fear are the release of adrenaline, cortisol, and other chemicals into the body. We can't see this happen, but we can see the change in the dog's body language and behavior. If given the opportunity, the dog's first reaction to fear is to try to move away to increase the space between him and the fear-producing situation or thing. The overall body language is low; the dog tucks his tail, avoids eye contact, and will pull or flatten his ears into a backward position. His eyes may be dilated, appearing big, black, and wide open. If startled suddenly, the dog might urinate or defecate. Dog owners often believe their dogs have been abused if they react fearfully to harmless stimuli or situations. While this may occasionally be the case, it is more likely that the dog has not been well-socialized. Freezing, trembling, panting, or whining are other common fearful behaviors. When dogs are afraid, they may be reluctant or refuse to approach any unfamiliar dog or person.

In a class, these dogs may be pulling toward the door or attempting to get to a far corner of the room, as far away from other people and dogs as possible. Fearful responses are also characterized by attempts to hide under chairs and other objects, or behind the owner. Fearful dogs may be unwilling to enter the building, may freeze in one spot when they arrive, or slowly creep around the room a step at a time.

## Reactive, Excitable Behavior

Some individuals have an unreasonably strong reaction to events in comparison with other dogs. For example, a highly reactive dog may do spins and jumps while watching dogs enter and waiting for class to start. A less reactive dog would not exhibit such extreme behaviors. If you bring out a strange item for a game, a pile of hula-hoops for example, one dog may cringe on first sight of these new objects. A more normal response may be for the dog to take notice and attempt to investigate. A dog is considered reactive if he displays any behavior (fearful, aggressive, friendly) that goes beyond the behavior of a "normal" dog in frequency, intensity, or duration. Reactive dogs have poor impulse control. Their energy builds up and if untrained, is not always released at the appropriate time. They will bounce into action when they feel the need, like the whistle blows to relieve the pressure on a teakettle. Standing around in class while the instructor talks may be difficult for this dog. Class instructors should be ready to intersperse active exercises with stationary ones.

## Ambivalence

Ambivalence means being in conflict. The dog is unsure, unclear, undecided, and the body postures might show both offensive and defensive components at the same time. For example, a dog may be staring, but he is backing up in a defensive position. Then he may lunge forward. Or, in a greeting situation, a dog can display mixed language that indicates he is friendly, and also language that indicates he is fearful. The way the dog will go, friendly or fearful, often depends on the environment and how the other individual responds to the greeting.

## Displacement Behavior

Displacement behaviors are important because they are signs that the animal is unsure of herself or anxious about how to behave. They can be early warning signals telling you the dog is feeling threatened or fearful. They are signs that a dog is in conflict or frustrated and trying to "hold it together" while deciding what to do. Perhaps she is thinking of fleeing, but realizes she is in a corner or on a leash. If retreating isn't an option, she may be considering a threatening motion forward to try to increase the space around her. In class, dogs in this state should be placed in an area with a solid wall or corner behind them so they realize no one can approach from the rear. At the same time, there should be adequate space between them and this safety backstop so that the dog can retreat if need be. Give this dog enough room to assess the class situation as a safe one. The undecided dog may display behavior that is irrelevant to the situation. Common displacement behaviors in dogs are yawning, lip licking, and scratching. These behaviors can occur for other reasons, but when they seem out of context for the situation in which they are occurring, they are usually displacement activity. When these behaviors occur as displacement, they usually occur at higher rates than for other motivations. For example, a comfortable dog might occasionally yawn, but repeated yawning is more common as a displacement activity, especially when the environment of the dog is changing. Displacement behaviors indicate the dog is in conflict; all is not well.

## The Slide-of-No-Return Analogy

Help owners read their dog's body language. Not just the easily recognized more obvious "**bold print**" language, but also the easy to overlook "fine print" language. It's fairly easy to tell when a dog is shouting out a message with his body. If we can interpret the subtle whispers that often precede the obvious shouting of information, we can step in and help avoid problems. That intervention might be giving the dog more space, changing the method of instruction, or altering the interaction between the owner and pet to a more manageable situation for the dog. I talk to my students about sliding boards. When you are approaching the board, perhaps with just one step on the lowest step of the ladder, there is still time to change your mind and do something else. When you are at the top of the slide, you can still change your mind, but it's more difficult. If we can read the dog's signals at these two preliminary stages, intervention has a better chance of working. If the dog is already on the slide down, it's an easy sign to see, but very difficult to stop or to reverse the action. Class instructors should be able to identify a dog at the top of the slide, or before they start to climb the ladder.

Worried dogs need to communicate to others that they are not a threat and will do no harm. Their actions might be displays of escape intention, such as turning the head or body to the side, or a sudden sit. Displacement activities can serve this purpose. Ethologist Nikolaas Tinbergen, in the book *The Study of Instinct,* describes similar actions as cutoff signals. The signals suggest a compromise between potential adversaries. It's a means to postpone or break off agonistic conflict or an expressive compromise between fighting and fleeing. The problem arises when different people have different terms for the same or similar signals. Some of the typical cutoff signals have been previously mentioned as appeasement or displacement displays. In a personal conversation with Sue Sternberg, she describes these displays as "holding it together," that is, the dog is keeping self-control in a difficult situation. Others define the same signs as a deviation from homeostasis—the dog begins moving away from neutral, something is about to change. P. Leyhausen (*Motivation of Human and Animal Behavior: An Ethological View.* New York: D. Van Norstrand, 1973) reports that the compromise signal is not a submissive gesture, but an opportunity for the contestants to call a draw and walk away without loss or gain of status. Dr. Suzanne Hetts reports that the group of signals labeled "calming signals" by Turid Rugaas is a mixture of several types of behavior, including submissive, appeasement, and displacement behaviors.

## Calming Signals

Norwegian dog specialist Turid Rugaas is credited for coining the term "calming signals." She explains calming signals as cues that produce pacifying effects on the animal exhibiting them. Rugaas believes that the signals have a mutually pacifying effect that curtails hostilities before they have a chance to escalate into more serious conflict. Calming signals do not necessarily carry status significance. They simply function to smooth over agonistic tensions. In a recent personal communication, Turid reported these signs are often associated with an attempt to resolve a social conflict. They might appear to pet owners as out of place for the context. Clusters of calming signals will alert you to observe carefully. Adjustments to the environment, such as increasing space between individuals, are in order.

- **Yawning**—Dogs yawn when things are getting tense. Perhaps the dog was holding his breath and the deep inhalation and subsequent exhalation of a yawn acts to increases oxygen intake.

- **Stretching the Tongue**—A quick little flick of the dog's tongue often goes unnoticed because it is clouded by more obvious signals. It's another way for a dog to convey the same calming message. Both yawning and tongue flicking will often appear in photographs because posing for a photo session can be stressful.

**Sniffing**     **Yawning**     **Blinking**

**Licking**     **Turning Away**

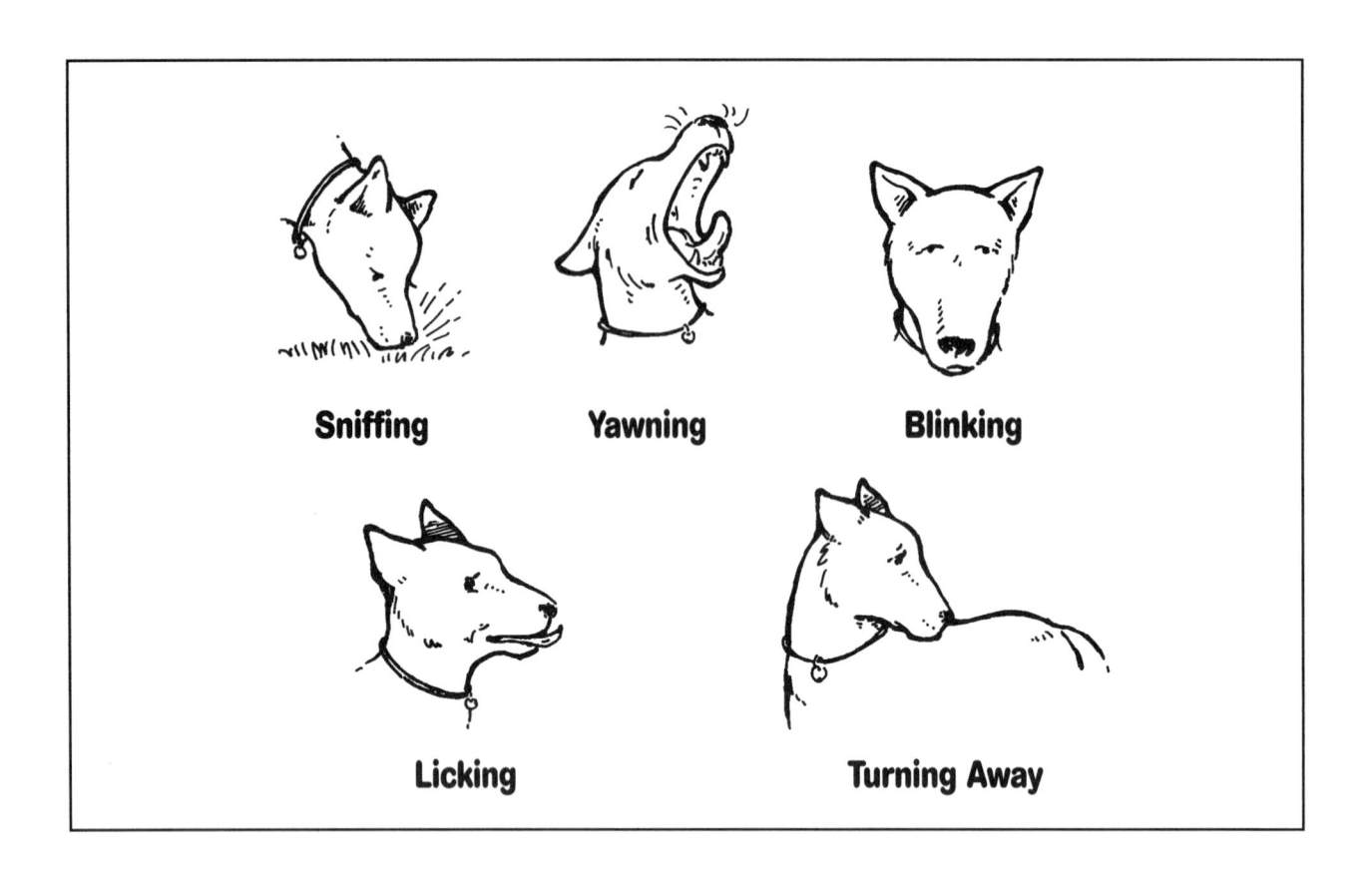

- **Scratching**—A dog that scratches himself even though he doesn't have itchy skin may be diffusing a potential conflict. This is often seen in situations where a little itch would be inconsequential, for example, in the face of a confrontation.

- **Turning Away, Curving**—Dogs will turn their eyes, head, or their entire body away from a problem. This curving away seems to indicate a less threatening demeanor. People can convey this message by curving away themselves. It may also show submission, the opposite of face-to-face contact.

- **Sniffing**—Dogs use their noses to explore their environment, but excessive sniffing can be a calming signal. This dog is not quite sure about what is going on. It's a stalling tactic that can be seen after giving a cue to "Come," for example.

- **Blinking, Averting Eyes**—Dogs approaching each other look away or make exaggerated eye blinks as a coping behavior. You can gain the confidence of a worried dog more quickly by avoiding direct eye contact and turning away.

- **Splitting**—It's interesting to see a dog walk between two dogs interacting with each other. It's as if the dog wants to come between and split up the focus. Stepping between two dogs staring at each other is often enough to end the interaction.

*Coaching People to Train Their Dogs*

Turid Rugaas theorizes that humans can communicate with and can calm dogs by mimicking the displays dogs use to cut off others. Training class instructors should take note when dogs are trying to communicate in this manner.

## AGONISTIC BEHAVIOR: CONFLICT RESOLUTION

Animals living in groups depend on each other for survival. It's in the group's best interest to co-exist peacefully. Groups need a means to avoid or resolve social or competitive disputes without injury. An injured member affects the well-being of the entire group. Two general categories for resolving social conflict are fight or flight.

In ethological terms, behaviors used in response to social conflict or competitive encounters are called agonistic behaviors. In everyday language, these behaviors are sometimes incorrectly lumped together as aggressive behavior. Aggression is an extreme example of agonistic behavior, but the following categories, which are all forms of agonistic behavior, are more helpful in dealing with dogs.

Here are some options dogs have to resolve social or competitive disputes:

### Avoidance

One choice of agonistic behavior is to simply leave or flee, and avoid a threatening situation altogether. Dogs signal their intention to flee in class by backing away, or getting under or behind a chair or the owner. In a training class, dogs are often prevented from backing up by a tight leash or by their position against a wall or other obstacle. Dogs in this situation are forced to select another option.

### Appeasement

Another choice dogs can make to resolve social conflict is to display behaviors with a goal to turn off or inhibit perceived threats from others. These actions are often labeled as "calming signals."

### Submission

Different from appeasement, behaviors labeled as submissive are shown toward people or dogs that have an established relationship with the dog. While respect for his leader is important, an overly submissive dog could pose a training problem. Positive methods and a change in relationship are in order and can be very effective in training this dog. Submissive dogs may be conflicted. These dogs may be willing to approach unfamiliar individuals and then may act submissively when they do.

Some submissive gestures are similar to those meant to communicate anxiety (fear, stress). Gestures of lower rank are not necessarily signals of fear. Fearful behavior can be a reaction to something in the environment—loud noises, strange sights. Freezing, shaking, and defecation, which are components of fearful behavior,

**Active Submission**

*(Labels on illustration: Tail down; Body lowered; Ears back; Forehead smooth; Licks at mouth of superior dog; Corners of mouth back; Grovelling movements)*

**Passive Submission**

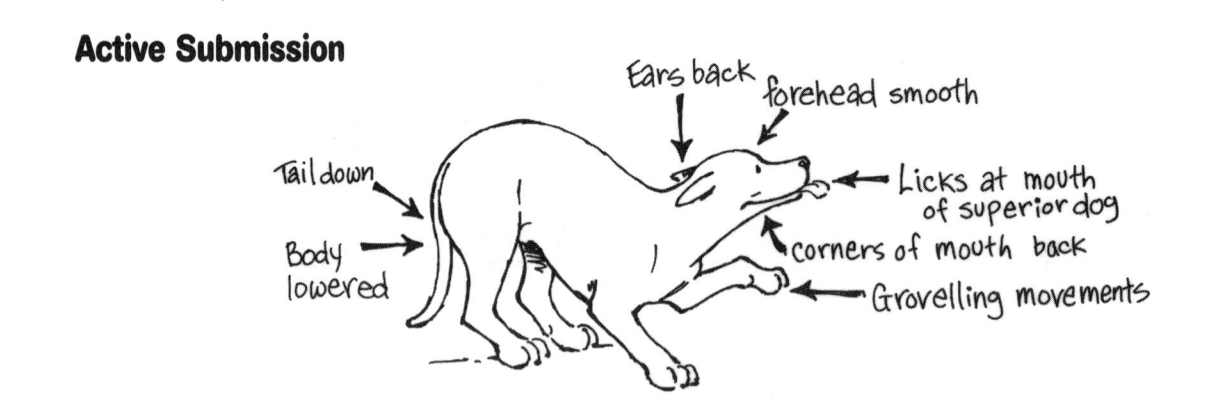

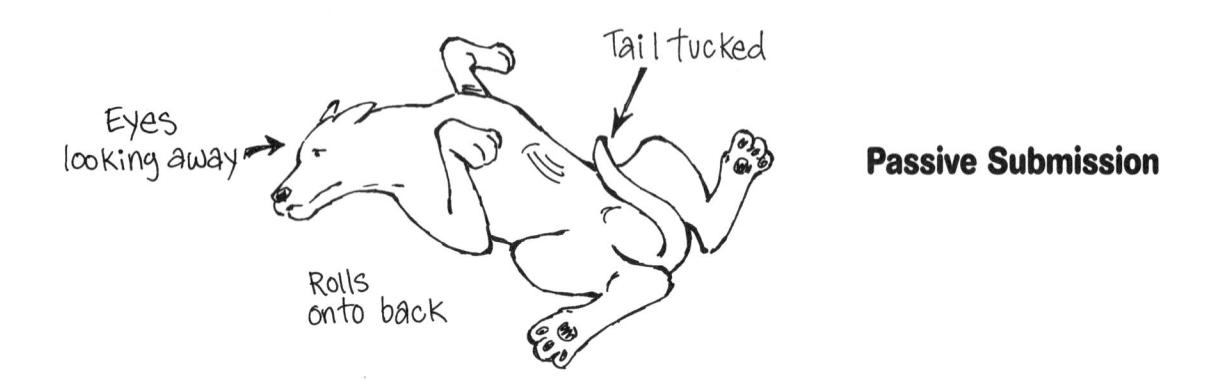

*(Labels on illustration: Eyes looking away; Rolls onto back; Tail tucked)*

are not usually seen in submission. Means to identify and reduce fear reactions are mentioned in upcoming chapters and are important tools in any instructor's toolbox.

Submission includes a wide range of postures, which are often sub-categorized as active or passive submission. Dogs assume submissive postures and may even urinate while doing so in an attempt to inhibit threats coming from another. Most, but certainly not all, dogs "play by these rules." An instructor cannot depend on dogs to diffuse threats by submissive posturing. The instructor is the advocate for each and every dog in class. Maintain suitable spacing and keep arousal levels within reasonable bounds by coaching appropriate exercises for the demeanor of the class.

## *Threats of Aggression and Aggression*

A dog that feels in danger in the presence of another individual may try to keep that scary individual away. One way to do so is by warning of possible future aggression. The goal of this threat of aggression is not to cause physical injury but simply to warn the other to stop. Threatening dogs can be quite dramatic with lunging, snarl-barks, and even snapping—just short of bodily contact. Air snaps are inhibited bites. A dog could have connected an air snap and done harm, but chose to threaten only. Threats and aggression are on a continuum anywhere from a subtle warning to an all-out attack. Aggression is often the result of frustration or some inner conflict, so keep that in mind when planning your training environment.

What a dog chooses to do depends on the available options. If the dog is in a confined area or held on a tight leash, she might go right into full-fledged aggression knowing there's no backing up or getting away. An instructor needs to pay attention and respond to these most subtle precursors because threats can quickly escalate into a change of behavior—aggressive behavior—making contact with the intent of doing harm.

### Offensive Motivation for Threats/Aggression

The offensively threatening or aggressive dog is fearless, assertive, and self-confident. The body in general appears to be up and forward from the dog's neutral body posture. However, one must take into consideration each individual dog's conformation. Boxers and Doberman Pinschers, for example, are naturally up and forward in posture. In general, the offensively threatening dog makes herself look larger and faces the problem straight on. The hackles (hair) along the back of the dog may be raised. The tail might be elevated higher than neutral position and wagging slowly. The ears will be up and forward. The dog makes eye contact. The dog may show her teeth, growl, or bark. If given options, the offensive dog will be willing to lunge at and chase people and dogs out of her critical zone. Challenge her, and she'll probably lunge, chase, or bite if given the opportunity. Sometimes it's hard to know what a particular dog considers a challenge. Sometimes it might be as simple as walking too close to "her" area in class.

Think about warriors. A warrior carries both a shield and a spear. If she uses the spear, she is being offensive, ready to attack others. If she uses the shield, she's simply trying to hide or fend off the problem to protect herself. The offensive one is calling the shots and commanding the situation. While an offensive dog can be trained to be a good companion, the average owner lacks the skill needed to manage the dog in all situations. Fortunately, offensive dogs are in the minority. The offensive dog is an unnecessary risk in a class situation. Help the dog and owner in another way.

### Defensive Motivation for Threats/Aggression

A dog displaying defensive postures looks the opposite of the offensive dog. He doesn't want to use a spear. He is very much into staying behind his shield. The dog is hesitant, nervous, distrustful, fearful, and hopes the scary thing goes away. He's trying to protect himself from real or perceived harm. The body will be low to the ground, as if he is trying to protect vulnerable parts of his body. The hackles may be up. Defensive dogs usually avoid eye contact. The ears and tail will be down, and the eyes may be dilated. Defensive dogs may also growl and bark, or whine and whimper. Defensive dogs may take a little lunge forward, but then back up. Although the actions of a defensive dog may be misinterpreted as bold, these actions are based on fear. The dog may have learned from past experience that an offensive looking picture works to keep threats at bay, or the dog may be confused and ambivalent. The owner of this dog might say, "He's protecting me," but the dog is behind the owners: not the ideal place to protect the owner. The dog probably hopes his owner will help get rid of the scary thing.

## Conflicted or Mixed Motivation for Threats/Aggression

Similar to humans, some dogs can't make up their minds. They shift back and forth between offensive and defensive actions. The body language reflects this confusion and in turn can be difficult to interpret by instructors. Our immediate response is not to ponder WHY, but do something to quickly diffuse threatening behavior for any reason. One of the best neutralizers is space. Another is keeping the dogs in your class focused and busy on a rewarding task. It is important to evaluate why the threat occurred to make sure that situation is not repeated in your classroom.

## Triggers, Categories, and Reasons for Threats/Aggression

Once again we become mixed up in our own human language, let alone the dog's language. Following are various terms used when referring to reasons for aggression. Categories of aggression are arbitrary, and they overlap. Some dogs are aggressive due to triggers from more than one category occurring at the same time. It seems that the motivations are similar whether we are talking about dog-to-dog interactions or dog-to-human interactions. It's important to describe the behavior rather than label it. The following behaviors might be seen in a classroom situation. They are fluid. Some fade from one into another without distinct boundaries. The words "it depends" keep popping into my mind:

**Fear**—Fear is a defensive type of aggression that occurs when an animal perceives his physical safety is threatened or when his critical distance is invaded. In the popular literature, an animal displaying this type of aggression is referred to as a "fear-biter." Fearfully aggressive animals will not generally chase their opponent or continue an attack once the opponent has retreated outside the critical distance. Fear-motivated aggression is associated with defensive body postures. Components of fear or defensive behavior may be combined with other types of aggression. I've listed fear first as, in my experience, it seems to be the main trigger of threats and aggression.

**Dominance**—This term is heard often and seems to be a popular label for threats and aggression. When reported by an owner, it's usually not well-defined. Ask for details. Ask the owner to paint a word picture. This type of aggression can be triggered when another individual in the social living group fails to display the proper appeasement behavior. It can be triggered when another attempts to take possession of a valued resource: the bone, the couch, or the ball. This is not a personality trait or emotion but a reaction to a social situation. The body language appears more offensive than defensive. Aggression to others in the social living group may be caused by reasons other than dominance.

**Possessive**—Possessive aggression occurs when a dog has a valued resource such as a bed, toy, or food and does not want to share! Some authorities combine this category with dominance aggression and I've seen it described as territorial or guarding behavior. Possessive aggression can be directed toward other dogs or humans. This type of aggression may have offensive or defensive components.

**Protective**—When an animal is defending one or more members of its social group, it might be termed protective aggression. Some authorities include maternal aggression in this category. Others include territorial aggression as a special type of protective aggression that includes the defense of a home or breeding area. Protective aggression may have offensive or defensive components.

**Territorial**—Territorial aggression is shown when a dog is defending his or her home area or social group. Is this possessive aggression or protective aggression? These are gray areas. Territorial aggression may have defensive as well as offensive components. A dog's sense of territory may extend well beyond what you or the owner consider appropriate. A dog may extend home property lines such as fences, gates, and doorways to include the park he visits every day. If the dog is in his car, the car and immediate area around it could be considered territory. In class, the place the dog has settled with his owner may quickly be considered territory.

**Pain-related**—This is defensive aggression seen in response to physical pain or discomfort. This is sometimes classified as fearful aggression. Some authorities put punishment-elicited aggression in this category. Be alert for a dog that might be in pain. Don't diagnose or speculate, but as a pet professional, you can draw the owner's attention to your observation.

**Redirected**—If a dog is prevented or blocked from attacking her primary target, that aggression can be directed toward any individual who is handy. Hopefully you have screened out dogs with such propensities through your orientation or profiling procedures. This is important because owners, the next dog in line, or the nearby instructor can be the target of the redirected behavior.

**Socially-Facilitated**—This is sometimes called pack-facilitated aggression. If one or more dogs in a group display aggressive behavior, it is easier for the others in the group to follow suit. This process is seen in other areas of behavior, such as barking and howling.

## *Predatory Behavior*

Predatory behavior is sometimes listed as a form of aggression. Most authorities do not consider predatory behavior to be aggression because the intent is to obtain food. It is not displayed as a reaction to social conflicts; it's directed toward individuals or objects moving away such as joggers, bicyclists, or skateboarders, which stimulate predatory-like behavior. Dogs will also display predatory behavior toward small mammals such as cats, mice, and birds. Some dogs will chase a cat if the cat runs. If the cat stops, the dog does nothing. The trigger is gone. Some attacks on children are probably motivated by predatory behavior. The dog perceives the quick, jerky movements and high-pitched vocalizations of children as similar to the behavior of prey animals.

Stalking, chasing, and nipping at the legs or ankles are characteristics of predatory behavior. A Border Collie working a herd of sheep is engaging in the initial stages of predatory behavior.

Predatory behavior has nothing to do with malice. The fisherman doesn't hate the fish; he just wants to catch a meal. Catching prey is not an emotional occurrence. It is business-like and based on instinct.

The term predatory drift most often refers to dog-to-dog interactions. Dogs can be getting along fine, when suddenly something causes a heightened arousal level, which triggers a limbic response, making one dog regard the other as prey.

## WHAT'S AN INSTRUCTOR TO DO?

The Class Organization chapter contains strategies on how to avoid having aggressive dogs in class and how to help them otherwise. There is always the potential of an offensive or defensive threat. Some situations to pay attention to in class may be:

- Someone arriving late to class
- A vocal or physical outburst of energy from another dog

- Moving exercises such as "Come" and heeling
- Use of toys
- Excitement and arousal when playing games
- Owners obviously not focusing on their dogs
- Anything happening around a doorway
- Body language showing signs of stress
- Dogs and owners drifting too close together in class
- Assistants reaching over dogs in an attempt to help

## *Biting Is a Natural Option*

Some dogs have very good reasons for biting. That doesn't make biting an acceptable behavior in our society. And we must avoid this situation at all costs in class. Sacks and Lockwood reported in the *Journal of the American Veterinary Association*, that on average 4.7 million people are bitten by dogs each year in the United States. Of these, approximately 800,000 people require medical attention.

Before you decide you can help a dog that is a potential biter or has bitten, consider these concepts:

- First do no harm. Will working with the dog and owner put the dog, the owner, or others in danger? A questionable dog should not be enrolled in class.

- Can you give adequate information to the owner and gain immediate and complete owner-compliance with appropriate confinement and control of the dog? Will the owner let down his or her management guard if the dog is perceived to be "better"?

- Will you be available for the long-term follow-up needed for this client?

- Do you feel confident in your knowledge to identify why the dog is behaving this way? Do you feel confident in your ability to safely resolve the situation? If not, you should refer the client to someone with more expertise.

- Owners of dogs known as biters or anticipated to be biters
  - should not bring the dog into a class situation,
  - should consider a referral to a canine behavior specialist,
  - should be made AWARE of the potential danger and liability, and
  - should be given realistic information about the possibility of complete rehabilitation.

## *Classifying Bites*

Dr. Ian Dunbar, popular writer and presenter on pet dog training, came up with this standardized way to evaluate bites. His evaluation procedure has been recently revised and is used by some animal control agencies in the United States.

## DR. IAN DUNBAR'S BITE EVALUATION SCALE

**LEVEL ONE BITE:** Air snap. This is a warning bite that doesn't connect. The dog intentionally inhibited his bite and "missed" on purpose. The dog is doing everything possible to get your attention and tell you that all is not well. There were probably many signs leading up to this snap.

**LEVEL TWO BITE:** Air snap with skin contact. There might be a red mark or slight bruise, but no skin is punctured. The dog has purposely not bitten down hard. The dog is inhibited to bite, but could be losing that inhibition. If Level One and Two snaps aren't working for him, he could escalate to Level Three.

**LEVEL THREE BITE:** There may be one to four puncture holes from a single bite. Skin punctures are no deeper than HALF the length of the dog's CANINE teeth.

**LEVEL FOUR BITE:** One to four holes from a single bite, deeper than half the length of the teeth. There is soft tissue damage such as (a) severe bruising telling us the dog clamped down HARD, and/or (b) slashes in both directions from the puncture indicating that the dog bit and shook his head.

**LEVEL FIVE BITE:** Multiple level four bites with deep punctures or slashing due to clamping down, shaking, or repeated gripping in an attempt to move the bite to a "better" advantage.

**LEVEL SIX BITE:** The victim died as a result of the attack.

**DR DUNBAR SUMMARIZES:** 99% of all dog bites are levels one through three, and mostly ones or twos.

Hopefully you will never experience a bite in the course of your dog training career. Comply with the dog bite laws of your community. You may, by law, be required to report any bite that you know about. All five of Dr. Dunbar's levels should be dealt with outside of a group class situation. Level three, four, and five bites at the very least, should be referred to a dog bite (aggression) specialist. Levels 1 and 2 might respond to a program of desensitization, counter conditioning, supervision, environment and mental changes, and strict compliance with safety measures. A general pet dog class situation is not the best environment for a biter or potential biter. I view Levels One and Two as a big neon sign in capital letters. The dog is saying, "something has to be changed for me to be okay." Pet professionals need to identify the subtle body language that leads up to such bold statements from the dog.

# Chapter 2 Review Questions

1. In dog breeding, if you select for a change in looks, you also get
   a. hip dysplasia.
   b. rich.
   c. a change in behavior.

2. Some people say canine behavior is divided into three categories: reproductive behaviors, hazard avoidance, and
   a. food acquisition.
   b. tennis ball chasing.
   c. burying bones.

3. A dog's temperament is exactly half the result of genetics and half environment.
   a. True
   b. False

4. A defensive dog
   a. is afraid of something.
   b. will never bite anyone.
   c. makes the best pet for children.

5. Which sex will mark territory?
   a. Castrated male
   b. Female
   c. Intact male
   d. Any of the above can be true

6. Assigning human traits and motivations to animals is:
   a. Polymorphism
   b. Egocentrism
   c. Anthropomorphism
   d. Anthropocentrism

7. Early experience is vital because it
   a. affects the brain's development.
   b. is the first learning experience.
   c. affects the number of brain cells.
   d. affects the growth plates.

8. The limbic system is involved with emotions, such as fear.
   a. True
   b. False

Answers: 1. c  2. a  3. b  4. a  5. d  6. c  7. a  8. a

## ADDITIONAL READING/RESOURCES

Animal Behavior Associates, Inc., 4994 S. Independence Way. Littleton, CO 80123 (Dr. Suzanne Hetts and Dr. Dan Estep). *AnimalBehaviorAssociates.com*

Beckoff, M. and Jamieson, D. (1996). *Readings in Animal Cognition.* Cambridge, MA: MIT Press.

Booth, S. (1992). *Schutzhund Obedience, Training in Drive.* Ridgefield, CT: Podium Publications.

Breland, M. and Breland, K. (1961). "The misbehavior of organisms." *American Psychologist Journal,* Nov. 681–684.

Coppinger, R. and Coppinger, L. (2001). *Dogs.* New York: Scribner.

Dodman, N. and Shuster, L. (1998). *Psychopharmacology of Animal Behavior Disorders.* Malden, MA: Blackwell Science, Inc.

Fox, M. (1972). *Understanding Your Dog.* New York: Conard, McCann, Geoghegan.

Hare, B., Brown, M., Williamson, C., Tomasello, M. (2002). The Domestication of Social Cognition in Dogs, *Science* 298: 1634–1636.

Hetts, S. and Estep, D. (2000). *Canine Behavior.* ACT Humane Society of the United States.

Klinghammer, Erich, Ph.D. Director, Eckhard H. Hess Institute of Ethology, Wolf Park, Battle Ground, IN 47920.

Leyhausen P. (1973). *Motivation of Human and Animal Behavior: An Ethological View.* New York: D. Van Norstrand.

Lindsay, S. (2000). *Handbook of Applied Dog Behavior and Training,* Vol. I, Adaptation and Learning. Ames, Iowa State Press.

Lindsay, S. (2001). *Handbook of Applied Dog Behavior and Training,* Vol. II, Etiology and Assessment. Ames, Iowa State Press.

Lorenz, K. (1948). *Man Meets Dog,* Reprint Edition (1994). Tokyo: Kodansha International.

Lorenz, K. (1982). *The Foundations of Ethology: The Principle Ideas and Discoveries in Animal Behavior.* New York: Simon & Schuster.

McConnell, P. (2002). *The Other End of the Leash.* New York: Ballantine.

Neilson, J. C., Eckstein, R. A., and Hart, B. L. (1997). "Effect of castration on problem behaviors in male dogs with reference to age and duration of behavior." *Journal of the American Veterinary Medical Association,* 211(2): 180–182.

O' Farrell, V. and Peachey, E. (1990). "Behavioural effects of ovariohysterectomy on bitches." *Journal of Small Animal Practice,* 31(12): 595–598.

O'Farrell, V. (1992). *Manual of Canine Behavior.* Sussex: British Small Animal Veterinary Association.

O'Heare, J. (2002). *Canine Neuropsychology.* Ottawa, Canada: DogPsych Publishing.

Pfaffenberger, C. J. (1963). *The New Knowledge of Dog Behavior,* Howell, Reprint Edition (2001). Wenatchee: Dogwise Publishing.

Sacks J., Kresnow M., and Houston, B. (1996). "Dog bites: how big a problem?" *Injury Prevention,* 2:52–4.

Sacks, J., Sinclair, L., Gilchrist, J., Golab, C., and Lockwood, R. (2000). "Dog bites." *Journal of the American Veterinary Medical Association,* 217:836–840

Scott, J. P. and Fuller, J. L. (1965). *Genetics and the Social Behavior of the Dog.* Chicago: University of Chicago Press.

Tinbergen, N. (1974). "Ethology and stress diseases." University of Oxford, *Oxford England Science,* 185:20–27.

Tinbergen, N. (1951). *The Study of Instinct.* London: Oxford University Press.

Trut, L. N. (1999). "Early canid domestication: The farm-fox experiment." *American Scientist,* Vol. 87, 2:160–169

Wayne, R. K., et al. (1997). "Multiple and ancient origins of the domestic dog." *Science,* 276:1687–1689

Wayne, R. K. (1993). "Molecular evolution of the dog family." *Trends in Genetics,* 9:218–224.

Whitney, L. (1971). *Dog Psychology; The Basis of Dog Training,* New York: Howell.

Wolf Park, North American Wildlife Federation, Battle Ground, Indiana. *www.wolfpark.org.*

Zink, M. C. (1998). *Peak Performance, Coaching the Canine Athlete®,* Maryland: Canine Sports Productions.

Zimen, E. "Social dynamics of the wolf pack," in M. W. Fox, ed., *The wild canids:their systematics, behavioral ecology and evolution,* pp. 336–362. New York: Van Nostrand Reinhold Co.

# CHAPTER 3

# THE SCIENCE OF LEARNING

"*Practice doesn't make perfect—
Perfect practice makes perfect.*"

—Steve White

# LEARNING THEORY BASICS

## Training Is a Science, an Art, and a Mechanical Skill

Think of the science behind training as the hardware in your computer. It's the framework or skeleton. Think of the art of training as software. Software is the stuff that makes the computer easy to use and fun to be with. Think of the mechanical skill of training as practice. To do a good job at the computer, you need to teach your fingers to fly accurately and quickly over the keyboard. Science, art, and mechanical skill are all important in dog training. This chapter will explore the science of learning.

Why is learning theory important to a dog trainer when dog training is a very "hands-on" task? Let's use the example again of driving a car. It's pretty quick and easy to learn how to use the steering wheel and operate the pedals. Everyone is doing it. But what happens if the car unexpectedly makes a funny noise or stops running? Can the driver fix it to run smoothly again? It's my goal that my students understand dogs and have enough skill to work independently and successfully through rough times with their dogs.

Learning theory is not a mystery. Learning is a process that results in the dog recognizing relationships between events and hence causes his behavior to change. Some learning principles are introduced in this chapter. In subsequent chapters you will be given examples and exercises reviewing these principles. This book will attempt to present the science of learning in an easy-to-use form. However, you might find the need to refer back to this chapter. It is possible for your students to train their dogs appropriately without knowing any of the scientific and practical reasons behind your methods. However, an instructor needs to know these things. Don't feel as though you must teach this language and these principles to your students. As long as you understand how behavior and training works, you can present it to your students in an easier, user friendly format.

Here is an example of a common mistake: A person might say, "I'm going to train the new way, the operant conditioning way, the nice way with food and a clicker." This statement gets high marks for enthusiasm, but is scored low for correctness.

- Operant conditioning is not new. It's been around for years.
- The real definition of operant conditioning includes things that are not necessarily nice.

- Classical conditioning, as well as operant conditioning, plays a big part in dog training.
- You don't need to use food—or a clicker—to use operant or classical conditioning.

Dogs learn by association, but there are different kinds of association. Following are definitions that include an explanation of operant (Skinnerian or instrumental conditioning) and respondant (Pavlovian or classical conditioning).

Bob Bailey began training animals in 1957. He joined Keller and Marian Breland (Marian was a graduate student of B. F. Skinner's) in Animal Behavior Enterprises (ABE), a commercial animal training organization that produced the first training directors for Sea World. ABE also worked with the United States government training a variety of animals for national defense purposes. Bob explains, "In the operant paradigm, an organism can experience three outcomes or consequences of its behavior: something good, something bad, or nothing at all. All three have respondent and operant components, and many of the words we use today to describe these results are derived from Pavlov's work. . . . The fact that animals will do things that work, and do less of things that don't work, indicates that the animal is changing its behavior based on consequences—the better the consequence, the more likely the behavior is to occur, and vice versa."

# CLASSICAL CONDITIONING

*Classical conditioning is the learned association between two events: One event is neutral and one event elicits an unconditioned response.*

Around 1900, Russian scientist Ivan Pavlov was studying the physiology of the digestive glands using dogs as research models. To conduct his experiments, he presented his dogs with food, a primary (unconditioned) reinforcer. The dogs' natural reflex was to salivate. Pavlov did not teach the dogs to drool. During the course of his salivation experiments, Pavlov observed that the dogs salivated as soon as he or one of his assistants entered the laboratory wearing a white coat. The dogs' response wasn't dependent on whether or not the staff had meat to offer them. The dogs had come to associate a person wearing a white coat, a secondary (conditioned) reinforcer, with the experience of being fed. The dogs were not born knowing white coats predicted food. It was a learned association. Pavlov continued experiments by ringing a bell before presenting the food. Soon the dogs salivated when they heard a bell . . . with or without meat in the offing. Pavlov went on to win a Nobel Prize for his work on digestion, and then spent a great deal of his life studying classical conditioning, the learned association between two events.

**EXAMPLE:** You just adopted a dog from the shelter. He loves to eat. You gave him a few tidbits while in the dining room. Very soon he learns to become excited when you enter the dining room. At first, it was just one room of many in your home. Now the dog has learned a special meaning for this room. This is classical conditioning.

**EXAMPLE:** Milk cows look forward to being milked because milking feels good, it relieves pressure on the cow's udder. You visit your friend who works in a dairy barn. You notice that as soon as the milk suction machine is turned on and the cows hear that noise, they begin to drip milk. Cows are not born knowing what a milking machine sounds like. Hearing the sound and letting down their milk is a learned association. It's classical conditioning.

**EXAMPLE:** To a dog, the sound of a clicker is unimportant (unless of course she's sound sensitive!). The click has no real meaning at first, but that sound becomes a good sound if it is quickly and regularly followed by a bit of desired food. It's a learned association. It's classical conditioning.

**EXAMPLE:** In Legacy's DogSense courses, we play Pavlov's dog by presenting a cue (a yellow flag for example) before asking volunteers to place a slice of lemon in their mouths. Very soon the sight of the flag has the students puckering up. It doesn't take many repetitions for students to report that they begin to drool when they see the lemon container, or when I ask them to line up for the experiment, and when they first see me in the morning.

## Classical Conditioning Working Against You

Classical conditioning occurs frequently in dog training. You can use it to your advantage, but sometimes it is the cause for behavior you don't want. Think of it as Pavlov coming back to haunt you. For example, say you want your dog to sit still and wait while you throw a ball for him. You then want him to run after the ball when you say, "Fetch." When you pick up the ball, he dances out ahead because he's made the association of what will be coming next. Trainers might call this a mistake, or anticipation, or a poor "Sit Stay." It's classical conditioning. Perhaps you didn't want that behavior, but the dog has been conditioned to do it. It is a mistake, a mistake of the trainer, not the dog.

## Conditioned Emotional Response

Some unwanted behaviors, such as avoidance or aggression, are the result of fear, which is an emotional state. Emotional states are influenced by classical conditioning. A dog might learn to associate certain cues with certain other unpleasant events. If the dog is riding in a car and suddenly hears another car backfire, the fright of the noise might be associated with car rides. This is a conditioned emotional response (CER). The CER might result in a dog that balks, tries to escape, or a dog that snaps when being placed in a car by his owner. The good thing is that while time consuming, it is possible to counter condition that conditioned emotional response. Some examples appear in Chapter 8. There are many more examples of classical conditioning throughout the textbook. But let's move on to the next important concept.

# OPERANT CONDITIONING

*Operant conditioning is learning by association with what happens after the behavior.*

The short explanation of behavioral consequences is: Behavior is a function of its consequences. What is reinforced will occur more often. What is punished will occur less often.

Early in the 1900s American researcher Edward Thorndike was interested in the principles of learning and behavior. His Law of Effect plays a critical part in learning. Paraphrased, that law states: "Responses that are made just prior to a pleasant (satisfying) event are more likely to be repeated, while responses that are made just prior to unpleasant (annoying) events are more likely to diminish." However, Thorndike eventually abandoned the punishment part of the Law of Effect. Experiments suggested to him that punishment did not weaken the bond between a stimulus and response. Instead, punishment seemed to increase the variability of behavior and led to the emergence of a new response that brought about a satisfying state of affairs. The animal then performed this new response without actually unlearning the punished response. The Law of Effect then became a statement about positive reinforcement only, and it was in this form that it had the most impact on modern day training.

Hergenhahan (University of Cork, Ireland, 1992) says: "Skinner added to Thorndike's theories of teaching when he addressed positive reinforcement vs. punishment. Skinner attacked the subject in depth, coming up with the conclusion that while punishment will fix a temporary problem, it tends to be the wrong way to go about doing things. His reasoning was that punishment does a good job of telling the rat what not to do, rather than what they should do. Skinner placed his emphasis on positive reinforcement." Dr. Burrhus Frederic Skinner popularized four areas of learning, which together are called operant conditioning. The premise in operant conditioning is that the dog's **behavior** can "operate" on (make a difference in) his environment. Notice the word behavior is stressed, not the word dog. The dog doesn't necessarily assume consciousness of learning. Operant conditioning is different from classical conditioning in that the animal must perform a behavior in order for the consequence to occur; the behavior operates on the environment to produce the consequence. Classical conditioning forms an association between two stimuli. Operant conditioning forms an association between a behavior and a consequence.

Chapter 3  The Science of Learning

# ABC's of Learning

Here's another way to think of training:

### A = ANTECEDENT
An antecedent is any stimulus present in the environment before the behavior occurs. It doesn't have to tell the dog anything. But, an antecedent can be used to tell the dog to do a behavior. Humans plan cues like the word "Come" as an antecedent. The problem is, anything the dog notices can be an antecedent. If the dog can notice it, it can be a cue.

### B = BEHAVIOR
Behavior is anything a dog does. Dogs are constantly emitting behavior: breathing, walking, barking. Behavior happens whether or not the dog notices an antecedent. We can begin training by ignoring A's but selectively reinforcing the B's we like. Neither we nor the dog has to attend to A's for this process to work.

### C = CONSEQUENCE
Anything that happens to the dog as a result of the behavior is a consequence. It can be something good or bad or nothing at all. It must be the actual consequence of behavior, not what the owner planned to have as a consequence! All dog trainers should remember these three words: "Consequences drive behavior."

| ANTECEDENT | BEHAVIOR | CONSEQUENCE |
| --- | --- | --- |
| Dog hears refrigerator open | dog goes to refrigerator | owner gives dog a bite of ham |
| Dog hears word "Come" | dog runs within reach | owner gives dog a piece of cheese |
| Dog sees high five sign | dog does high five | owner praises and pets dog |
| Dog is shocked by lamp cord | dog removes mouth | shock stops |
| Dog smells drugs | dog barks | handler plays tug with dog |
| Dog hears word "Come" | dog runs to trainer | owner hits dog for being in trash |
| Dog hears door bell ring | dog sits politely | owner opens door |

## Four Important "Learning" Terms

▶ **Reinforcement "R"**—In the training context, this is an appropriate way to think about the word reinforcement: When you add steel reinforcement bars to wet concrete, the concrete is stronger. Reinforcement and reward are sometimes used interchangeably, but you reward a dog, you reinforce a behavior. It's not a reward unless the dog desires and will work for it. Dogs decide what stimuli are reinforcing; owners can only make educated guesses, based on observing their dogs. An objective observer should be able to say, "This dog's behavior is getting stronger, more frequent, more intense, longer, or more resilient to extinction, or not."

▶ **Positive "+"**—In the training context, this is a math term. Positive means to add something. In training language, positive is not an emotion. It's not something pleasant.

▶ **Negative "–"**—In the training context, this is a math term. Negative means to take something away. In training language, negative is not an emotion. It's not something aversive or unpleasant.

▶ **Punishment "P"**—In the training context, this is how to think about the word punishment. It's anything that stuns, stops, or decreases a behavior. It's not necessarily something you think is aversive. It simply means anything that will make the dog, from his own point of view, stop a behavior. Whatever it is, if the resulting effect is that the dog stops the behavior, it's a punisher.

Actually, there are five possible consequences of behavior. Absolutely no consequence (neutral), or one of the four consequences outlined in the operant conditioning diagram below.

---

## APPLICATION OF BEHAVIORAL CONSEQUENCES
## AN OPERANT CONDITIONING DIAGRAM

(Instrumental Conditioning or Skinnerian Conditioning)

AN EXAMPLE:
*Ruff Loves to Be Greeted by Granny.*
*Behavior Wanted: Ruff to Sit When Granny Approaches.*

|  | **ADD +** | **REMOVE –** |
|---|---|---|
| **SOMETHING GOOD** | *Positive Reinforcement (R+)*<br>Ruff sits: Granny pets<br>Sit for greeting INCREASES | *Negative Punishment (P–)*<br>Ruff stands: Granny leaves<br>Standing for greeting DECREASES |
| **SOMETHING NASTY** | *Positive Punishment (P+)*<br>Ruff stands: Granny uses squirt gun<br>Stand for greeting DECREASES | *Negative Reinforcement (R–)*<br>Ruff stands: Dad pulls up on Gentle Leader®. When Ruff sits: Dad releases pressure<br>Sit INCREASES |

Chapter 3   The Science of Learning

## What Could Be Confusing about R+, P+, P–, and R–?

Behavior is on a continuum. The category of the consequence depends on *which behavior* you attempt to change. The category of the consequence depends on what *instant in time* you are referring to.

- **It is nearly impossible to use R+ without also using P–**

    *At the instant Granny adds something good, she positively reinforces sitting*

    But,

    *In the next instant she takes away something good, she negatively punishes standing*

- **It is nearly impossible to use P+ without also using R–**

    *At the instant Granny adds something nasty, she positively punishes standing*

    But,

    *In the next instant she takes away something nasty, she negatively reinforces sitting*

You will see many examples of operant conditioning used in the training exercises in this book. It is most important for instructors to understand how and why the dog is processing information. But as professionals, we should also familiarize ourselves with the appropriate terms.

**Positive Punishment—More Examples.** In positive punishment (P+) an aversive is added.

> Dog barks. The electronic collar she is wearing gives her a shock. Barking is stunned. Silence is golden, barking is yukky. Adding an aversive stops (stuns) barking behavior—if the dog made the desired association.

> Human child is late coming home. Mom and Dad holler and scream. Adding an aversive stops coming-home-late behavior—OR it may stop coming home behavior altogether—think of the dog that doesn't want to come when called.

> *Note:* The effectiveness of punishment is under question (Sidman, M. 1989, *Coercion and Its Fallout*). A copy of the client handout Legacy is currently using to teach students about positive punishment (and aversives in general) appears in the Appendix as PDM1Aversives.doc, "About Punishment (Aversives) In Training."

**Negative Reinforcement—More Examples.** In negative reinforcement (R–) an aversive is subtracted.

> Dog is put into the "Down" position by running the leash under your foot and pulling up on it, exerting a downward pull on the dog's collar. When the dog lies down, you stop pulling. "Down" position gets the desired result—stop the choking of the collar. Subtracting an aversive increases lying-down behavior.

Human is speaking in front of a group and gets loud and very annoying static feedback from the microphone. The noise stops when the speaker moves to the left side of the stage. Speaker has options of where to stand to control the noise. Subtracting the aversive increases standing-on-the-left-of the-stage behavior.

**Negative Punishment—More Examples.** In negative punishment (P–) a reward is subtracted.

Dog is whining and finds your eye contact and the word, "Hush," rewarding. Remove your eye contact, say nothing. The dog can whine, or not. If the dog is quiet, whining has been negatively punished.

Human child is eating ice cream and making rude slurping sounds. Dad takes the ice cream away. Eat nicely or not. If the behavior is eating nicely, taking away a reward stopped (negatively punished) slurping behavior.

**Positive Reinforcement—More Examples.** In positive reinforcement (R+) a reward is added.

Dog is sitting near you. You scratch his chin and give him a liver cookie, which he loves. Adding a reward increases sitting-beside-you behavior.

Husband is cleaning garage. Spouse begins to sing, delivers a beverage to husband, puts husband's favorite dinner in the oven, and helps with the garage chores. Husband may not be making a conscious choice, but adding a reward increases cleaning behavior.

---

**Examples of Positive Reinforcement Working to Build a Desirable Behavior:**

- Your dog sits by the door when you say, "Sit." You open the door, go out, and play fetch with him.
- Your dog lies down on his rug instead of begging at the table. You go to him and give him cheese.

---

**Examples of Positive Reinforcement Working to Build an Undesirable Behavior:**

- Your dog tips over the kitchen trash container. She finds a delicious steak bone.
- Your dog barks because he wants the mailman to go away. The mailman goes away.

# Extinction—Operant and Classical

The term *extinction* is used in both operant and classical conditioning, but it refers to different processes. Animal behavior specialist Kathy Sdao frequently teaches the learning theory section of Legacy's DogSense course. Kathy has been a zookeeper, a marine mammal trainer, and she has an advanced degree in experimental psychology. She also teaches pet dog classes. Kathy gives this explanation of extinction: "We're most familiar with extinction in operant conditioning, where it is the procedure of withholding the reinforcers that maintain behavior. Note that it is **not** simply ignoring a behavior by providing no consequences. Extinction works when the behavior you want to eliminate has previously been reinforced by contingencies over which you have some control (e.g., attention, food, freedom)." In the jumping on Granny example in the diagram for operant conditioning, previous attempts at jumping on Granny have produced lots of attention, a big fuss, and perhaps even food bribes to get the dog to stop. Attempts to extinguish jumping would involve ensuring Granny's safety (with barriers, etc.), but so will actively ignoring all aerial displays by the dog, who will tire of this game when it doesn't pay. The important thing about extinction is that there has to be a previous history of R+ behavior. You only extinguish behaviors you've first fueled with attention, food, physical contact, freedom, or other rewards. A good way to remember extinction is by thinking of the word extinguish, which means to put out a fire. Before you can put out a fire, you first need the fire. That is, you need a behavior with some reinforcement history where the reinforcers are under your control, at least to some extent. It's only then that the removal of R+ (like the removal of oxygen near a fire) has an effect. In classical (or Pavlovian) conditioning, extinction is the procedure of repeatedly presenting a Conditioned Stimulus (CS) without the Unconditioned Stimulus (US). For example, Pavlov would ring the bell over and over again, without presenting the dog with food immediately after each trial. In both cases, the procedures are intended to eliminate (or at least weaken) a learned response (or behavior). In the case of operant conditioning, the learned response is allowed to occur without reinforcement. In classical conditioning, the conditioned stimulus loses its power to elicit a conditioned response (i.e., the dog will no longer salivate in response to the sound of the bell; the bell has lost its predictive value). The term extinction can also refer to the actual decline in response produced by either type of extinction procedure."

The following graph shows six extinction trials. Think of them as the next six times Ruff encounters Granny. Notice the extinction burst. Ruff gets worse before he gets better, but he eventually quits. Notice the spontaneous recovery. Each time in the near future that Ruff sees Granny, he tries jumping on her again. Over time, that jumping behavior is weakened in frequency, duration, and/or intensity because the reward (attention) was taken away. Sometimes there can be a dramatically strong spike of spontaneous recovery as shown in trial five. Keep going; extinction will work.

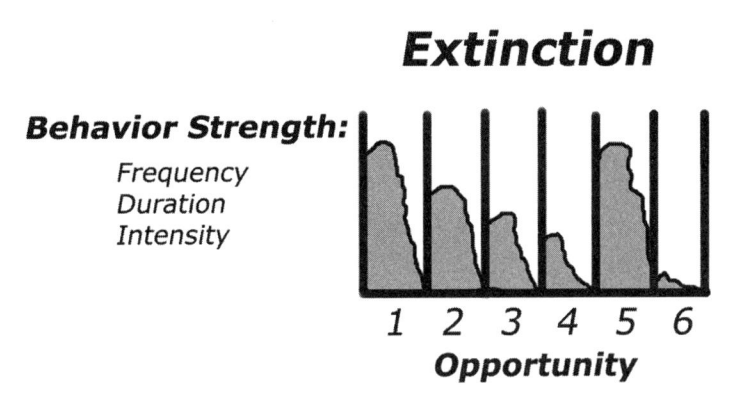

**Extinction**

Behavior Strength:
Frequency
Duration
Intensity

1 2 3 4 5 6
Opportunity

## *Extinction Burst*

The term extinction burst describes the phenomena of behavior temporarily or briefly getting worse, not better, when a previously rewarded behavior is not rewarded.

- **Begging Example:** Your client has been slipping her dog tidbits during dinner. One night she does not give a tidbit. Her dog will get worse before he gets better. The begging behavior will temporarily increase in frequency, intensity, and/or duration before he begs less. It's important for clients to know and expect this. My usual comment is, "Great! He got worse! That means extinction is working!"

- **Insert-Money-Push-Button Example:** If you stop by the soda machine every day at lunch time, put in your money and push the button, you are rewarded with a can of soda. The insert-money-push-button behavior has a reinforcement history. One day the machine jams. Your button pushing behavior becomes stronger! You will push the button with more intensity, frequency, and duration than normal. Eventually, your button pushing behavior goes into extinction, and you walk away.

## *Spontaneous Recovery*

Behavior affected by extinction is apt to recur in the future when the trigger is presented again. This is known as spontaneous recovery or the transient increase in behavior. Prepare your students for this eventuality. Tell them it's a sign that extinction is working! It's a little test for you, so be prepared to pass the test! Continue to withhold the reward or you will have placed your dog on a variable schedule of reinforcement. The dog will play the odds.

- **Begging Behavior Example:** The owner has been slipping her dog tidbits during dinner. If she stops, the dog will beg with more frequency, or with more intensity and/or duration before she begs less. Even though the behavior is lessened and perhaps stops all together, there is always the chance that begging could return again at the next meal or at a meal several days later. In other words, with no reward, begging will gradually disappear, but may recover again at any time should the trigger be presented.

- **Insert-Money-Push-Button Behavior Example:** The next day at lunch, you walk past the soda machine. You might give it a try once, but if it doesn't work, you'll probably not spend as much time on insert-money-push-button behavior as you did the day before.

Extinction and positive reinforcement are the two principles most often used in Legacy programs.

---

### BOB BAILEY ON EXTINCTION

"Extinction is a process, just as reinforcement is a process, and aversives is a process, all involving the results of interaction with the environment. In the 'old days,' Skinnerian psychologists tried very hard to separate operant and respondent behaviors and processes—not too much anymore, since most recognize how intertwined the processes are. And, of course, Pavlov is always on our shoulder, so there is a respondent component to reinforcement, extinction, and aversives. You might say that an animal would never "choose" extinction, or do anything that would result in extinction, but it is not necessary in operant conditioning for an animal to have control, only that there be a result of its behavior, thus influencing the probability of the behavior reoccurring. An animal goes hunting. It tries many schemes to get food. Some work, and some don't. Those that don't work face extinction; those that do, get stronger."

---

## How Extinction Differs from Negative Punishment

Extinction sounds like, but is different than, negative punishment. To use P– to stop a behavior, you don't need a reinforcement history. You're working with the situation as it exists in the moment. You're removing a goodie for which the dog has access. You're taking away his freedom (by crating him, maybe), taking away the tennis ball he's holding, removing the piece of liver from in front of his face, or taking away your hand that had been scratching his ear. You are removing a currently available treat. Back to the Granny example we used for the operant conditioning diagram: Granny enters the room, the dog's front feet lift off the ground in preparation for jumping on Granny, his favorite activity. Granny leaves. Her departure is an unconditioned negative punisher.

*Note:* You can establish a conditioned negative punisher much the same as you would establish the conditioned positive reinforcer. Some trainers refer to this as a "no reward marker" or a "signal of no reward."

# WHAT TO USE AS A PRIMARY REINFORCER

A primary reinforcer is something the dog naturally values and will work to get. In most animals it is considered something necessary for survival, such as food, water, proper temperature, or reproductive opportunities. Many people agree that for social animals, effective rewards have a larger range. Some dogs, for example, would rather play a game of fetch with the owner than receive a treat to eat. The important qualification for a reinforcer is that its use increases the behavior in frequency, duration, and/or intensity.

All training procedures, whether they rely on rewards or aversives, have the potential for misuse if not applied according to the correct principles of learning. Rewards, however, pose little bodily risk to the dog or danger to your relationship. Training with positive reinforcement does not imply permissiveness. Dogs still must learn limits to their behavior. This can be accomplished by replacing bad habits with desirable behaviors. Previously, you scolded your dog, now you can reward your dog.

Use a high rate of reinforcement—lots of properly timed rewards—in the first stage of teaching. But what will those rewards be? Owners should experiment and see what their dogs like best. A good reward will catch and maintain interest even if slight distractions are taking place. An owner might be attracted to a cute squeak toy, when in fact the dog prefers a plain old gummy tennis ball.

## Food as a Reinforcer

For the vast majority of dogs, the reward of choice is food. It's a primary reinforcer. To eat is to live. We can use survival instincts to help us in training. To survive, an animal needs to be highly receptive to information associated with food acquisition. Dogs no longer need to figure out how to catch their own dinner, but most are still alert and responsive when food is in the offering. Let's take advantage of it!

**More about Food.** When a dog receives food, it activates the animal's parasympathetic nervous system. We humans experience times when our parasympathetic nervous system provides us with nice warm feelings such as relaxation and contentment. We call it comfort food. There's nothing better than a good book and a bowl of fresh popcorn. Food can calm a dog, make him less fearful, or cause the whole training process to be a happy experience. A handout with details of how to help your clients select and use food as a reward appears in the Appendix as PDM1Select/UseRewards.doc, "The Selection & Use Of Training Rewards."

# Important Considerations About Reinforcement: Timing (When), Criteria (What), Rate (How Often), and Value (Quality)

## Timing of the Reinforcer

A reward should be given at the same time the target behavior is shown. This is often impossible for practical reasons, so the compromise is that the reward should be given as close as humanly possible after (not before) the desired behavior occurs. There is a high likelihood that a reinforcer delivered several seconds too late will modify a subsequent behavior, not the behavior you THINK you are working on. Practice will help your owners be consistent and smooth in the timing and delivery of reinforcers. Timing exercises are in the Appendix listed as PDM1YesCommunication.doc, "'YES!' As A Marker."

## Criteria Selection in Reward-based Training

*Criteria* is the term used for the specific, trainer-defined responses wanted. The instant the dog achieves the criterion, that response is rewarded (reinforced). There is usually more than one dimension of a behavior. Let's use the "Sit" cue as an example. Most owners care about:

- *Physical Response:* Dog puts rear end to the floor in a "Sit" position
- *Latency of the Response:* How fast "Sit" occurs when the cue is given
- *Duration of the Response:* How long dog sits

When teaching something new to a dog, there are decisions, decisions, and more decisions to be made by the trainer. Intuitive dog trainers can make snap decisions about when and what to reinforce. An instructor's job is to help her students gain this skill. Behavior analysis should be done on all exercises in your class. Split the behavior into steps and decide which step (criterion) will be rewarded during a given training session. Then you need to put the behavior into an easy-to-do training sequence for the owner.

**Temporary Criteria—When Perfect Is Not Better.** The dog and trainer should move quickly through the steps of an exercise (the temporary criteria) and not perfect those intermediary steps on the way to the goal. For example, in the beginning of teaching "high five," there might be 10 or more steps to shape the behavior.

1. Reward when dog shifts the weight of one front paw to another.
2. Reward shifting weight *and* bringing the paw up from contact with the floor.
3. Reward for a higher paw lift.

If the dog is rewarded too many times at one step, he might not be willing to offer anything else. The dog might decide to stay at the behavior that received so many rewards. Help your students realize that temporary criteria should be trained only to about 80% reliability before adding a step or changing criteria. If a temporary criterion is reinforced for too long, the animal may be reluctant to change the behavior. The rewarded behavior of weight shifting will have to go into extinction, which, in most cases, means getting stronger before getting weaker; only then can the trainer successfully move on.

**Permanent Criteria—The Finished Product.** Permanent criteria, the final goal, should be trained to a higher level of reliability than temporary criteria. Here we use the term *fluency* to mean the dog will respond appropriately when given the cue, not respond when the trainer doesn't give the cue, and not give a different response to the cue! Further, a fluent dog will perform quickly and within any other dimensions the trainer imposes as important criteria. For example, "Sit" with both hind legs under, rather than in a hip "Sit." The fluent dog is not distracted by changes in the environment.

## Rate of Reinforcement

There are rules about how often the dog should be rewarded. Those are covered under schedules of reinforcement. In the beginning, the learning stage of a behavior, a very high rate decreases the chance of distraction and speeds the learning process.

## Value of Reinforcement

Owners should be able to list a ranking of their dog's favorite reinforcements. Make sure owners understand the state of the animal can change the value of the reinforcement. A hungry dog will value food more than a dog that is full. A distracting environment will compete with the value of the reinforcement. It never hurts to bring out your own very enticing reinforcement to show owners that their dogs ARE interested.

## One More Important Point about Reinforcement

This point is so important it deserves a paragraph of its very own. It seems obvious, but my highly respected teacher Mr. Bob Bailey stressed it with me and I believe we must do a good job of passing this point on to our students: "Do not feed, or otherwise reinforce unwanted behavior during training. One of the biggest obstacles to getting desired behavior is reinforcing unwanted behavior. Some people worry so much about missing a reinforcement (missing the good behavior), while it is actually the reinforcing of what is not wanted that is more damaging. Even if a trainer does not increase the number of good reinforcements, training time can be cut dramatically by reducing the number of ill-timed or erroneous reinforcements."

# Schedules of Reinforcement

Exactly WHEN should we give a reward? There are many different schedules of reinforcement. Different training goals require different techniques. For our purposes, it's simple to divide training into two different schedules of reinforcement.

## Continuous Schedule of Reinforcement for Acquisition

To help the dog get the idea of what is being rewarded, the dog should be reinforced for every correct response. The instructor and trainer try hard to prevent the dog from making a mistake by thoughtfully planning the training exercise. The dog will learn with minimal frustration and maximum attention; one behavior, one reward; another behavior, another reward.

## Variable Schedules of Reinforcement (VSR) for Fluency

(Also known as partial reinforcement or intermittent schedule of reinforcement.)

**Random Reinforcement Is a VSR.** Even if we choose to give the dog a continuous schedule of reinforcement, real life dictates that we humans will be random. We won't be able to reward every single behavior consistently unless the dog lives in a vacuum.

A random schedule of reinforcement simply means that the reward is not given every time the dog offers the behavior. The dog is not able to predict just which behavior will be rewarded but receives the reward intermittently and unpredictably. There's no set pattern, but when the reward is given, it's given immediately in conjunction with the behavior. The trainer does not single out good or better responses. The reward is totally random. This is best to perpetuate a learned behavior. You might hear the term two-fers, or three-fers. It's just slang for how many behaviors the dog must perform to get his pay off. Most trainers start with two-fers, asking for the same behavior two times in a row before the dog gets the reward, then immediately go back to one-fers, then perhaps three-fers. When using two-fers, three-fers, and one-fers, it's important to use them randomly. Ping-pong back and forth between them with no set pattern.

Help students with random reward in each exercise. Formalize it for them by asking that they take their bait bags off and hold only three pieces of food in their hand. Then do an exercise that has five repetitions. At first, an instructor or assistant can call out, at random, which three of the five behaviors to reward. Later the student can decide for himself.

- **EXAMPLE:** Japanese pachinko machines or slot machines found in any country are examples of the variable schedule of reinforcement called random reward. Sometimes they give the gambler a reward, sometimes not, but people still play in hopes of the big payoff. Intermittent reinforcement teaches the dog not to give up and to be persistent. It's the principle that keeps people going fishing. Fishermen will fish all day and not get a bite, but will return the next weekend and try again. Why? Because eventually something great will happen. It's the same with your dog. One of the biggest mistakes in reward-based training is failure to wean the dog to a random reinforcement. Be sure your training plans take that into consideration.

- **EXAMPLE:** If you graduated from reinforcing every behavior to reinforcing every other behavior (two-fers) and stayed on two-fers, this wouldn't be a truly random reward. The dog will quickly learn that this is a fixed schedule of reinforcement and will know exactly when the reinforcement will occur—every other time.

Because dogs live in a complex environment where more than one thing is going on at the same time, there are certainly going to be times when the dog is NOT reinforced for each correct behavior. One could argue (Bob Bailey) that rewards need not intentionally and specifically be placed on a random schedule since they are delivered at random anyway in our pet dog family environment.

**Differential Reinforcement Is a VSR.** Differential reinforcement is a different application of variable reinforcement. Instead of being truly random, coach students to begin looking for the best examples of the behavior and reward their dog, ignoring other offers. It's up to you to define "best." Have it clear in your mind and in that of the owner's mind. Work on only one clearly defined criterion and improve that. Other criteria can be relaxed, lowered, or temporarily ignored during this time.

- **EXAMPLE—HEELING:** The trainer does not care about speed, eye contact, forging, or bumping. The trainer is concentrating now on heel position without lagging. Reward that position, ignoring less than acceptable responses.

After careful coaching and when the student skill level is up, team up the students and they can take turns saying "now" for the best behaviors.

**Limited Hold Is a VSR.** Limited hold is a *variation* of differential reinforcement. The term *limited hold* means the trainer is concentrating on rewarding the criterion of speed of response (also called latency). It's rewarding in class to pick speed as a criterion because the people and dogs are usually successful. Choose one exercise, for example, "Sit," and work latency on that. Two to three seconds is reasonable. Don't let the students guess. Count it out for them. The dogs catch on to limited hold quickly, and, as a bonus, they seem to be able to generalize speed of response to other exercises as well.

- **EXAMPLE—SIT:** Pick a certain time limit, for example three seconds. The dog must sit within a count of three (you count it out for the student!) or the reinforcement will be withheld. Students must forget about all other criteria but speed of response. This dramatically increases a dog's motivation to work quickly.

**Jackpots.** Jackpots could be considered a type of VSR. Trainers apply the jackpot principle in different ways. In general, a jackpot is an unusually large or valuable, unexpected reward. Trainers enjoy using jackpots as a message to the dog that she has done something really, really well. Some trainers save jackpots for big breakthroughs, but jackpots can occasionally be used to reward average performance, not just super efforts. Remember that people win slot machine jackpots randomly, not when they pull the lever especially well!

- **EXAMPLE:** If you feed a small piece of kibble as a reward, several large pieces of liver (higher value) will be a jackpot. Some trainers claim a jackpot should be ten times the value of a typical reward. My dog thinks it's extra wonderful if, instead of giving him a training treat, he is allowed to put his nose in the treat pouch and help himself! I might bring out the bag from hiding and let him dip his nose in to reinforce a really, really speedier than normal "Come" when called. Jackpots can be a combination of rewards given in rapid fire, all within a second—words of praise, a bit of food, and the tug toy. Jackpots are best used sparingly.

Try previewing a jackpot as a primer for a good behavior. If the dog is working for kibble, ask the owner to give the dog a peek at the yummy liver in her pocket. The dog will try to operate the owner to figure out how to get her to deliver that great stuff.

# SECONDARY REINFORCERS: THE CLICKER AND OTHERS

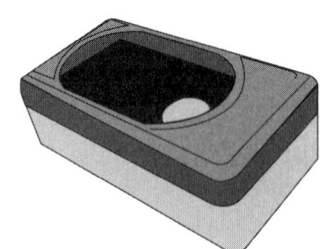

*Also known as*

- CONDITIONED REINFORCER
- BRIDGING STIMULUS
- BRIDGE
- PROMISE
- PREDICTOR
- MARKER

A conditioned, or secondary, reinforcer is an event that marks a behavior as rewardable and promises the delivery of a reward in the near future. Many dog trainers establish the sound of a clicker as a secondary reinforcer. A clicker is a small handheld device that emits a succinct click when depressed. However, the scope of secondary reinforcers is **much** broader than just marker sounds such as a click. Secondary reinforcers include any stimuli that gain reinforcing properties by their association with primary reinforcers such as food. Some examples are the movement of the trainer's hand toward the bait bag, a smile, or a nod.

The secondary reinforcer spans the time between marking a behavior as rewardable and delivering that promised reward. It's a great communication tool for all sorts of training and especially helpful for training dogs at a distance. If the primary reinforcer can easily be delivered, within a second or two, one could question the need for a secondary reinforcer. Just give the food.

Dogs learn secondary reinforcers all the time all by themselves:

- **EXAMPLE:** The dog responds happily when he hears the family's car pull into the drive. This, by the way, is an example of classical conditioning. **All secondary reinforcers are learned through classical conditioning.** The secondary reinforcer is repeatedly paired with a primary reinforcer and gains salience through that association. At first the sound of the car has no meaning, but now it predicts the company of his people. We take advantage of this natural principle in training by specifically pairing a special sound with the presentation of food. Initially the sound, the secondary reinforcer, has no meaning. When the sound is paired with a primary reinforcer (food), the sound becomes a reliable predictor of food and is reinforcing in itself.

Dogs learn best in black and white, not shades of gray. The sound of the secondary reinforcer establishes a clear message of approval. Most pet dogs have received generalized, random praise and rewards in the past; praise for being good, for being cute, or just for being there. That's fine, but good training dictates a more exact pinpointing and rewarding of the behaviors we are teaching.

## *More about Clickers and Clicker Training*

The principle behind clicker training, establishing a bridge, has long been in practice by animal trainers. The term *clicker training* and use of a clicker with dogs, has become popular within the last 20 years. Karen Pryor is largely responsible for popularizing the use of clickers among dog trainers. Trainers find clickers advantageous because they are non-emotional, quick and, unlike the human voice, a click is a new and interesting sound for dogs. As an instructor, you might find problems with owners remembering their clicker, having good coordination with a clicker, and having enough hands left over to use a clicker. Be prepared to spend time teaching your students (as a separate exercise from training) the mechanical skill of correct timing of the clicker and the delivery of the food. Some exercises are shown in the Appendix listed as CONT.EDClickBasics.doc, "Click! Clicker Basics."

## *A Special Word ("YES!")*

Another commonly used secondary reinforcer is a succinct word, such as "YES!" It should be said in a clear and enthusiastic tone and not lost in a muddle of other words. A distinct "YES!," is much more meaningful than the vague and lengthy, "YES! you surely were a good girl." The word "good" is too common and may already have an ambiguous meaning for the dog. Students might find "YES!" more readily available and it addresses the problem of "not enough hands."

Dogs don't automatically know what the secondary reinforcer means. People are prone to using bridges incorrectly. Such a powerful tool needs to be carefully taught in sequential steps, just like any other behavior. Legacy's formula for establishing the bridge, or "loading the clicker," or empowering the word "YES!" is found in the Appendix listed as PDM1Yes.doc, "YES! As a Reward Marker," and CONT.ED Click.doc, "CLICK! Clicker Basics."

I have found that an easy transition in helping students with timing is to hold the clicker myself. The owner has the food and the dog. I decide what to reward, and then I click. The owner gives the reward. Yes, this is sort of like clicker training the owners! Make the transition to the owner making reward decisions, marking, and rewarding their dog's behavior as soon as possible.

Be careful with the choice of your words. The term *secondary reinforcer* can confuse owners because it comes first! And the primary reinforcer is delivered second! The words *promise* or *bridge* are much more descriptive. Help owners remember by saying, "Remember that the new thing always comes first to predict the old thing." This is a good way to remember how to add or change cues as well.

# BEHAVIOR ANALYSIS

All types of training require making a plan. What are you going to teach and how? Teach students to observe their dogs. The dog's condition is one factor that will influence the effectiveness of the training. For example, if the dog is aroused, physically unfit, or thirsty, the outcome of training will be affected. Are trainer and dog in a distraction-free environment, or will competing stimuli vie for the dog's attention? Is the reinforcer adequate for the task considering the state of the dog at the time and place of training? These considerations can help owners stack the deck in their favor.

"Be a splitter, not a lumper." I believe I first heard "split, don't lump" from the late Marian Breland-Bailey during a Legacy Chicken Training Camp* in 1994. "Split, Don't Lump" became the mantra at our early dog and chicken training camps. Complex behaviors can be reduced to smaller components. To determine just what the components of a behavior are, observe the dog. What goes into lying down? Look at the little pieces of sequential behavior: dipping the head, flexing the shoulder muscles. Are your chosen behavior bits easy to identify and easy to reward? Use that knowledge to help you set criteria for reinforcement. One of the benefits of secondary reinforcers, especially the clicker, is that you can pinpoint the exact bit of behavior you want to reward. The clicker is like a snapshot. It marks an instant in time.

---

*Training a chicken is a great way to practice timing rewards for your dog. Chickens are FAST! Good chicken trainers make great dog trainers, and humble ones too. A little slower paced, but cuter, rats have played an important part as training subjects at Legacy camps. Both species are good instructors of the finer points of classical and operant conditioning.

# Getting the Behavior

## Methods to Get Behavior—Acquisition

A great deal of this chapter has to do with reinforcement. How do we GET a behavior we want in the first place? For the purposes of Legacy classes, we have two main categories for getting a behavior to occur.

1. The behavior can be emitted—offered spontaneously by the dog.
2. The behavior can be elicited—trainer helps dog to perform the behavior.

Sometimes there is one method that stands heads and shoulders above the others for a particular behavior. At other times it's a toss up. Depending on what you are trying to get, a particular method could be counterproductive. Here are Legacy's main strategies for getting behaviors. If one doesn't work, we quickly try another approach.

## Physical Modeling

I mention modeling because, over the years, it has been one of the most common ways to elicit a behavior. Think of modeling clay. A person molds the clay into the desired shape. In modeling, the trainer physically manipulates the dog into the desired position. Modeling can be used for most behaviors, but it is not necessarily the best method for getting a behavior.

**Physical Modeling Applied to "Sit."** In this drawing the trainer gently reaches behind the dog and quickly but gently folds the dog's hind legs into a sitting position. At the same time, he guides the dog's head backward. Imagine someone applying quick but gentle pressure behind your knees. You would probably begin to fold up into a "Sit" just as the dog would.

**Pros and Cons of Physical Modeling.** For those owners with good timing and coordination, modeling can be a swift, therefore gratifying, way to get the behavior. Some dogs are distracted from the task if they feel hands on their body. The attention to hands might overshadow any other intended cues. The dog attends only to the touch. Also, take into consideration the opposition reflex (Chapter 2). If the trainer pushes one way, the dog will push the other. Some students get carried away if allowed to model. This drawing does not illustrate modeling. It's an example of dog abuse.

Chapter 3 The Science of Learning

## Luring and Fading Lures

Luring is a popular tool with trainers for getting dogs to elicit a position. The trainer selects an interesting object upon which the dog should focus. In Legacy classes, most of the exercises require food, but some require a toy as the object of attraction.

**Luring as Applied to "Sit."** When the dog's eyes and/or nose are focused on the lure, draw the lure over the dog's head. Control the head, control the dog. As the dog's head follows the lure, the law of gravity makes "Sit" happen.

**Pros and Cons of Luring.** Luring is easy for almost anyone, and no force is involved. Luring makes lots of behavior happen quickly, providing the trainer with lots of opportunity to reinforce. Reinforcement drives behavior. Instructors should carefully coach students on the use of the lure. Be sure to include in your instructional format a means to eventually fade the lure. Lures are addictive! The movement of a luring hand, even without food, might also be a cue for the behavior. Take that into consideration and plan to add a verbal cue BEFORE, not during, the movement of the hand. Some dogs cannot concentrate on two things at once and only one, usually the familiar hand signal, will be attended to. You will find luring basics in the Appendix listed as "PDM1SitHappens.doc, "Sit Happens . . . . Using A Lure."

## Target Training Nose, Paw, and Rear End

A target is an object that an animal has been taught to touch with a certain part of his body. The target can then be used as a tool to position the dog

**Target Training as Applied to Rear End.** Also known as station training, the trainer will chain behaviors. Chaining means splitting a complex behavior into many smaller segments, with each step (link) trained individually and then put together sequentially. A behavior might be to require the dog to find and sit on a small mat for a reward. This is good canine traffic control when the doorbell rings. The bell becomes the cue for the behavior.

**Target Training as Applied to Nose.** The trainer will teach the dog to touch her nose to the end of a dowel. Control the head, control the dog. The dog's head can then be guided with the target stick into a variety of positions.

**Target Training as Applied to Paw.** The dog will be taught to touch a sticker with his paw. The sticker can then be moved around and combined with other objects. The dog can touch a bell hanging from the doorknob to signal he wants to go out into the yard.

**Pros and Cons of Target Training.** It's helpful for owners with a limited range of motion in their arms. It requires another piece of equipment for the students to handle and might figure into the "not enough hands" problem. However, you don't necessarily need a prop or a clicker: Trainer and instructor Dawn Jecs has a very thorough and successful method of dog training called "Choose to Heel™". Part of her program teaches students to use their hand as a target for heeling. Dawn's students are skilled at delivering a primary reinforcement in a timely manner.

A target stick handout is included in the Appendix as "CONT.EDClicks& Sticks.doc, "How To Start Target Stick Training With A Clicker."

## Catching a Behavior

The trainer can be observant and wait until the behavior, or parts of the behavior, is offered spontaneously (emitted) and reward the behavior.

**Catching a Behavior as Applied to "Come."** Tell students to be opportunists. If the dog happens to run up, catch her in the act and reward her!

**Pros and Cons of Catching a Behavior.** Dogs naturally offer behavior such as running up to their people or sitting. Those two behaviors lend themselves easily to the "catching" technique. Other behaviors, such as "Down," might take longer to catch with regularity. With repetition, the dog will understand how the behavior is to be executed in order to get the reward. For example, if "Come" is rewarded, does it make a difference how fast or in what position the dog arrives? If so, a method for selecting and rewarding specific criteria must be employed.

## Shaping

In shaping, the trainer will reward the dog for successive approximations of the desired behavior. This is especially useful in complicated behaviors. Choose a criterion that is a small or preliminary step toward the goal behavior, then successively reward only better and better steps. In other words, raise the criteria for reward. As generally used by dog trainers, it's a hands-off process and is most often used with a secondary reinforcer. Although some dog trainers refer to free shaping, this term is rarely found in the training literature.

**Shaping as Applied to Jumping through a Hoop.** One plan would be to stand a hoop on end with one hand or get a friend to hold it. Reinforce any behavior that shows interest in the hoop. You might reward a glance in the direction of the hoop, a step toward it, a sniff of it, a nose on it, or foot pawing on it. Once the dog knows the hoop will pay off, teach the dog exactly what to do to make it pay. Choose one criterion, perhaps "foot step toward hoop" or it could just as well be "nose touching hoop." Try very hard to stay with one criterion per session, but sometimes you need to grab whatever the dog does that is helpful to the end goal. Decisions, decisions! Keep raising criteria until the dog is walking through, then jumping through the hoop, raising the hoop a bit more each time. Determine the goal, and then break it into easily trained steps.

*Chapter 3   The Science of Learning*

**Pros and Cons of Shaping a Behavior.** The dog becomes a full partner in training, constantly working to see what will generate a reward. Dogs trained this way are usually eager for training sessions and less concerned with what is going on around them. Trainers need to be able to break behaviors down into small pieces and be quick to reward them. The trainer with good observation and decision-making skills will do best at shaping. If one moves along through the steps too fast, the behavior may deteriorate. The trainer is asking too much too soon. If things go too slowly and the dog doesn't get enough reinforcement, the behavior will deteriorate because there's nothing to keep the dog interested. A good measure of when to raise criteria is when the dog is performing well 80% of the time at the current step. Holding out for 100% accuracy at each step is not only unrealistic, but students might have difficulty changing criteria that has been reinforced so much. In fact, that step might have to go through the extinction process before moving on. This wastes time and effort for the dogs, and the trainer too!

## Chaining

Chaining is helpful for complex behaviors. A behavior is broken down and each component is taught separately, usually in small, sequential steps. When put together, each step the dog performs is a cue for the next behavior to begin.

**Chaining as Applied to the Formal "Come-When-Called."** In obedience trials, the recall requires:

- dog sits still while trainer walks away
- dog waits for a cue
- on cue the dog runs to the trainer
- dog sits in front of trainer
- dog waits for a cue
- on cue the dog moves into position at the trainer's side

Each preceding behavior is a cue for the next step. The dog is rewarded only after the last step is performed.

**Pros and Cons of Chaining.** Chaining enables immediate success for both the dog and owners because work is completed with one simple segment of a behavior at a time, consistent in the order of events. Clients often fall into the habit of wanting to skip a step or lump steps together, so be clear in your instructions.

## Backward Chaining

This is nearly the same concept, but the complex behavior is started with the last step (the goal) and worked backward. The concept is that learning is easier by working from a newly acquired step of a behavior to an already learned, comfortable step of the behavior.

### Backward Chaining as Applied to "Retrieve"

- First the dog holds and releases the toy back to your hand
  - Next the dog must reach for it, hold, and release to hand
    - Next the dog must pick it up off the ground, hold, and release
      - Next pick it up, take a step while holding, and release
        - Build step by step until an appropriate distance is achieved

Because the dog is rewarded so often for releasing the toy to you, it's the strongest link in the behavior chain. Most trainers agree that working from a new, unknown behavior to a known one helps decrease the stress level. This is an application of the Premack Principle. A handout on backward chaining the "Retrieve" is included in the Appendix as CONT.EDFetch.doc, "Fetch!"

# PREMACK PRINCIPLE

Behavioral psychologist David Premack identified the Premack Principle. This principle can be used to our advantage: A high-probability behavior, something the dog loves to do, can be used to reward a low-probability behavior. The opportunity to engage in a desirable activity reinforces the behavior required to engage in the less likely activity. In other words, a trainer can increase the frequency of a low-probability behavior by following it immediately with the opportunity to do a high-probability behavior. Remember that the value of any reward depends on the state of the animal. A hungry animal can be rewarded by food. By the same token, the probability of a behavior depends on the state of the animal. A tired dog is perhaps more apt to lie down than a very alert, excited dog.

**EXAMPLE:** Dog is excited and anxious to be let out of the car at the community dog park. Leaving the car and running with friends is a high probability behavior. Sitting in the car while the door is opened is an okay behavior. Dog has to "Sit" and "Stay" while the door is open for three seconds and then will be released to jump out and romp with his friends.

**EXAMPLE:** Parent to child at dinner time: "If you eat your spinach, you can have ice cream for dessert."

# Cueing Behaviors

A cue is also known as an antecedent, a stimulus, a command, a signal, or a request. Different trainers have different words for the same concept! The most often used word in pet dog training to replace the rather strong term "command" is the word "cue." A cue comes before the behavior (antecedent) and tells the dog to do the behavior. In training, the word *stimulus* is used interchangeably with the word *cue*. A stimulus or cue can be any object, event, or perceivable change in environment by the animal. The most common cues dog trainers think about are spoken words like Sit, Down, Heel, and Come. Other sounds can also be cues—the jingle of car keys produces run-to-the-door-behavior. A cue can be a silent hand signal instead of a word. The owner getting up and walking toward the door can be a silent cue for run-to-the-door-behavior! Ask dog owners for new and interesting cues their dog has learned. We had a demo dog that would run over to a box of tissues and retrieve one when the instructor faked a sneeze! It was taught as a trick, but is a good illustration of environmental cues.

## When to Introduce a Cue

In class, owners will be tempted to give verbal cues before they are appropriate. They should not bother with words until they can get the behavior repeatedly and predictably. Your lesson plan should indicate when it's okay to start using a verbal cue. For example, in Legacy classes we play the magnet game. By not calling it a Sit, Down, or Stand, owners are not tempted to label it. It's simply a silent magnet game. The usual magnet is a piece of food. Full instructions for the magnet game appear in the Appendix as PDM 1 SitHappens.doc, "Sit Happens! Using a Lure—The Magnetic Sit Exercise."

---

**SPECIAL NOTE ABOUT FOOD AS A CUE**

Many programs use food lures to get behaviors at first. This is fine for the first few repetitions, but your program should provide for the fading of these food lures/cues very quickly. This will lessen the problem of the behavior being contingent upon seeing the food. The major complaint lodged against training with food is that if you don't have food, the dog won't respond. This is a fault with the trainer, not with the technique. Therefore, the ultimate responsibility is on THE INSTRUCTOR. Too many people continue using the food as a lure or bribe well past its usefulness. It seems a small point, BUT IT IS ONE OF THE MOST IMPORTANT CONCEPTS in good dog training. The training strategies in this book take this into consideration. You will see references to phasing out the food and toys as lures and turning them into occasional rewards.

## Stimuli Packages and Environmental Control

The problem with stimuli is that trainers are not machines and we don't live in a sterile environment. In training, a person might give the dog a verbal cue, for example, the instruction to "Stay." At the same time the trainer might change the tone of her voice, lean forward, look at the dog, and give a hand signal. All these things together are called a stimuli package. Quite simply, anything going on while the trainer is working with the dog can be considered by the dog as an important feature and can become a cue. Remember the story about Clever Hans in Chapter 2? The horse responded to very subtle cues that no one else noticed. This can be a drawback when it comes to training, but it can also work to your advantage when you use environmental cues to help train your dog.

**Environmental Cues.** Cut out the middleman! Help your students teach their dogs practical, everyday cues for useful behavior. The cues are there anyway; they might as well use them.

| | | |
|---|---|---|
| *Environmental Cue* | → | **Doorbell**—Dog sits on a certain mat before seeing the visitor. |
| *Environmental Cue* | → | **Hand on car door handle**—Dog sits before being allowed to jump out. |
| *Environmental Cue* | → | **Leash comes off rack**—Dog sits quietly. |
| *Environmental Cue* | → | **Food bowl preparation**—Dog goes to special place to eat. |

## Cues: Overshadowing, Blocking, and Salience

Here are some details to keep in mind as you develop your lesson plans.

Overshadowing is when the most important detail in the environment—from the animal's point of view, not yours—can cover up other details present. Try to avoid the possibility of overshadowing when you establish cues by making the cue you want the dog to attend to the most salient.

For example, if you call your dog with a verbal "Come" and at the same time, swing your arm in a hand signal to Come, one might dominate (overshadow) the other. If taught separately either one would be effective. But if taught together, the dog might only zero in on one. Which one? You never know, but in this case I would wager that the hand signal would overshadow the verbal cue. Dogs are naturally observant, nonverbal communicators. If this is true, when you teach "Come" with both hand signal and verbal signal simultaneously, and then you leave out the verbal signal for the behavior, the dog will still come. If you leave out the hand signal and only say "Come," the dog will more than likely sit there. To the dog, the motion is more salient (noticeable) than the verbal. Aha! Then the trainer realizes the dog needs more work. Trainers call that dog green, unfinished, and in need of proofing. This problem is easy to train through, but a thoughtful trainer will train each cue separately and then put them together, if needed.

A similar result might occur when a previously learned cue conflicts with a newly learned cue. This phenomenon has a different name. If both are presented simultaneously, the previously learned cue is said to block the new cue. Dr. Pam Reid has an excellent example in her book *Excel-erated Learning,* "Blocking is a frequent problem for agility trainers attempting to teach 'left' and 'right' responses to their dog. Typically, a trainer will start the dog by giving plenty of body language to help him choose the correct jump (out of a number of choices). If the dog is to take the left jump, the handler might start by standing to the left of the dog, command the dog to jump while running alongside, then ducking off to the left, giving the command, and a visible arm movement toward the correct jump. Eventually, a lot of the extra movement is faded out. However, often the handler will continue to stay on the side of the dog that is consistent with the turn, even though when running a course, this may not be feasible. Unfortunately, the majority of dogs pick up on the body language, which is very salient, and they never pick up on the verbal commands, which are blocked from learning. Because the owner is already standing on the correct side, why should the dog bother to learn the verbal command?"

Over the years, most trainers and class instructors have dealt with blocking and overshadowing. In my own classes and with my own dogs, I would expect that this might happen. I test for it. If the dog didn't understand the cues separately, I'd just train through and fix it. I called it proofing. Aha! With age comes wisdom! It's possible to avoid those problems in the first place!

## Stimulus Control: Discrimination, Generalization, and Context Learning

*Stimulus control* is a term referring to several dimensions of how a dog responds to a cue. A dog is said to be "under stimulus control" if the dog does not:

- Refuse to give the behavior when cued to do so
- Give the behavior if not cued to do so
- Give the behavior for a different cue
- Give a different behavior on the cue

The dog needs to discriminate between relevant stimuli and all other stimuli available to the dog at the time the behavior was marked and rewarded. Dogs in Legacy's Pet Dog Manners classes tend to err on the last three. I call it enthusiasm. They offer behaviors, seeming to enjoy the game, and have a look that seems to say, "What can I do to get the cookie?"

A dog that has learned a behavior in one context will not necessarily perform it in another. Trainers say the dog is not fluent or has not generalized the behavior. When a dog goofs in class, the owner might say, "But he does it perfectly at home." Tell them that's fine, you believe them, and it's to be expected. The dog is performing to expectations within a context. The classroom is a different environment from the living room at home. When any element of the context changes, many dogs view that as a different exercise. The dog might sit perfectly in the living room, but when you have guests he "forgets" how to sit. He has not been trained to sit in the living room with guests. Perhaps he has been trained to sit in the living room, in the living room with guests, and in the dog training classroom. But he still can't sit on wet grass. Perhaps he'll respond to the word, "Sit" if Mom says it but not if he hears it from Dad. Create a training program where the dog will learn to perform the behavior in a range of different contexts. Explain discrimination and generalization to your students so they know what to realistically expect from their dogs. The lessons plans in the Appendix take these issues into consideration.

**When the Trainer Generalizes and the Dog Doesn't.** Legacy camps and five-day courses always include a welcome dinner. Campers were coming to our home for a welcome barbeque one night. Earlier in the day I had taught a section on how to train competing behaviors for common household crises, such as the doorbell. I gave my own dogs as an example of sitting on a carpet square quietly rather than dashing around at the door when the bell rings. A group of students arrived at our home and KNOCKED on the door instead of using the bell. Our dogs went ballistic, forgetting about their doorbell station. I made the official-sounding excuse, "My dogs have not generalized the behavior to knocking."

## Superstitious Behavior

*Superstitious behavior* is a term for coincidental learning of some irrelevant behavior along with the desired one. It's a behavior unrelated to the consequence, but is nonetheless exhibited by the dog as if it were required for earning the reinforcement. It's usually the result of accidental reinforcement. The cue you have intended is not the one the dog learned. Following are some examples of superstitious behavior:

- When a dog hears, "Down," he lies down and puts his head on his paws (the owner didn't care where his head went as long as he was down). Now he puts his head on his paws AND lies down when he receives the "Down" cue.

- A handler wears her " lucky shirt" to the next obedience trial (she wore that shirt last week, her dog got a perfect score). Of course, the shirt had nothing to do with the score; it was a coincidence.

- A dog is rewarded for "speaking"; he now speaks and wiggles his rear when he speaks because both were rewarded in the first place.

- A man buys a lottery ticket every week. He finally wins some money. Now he will buy only from that "lucky" store. He associated the lucky tickets with the place where he bought it.

Dogs are contextual learners. Although we never know for sure the exact association a dog is making in training, try to plan all lessons to increase the odds that students will communicate successfully with their dogs. Here is an example of how my dog learned one thing, but I was teaching a different thing.

Once upon a time eight-week-old Lacey, an English Cocker Spaniel, arrived at our house. We began to toilet train Lacey, as we had all of our other dogs. The idea was for the dog to sit by the door and wait for someone to open it. Then she proceeded to the designated toilet area at one side of our fenced yard. It was winter in Eastern Washington during the snowiest year of the century. All seemed to be going well except when snow would build up on the deck. On those days, Lacey sat to be let out as usual, but instead of walking off the deck into the yard to toilet, she went potty right on the deck. The family began to call it the Poop Deck. What could be going wrong? This was a tried and true method. All of our other dogs were successful. "Should have gotten a real dog," said a not-too-helpful family friend. He was referring to the fact he still, and I previously, lived with German Shepherd dogs. "No, I wanted something small and sporting," I replied. "Should have gotten a Corvette" he retorted. "She's being wimpy," my son volunteered. "She's not as smart as my Golden Retriever, Mom," my daughter offered. "She's cold" my husband suggested. "Shouldn't take so much fur off when you groom her, better buy her a coat." Pride and love of this puppy (she was much cuddlier than a sports car) urged me to get to the bottom of the problem. She was okay unless it was really snowy. A good clue, but how could I use that information to solve the problem?

THE POOP DECK

With careful observation and documentation the mystery was solved. When it was snowy, the deck was completely covered with snow . . . just like the backyard. When it warmed up, the snow melted or we had swept it off the deck. During the backyard training sessions she had been rewarded for toileting in the snow since there was snow everywhere. When it snowed again and covered the deck, the deck was then fair game in her mind. When the days warmed up, the snow on the deck melted. On those days, she stepped down into the yard like a good girl . . . in search of snow. Lacey's association was on snow not "in this area" as I thought I was teaching her. When we caught on, the jokes were flying about the spring thaw! As the snow started to disappear, Lacey went farther and farther into the shady parts of the yard to find some snow. Spring came, and she figured out that grass was okay, too.

# CHAPTER 3 REVIEW QUESTIONS

1. The word punishment means to inflict pain.
    a. True
    b. False

2. Dogs learn from
    a. operant conditioning.
    b. classical conditioning.
    c. both operant and classical conditioning.

3. In the ABC's of learning, C stands for Consequence.
    a. True
    b. False

4. Select the best definition of the word *positive* as used in operant conditioning.
    a. Add something
    b. Be sure of yourself before you train your dog
    c. Say "good dog" in a nice voice

5. In operant conditioning the word *reinforce* means to make stronger.
    a. True
    b. False

6. The training slang term "two-fers" means
    a. only practice each exercise for two minutes.
    b. two people training the same dog.
    c. dog must do two behaviors to receive one reward.

7. If you use a hand signal and a verbal cue at the same time.
    a. the dog might focus on one and not the other—overshadowing.
    b. the dog will turn his head away and wait for you to make up your mind.
    c. the trainer will get tired too quickly.

**Answers:** 1. b  2. c  3. a  4. a  5. a  6. c  7. a

## ADDITIONAL READING/RESOURCES

Breland, M. and Breland, K. (1961). "The misbehavior of organisms," *American Psychologist Journal,* 16:681–684

Burch, M. and Bailey, J. (1999). *How Dogs Learn.* New York, Howell Book House.

Dogwise, A Direct Book Service, 701 B Poplar, Wenatchee, WA 98801, 1(800)776-2665, *mail@dogwise.com* (Terry's books and others).

Jecs, D. (1995). *Choose To Heel "First Steps."* Puyallup, WA: Choose To Heel™, *www.ChooseToHeel.com.*

Legacy Canine Behavior and Training, Inc. Courses: Practice principles of learning by training rats, chickens and dogs. *www.LegacyCanine.com,* 360-683-1522.

Miller, P. (2001), *The Power of Positive Pet Dog Training.* New York: Howell Book House.

Pryor, K. (1984). *Don't Shoot the Dog.* New York: Bantam Books/Simon and Schuster.

Reid, P. (1996). *Excel-erated Learning.* Oakland, California: James and Kenneth Publishers.

Ryan, T. (2004). Sounds Good, CD Series for Sound Desensitization. *www.LegacyCanine.com,* 360-683-1522, P.O. Box 3909, Sequim, WA 98382.

Schwartz, B. (1989). *Psychology of Learning and Behavior.* New York: W.W. Norton & Company, Ltd.

Sidman, M. (1989). *Coercion and Its Fallout.* Concord: Cambridge Center for Behavioral Studies.

Skinner, B. F. (1938). *Behavior of Organisms: Experimental Analysis.* New York: Prentice Hall.

Tawzer Dog Videos and DVDs, P.O. Box 423, Meridian, Idaho 83680, 1(888)566-3003, *Tawzer2@msn.com* (Videos and DVD's of Terry's programs and others).

# CHAPTER 4

# HUSBANDRY

*" First, do no harm."*
—Hippocrates

# ABOUT PART I: HEALTH AND WELLNESS INFORMATION

*"First do no harm"*
—Hippocrates

The authors of the physical and behavioral health and wellness material in Part I are:

**Margaret M. Duxbury DVM, DACVB**

Dr. Duxbury has broad experience as a veterinarian in small animal and equine practice in Minnesota and Wisconsin. Following this, she spent 5 years in postdoctoral studies in animal behavior completing a behavior residency program. After completing this program she passed an examination offered by the American College of Veterinary Behaviorists to become certified as a Veterinary Behaviorist. She is also the senior author of a peer reviewed epidemiologic study published in the *Journal of the American Veterinary Medical Association*, Vol. 223, No 1, pp. 61–66. She currently holds the position of Assistant Clinical Professor, Behavioral Medicine Service in the Veterinary Medical Center, College of Veterinary Medicine, University of Minnesota.

**R. K. Anderson DVM, MPH, DACVPM, DACVB**

Dr. Anderson is Professor Emeritus and currently Director of the Center to Study Human Animal Relationships and Environments in the College of Veterinary Medicine and the School of Public Health, University of Minnesota. He has received the Waco Childers Award from the American Humane Association and a Life Time Achievement Award from the American Society for Prevention of Cruelty to Animals. He is one of the founders of the national Delta Society and received the Leo Bustad Award as Companion Animal Veterinarian of the Year 1987. He is also a co-inventor of the Gentle Leader® headcollar for dogs along with his colleague Ruth Foster to whom this book is dedicated by author Terry Ryan.

# PART I: HEALTH AND WELLNESS INFORMATION

## PUPPIES

Puppies are wonderful and capture our attention and affection with their soft cuddly bodies, looks, energy, curiosity, and desire to learn. To achieve our goals of helping puppies develop into mannerly and healthy dogs, puppies need to have the help of the mother dog, the breeder, the new owners, veterinarians and trainers. They form an important team to assist new owners with learning about physical and behavioral health to enhance the human animal bond.

Socialization is a very important part of bringing a puppy into human society and should start with the breeder. For the first 7 to 8 weeks of a puppy's life the breeder is responsible for providing an environment that will help the puppy learn to cope with novelty in sounds and sights and with other puppies, other dogs and with as many people as possible. When puppies go to new homes at 7 to 8 weeks of age, owners need advice and instruction from breeders, veterinarians and trainers so that they can "pick up the torch" immediately to continue this socialization.

Dogs benefit from regular social experiences all their lives. But from 3 to 14 or 16 weeks of age, the brain is biologically ready to make long-term change in response to social input. This window of temporary open-mindedness is too important to ignore. Under old training methods, puppies didn't start "school" until 6 months. Many owners still have this mindset and don't understand the importance of starting socialization 'school' right away. Along with the crate, the toys, the collar and the leash, new owners should prepare for a new puppy by locating and enrolling the puppy in class at 8 weeks of age, or as soon as possible after this age. Breeders and veterinarians are perfectly situated to deliver this important information. They can recommend trainers and training programs where owners can learn to manage behavior and provide important socialization experiences for their puppy.

Puppies should have their first visit to a veterinarian for a physical exam and begin a vaccination program starting at 6 to 8 weeks of age. At this time they should plan a wellness program that includes prevention of problems in nutrition, dental health parasitism, infections, and behavior. This includes enrolling the puppy in socialization class at 8 weeks, or as soon as possible after this age. Some veterinarians and owners restrict socialization opportunities until after the puppy

*Chapter 4   Husbandry*

is 16 to 18 weeks of age or at least 2 weeks after it has received its last dose of distemper, parvo, or adenovirus. Preventing or limiting socialization greatly increases the risk that those dogs will develop unwanted or even dangerous behaviors.

Of the several million dogs that die in animal shelters each year, several hundred thousand have unwanted behaviors, many associated with lack of appropriate socialization and training. In stark contrast there are few to no reports of dogs dying of canine distemper or canine parvovirus because they became infected while attending a puppy socialization class. We have gathered data from 3 areas across the U.S. (east coast, west coast and Midwest) showing no cases of parvo-distemper disease in puppies attending these specific early socialization classes. These puppies have completed 22,147 weeks of puppy class exposure with no associated illness.

In our judgment puppies should continue socialization activities and begin training classes while receiving their puppy vaccinations. Puppies should start group classes one to two weeks after receiving their first dose of vaccine for distemper, parvo and adenovirus. The data presented above, which was collected from some of the largest puppy socialization and training programs in the U.S., supports our assertion that this is safe practice. Additionally, published research supports the benefit of puppy socialization classes beginning at 8–12 weeks of age.

# Disease Prevention/Wellness

Disease protection is an essential responsibility for the dog owner. The beginning owner may not understand this, and may try to bring their puppy or dog to you for training without adequate preventive measures. By requiring proof of vaccination and parasite control, you can help yourself, your clients and their dogs. Remind owners that for early disease protection, a veterinarian should examine their dog at least once yearly.

## *Infectious Diseases*

Adequate vaccinations are an essential part of a preventive health program. The body is pretty good at recognizing the different "bugs"—as long as it gets a good look at them the first time. Vaccines are the safest first exposure. Initial vaccines and boosters are attenuated, which means they are altered in some way and can't induce serious disease—like the bad guy with his hands tied behind his back. Once that 'face' makes the body's "most-wanted list," subsequent exposure—either in the form of booster injections or the real thing—induces an amnestic, or "I remember you" response, and the body fires up its protective forces. Periodic booster shots ensure that the body stays on security alert and is not caught unprepared if the real bug shows up.

The timing of initial vaccines and boosters is especially particular for puppies. Puppies are born with a supply of antibodies from their mothers. Until these maternal antibodies fade away in the first few months, they will cancel out any vaccines. Since we don't know exactly when those maternal antibodies disappear, the puppy must receive several boosters to ensure adequate protection.

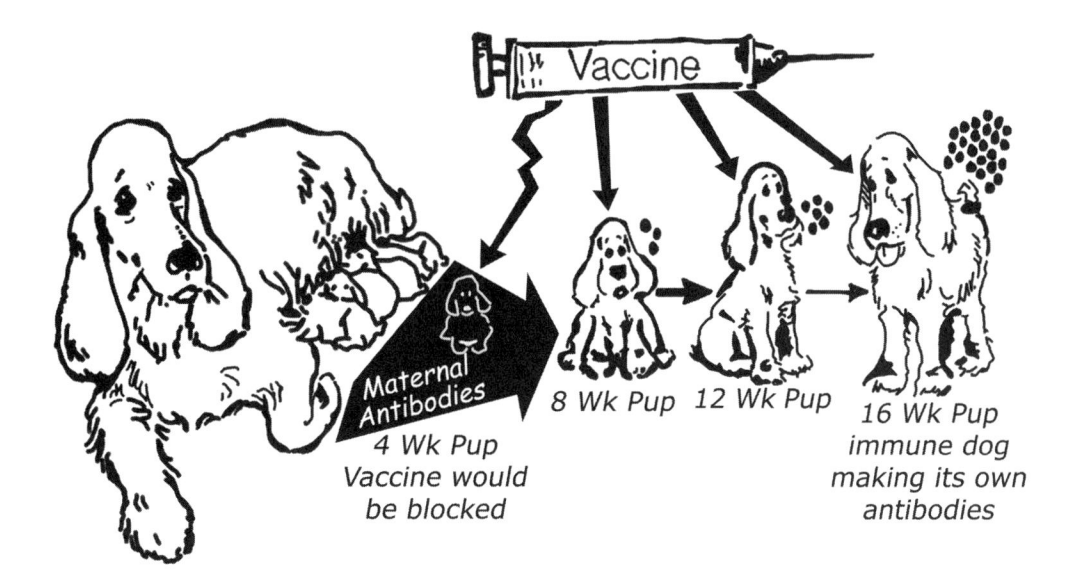

According to the 2006 American Animal Hospital Association Vaccine Guidelines, core vaccines are those recommended for all dogs, and should be given according to the following schedule. Distemper, hepatitis, and parvovirus vaccinations must be given every 3 to 4 weeks starting at 6 to 8 weeks of age until the puppy is 12 to 14 weeks of age. These vaccines are "boostered" at one year of age, and then repeated every three years. Rabies is given once in the first year—at 12 weeks of age or older, followed by a booster when the dog reaches one year of age. Subsequent boosters are repeated every 1 to 3 years, depending on the product.

In certain geographic areas, or for dogs that engage in certain activities, additional non-core vaccines may also be recommended. Examples include vaccines for Lyme disease, leptospirosis, and for bordatella and parainfluenza (parts of the kennel cough complex).

Complete vaccination is very important. These diseases are not ghosts from a bygone era, but rather are credible continuing threats to unprotected animals.

## Internal and External Parasites

Parasites are another important cause of illness and disease in dogs. The type of illness produced depends on whether the parasite lives inside (internal parasites) or outside the body (external parasites).

*Heartworms* live inside the heart itself, wreaking such havoc on the heart, lungs and circulation that careful proactive measures are warranted to prevent infection from ever occurring.

*Gastrointestinal parasites* are also important because they can damage the gastrointestinal tract and impede the absorption of proper nutrients from the diet. Many puppies are born with roundworms and hookworms, so this problem needs to be addressed early. Both of these gastrointestinal parasites can cause illness in people—children are especially vulnerable.

*External parasites* such as fleas and ticks can be both the cause and the source of other diseases. For example, fleas ingest a blood meal each time they bite. The bites can cause severe allergic skin reactions. If the bites produce enough blood loss, the dog becomes anemic. Fleas may also harbor tapeworm eggs, which become infective if a dog ingests them while grooming itself. Ticks transmit a number of important infections that may cause lameness, fever, and systemic organ dysfunction.

## Environmental Hygiene

Disease prevention cannot be left entirely to vaccines. Whether or not a dog becomes ill after disease exposure depends on the dose of contagion as well as the animal's immune status. Any puppy or dog showing signs of illness should not be allowed in class. Parvovirus can be deadly—and may first appear as a puppy that is depressed, vomits or has diarrhea. Dogs do not get 'colds', so be especially aware of any dog that is coughing. Infectious canine tracheobronchitis or kennel cough can spread like wildfire and become established in the environment—especially if hygiene is poor.

Good environmental hygiene reduces exposure to disease causing agents. Training facilities should be kept free of hair and debris, and cleaned regularly with disinfectants. Puppies and nervous dogs may eliminate in the training area. Areas of fecal soiling should be cleaned up immediately and the area treated with a solution of 1:30 bleach, which is effective against parvovirus. Your clients will appreciate your efforts to keep their dogs or puppies safe from contagious disease. Professional policies such as requiring proof of immunization and examination by a veterinarian, keeping your training area clean and free of odor, and refusing sick puppies will encourage client trust and respect.

## PREPARING FOR EMERGENCIES

At some point, you may find it necessary to administer first aid to a dog in your class. It is wise to have emergency supplies on hand and an action plan in case an emergency arises. Your local veterinarian may be willing to instruct your staff in appropriate emergency protocols.

Remember that a hurting or frightened dog is more likely to bite. Be aware that looming over the dog's head, especially from the front, or allowing crowds of concerned people to surround the dog may be extremely threatening to the dog and trigger a bite. If an emergency happens in your class, people will take cues from you on how to respond. Stay calm so that you encourage others to stay calm. Move slowly, breathe, and keep your shoulders loose so that your body and mind stay clear to handle the emergency well.

# HEALTH MAINTENANCE

Before beginning any strenuous athletic activity such as flyball or agility, dogs should have a complete physical exam performed by a veterinarian. An examination is especially advisable for any dog that is overweight or has been sedentary. Furthermore, certain breeds have special concerns (e.g., a higher incidence of heart problems, respiratory problems like laryngeal paralysis, or musculoskeletal problems such as hip or elbow dysplasia).

Maintaining a healthy body weight is important, especially for dogs that are active or still growing. Obese dogs have a higher risk of cardiovascular disease and certain metabolic illnesses such as pancreatitis. Excess weight will magnify the stresses placed on joints and limbs and contribute to lameness. Nutrition is also important for canine athletes. Like all dogs, canine athletes should receive a well balanced diet in an amount that maintains ideal body weight and condition.

Dogs in ideal body condition will have a "waist" or hourglass shape when viewed from the top and from the side. Their ribs can be felt but not prominently seen.

If we use ourselves as comparisons, it's easy to overestimate the amount of food a dog needs each day. This is especially true for small dogs as with today's nutrient-dense dog foods they may require extremely small volumes. With even a few extra pieces of kibble or the crust off the morning toast, it can be easy to overshoot the daily caloric requirement and promote weight gain. The caloric impact of food rewards used in training must also be considered.

Food is an important primary reinforcer—i.e, it is inherently motivating, which is why it can serve as an effective reward in training. Its effectiveness depends on the dog's satiety vs hunger level. A satiated dog may not be motivated to work for food, where a hungry dog will. Within reason, you can ask your owners to make sure their dogs are truly hungry during training sessions—so the dogs are best ready to learn. Dogs originated as pack animals whose ability to eat depended greatly on problem solving skills and communication among members. In some ways, training simulates a biologically natural situation for the dog—that is a hungry dog using communication and problem solving skills to attain food. Before owners manipulate their dog's feeding schedules, they should discuss it with their veterinarian. This is especially true if the dog has any medical problem or is a member of a deep-chested breed with a high incidence of gastric dilatation/volvulus.

# THE ROLE OF SPAYING AND NEUTERING

In current practice, dogs are spayed or neutered anytime after 6 to 8 weeks of age. What's most likely to matter in terms of behavior is whether the surgery takes place before or after puberty. Male and female hormones have both organizational and activating effects. Male or female hormones act very early in a puppy's development to *organize* the brain circuits. These circuits in the brain can then spring into action when *activated* by hormone surges at puberty, resulting in the behavior patterns of the adult male or female.

# Nestlé PURINA
## BODY CONDITION SYSTEM

**TOO THIN**

**1** Ribs, lumbar vertebrae, pelvic bones and all bony prominences evident from a distance. No discernible body fat. Obvious loss of muscle mass.

**2** Ribs, lumbar vertebrae and pelvic bones easily visible. No palpable fat. Some evidence of other bony prominence. Minimal loss of muscle mass.

**3** Ribs easily palpated and may be visible with no palpable fat. Tops of lumbar vertebrae visible. Pelvic bones becoming prominent. Obvious waist and abdominal tuck.

**IDEAL**

**4** Ribs easily palpable, with minimal fat covering. Waist easily noted, viewed from above. Abdominal tuck evident.

**5** Ribs palpable without excess fat covering. Waist observed behind ribs when viewed from above. Abdomen tucked up when viewed from side.

**TOO HEAVY**

**6** Ribs palpable with slight excess fat covering. Waist is discernible viewed from above but is not prominent. Abdominal tuck apparent.

**7** Ribs palpable with difficulty; heavy fat cover. Noticeable fat deposits over lumbar area and base of tail. Waist absent or barely visible. Abdominal tuck may be present.

**8** Ribs not palpable under very heavy fat cover, or palpable only with significant pressure. Heavy fat deposits over lumbar area and base of tail. Waist absent. No abdominal tuck. Obvious abdominal distention may be present.

**9** Massive fat deposits over thorax, spine and base of tail. Waist and abdominal tuck absent. Fat deposits on neck and limbs. Obvious abdominal distention.

The BODY CONDITION SYSTEM was developed at the Nestlé Purina Pet Care Center and has been validated as documented in the following publications:

Mawby D, Bartges JW, Moyers T, et. al. *Comparison of body fat estimates by dual-energy x-ray absorptiometry and deuterium oxide dilution in client owned dogs.* Compendium 2001; 23 (9A): 70

Laflamme DP. *Development and Validation of a Body Condition Score System for Dogs.* Canine Practice July/August 1997; 22:10-15

Kealy, et. al. *Effects of Diet Restriction on Life Span and Age-Related Changes in Dogs.* JAVMA 2002; 220:1315-1320

Call 1-800-222-VETS (8387), weekdays, 8:00 a.m. to 4:30 p.m. CT

Nestlé PURINA

*Coaching People to Train Their Dogs*

Prepubertal neutering does not prevent the organizational effect of these hormones. A male puppy's brain is masculinized at birth—and just like an unneutered male, a neutered male will rate slightly higher than a female for traits like activity level and playfulness. Neutering does not affect athletic ability, watchdog tendencies or trainability, nor will it "calm the dog down."

Prepubertal neutering does prevent activational effects. The dog will not go through puberty, so sexually dimorphic behaviors (behaviors associated with mating that differ between males and females) do not develop. For males, these include roaming, mounting, urine marking, and fighting with other male dogs. Neutering *after* the onset of puberty may still reduce these sexually dimorphic behaviors. Studies show that urine marking, mounting, and fighting between males decrease in response to neutering in 50–60% of the cases. Roaming behavior decreases after neutering in approximately 90%.

Both females and males gain huge health benefits from their respective procedures. Spayed females are protected against serious diseases of the reproductive tract including uterine cancer and pyometra (a life threatening uterine infection). Females spayed before their first heat cycle have a dramatic decrease in their risk of mammary cancer—an otherwise common condition. Neutered males show reduced risk of infection and benign overgrowth of the prostate. The risk of testicular cancer is eliminated.

# FACTORS THAT INTERFERE WITH LEARNING

When a dog seems to learn slowly or appears difficult to teach, the problem often lies with the person trying to train the dog. Timing mistakes and other owner handler errors are very common reasons for poor response to training. But they are not the only reasons; medical and emotional factors can also affect a dog's behavior and its ability to learn.

## *Medical Conditions*

Medical conditions impacting behavior may be detected on physical examination, but more often require laboratory testing to identify. These conditions may be congenital or acquired—meaning they are either present at birth—or develop sometime after the puppy's wriggling, wet and helpless arrival through the birth canal. Some of these conditions are listed below. This is not intended to be a complete list of medical conditions affecting behavior—but rather to alert you to the variety of conditions possible, and the importance of frequent veterinary examinations.

Hydrocephalus results when excessive cerebrospinal fluid accumulates in the brain. The brain is normally protected by the skull (its own private hard hat) and by the cerebrospinal fluid, which shields the brain from slamming into the skull itself. Cerebrospinal fluid also bathes the brain with nutrients and natural disease-fighting cells—kind of like a 'day at the spa' for the brain. Like a flowage, this fluid seeps into and drains out of spaces in and around the brain. While a flowage would overflow to other areas if its drain backed up, cerebrospinal fluid is tightly contained and has no place to go. When the drains clog, the fluid pressure builds and builds—in severe cases squeezing the life out of the soft spongy tissue of the brain. Brain drains can clog because they didn't form correctly in the first place (congenital), but can also fail after trauma, inflammation or infection in the brain (acquired). Hydrocephalus can cause learning delays or failures (e.g., slow or absent house training) and irritability or aggression. Congenital hydrocephalus is more common in very small (e.g., Chihuahua, Yorkshire Terrier, and Pomeranian) or brachycephalic or flat-faced breeds (e.g., Pug, Pekingese, and English Bulldog).

Congenital or acquired abnormalities of the brain or brainstem can impair the voluntary control of urination, or lead to precipitate voiding—where the dog frequently voids small amounts of urine without warning. These conditions are not common and are often accompanied by other neurological signs, but should be considered in dogs that fail to housetrain despite well-implemented training.

Epilepsy is a brain disorder characterized by intermittent bursts of abnormal brain activity resulting in seizures. Seizures can take many forms including convulsions and loss of consciousness. In certain less common forms, they can also produce sudden changes in behavior. These "psychomotor seizures" often originate in the limbic or emotional areas of the brain and can produce sudden out-of-context episodes of aggression, salivation, or hallucinations (e.g., flybiting). Behaviors associated with psychomotor seizures will not improve with behavior modification since they are not under the dog's voluntary control. Anticonvulsant therapy may be helpful in some cases.

A variety of metabolic disorders can lead to changes in behavior. Hepatic encephalopathy can result from either congenital or acquired conditions of the liver that render it unable to perform two important functions: removing toxic byproducts that enter the blood from the gut, and producing the amino acids and other factors necessary for neurotransmission. Behavior changes resulting from liver disease may be most obvious in the few hours after eating—especially if the meal contains a large amount of protein. Pacing, mental dullness, increased irritability or aggression and seizures are possible. It's hard to interfere with the functioning of such a highly important organ as the liver without seeing an effect beyond behavior. Loss of appetite, vomiting, weight loss, and increased water consumption and urine output are common. Some animals are better able to compensate than others, so these changes may be subtle.

A potentially fixable cause for this kind of hepatic dysfunction is a portosystemic shunt—a congenital defect that sends the blood supply from the gut zipping past its usual target (the liver) and on to the body's main circulatory system. Toxic byproducts absorbed from the gut—which are usually filtered out by the liver—are instead dumped directly into the systemic blood stream. Portosystemic shunts are seen more commonly in young purebred dogs. Depending on the anatomical location of the shunt, surgical repair may be possible.

***Hypoglycemia.*** Unlike most other body tissues, the brain does not use insulin to get sugar or glucose into its cells, and has no mechanism to 'store it up for later'.

The brain needs sugar. It needs it fast and it needs it constant, or it quickly starts to malfunction. This makes the brain very dependent on the mechanisms that normally keep blood sugar stable. Signs of hypoglycemia depend on how low the blood sugar is, and how fast it dropped. In dogs whose ability to maintain their blood glucose is impaired, strenuous exercise, a high level of excitement or lack of food may cause a quick drop in blood sugar and result in seizures. When the drop occurs more gradually, the animal may be weak, disoriented, irritable, or fail to process information well. Treatment for hypoglycemia depends on the cause. Young puppies and some toy breed dogs are at risk for hypoglycemia if they are subjected to improper nutrition, a heavy parasite load, or stress. Hunting dogs will sometimes use up so much glucose while in the field that their compensatory mechanisms fail and signs of hypoglycemia appear. A diabetic dog given too much insulin or exercising too heavily could become hypoglycemic, as could an adult dog with an insulin-secreting tumor.

## Hormonal Diseases

*Hypothyroidism.* The thyroid gland secretes hormones important for growth and metabolism. Overactivity of the thyroid gland—or hyperthyroidism—is uncommon in dogs, but hypothyroidism, or underactivity, is common especially in certain breeds. The thyroid's role in behavior problems is somewhat controversial. In the author's experience hypothyroidism is an uncommon but occasionally important contributor. Problems include aggression, irritability and anxiety related disorders. Sustained use of certain psychotropic medications can affect thyroid test results so it is important to establish a pretreatment baseline.

In Cushing's disease, the body produces too much cortisone, which can contribute to irritability and increased reactivity. Most cases of Cushing's disease occur in middle-aged to older dogs.

## Drug Effects

Irritability and increased reactivity are sometimes observed while dogs are on certain medications including some tranquilizers and corticosteroids. The benzodiazepine medications can disinhibit aggression. This means that certain dogs may be more aggressive on the drug than off—for example the dog appears to overreact to a stimulus it previously tolerated.

## Issues of Aging

*CDS.* With advancing age comes the possibility for age related changes in mental functioning and behavior. Cognitive Dysfunction Syndrome is a well-recognized problem of older pets. Structural brain changes are associated with signs of disorientation, change in the way the dog interacts with its social group, disruptions in the sleep/wake cycle, and loss of known 'rules' leading to problems such as house soiling. In older dogs, irritability may be a sign that they hurt (see chronic pain below). The dog may startle more easily due to loss of vision or hearing.

***Chronic pain.*** When we suspect that a dog is suffering from chronic pain or malaise (not feeling well), oh how we wish that dog could talk. Pain can be described by the sufferer but not measured by another individual. Do dogs get headaches? How would we know? Pain is experienced subjectively and can exist with no outward localizing sign to point us to its cause. While in most cases, we work diligently to avoid anthropomorphism (assigning human feelings to a non-human species), most people can relate to the potential effect of long term pain or illness on mood and reactivity patterns. Chronic pain can reduce a dog's motivation to learn or take risks. It can increase irritability so that the dog reacts aggressively to benign stimuli. Dogs that hurt may have a heightened need to protect themselves and decide that "the best defense is a good offense." A careful physical examination, laboratory work, and in some cases a trial course of pain medication can be important for any dog who is not responding well to training, or who appears to backslide.

The previous discussion illustrates the point that many medical problems impact behavior. Our goal is to encourage a partnership between trainers and veterinarians. A trainer, who may be the first professional an owner talks to about a problem behavior, can refer the owner to a veterinarian for diagnosis and treatment of any contributing medical problems.

## *Emotional Issues*

Like pain, complex emotions can be described by the sufferer, but not independently measured by an observer. Since animals can't talk to describe their feelings, controversy exists about whether dogs have complex emotions equivalent to those of humans (e.g. jealousy, love, respect). But we can observe consistent physical signs among dogs in certain settings, leaving little doubt that dogs can be fearful, anxious or aroused (fight/flight).

Anxiety, fear and arousal cause dogs to behave in ways that cause problems for people. Examples include destructive escape attempts, or aggression directed towards people or dogs. These behaviors may lead to relief of the dog's fear or anxiety (the dog comes closer to escaping or the threatening person pulls away). This success reinforces the behavior making it more likely to be repeated. Punishment can make the problem worse by further increasing fear and anxiety in the problem setting. Fearful or anxious dogs are in a self-preservation mode—and thus more likely to interpret even benign stimuli as threats, further worsening the problem. For these reasons, behavior problems that are rooted in fear or anxiety require more expertise to solve.

## *Pscyhotropic Medications*

In some cases, appropriate administration of psychotropic medications can improve the response to treatment for behavior problems. These medications should be prescribed by veterinarians who have themselves examined the dog and made their own diagnosis. Veterinarians with advanced behavior training will best accomplish this. More veterinarians in general practice will be prepared to make prescription decisions as increasing numbers of veterinary schools include behavior education as part of their core curriculum. Psychotropic medications represent only part of a complete treatment plan.

## Professional and Certifying Organizations

There are a number of ways that trainers, veterinarians and behaviorists develop expertise, and several credentialing options. If people in these different groups perceive they are competing for the same 'turf', there may be a tendency for competition to develop. This is unnecessary. Every dog can gain from having professionals working to prevent or treat behavior problems. And professionals can all benefit from each other. Trainers need veterinarians with behavior education to rule out medical problems that may impact behavior in dogs they work with, and to choose appropriate psychotropic medications if indicated as part of a complete treatment plan. Veterinarians benefit enormously from skilled trainers who can work with clients to implement behavior modification recommendations. Behaviorists with advanced training contribute a broad based ethological perspective recognizing the impact of both past biology and learning on current behavior, as well as any medical contributors if the behaviorist is also a veterinarian.

**For trainers:**

A number of different professional organizations exist for trainers seeking a scientifically based and humane approach to dog training.

- The Association of Pet Dog Trainers (APDT) is an educational organization for dog trainers seeking to ever-improve their training skills. APDT members are encouraged but not required to use dog-friendly, scientifically based training techniques. Many educational opportunities are offered. More information is available at *http://www.apdt.com/*.

- The Certification Council for Pet Dog Trainers (CCPDT) provides professional testing and certification for professional dog trainers who have been trained in scientific and humane training techniques. To maintain their certification, Certified Pet Dog Trainers (CPDT) must follow a stringent Code of Ethics and earn a prescribed number of continuing education credits. More information is available at *http://www.ccpdt.org/*.

- Certification for behavior consultants that work with many species is possible through The International Association of Animal Behavior Consultants (IAABC). IAABC also promotes professional ethical standards, research and continuing education. More information is available at *http://www.iaabc.org/*.

- The National Association of Dog Obedience Instructors (NADOI)—NADOI is the oldest group of its kind in the world. Their mission is to endorse dog obedience instructors of the highest caliber; to provide continuing education and learning resources to those instructors; and to continue to promote humane, effective training methods and competent instructors More information is available at *http://www.www.nadoi.org*.

***For those with advanced degrees:***
The Animal Behavior Society was founded to promote the scientific study of animal behavior, both in the lab and in the field. Its Certified Applied Animal Behaviorists (CAAB) have either a PhD in a behavior related field and years of clinical experience treating behavior cases, or are veterinarians who have completed formal training in animal behavior and have several additional years of clinical behavior experience. More information on the Animal Behavior Society and its certification programs can be found at *http://www.animalbehavior.org*.

The American Veterinary Society of Animal Behavior has organized to provide a forum and educational information for veterinarians with interest in animal behavior and clinical behavior cases. Their membership includes both board certified veterinary behaviorists (see below) and veterinarians who are interested in behavior but have less formal training in the field. More information is available at *http://www.avsab.us/*.

Veterinary behaviorists (Diplomates of the American Board of Veterinary Behaviorists) are trained to identify and treat both medical and emotional factors impacting behavior, and can prescribe psychotropic medications where they are clinically indicated. In accordance with specialty practice requirements of the American Veterinary Medical Association, the term 'behaviorist' is reserved for those who have attained board certification. They have received extensive training in ethology, learning theory, the effects of disease on behavior and psychopharmacology. They've completed a supervised residency program with responsibility for over 400 clinical cases under the supervision of another Diplomate, and passed a rigorous specialty board examination. For more information or to contact an ACVB Diplomate go to *www.dacvb.org*.

# PART II: TRAINING EQUIPMENT

This section describes Legacy's training equipment preferences—what we recommend for our clients at the present time. It is not meant to be an all-encompassing objective guide to all types of equipment.

## WHAT IS YOUR EQUIPMENT POLICY?

Do you have a stated policy on equipment? For example, Legacy requests that owners do not use a retractable leash while in class for training. We have a supply of appropriate leashes to lend to clients. We use mostly buckle collars in our classes, Premier martingale collars, and Gentle Leaders®. We don't recommend or sell slip collars (choke collars, choke chains) or prong collars (spike collars, pinch collars, German choke). At our orientation session we talk about training equipment. The orientation is mandatory and is held before the first class with dogs. Most students acquire suitable equipment before the dog comes to class.

We no longer allow participants into advanced Legacy classes who have not completed an entry level Legacy class. However, at some workshops and seminars we accept unknown dogs and owners. Participants know ahead of time what our expectations are for their behavior and the behavior of their dog during the seminar, but we don't state that only certain collars are allowed. If these folks arrive using other collars, our mindset and policy on other collars is as follows: Should someone have a slip or prong collar on their dog, they probably have a good reason for it. To simply ask that the collar be replaced with a different one could alienate that person. It could be a form of "bashing" their home class or trainer. Participants might be apprehensive when groups of unknown dogs get together. To take away that person's symbol of control might shake his confidence. It might increase worry that his dog will not be "good." When an owner feels anxious, that feeling seems to be communicated to his dog. Once that owner sees other students working their dogs successfully he may be more open to change. It's still your workshop. You are in charge. Be alert for a good time to ask how the collar is working. Has he tried other collars? Would he like to borrow something different and try it out? If he says yes, the success of that person and dog are your responsibility. Supervise and coach them so that they are successful and safe with different equipment.

Consider including a collar and leash in your registration fee or at least have high quality, reasonably priced equipment available for sale. You are a pet professional; you may be asked questions about all sorts of equipment. Be aware of new products on the market. If you have not tested them yourself, know how they have been received by your peers.

# Collars—Friend or Foe?

When you recommend a collar, remember, it's the human on the other end of the leash that is key to the effectiveness of that collar. Your job is to coach that trainer to use the equipment efficiently, humanely, and successfully.

Collars are a means of control—a handle on a dog. Every effort should be made to help clients understand that collars and leashes are imperative to safety in most of our modern lifestyles. The collar provides a means for identification, an important safety issue should the dog become lost. A frightened dog that is running loose can be more easily caught if wearing a collar. On the other hand, almost any collar can accidentally get caught on something, presenting a serious problem to an unsupervised dog. Have information available about microchips or tattoos, whichever is recommended as an additional method of ID in your area. Help the client weigh the pros and cons about keeping collars on home-alone dogs.

With few exceptions, Legacy classes use the first three types of collars listed below. An explanation of other collars clients might own or see in stores is also included.

## Belt-Type Collar

Many dogs and most puppies will respond very nicely in Legacy classes on their usual everyday belt-type collars. Made of a variety of materials, they have conventional buckle or snap release fasteners. There may be a problem of security with buckle collars. Because the collar does not restrict when pressure is applied from the leash, it's possible a dog could back up and pull free. One must find the right balance between a collar snug enough so the dog can't pull out of it and loose enough to be comfortable. Dogs with narrow heads and small ears, such as Greyhounds or Dobermans, are more at risk for backing out of collars. Dogs with big heads and ears, like a Cocker Spaniel or Basset Hound, will have more difficulty getting free. Many puppies and adults wear belt type collars in our program.

## The Limited-Slip Collar

Usually made of nylon, this collar, also known as a half-check collar or martingale, restricts slightly when tension is placed on it. This prevents the dog from pulling free, but is loose enough to be comfortable with a slack leash. It's much safer than the traditional slip collar because it cannot restrict any further than the safety loop. This collar works very well with motivational training methods. It's a favorite collar in our program. At Legacy we refer to this as the Premier Collar because the collars we use are made by Premier Dog Products, Inc., owned by a friend of ours, Sharon Bennett. Sharon designed this collar for use with her rescue greyhounds. She started by sewing collars for her own dogs in her bedroom. Premier now has a large factory that employs 45 people! In 2003, the United States Small Business Administration awarded Sharon Bennett "National Small-Business Person of the Year."

## Gentle Leader® Head Collar

There are various brands of head collars or head halters. Legacy has tried most of them. We use and sell the Gentle Leader® brand. Friends of Terry's, professional trainer Ruth Foster (this book is dedicated to Ruth) and board certified veterinary behaviorist R. K. Anderson, joined forces to produce the Gentle Leader® head collar. Legacy was one of the official field testers of the device and has continued to use the Gentle Leader® in classes ever since. It's like power steering—where the dog's head goes, the dog will follow. If you recommend Gentle Leaders® in your class, I suggest that you invest in a few of the Gentle Leader® videos. Send one home for the entire family to view. If a Legacy client decides to try a Gentle Leader® we include a private 20-minute fitting and use lesson free of charge.

**Why Use a Gentle Leader®?** People have been using halters to lead animals for centuries. Which is easier—leading a horse wearing a head halter or one with only a rope around its neck? Similar to a halter, the Gentle Leader® does not put pressure on the dog's throat; it fits up higher and rests on the jawbones of the dog.

**How the Gentle Leader® Works.** The Gentle Leader® works in the natural manner of canine communication. In addition to physical help in controlling the dog, the strap around the muzzle delivers a psychological message as well. In watching a group of dogs, you might see a higher ranking dog encircle the muzzle of another dog with his or her own mouth. Gentle Leaders® use this instinctual muzzle control to make a statement of rank. Most dogs recognize the muzzle strap as an extension of your leadership and will often settle into a mellower attitude with minimal training.

**Introducing and Fitting the Gentle Leader® to the Dog.** Gentle Leaders® are available in several sizes and each size is fully adjustable. Gentle Leaders® fit most dogs nicely. Possible exceptions are short-nosed dogs such as Pugs, Pekingese, or Boxers. Some dogs act up when the Gentle Leader® is first put on them. Usually, the dogs that do so are the ones who need a Gentle Leader® the most! These are dogs that do not want to be restricted in any way! The video will have made the client aware of this. Your personal attention in fitting and using the Gentle Leader® is invaluable in helping the dog and owner work through any possible resistance quickly and humanely. Ask the owner to apply pressure to his throat. It's tender. This is where a regular collar rests. Then ask him to apply pressure to his jawbones. The jawbones are not as tender as the throat. This is where the Gentle Leader® rests.

The first few minutes of class are not the appropriate time to fit the Gentle Leader®. Meet with the dog and owner before or after a class when you can take your time. For safety's sake, when you fit the dog, the regular leash and collar should remain on with you or the owner hanging on to the leash. An additional leash can be snapped to the ring of the Gentle Leader®. The weight of the leash on the Gentle Leader® shows both you and the owner "which end is up" during the fitting procedure. The owner should have a handful of really good treats.

**Start with the Neck Band.** Unless the dog is very comfortable with you, do not face and reach over the dog. Have the dog at your side, it's less threatening for the dog and requires less reach on your part. The owner can be in front of the dog with treats. Fit the neckband first. Attach it high, at the base of the ears, and buckle. As you fasten it, admire the dog, and encourage praising and treating from the owner. Keep it on for less than 15 seconds. When you take it off, all praise stops. Say nothing and disengage attention from the dog. Never praise when or directly after you take it off. If the dog struggles, wait for a few seconds of calmness before taking it off. Never take it off while the dog struggles or directly after the dog struggles. Repeat this a few times until the neckband is accepted, then check for proper neckband fit: The band needs to be as high up behind the ears as possible. It should be very snug, like a watchband, a shoe, or the cinch on a horse. Only one finger should fit in the collar. If it does not fit snugly, the dog can back out of it and will be in danger. Almost as bad—the dog has learned it's worth it to struggle. The struggling lottery sometimes pays off! One of the biggest mistakes is not fitting the Gentle Leader® snugly enough.

If the dog's coat type makes it difficult to fasten the collar without snagging some of the hair, lay a paper napkin on the back of the dog's head. It will keep the hair down and in place. Should you catch the napkin in the fastener, just pull the bits of paper out, but be sure the fastener is secure!

**Choices for Fitting the Nose Band.** There are two alternatives when introducing the nose band in combination with the neck band. Choose the one that appeals to your client. Either way, go through the fitting process first!

1. **ALL AT ONCE**
   Put it on and if he doesn't like it at first, simply work through it; don't give in by taking it off while the dog is opposing it. The dog may rub his nose with his paw, scoot his nose along the floor, or otherwise act like a flopping fish. This is sometimes hard for the owner to watch and often difficult for the owner to do. It may work best if you get permission from your client to fit and handle the dog yourself for the first few minutes. Point out that the dog has a choice. He can put his body in a position where the Gentle Leader® is less restrictive. When there he gets treats, treats, and more treats and lots of praise. If he bucks, he is ignored. At any time, if the dog voluntarily starts to slacken the leash, give him even more slack and start treating. You can use food in your hand as a dispenser for him to nibble his way along for a few steps. He will learn by a few quick trial sessions. Most dogs quickly realize that they might as well put up with it

because it's linked with rewards. In short: A quiet dog turns on the owner's attention, and cues the owner to put even more slack in the leash. Acting up gets no attention at all.

2. **LITTLE BY LITTLE**

    If the client would rather you take the slower route, take these preliminary steps to ensure acceptance. Do the following several times a day. At the end of the day, most dogs look forward to wearing the Gentle Leader®. Even stubborn dogs are habituated to it in a couple of days.

    *Start with the Nose Band.* Take a little time to stroke the dog on her nose. Get her used to your hands being there before you start with the band. Don't worry about fit. Extend it to the full size and lay it over the dog's nose a couple of times. If you have trouble with the clasp, insert a dime and twist. The owner can give treats "through" the Gentle Leader®. Take the collar off and the treats and attention go away. Repeat. If you are lucky, just a couple of reps and the dog will be stabbing her nose through the loop in anticipation of the treat. You can start to "eyeball" the fit and adjust slightly between repetitions.

    *Fit the Nose Band and Neck Band Together.* The nose band should fit in front of the dog's eyes, but behind the corners of the mouth. The dog should be able to pant, drink, eat, and bark. The nose band should be able to slide almost to the black part of the dog's nose tip. If it is too loose, the dog can rub her nose on the floor or use his front paw to get it off. Now, this is where your coordination and mechanical skill comes in. Slip it over the dog's nose and quickly fasten it behind the ears. As soon as the nosepiece goes on, the owner can start treating and praising the dog. A quick check and you'll probably find you need to adjust it. Take it right off, and stop the attention, praise, and treats. Adjust and repeat the above. It often takes a few tries to get it right. You might have to readjust the neck band before everything fits properly.

    *Go for a Walk!* When you think you've got it right, either coach the owner or do this yourself: With a good treat in one hand, move several steps forward and turn into the dog, feeding all the way. Help the client remove the Gentle Leader®. When the Gentle Leader® is off, the dog receives no treats, and no attention. The dog is safe on his regular collar and leash.

    *Final Fit.* After a few "test drives," mark both Gentle Leader® fasteners with a pen so everyone knows the proper fit. The neck band was designed to be very large. Once it is fitted properly to the dog, there is apt to be lots of leftover strap. Tell the owner to allow a little extra for growth and cut off the excess. The nylon material can be "sealed" with the flame of a match. This might seem silly, but remind them to take the collar off their dog first!

## Gentle Leader Easy Walk™ Harness

These harnesses are designed to keep the dog from pulling forward on the leash. There are various manufacturers and designs. A control harness is a collar with straps attached that pass under the dog's front legs to form a device similar to a harness. The leash is attached to a ring on the back of the dog. It's easy to use because the dog does all the work. The owner does not jerk or pull the dog, but simply holds on to the leash quietly and allows the dog to experiment. The dog will walk into the harness and stop when tension is felt. With gentle guidance, the dog can then be encouraged to walk in the direction the owner had in mind and is praised as if it were all the dog's idea. The main function of the harness is to prevent the dog from pulling on the leash. It's not very effective as an aid to teaching other behaviors, and, since it must be removed when the owner is not walking the dog, an additional collar is needed for ID or other purposes. Our program uses control harnesses on occasion.

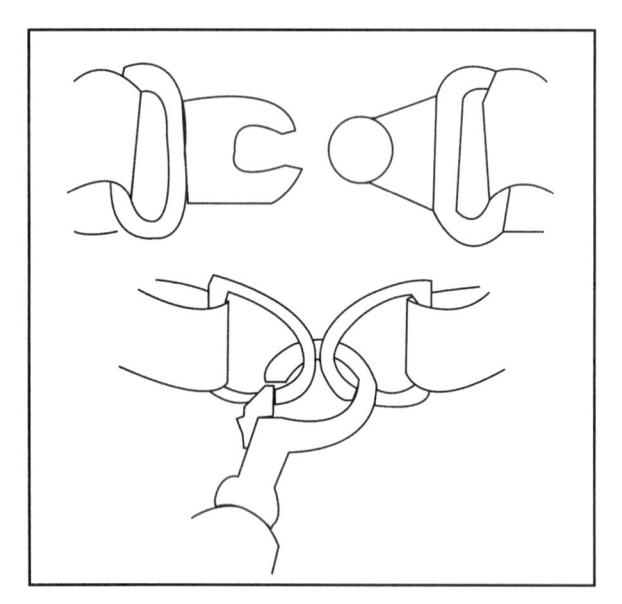

## Break Away Safety Collar

Any collar, regardless of type, can get caught on a nail on your deck or stuck in an opening in a heat vent in your home. It's not uncommon for two dogs playing to become twisted and stuck together by their collars. Each year many injuries and deaths occur by such accidents. The KeepSafe™ break away collar has a segment that will come apart if undue force is applied to the collar. The same collar can be used to safely walk your dog by attaching the leash to two sturdy rings that span the break-away device. This collar is sold by Premier Pet Products.

*Note!* Remind owners that any collars can become a trap for their dog. Some owners opt never to leave any sort of collar on their dog unless supervised. This is a personal choice. A dog without a collar is more difficult to identify or catch should she get away. Ask owners to think carefully about their lifestyle and decide what is best for their dog.

### Choke Chain Collar (Slip Collar)

In days gone by, the term *choke chain* was synonymous with obedience training. Recently, more trainers are going by the motto, "Use brains, not chains," meaning there are ways to train dogs that don't rely on brute strength or intimidation. Dogs need a collar and a leash as a safety measure more than as a training aid. It's not necessary to jerk and pull our dogs into position. Choke chains are sometimes called slip collars or training collars. They can be made of other materials such as nylon or leather. A dog should never be tied or left unsupervised while wearing a slip collar. Death by asphyxiation can occur.

### Pinch Collars

Pinch collars are also known as prong collars. Some trainers refer to them as German choke collars because the good ones are made in Germany. It is a limited slip collar made in segments that end in blunt-ended prongs. If the dog or the owner pulls on the leash, the prongs pinch the dog's neck. Because the collar works by causing pain, the dog may become very confused and identify the pain with something he sees at the time of the pain. When the collar is tightened the dog may lash out at whatever is close, including the handler. Some owners mistakenly use pinch collars for dogs that lunge at others. This might result in a dog becoming more reactive when he associates the pinch with the person or dog approaching. Pinch collars can come apart at the connections if not fastened properly. Some dogs appear to learn very quickly on this collar due to the surprise effect. In many cases, the dog reverts to previous behavior when the collar is removed. In other words, no real training took place. Legacy does not use choke chains or pinch collars in its training programs.

### Body Harness

It's possible to use a regular body harness in class. Dogs tend to pull against a harness, but since we are using motivation, that is not usually an issue. See how the owners do and then suggest something different if appropriate.

## LEASHES

The trouble with leashes is that they can work against you—literally! Clients need a leash for safety and for training, but unfortunately many dog owners use the leash to yank and jerk their dogs into position. Not only is it unnecessary and disagreeable, it's counterproductive due to the dog's natural opposition reflex. Ask your client to test it out. Have her slip her finger in her dog's collar and pull slightly. Does the dog move away from or into the pressure? Unless overpowered or successfully trained otherwise, dogs instinctively oppose force. With this demonstration, the family can see why the dog continues to pull on a walk! It's much easier to go with natural instincts than against them.

## Training Leash

A six-foot long leather or fabric leash is the most versatile for training. Legacy recommends it as a first training leash. It's long enough to allow some distance between the owner and his dog when practicing stays, but not so bulky that it can't be gathered for close work. A four-foot leash might be easier to handle, but doesn't allow any distance from the dog for stationary exercises. You might ask the owner if you can tie a temporary knot in the middle of her six foot leash as a marker. In the beginning, that knot designates the end of the leash. I've found this to be a good means of traffic control and to protect personal space between dogs. Nylon or chain leashes can cut and hurt, especially if the dog pulls. Have a box of loaner leashes available and/or for sale. If you don't sell leashes, make sure you know what the shops in your area carry so you can make a recommendation.

## Retractable Leash

A spring-loaded retractable leash is great for casual walks. The dog is safe, but has quite a bit more range to explore. The spring-loaded mechanism keeps constant pressure on the lead as the dog moves to and fro, lessening the chance of the dog stepping over the line and becoming tangled. While you are teaching loose leash walking and/or heeling, your client will still need to take his dog for a walk. A retractable leash can be used as a signal to tell the dog it's not a training session, but a relaxed walk. Because of that association and to maximize safety, retractable leashes are not used in class.

## Long Line

Perhaps you rely on long leashes for "Come-When-Called" exercises in class. If you will be preparing your students for the the American Kennel Club "Canine Good Citizen" (AKC CGC), you might as well help them get used to the long line early on as it's a requirement for the test's recall.

# SELECTING TRAINING REWARDS

Other than for reasons of safety, training rewards are of more importance than collars and leashes. You may be interested in seeing what we say to our students on orientation night about rewards. The handout is in the Appendix as PDM1Select/UseRewards.doc, "The Selection and Use of Training Rewards." It covers toys, food, and interactions that can be used as rewards. The handout reminds students that they will need clothes with pockets. Some dog trainers select their wardrobe not for style, but for the size of the pockets! The timing of rewards is critical. The Legacy spring-loaded pouch stays open but can be closed with a nudge, so that food does not spill out if you bend over.

Although clients are responsible for providing their own treats and toys, we have a bin of small loaner toys in our training room. It's an easy way for the client to see just what type of toy turns her dog on! We also have a variety of packaged food treats. Because it's offered in small sealed packaging, the client can read the contents and not worry about what he's feeding his dog. Sealed treats give you freedom from preparation, refrigeration, and storage!

# REMOTE OR HAND-HELD ELECTRONIC TRAINING DEVICES

These devices require the dog to wear a collar designed to deliver an attention-getting stimulus. Some collars will vibrate, like some cell phones do. Other collars deliver a sound that can be used as a secondary reinforcer to convey approval and mark the behavior as rewardable. Other models use an aversive high-pitched sound as a punisher. Some use shock to communicate with the dog; invisible perimeter fences work on these principles. Our program might, on occasion, use vibrating collars for deaf dogs. More information can be found under the topic "Deaf or Blind Dogs," in Chapter 7.

## Citronella Release Devices for Barking

We might recommend a Gentle Spray™ collar as an anti-barking device for home use. It comes in a model that automatically releases a spray of citronella, a harmless but aversive scent. It's similar to the smell from a freshly peeled orange. We don't recommend this aversive if the dog is barking from fear or anxiety. We help the client evaluate the reason for the barking. There is a brief overview of the information found in our book, *The Bark Stops Here,* listed in the Appendix as INFO Barking.doc, "The Bark Stops Here." Sometimes wearing the collar, even though it is "out of juice" is enough of a reminder for a dog to be quiet. Some dogs will never bark again if they SEE the collar. A collar lying on the windowsill, for example, is enough for some dogs to be quiet even if they may have experienced the smell only once.

# CRATES

Crates are becoming more common with pet owners. We do crate training in puppy classes by letting the pup hang out in a crate for a few minutes while the owner is sitting alongside. Various uses of these versatile portable kennels are outlined in the Appendix handout PUPPYCratesHousetrain.doc, "Crate Training and Housetraining."

# A Word about Electronic Containment Systems

Electronic fencing systems use a radio signal transmitted to a remote receiver device on the dog's collar. When the dog approaches a boundary line (usually underground and invisible) determined by the owner, the radio signal activates the device on the dog's collar and the dog is shocked. Not all of these systems function well or consistently. Investigate. Ask questions before you suggest this type of fencing. Ask the client to do homework too. Can the shock level be accurately controlled? Will the strength of the shock give information to the dog as intended rather than poorly timed punishment? How good is the company representative who installs the fence and instructs the family on how to use it? Will the owners be compliant with the training needed to make this system work well? Is it really a good idea to leave a dog in the yard unsupervised? Unlike traditional fences, neighbors, other dogs, and wildlife can readily enter the yard. What special measures will need to be taken when the family wants the dog to cross the line, such as taking their daily walk around the neighborhood? Consider the ramifications of that possibility. Will family members remember to turn the fence on? What if the dog becomes highly stimulated when, for example, a cat passes through the yard? The dog might cross the line in her excitement, but then not have equal motivation to cross through the shock again to go back into the yard!

# CHAPTER 4 REVIEW QUESTIONS

1. Normal body temperature for a dog is
   a. the same as humans, 98.6°F.
   b. normally in the range of 100.2° to 102.8°F.
   c. so varied that there is not a normal range.

2. "Natural" written on a bottle of medicine means
   a. it's perfectly safe to give your dog any dose.
   b. it's made by hand.
   c. it's not necessarily harmless.

3. Spaying a dog
   a. is complete surgical removal of the uterus and ovaries.
   b. is a tubal ligation.
   c. makes her dislike puppies and young children.

4. The common household item best suited to combat the spread of parvovirus is
   a. lemon juice at full strength.
   b. white vinegar diluted by water.
   c. a bleach solution.

5. Castrating a dog is
   a. not a good idea for any dog over two years of age.
   b. the surgical removal of the testicles.
   c. the same as a vasectomy in humans.

6. The Gentle Leader® head collar closes the mouth and prevents a dog from biting.
   a. True
   b. False

7. Which statement is true?
   a. Slip collars are the only collars that can actually kill a dog.
   b. No properly fitted collar of any kind can kill a dog.
   c. Most collars have the potential to kill an unsupervised dog.

**Answers:** 1. b  2. c  3. a  4. c  5. b  6. b  7. c

## ADDITIONAL READING/RESOURCES

### Part I: Veterinary Information

Jevring, C. and Catanzaro, T. (1999). *Health Care of the Well Pet.* New York: W.B. Saunders.

Animal Behavior Network, 15340 Pastrana Drive, Suite 100, La Mirada, CA 90638 (800) 372-3606, *www.AnimalBehavior.net*
A network of behaviorists, veterinarians, veterinary technicians, groomers and trainers who have agreed to share information, and offer to help pet owners with their pet behavior concerns.

### Part II: Equipment

Delta Society. (2000). *Professional Standards for Humane Dog Training.* Washington: Delta Society. This manual has a section describing various training equipment and it's use.

The Delta Society, 580 Naches Avenue SW Suite 101, Renton, WA 98055-2297; (425) 226-7357 and (425) 235-1076 (fax), *info@deltasociety.org.*

Kong Company, 16191 Table Mountain Parkway, Golden, CO 80403, *www.kongcompany.com.* This company has a variety of toys and training treats.

Premier Pet Products, 406 Branchway Road, Richmond, VA 23236, *info@premier.com.* This company carries most of the collars and leashes mentioned in Part II: Equipment.

# CHAPTER 5

# THE BUSINESS

> "Those who dance are often thought insane by those who hear not the music."
> —Unknown

In a perfect world, instructors get to instruct. They don't have to be a secretary, a bookkeeper, a graphic artist, and a janitor all in one. Most of us find ourselves in the do-it-all mode. Business might not be your strong suit. Get help. Use the library as a resource. Books on the subject of managing a business are plentiful; find the management approach that fits your style. What follows are lots of questions for you to consider. Recruit local professionals to give the right answers.

## SETTING UP YOUR BUSINESS

Veronica Boutelle runs dogTEC, a continuing education and professional support service center for dog trainers. She is an outstanding resource, many of her ideas are included here.

Veronica differentiates the choices one has in setting up a business. First, decide how you want your small business to run. There are several options. The first is the sole proprietorship (a single owner) or a partnership (several owners). In these, taxes are straightforward and the paperwork is minimal. The downside is that all business liability includes personal liability. For instance, if a dog bite occurs in a class you're teaching and a client chooses to sue you, then not only are the assets of your business at stake, but also your personal assets such as your house and personal bank account.

A second option is the corporation, a more complex set up that entails much more paperwork. In a corporation, business assets and personal assets are separate, which mean liabilities remain only with the corporation and do not include your personal assets.

A third option, the Limited Liability Company (LLC), offers the positives of both the proprietorship/partnership and the corporation. Veronica explains, "As an LLC, you maintain the simple pass-through tax status of a sole proprietor (or you can opt to be taxed as a corporation if you or your accountant find this would be to your advantage) and have relatively few and easy paperwork requirements, while also receiving the liability protection enjoyed by corporations."

The LLC option is available in all 50 states. Before you file for your LLC, you need to search the database at the Secretary of State's office to make certain you aren't duplicating another business name.

If you opt to run your business as an LLC or as a corporation, make certain to file with the Internal Revenue Service (IRS) for an Employer Identification Number (EIN). You'll need this even if you don't have employees. It's much like a social security number for your business.

After you decide the organization of your business, make certain you apply for a business license within your town/city. Even if the city/town does not require one, check with the county before concluding you don't need one. Read carefully all material describing your city's or county's requirements.

# Your Business Plan

Be organized—have a plan. If you are not prepared, the details of running a business can be overwhelming. Here are some categories included in a typical business plan. Business plans are especially important if this is to be your full-time work and not a hobby.

### *Profile*
The business profile describes your business and its goals. Short-term and long-term plans state your goals for the business after certain periods of time. Those goals can be financial or otherwise.

### *Competition Analysis*
An analysis of your competition is a realistic survey of who's doing what in your field in the population you plan to serve. Does a significant market demand exist for your service in your geographic area?

### *Identity and Marketing Plan*
A marketing strategy should be included. Will the rates you intend to charge hinder the ability to attract clients? Will your good service make what you charge worth it to the consumer? Your selection of name, logo, even typestyle should reflect your identity and be consistent. Veronica Boutelle of dogTEC has advice about names; in particular, fictitious business names: "The fictitious business name (FBN) is also called a 'doing business as' statement (DBA). If your business name is different from your personal name, your county might require you to file your FBN. (Occasionally, an area, for example an unincorporated township, doesn't require an FBN, but this is rare.) The FBN ensures that there are not multiple businesses in a single area using the same name and, once you have it, prohibits other businesses in your county from using your name. It also creates a public record of who owns your business. The FBN is relatively inexpensive and lasts longer than business licenses—usually about 10 years. After you have filed, run a listing in a local paper announcing you have filed. If you want to protect the name of your business, you can get a state or national service mark to protect your business name."

### *Staff*
Who will be needed to operate your business at start up? At the end of your first short-term goal period? Will they be paid or volunteer? Include an overview of your staff qualifications, which at first, if you don't have staff, will be a list of your own experience, strengths, and credentials.

### *Financial Chart*
*Start-up Expenses.* Before your first class you are apt to have expenses that include but are not limited to legal work, logo design, brochures, site rental or improvements, and advertising. Keep all business related receipts; they will be needed when filing your Federal/State income tax returns. If you currently

prepare your own tax returns, you might consider hiring a professional tax consultant to file your returns the first year in business. Tax consultants have more knowledge and experience in business tax laws than the average person.

*Start-up Assets.* Typical start-up assets are cash you are willing to commit to the project. It also includes fixed assets such as furniture, matting, audio system, computer, or copy machine.

*Start-up Financing.* This includes both capital investment and loans. The only investment or loan amounts that belong in the Start-up table are those that happen *before* the beginning of the plan. Whatever happens during or after the first month should go into the Cash Flow table, which will automatically adjust the balance sheet.

### Profit or Loss during Start-up?

Will projected business revenues be sufficient to pay for your operating overhead and still allow a net profit? A start-up loss is common and normal. A net profit should be attained within an acceptable period of time to allow you to pay your bills and to pay back your initial investment or loans.

You don't have to re-invent the wheel! Consider approaching small business owners in your area to ask advice about the pitfalls of starting a new business. Contrary to what you might think, if you are not competing for their business, people will be more than glad to share their experiences, both positive and negative. Listen to what they say, and see if it applies to your new venture. After your plan is complete, it will be the template for your business. It will help you stay focused and get you where you want to go. Keep it updated as your goals or the market changes.

## LEGAL MATTERS IN GENERAL

In addition to all the start-up details, instructors must comply with all local, state, and federal laws applying to their activities and to the operation of a business. In the event of a dog bite, instructors must comply with laws about reporting bites. Be sure you know what the local and state laws are concerning injury to your students or their dogs.

## THE LEGALITIES OF HANDLING FOOD

If your orientation is longer than 50 minutes, schedule a break or two. This gives you and your staff a chance to visit with students and answer questions they might have about the material being covered. You might want to consider serving food and refreshments for special events. It's a friendly touch to provide coffee, tea, and other drinks as well as snacks. But, before you go all out and bake up some wonderful goodies, consider what the guidelines are for serving food in your county or state. Today, there are many regulations about serving food and beverages, even something as simple as coffee and cookies. Check the requirements in your area before you decide to serve food because you might need a food server's license.

# ETHICS AND PROFESSIONAL LIMITATIONS

Instructors should conduct themselves responsibly and honestly. What are the ethical guidelines of associations to which you belong? You can also get guidance from Delta Society's "Professional Standards for Dog Trainers, Effective, Humane Principles." Your advertising should be honest and to the point, making the goal of your various classes clear. Don't guarantee specific results that are unrealistic. When the needs of owner and dog are beyond your expertise, be ready to refer. Perhaps another instructor, an animal behaviorist, a veterinarian, or other animal professional can better serve your client. Do not misrepresent your own credentials, and make sure those in your referral network have reliable credentials.

Continue to grow professionally. Look for educational opportunities in your area and nationally. Network with other professionals. Money should be budgeted for continuing education and for membership in professional organizations.

Respect client privacy by not talking about their family, dog, or other business with others without the client's permission. Exceptions might be made if you suspect abuse or believe someone may be committing a criminal act. Take appropriate measures if you suspect these situations. Mention the matter in a nonjudgmental, neutral stance as an attempt to educate the owners. You may need to consider reporting your concerns to appropriate authorities.

Refrain from disparaging other pet professionals or clients. If asked about another instructor, veterinarian, or shop owner you don't particularly like, answer as neutrally as possible.

It is essential that clients sign a waiver form acknowledging the risks of dog training. A training contract should be required for private sessions and kept on file. Legacy's waiver is on the profile form clients are required to complete when they register for class and appears in the Appendix as MISC StudentProfileForm.doc.

# INSURANCE

Any time you work with the public and their dogs, you are working with an unknown. There is always a potential for misunderstanding. Since you may be considered responsible for the well-being of people and their pets while they are in your class, plan for unexpected occurrences by securing insurance protection for yourself and your assistants.

Check with the company that insures your home. You may be able to purchase a short-term policy of some type to cover your initial needs. However, it is very important to consult with an agent who specializes in insuring dog-related businesses. Is that agent familiar with the laws in your state? You might be able to purchase insurance or at least be able to receive an insurance discount because of your affiliation with national trainer organizations like the Association of Pet Dog Trainers and National Association of Dog Obedience Instructors. A good source of information regarding insurance is your local Small Business Administration office. You need insurance for the building or if you are renting for the contents of the building. If you hire independent contractors, hire employees, or work with volunteers, do they have insurance or will your policy cover them? "Umbrella" insurance should also be considered. This type of insurance policy offers extra liability coverage when the limit of your primary liability policy is reached.

# ONGOING MONEY MATTERS

Computers make life in this techno-business world easier. Do your research to determine which program will work better for you and your business. Quick Books Pro® is a good tool for recordkeeping, but how you keep books is less important than actually keeping books. Call your bank to check their requirements for opening a business account. Keep business and personal accounts separate. Credit cards or checks with your business name and address on them look professional, and it is an easy way to track business expenditures. The bank may ask for your business license number or your articles of incorporation. Consider employing an accountant a couple of days a month to help you take good care of your financial matters.

### Setting a Fee Structure

Do you need to cover your time spent on the phone and preparing handouts? Are your fees comparable to other schools in the area? It's not necessarily a bad thing if you are charging more than your competition. Your program just might be worth more than the others. Think about the services you provide and the quality of those services. Is this apparent to your future clients? Talk to other instructors. There are all kinds of ideas on how and what to charge. How about a package deal—one set of classes plus one private lesson or two hours of free doggy daycare? Consider offering a discount coupon for your retail shop or include a collar and leash with a paid registration fee.

### Payment

Do you ask for the entire payment before class? Legacy's experience has shown that it's appropriate to do so. It's a commitment. The few schools that allow students to pay as they go soon realize what they are really doing is paying students to stay away. How about credit cards? Accepting credit cards is a convenience for your clients. Can you justify the time and expense needed to process credit card payments?

## Refunds

What is your policy concerning refunds? It has been my experience that it is always better to give money back if you can't provide a service. If there has been a change in health or an accident with the dog, your student would certainly appreciate a refund.

## Compensation for Your Staff

If you are fortunate to have assistants, you must consider what your working relationship will be. Are your assistants volunteers? Are you providing them with experience and training in exchange for their help at your classes? Do they get free workshops and seminars or access to your library? Are you going to pay them? If yes, what are your tax liabilities? It is always wise to consult an experienced tax advisor when dealing with employees.

## Is It a Business Expense?

Talk to a tax adviser about this. You may be surprised what is classified as a business expense. Know the proper way to document purchases for submission as a business write-off.

# GENERAL SAFETY

Do everything possible to ensure the safety of clients, dogs, and visiting spectators. Turn a questionable area into a safe area with matting, baby gates, additional instructors, and creativity in the exercises you will teach. Arrange clients and their dogs at a comfortable distance while they are in class. Doors are often a high arousal area for dogs. If the area does not allow for an "IN" door and an "OUT" door, plan at least a 15-minute transition time between classes for safe entrances and exits. Instructors should ensure that dogs are kept under control at the training site and in the parking lot. Do not allow clients to tie their dog to a chair or any other unstable or unsupervised area. Some training buildings have tethering rings on the wall. These are helpful for a variety of exercises, but a dog should not be left unsupervised while tethered.

If you are teaching in a public place, such as the county park, don't depend on the park department employees to pick up broken glass, garbage, or other dangerous items. Walk around and look the place over just before your first class to be sure there is nothing on the grounds that could be harmful to your clients or their pets. Will a little league baseball game be scheduled next to you on training class night? Stray children, stray balls, and stray dogs might pose a problem.

Are you prepared if someone in your class needs medical attention, either because of a dog bite, a fall, or a health reason, such as a heart attack or stroke? Are you or someone on your staff trained to perform Cardio-Pulmonary Resuscitation (CPR)? Will you have a first-aid kit available? Do all the staff members know the location of the kit? Where is the nearest phone, and what is the number to call in case of a medical emergency? Have an action plan in place for emergencies. Our school instructors carry a cell phone with emergency numbers taped to the side of the phone. What will you do in the event of a fire? Where is the nearest fire extinguisher?

### *Good Samaritan Statute*

Does your state have a Good Samaritan Statute? This statute generally protects you from liability for damages occurring while you provide emergency or medical services. Ask your lawyer about the use of your car to transport students in an emergency or for any reason.

## ADVERTISING

There are always pet dogs in need of training. How do you let their owners know about YOUR school? Specific marketing strategies will depend on your goals. You don't want to spend a lot of money on advertising and get only two responses. You want to plan your advertising so you have enough time to attract customers and sign them up for your classes.

- Do you want more customers or steady customers?
- What is your competition doing? (Don't be afraid to check them out.)
- What kind of advertising and what media should be used, if any?
- Will advertising help increase your profit? (Definitely, if you are just starting out!)
- Publishing articles or writing a regular column for a newspaper or magazine is another form of advertising.

Avoid impulse advertising. What might seem like a great advertising price might target the wrong market. Be specific about the population you're trying to reach by investigating options that will actually reach potential clients at the best price.

Some things to think about when you advertise include:

- **Have proof to back up every claim you make**—support it with facts.
- **K.I.S.S.**—Keep it short and simple.
- **Package information nicely**—add color to the pages if you have the option: a colored line, a logo, or other spot of color on the flyer or pamphlet.

Here are a few advertising ideas:

- Place posters and brochures at veterinary hospitals, grooming shops, and pet stores.
- If you have a website, link your site to other pet-related sites.
- Mention your classes on Internet pet chat groups.
- If your website is popular, offer training tips.
- Take video or digital photos of your class showing clients doing great stuff and post "dog of the week" photos on your website.
- Have business cards that catch a person's interest.
- Get permission to do a demonstration at civic events, fairs, garden markets, and local celebrations.
- Let your local newspaper know when you are having a special event.
- Suggest the media attend "graduation night"—they might take photographs.
- Contact the newsletter editors of local schools or clubs.
- Volunteer to be a dinner speaker at community service clubs in your area.
- Let animal rescue organizations help you advertise . . . and you find a way to help them.
- Place an ad in the yellow pages.
- Donate plastic poop bags with a logo on them for use in the park.
- Give school T-shirts with your logo on them for people and bandanas for dogs.
- Prepare nice clipboards, notebooks, or folders with your school logo on it—these will be put to use long after your class is over.
- It's expeditious to follow up a telephone call with a written brochure or a client handout sheet to get people interested.
- Have information sheets or brochures ready to mail out.
- Prepare computer documents, but keep it short, not everyone has a fast computer. Graphics take a long time to download.

Sometimes media publicity can bring more credibility and visibility than advertising. Is there a local event involving dogs where you might be noticed by the media? How about making contact with a radio call-in show?

Join a professional organization in your field. Let friends and family and previous business associates know of your new venture. Your friends might not own a dog, but they usually know someone who does. Always keep lines of communication open.

# Registration Procedures

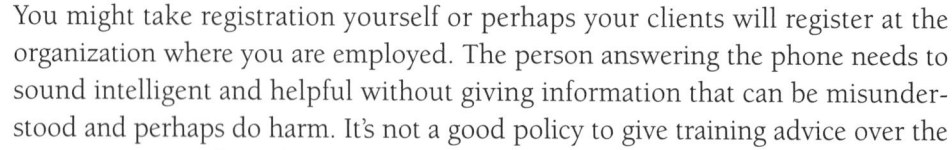

You might take registration yourself or perhaps your clients will register at the organization where you are employed. The person answering the phone needs to sound intelligent and helpful without giving information that can be misunderstood and perhaps do harm. It's not a good policy to give training advice over the phone because that advice can get pet owners into trouble. Will you register the person in name only or will payment be necessary? If payment is not required at registration, you may not know until the first night of class who you will have in class. It's difficult, but not impossible, to schedule classes efficiently if you don't know who is going to show up the first night of class. Talk to your service provider about on-line registration. A copy of Legacy's registration and profile form appears in the Appendix as MISC StudentProfileForm.doc, "Student Profile Form."

# Appropriate First Contact Information

The person who makes the first contact with the client has a big impact upon what that person thinks of your school. Be prepared to listen attentively and carefully to your potential client. Be respectful. Remember there are no dumb questions. Perhaps someone will talk with you at the grocery store, over the phone, via e-mail, or through your website. Give enough good, helpful information to catch their attention. But don't try to solve problems or elaborate on training methods until you have a good idea of your client's needs. If you suspect a behavioral problem, always refer them to their vet for a physical checkup first. If you don't have a class scheduled, tell the prospective client to consider a private lesson and explain why this might be a good option. Make sure you get their name, address, and phone number. Carry business cards with you at all times. Reply promptly to requests for information.

If someone contacts you by telephone, remember that you do not have the luxury of observing that person's body language. Be careful what advice you give. You won't have the visual cues available to you to let you know if what you are saying is being understood. If you are not sure if your message was interpreted correctly ask the person to repeat back what they thought you said. This feedback process will let you know if you both are on the same page!

E-mail is not private. What you write can be reprinted in other forms. You may be misquoted, or the information you give may be misrepresented. Be cautious about what you write.

# THE TRAINING SITE

## Site Selection

**Outdoors.** *The vision:* Blue skies, nice flowers, soft breeze, 70 degrees, smiling owners, and happy dogs. That's what an outdoor class can be . . . about 10% of the time! *The problems:* Outdoors is almost ALWAYS a bigger security threat. What if the dog pulls away from the owner? You cannot trust the owner not to have an accident like that. Can you get the dog back? Are there streets nearby? Are you using a park? Is there a ballgame going on? What are the chances of being hit by a baseball? Are the sprinklers going to be programmed to come on during your class? Or will the maintenance men decide it's time to mow the lawn? A fenced area with a double gate is good. The double gate creates a safety zone—one gate will be closed before the other is opened. This is a costly setup and it's not portable. Is it going to be too hot and/or sunny for the safety and comfort of people and dogs? Consider not only the ambient temperature, but also the surface the dogs will be walking on. Do you have to patrol to be sure there are no thistles, poison ivy, broken glass, or sharp rocks? What about spiders or mosquitoes? Might there be garbage on the ground the dog could eat? You will need a means to visually define where the class takes place; otherwise, children, loose dogs, or even adults might wander in and disrupt class. One of the dogs could cause injury to a visitor. What will you do if it rains? Do you have a call-in number so people can check to see if the class is postponed, cancelled, or if the location has changed? Can clients hear you outdoors? An instructor's voice doesn't carry very far when it's windy or when there is a children's playground nearby. Will you need a portable public address system? If you have your hands on a microphone or bullhorn, you are not able to do as good a job of teaching. Do you have permission and insurance to use this outdoor location? Cities sometimes have rules and restrictions regarding signage and parking access. Be sure to have your cell phone for emergencies!

**Indoors.** After reading the problems with outdoor locations, we have to be fair and say there are drawbacks to indoor training facilities. Most cities and towns create zones to protect residential, commercial, business, and manufacturing areas. Often in residential areas, businesses are not allowed. In some cities, there are zones for multiple uses. A real estate agent can help you decipher the zoning and permits required. It can be hard to find indoor facilities that allow dogs. When you find a good location, it might be a bit expensive, but the security and continuity of an indoor location makes up for it, especially if you live in an area that has inclement weather. You will need to bring in appropriate footing if the floor is too slippery. Matting can be very expensive and will need to be carefully cleaned and sanitized. Chances of dogs getting into trouble with other dogs too close to them increase in a building, simply because of space limitations. All things being equal, most instructors prefer the predictability of an indoor site. Vet clinics, school buildings, horse arenas, churches, community centers, club houses, parking garages, and pet shops are all possible locations for an indoor training area.

## Size: Amount of Space Per Dog

Whether training takes place indoors or outdoors, plan for large dogs, since it only takes one small, unruly dog to take up the same "space" as a large dog. A large number of registrants could be split into two or three classes. With assistants, half of the class can do stationary exercises while the other half does moving exercises. Baby gates or tables placed on edge sideways on the floor a few feet from the wall can make a comparatively safe "Come-When-Called" chute. There is no set formula for how many dogs will fit appropriately in a given space. There are many variables to consider when choosing a training space. In addition to the different personal space issues of each dog, the type of training you do will dictate how much space you will need. Moving exercises can be a problem, but heeling can be taught in a space the size of your bathroom. I know a gentleman who trained his young Samoyed to the AKC Novice Obedience level during the six months the dog was in quarantine—the old days in Hawaii. Within two days of release from quarantine, his dog was entered in three trials and earned qualifying scores. The average Novice Obedience competition ring is $40 \times 50$ feet. Kennel sizes at the Hawaii quarantine facility are about $12 \times 18$ feet. In Japan some of our most successful classes are operating from a veterinary waiting room no bigger than $9 \times 10$ feet. You will find some creative ways to use small spaces for "large" exercises in Chapter 7.

## Restrooms

If restrooms are available at your training facility, they should be clean, safe, accessible, and well supplied. Do you need to provide emergency supplies for your rental building restroom or do you have easy access to the onsite utility closet? Is the restroom accessible to handicapped people? Unfortunately, not all restrooms are. If your class is outdoors, a restroom located on the other side of the park will not be much help to your students.

## Water

Is water available for dogs and humans? If not, make sure students are aware of this ahead of time so they can bring their own bottled water. Beverage dispensers are a convenience if you have your own place. Just look in the yellow pages for vendors. Try to prevent dogs from sharing water bowls. Keep a stack of paper bowls handy. Be sure students are not planning on using the public restrooms as a drinking facility for their dogs. The veterinarians at the ASPCA Animal Poison Control Center (APCC) have found that water from toilets can upset a dog's gastrointestinal tract. Harmful residues from cleaning tablets and chemicals used to clean the toilets may be present. Announce your policies on water at your class orientation. Include bottled water and drinking bowls in the list of things students need to bring to class.

## Trash Containers

Are there trash containers in or near your training area? If so, are they conveniently located? Are they lined? Where are the extra liners? Is it your responsibility to empty them? Even if it's not your job to empty the trash, do so anyway. This can only ensure goodwill among fellow instructors or the landlord. Make sure students know the clean-up policy and have clean-up materials readily available for them to use.

## Signs

If you are using a borrowed space, fold up easel-type signs will help people find the training area and help designate it as "yours" in a public setting. Think about "In" and "Out" signs for the doorways. How about signs that show the location of the restrooms? People find arrows very helpful when trying to find a location. We sometimes use paw prints on the floor for traffic control.

## What's Under Foot?

The type of floor in your training facility will have an effect on how the dogs will react in class. A cold concrete or slippery vinyl tile or hardwood floor may be uncomfortable for the dog if he is not familiar with this type of surface. Large dogs may be reluctant to move quickly on this type of flooring. Dogs may have trouble remaining in a "Sit"; they may slide into a "Down." On the up side, if the dog has to work to keep the sitting position, it's actually a pretty good lesson! Dogs used to an indoor environment may not want to "Sit" or "Down" on wet grass, snow, or a graveled area.

Consider using mats if the floor in your training area is slippery. If you are fortunate enough to have a permanent facility you can put down seamless wall-to-wall matting. It's very easy to keep clean and most of the products are made of recycled materials. These mats come in a variety of colors and thicknesses. Check with pool installation companies and ask about the rubber matting used near pool side. The type that comes in a roll can be useful because they are portable, however, they're very heavy to carry and awkward to store. Most mats with slip-proof surfaces are difficult to clean. Mats with smooth surfaces are slippery when wet. As an alternative, you could consider interlocking mat pieces. These are colorful and can be used to make patterns for exercise and traffic control. For example, you can direct Jim and Fluffy to their station on a red square and Carol and Chief to a blue square. Indoor/outdoor carpet is also a possibility but it has many of the same drawbacks of mats, plus it collects hair and is prone to stains and odors.

Some schools ask clients to bring a small area rug for their dog's use in class. Others will have a stack of small rugs and students help themselves to them when they arrive. Again, be concerned about cleanliness.

## Acoustics

Our dogs are better at reading body language than they are at listening to our spoken language. Humans, however, need to be able to hear what we are saying in addition to watching what we do. If you have a client who does not hear well, it's better to place them at a spot that has the least noise interference. If indoors, placing someone who cannot hear well by a window or a door where outside noise can be heard may cause that person to miss important information. When speaking, it may be helpful to look directly at this person and be sure your face is not in a shadow, so he can lip-read if necessary. Be sure your assistants are aware of these clients because they may need a little different coaching than other class members.

## Public Address System (PA)

Is your training site equipped with a PA system? Outdoor classes create their own special problems, especially if in a public place. Can your clients hear you? Try to face a wall or trees, so your voice is not lost in large open areas. Also, consider what may happen to your voice if you are constantly straining to be heard over extraneous noises. Bullhorns have been used, but these are awkward and present the problem of "not enough hands" and, in fact, seem impolite to me.

Purchasing a good quality portable PA system with a cordless microphone is money well spent. Some considerations are: Will you wear a headset? Will you need electricity? Where are the electrical outlets located? Can the electrical cords be placed in such a way that you or your class members will not trip over them?

## Music

One of the greatest aspects of having a PA system (or CD player) is the ability to play music. Music can be used to create a calm environment. It can be a polite way to signal the beginning and end of class since the instructor does not have to talk over the conversations of the class to get everyone's attention. It can also be used to pep the owners up for some nice, fast, loose leash walking.

## Furnishings for the Training Area

Not only are chairs comfortable and friendly, but they are a good traffic control method for keeping students where you want them. If you are considering new chairs for your indoor facility, you might want to avoid padded, cloth seats since they are not easy to clean. Stacking plastic or standard folding chairs are easier to handle in large numbers if they are on a wheeled cart. What kind of legs does the chair have? How will they affect the surface of your training room? Will they poke holes through your matting? Tables are helpful in many ways. They provide a relaxed learning environment for orientations, private lessons and, of course, seminars and workshops. A table turned on its side will provide a barrier space between two dogs. Dogs can't easily see over the table, but their owners can.

Baby gates can be used to section off a play corner for the children of your clients. They can make an impromptu visual barrier between dog-reactive dogs.

To make more of a barrier, just throw a beach towel over it. With gates, you can separate a spectators' area, close off a dangerous hallway, or separate your training area into learning centers, each one with a different exercise and instructor.

## Supplies for the Training Site

Being sure you have all the needed equipment becomes especially difficult if you don't have a permanent location with on-site storage. You can organize equipment by dividing supplies into rolling suitcases. If you are lucky and have willing class assistants, you can put them in charge of one or two suitcases! They can take the cases home, and the contents can be checked against the list attached to the case. Here is a list of useful training class supplies:

### Loaner Leashes and Collars
A stash of used leashes and collars are handy to loan to a person who forgot and brought his dog on a flexi lead, or an unsafe collar. A supply of Gentle Leaders® videos and DVDs can be kept on hand for the student to view at home. Legacy offers a free private lesson on fitting and use of the Gentle Leader® as well.

### Loaner Goodie Tray
It's really best if the people bring their own treats, but you should have some "just in case" for owners who forgot or want to try something new and for dogs that think they need a better goodie! Beware of allergies. Beware of spoilage. It's safer to provide small, sealed packages of commercial treats.

### Loaner Toy Basket
This small basket of assorted toys is for owners who forgot to bring a toy or who want to try something new. The toys should be washed after each class.

### Loaner "Focusing" Kit
We keep a variety of sizes of KONGS® (hollow rubber chew toy), adapted with a loop of nylon rope to be used as a handle for the owner. (My family never realized that our water skiing tow rope was getting shorter and shorter.) A can of squeeze cheese and a tube of peanut butter completes the focusing kit. Check for allergies. When class is over, Kongs go home with the instructor and into the dishwasher or clothes washer for cleaning.

### Clean-Up Kit
Bring sanitary spray in a bottle that can be closed and is leak proof. Get a recommendation from your vet for the best product to use. Plastic bags, strips of cardboard for poop scoopers, and a roll of towels complete your kit and might be easier to manage than a conventional long-handled pooper scooper. Put items in a cute, colorful bucket or tote bag.

### Traffic Control Items
You are not a real instructor unless you have cones and hula hoops. Smaller versions of the orange traffic cones used by road construction crews are readily available in sporting goods stores. Cones can help establish perimeters and

destinations for heeling. They can double as place markers. Write the owner's name on an index card and tape it to the cone to show each student where his home base is for the class. There are very lightweight models that have holes in them like a whiffle ball—however I saw a dog get her foot stuck in one once. Hula hoops can show dogs where to sit and can be used for a variety of games. Pull-apart hula hoops can be made from plumbers tubing and the right sized cork! Masking tape, chalk, or another means to draw lines on the floor or ground will be helpful.

*Handouts*
Some sort of file container is helpful to organize homework sheets and handouts for Frequently Asked Questions (FAQ).

*Positive Reinforcement Stuff for Owners*
Don't forget a colorful container for Bonus Bones and prizes or whatever goodies you provide for your classes.

*Roster Notebook*
A three-ring binder is great for organizing your profile sheet for each student, by class. The same notebook can contain pens, "we missed you" postcards, and stamps.

*Misters with Lavender Water*
Spray bottles are used as interrupters and can be used in a pinch for clean-up water.

## Where Will Owners Put Their "Stuff"?

Owners often arrive with a wide array of things in addition to their dog, like spouses, children, food, coats, purses, toys, notebooks, water and water dishes, etc. Especially for indoor training areas, announce a location ahead of time where owners can put their stuff. The floor is not always the best choice. It may create an unsafe situation for people and the stuff may be distracting to the other dogs. For permanent locations benches with hinged seats for inside storage can be placed along one wall. The bench can double as a raised platform for working with small dogs or as an aid for owners with a bad back. Locker-like storage cubes along a wall work well as do hooks to hang outerwear.

## Where Will You Put Your "Stuff"

In an ideal facility, each instructor will have at least a drawer or shelf to call his own. Lucky ones have offices or a designated desk corner. You can create space for yourself using folding partitions. Home centers have three-fold screens designed with picture frames or bulletin boards on them. These are great to advertise, hang class photos, or list important class information.

# Records

What kind of records should you keep? There are dozens of computer database software programs available to adapt to your business requirements. You should research what is currently on the market and select one that fits your style and needs.

Information you might want to collect includes:

- Client profile information
- Attendance records
- Birthdays (clients and dogs)—this information can go a long way to promoting good feelings about you and your business

Having a database available also provides you with a list of current and potential customers to whom to advertise your classes. Student profile forms should be kept indefinitely.

For tax purposes, you need to retain basic record information to show the dates and names of people who attended and paid for your classes.

# Conclusion

Go back to the perfect world where you only train people and dogs. Hire a bookkeeper, an accountant and, of course, a lawyer. They are the experts. Let them do their job and that leaves you more time for what you do best.

### ADDITIONAL READING/RESOURCES

The Delta Society, 875 124th Avenue NE, Suite 101, Bellevue, WA 98005-2531; (425) 679-5500; *info@deltasociety.org.*

DogTEC, 5221 Central Ave #1, Richmond, CA 94804, *info@dogtec.org, www.dogtec.org;* Phone 510-525-2547.

Dogwise, A Direct Book Service, 701 B Poplar, Wenatchee, WA 98801, 1(800)776-2665, mail@dogwise.com (Terry's books and others).

National Office, Small Business Administration, 409 Third Street, SW, Washington, D.C. 20416. *www.sba.gov;* 1-800-U-ASK-SBA.

# CHAPTER 6

# PEOPLE SKILLS

*"He who dares to teach must never cease to learn."*
—Unknown

# Profile of a Great Instructor

An instructor is a teacher, a leader, and a mentor. Your own ability to train dogs is a major prerequisite to becoming a successful class instructor. However, it's not the only prerequisite. If you can't share some of your skills effectively with others, you will not be an effective class instructor. An instructor has to work with people. It's a different set of skills than those you use working with dogs. Instructors should strive to understand and treat the individuals on both ends of the leash with respect. The personality of a competent instructor can take many forms. Some people are born teachers. Others can learn communication techniques. All of us can work on improving our teaching skills. This chapter points out various attributes of effective instructors. It also presents information that will help you achieve your own personal goals for better interpersonal communication.

## *Some Attributes of a Good Instructor*

**Enthusiasm.** An enthusiastic instructor displays zeal, even passion, for training people and dogs. Enthusiasm is hard to define, but apparent when displayed. It's also contagious. Your personal enthusiasm for what you are doing can change the atmosphere of your entire class.

**Friendliness and Kindness.** Instructors can be both friendly and caring without smothering the class with parental-like attitudes. Condescending actions or language that infers "no-no, bad child" to your students can put them off, just as the drill sergeant's approach of "my way or the highway."

**Empathy**. Sincerely letting students know you understand the issues involved with their less-than-perfect dog is helpful. You haven't always been a skilled dog trainer yourself. Take the student seriously. If they have a problem that is overwhelming them, don't laugh it off and say everyone goes through that; it's no big deal. If it's a big deal to them, it should be taken as a seriously important issue for you also.

**Humility.** Remain humble. One way to do this is to volunteer at your local shelter and pick an out of control, poorly socialized dog with several well-established problems. Teach the dog something you've never attempted to teach before with methods you have never used. This is what the average dog training class participant is doing. Or try out a completely foreign activity; something you've never thought much about or have been interested in. Try something that involves mechanical skill. Experience being out of your own comfort zone. Perhaps a well-meaning friend signed you up for Scuba diving lessons as a birthday gift. Scuba really isn't your thing, but you find yourself in class. You are asked to do brand new things . . . like breathe! You're self-conscious; you don't want to seem like a dummy to the others in class or to the instructor. It's a somewhat distracting situation, and you have trouble concentrating on the lesson when suddenly . . . all eyes are on you. It's your turn to go across the pool. This feeling of being inept in a foreign situation is what your students may be experiencing.

**Patience.** If the student doesn't "get it" the first or second time, it's just as easily a fault of your teaching abilities as it is the ineptness of the student. Don't reply to a basic, boring question or statement with, "I wish I had a dime for every time I've heard that one." It's no longer an important issue for you, but it might be the entire focus for the student. Help yourself be patient by formatting your lessons into tiny, easily achieved pieces. For example, "Today we are going to work on 'Come-When-Called.' Say your dog's name enthusiastically and reward her for eye contact. That's great! You were all successful at this stage of the 'Come' exercise."

**Humor.** Jokes should be used judiciously. It may be what maintains your sanity as an instructor, but what is it doing to your student? Jim and Pete both have dogs that are a bit inattentive in class. In fact, at the moment they are very interested in each other and are pulling on the leashes to do a typical nose-to-tail greeting. Our comment is "Come on you guys, make yourselves more interesting than a dog's rear end." Jim might laugh and immediately get the message, remembering the joke each time in the future when his dog gets into a distracting situation, and remembering to up his "I'm the most rewarding thing in your environment" tactics. Pete, on the other hand, might be insulted and may not come back next week. Even worse, your message was not transferred into a positive, doable training principle to help his dog's inattention.

**Flexibility.** A good instructor will be comfortable enough with the material to adapt to each of the clients' learning needs. An important aspect of flexibility is to be able to say the same thing, only in a different way. If the students didn't understand the first time, it's not very helpful to simply raise your voice and repeat. People learn from repetition. Each time you repeat a message it can be in a slightly different mode: "Form a row facing the window, toes on the red line," or, "Jim and Buffy, please face me," or "Folks, find a hoop and stand in it with your dog," or, "Please stand by this cone, you and your dog facing the center of the room."

**Make Your Students Feel Special.** Be alert. Watch the door. Say hello and goodbye to each student individually. Make eye contact. Even in a large class, be sure to have a special comment for each student. It's easy to compliment an adept student. It's normal to give advice to a student needing help. Don't forget to single out the average student with a positive comment, too.

**Dress for Success.** Dog training class instructors are to be respected and should dress the part of a professional. Your clothing should appear neat and clean. This is sometimes difficult after two or three classes of being on the floor with puppies! Choose colors and materials that do not show dog hair and smudges. Pockets are a must. Comfortable, ready for action clothing and non-slip shoes are best. Instructors should consider wearing special shirts so they are readily identified. If you don't have a logo, get one and put it on your shirts. Add each instructor's name on the shirt with embroidery or an attractive name badge that can be read across the room. A vest might be more versatile in different seasons. A wardrobe of "logo clothing" is a good perk for overworked assistants. Have extra ones on hand just in case someone forgets.

**Punctual.** Set a good example and start class on time. Waiting for late arrivals encourages tardiness and penalizes students who are punctual. A professional instructor should be skilled enough not to allow class to run over time. The mechanics for accomplishing this appear later in the chapter.

**Responsible.** Your students deserve a safe, friendly environment in which to get as much help as is reasonable for them to train their dogs. Taking the actual responsibility to train is their job. Yours is to give them the best possible information and mechanical skills for success through good lesson planning and polite, effective intervention. They are depending on you. Make sure they get the expert instruction they deserve, even if that means you need to refer them to another instructor. Jack Volhard, a long-time mentor of training class instructors, said: "Put them in a position of success."

**Knowledgeable.** A good instructor will be eager to find continuous up-to-date information that can be applied to her classes. Networking with other trainers and instructors is a good place to start. E-mail makes this easier than ever. Keep in touch informally with friends or get on some chat lists. To get a different perspective on what you are doing, sign up for some courses in adult education. Many different organizations offer generic classes in team building, increasing self-esteem, and small business management. Check the public school system, parks and recreation sites, community colleges, or on-line offerings. Classes in Parent Effectiveness Training (PET) are particularly helpful. If there is a Toastmasters group in your area, members can give you a fresh outlook on public speaking.

Consider joining a kennel club, even if their main focus is conformation. Some of my best ideas came from people I've met at dog shows. If there is not a training club close by, start one! There are numerous national and international groups from which you could benefit. Most hold annual educational events. Once again, these groups have websites and chat lists. I have shelves and shelves full of books, but all you need now is one computer! Well, maybe not. I still buy books. Computers are hard to curl up with at night!

Use some of the principles discussed in Chapter 3 and train another species—a cat, a chicken, or a rat. For the faint of heart, there are computer games for rat training! *Sniffy, the Virtual Rat* (1995 University of Toronto) is a book and CD-ROM. Sniffy is in a Skinner box, an operant conditioning chamber named after B. F. Skinner. Sniffy can be rewarded for performing various behaviors. At Legacy seminars we train rats. We have one genuine Skinner box. Fellow instructor Lisa Dilling made several knock-offs for our students' use: a "lunch box," a "mail box," "Pandora's box," a "toolbox," a "glove box," a "Jack in the Box" (Lisa lives with Jack Russell Terriers!), a "jewelry box," and a "music box." Each homemade operant conditioning chamber is decorated in it's "box" theme. (No disrespect intended, Dr. Skinner . . .)

# LEARNING STYLES

This bar chart shows three important means of learning: listening, watching, and doing. Some individuals are more successful with one than the other. For example, seeing a task done is an easier way to learn for some people than to actually do it themselves.

*The least effective means of learning is auditory.*
The average person, after hearing verbal information such as a lecture, 48 hours later, will remembers only about 50% of what he heard. One week later, the average person accurately remembers only about 10% of what he heard. If you lecture for one hour, which six minutes will your student remember? The owner's stress of dealing with an unruly dog probably reduces that retention rate even further.

*Visual information is more successful than auditory.*
If an average person sees information as well as hearing it, his retention rate is increased to 35%. The student can see how it's done by demonstrations with a dog, a video, slides, posters, a chart, or handouts.

*Kinesthetic information is more effective than auditory or visual.*
Long-term retention is boosted to 50% if the student can also learn by manipulating tangible objects. Dog training to a certain extent includes mechanical skill. Work with the dog, but also practice in handling the leash, treats, clickers, toys, and other objects that are involved in your training program.

Individuals vary greatly, and dog training classes require repetition. Be sure to include all three means of learning in your lesson plans: AUDITORY *and* VISUAL *and* KINESTHETIC.

**Structure Your Teaching Style To Increase Student Success**

Tell Me, I'll Forget — 10% — Listening to a Talk
Show Me, I'll Remember — 35% — Watching a Demo
Involve Me, I'll Understand — 50% — Doing it Himself

Information Retention Rate

Chapter 6  People Skills  133

# TELL ME AND I'LL FORGET

Our job is to improve the relationship between dog and owner. First, we need to develop appropriate communication channels with the owner. Dog owners are sensitive about their pets and how they are perceived, so care must be taken. Here are several aids to help students remember what you say:

### Same-Letter Key Words
Elementary children learn the 3-R's in school: "reading, 'riting and 'rithmetic." Invent same-letter key words for anything you want students to remember. When I ask students to select criteria for an exercise, I talk about the "Four **D**'s: **D**istance, **D**uration, **D**ifferent Environment, and **D**elivery of Reward.

### Analogies and Metaphors
It's helpful to use a figure of speech where well-known and understood concepts can suggest a likeness to the points you are trying to make. They help clients understand a new concept by comparing it with a well-known concept. You will find many analogies and metaphors throughout this book. Here is an example I learned from behavior enthusiast and author, William Campbell. It's about leadership and communication: "Compare your dog's existence to a lifelong airplane trip—totally dependent on the pilot and crew for necessities, including one vital need: to feel SAFE. If the pilot appears incompetent and the crew isn't sure about what's going on, the passenger starts squirming with anxiety as the frustration of being unable to control the situation takes its toll. If the passenger tries to take control, he will be subdued physically or scolded roundly, which only heightens his frustration. This situation can be more frustrating if the crew can't speak the passenger's language fluently and communicates the wrong ideas."

### Acronyms
An acronym is a word formed by the initial letter or letters of a concept. Here's an example from Chapter 8 that I use all the time when I'm going through "The Toolbox" to try to find ideas to help a family live happily ever after with their dog: "HELM"

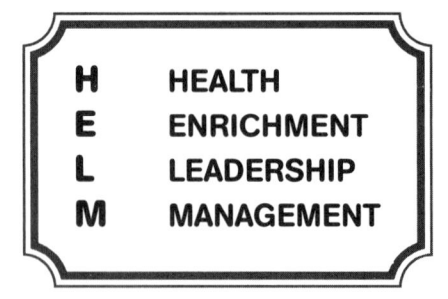

| | |
|---|---|
| **H** | HEALTH |
| **E** | ENRICHMENT |
| **L** | LEADERSHIP |
| **M** | MANAGEMENT |

### Well Put!
Over the years, I've heard many talented trainers and instructors say things in a way that is easily remembered. I've even come up with some of my own that

are helpful for me. I wish I could remember which was which so I could give appropriate credit!

***Don't Click without the Treat!***
For remembering good usage of a secondary reinforcer: "Think about bridging (clicking), as a full container of fuel. The container is divided into four parts. If you click without giving a treat, you have drained 25% of the power from your clicker. If you click twice without giving a treat, your clicker has lost half of its power." (You can add to the above word picture by using a chalkboard while you speak. Draw a glass full of water and erase one quarter of your drawing until the board is clean.)—Jan Fridge.

***Why Your Dog Acts "Crazy"***
His energy is like a tea kettle put on the stove. Pressure builds up until the whistle goes off. Give him things to do and avoid your *dog's whistle.*"—Adapted from Jean Donaldson's pressure cooker analogy.

***For Patience in Puppy Training***
"Training a puppy is like opening a savings account. At first, you spend a lot of time making deposits. Later you can relax a little and reap the benefits as your efforts are paid back, with interest."—Ted Turner

***For Getting the Food Lure Close to the Dog's Nose***
"This piece of cheese is magnetic. It sticks to your dog's nose until you turn it into a reward." (I often add to this by lifting a magnet off a nearby whiteboard. Then I let go and it smacks back on to the board. "Magnets stick tight.")—I think I made this one up.

## ROADBLOCKS TO VERBAL COMMUNICATION

Here are some tactics that might thwart successful communication:

- **Direct Warnings, Threatening Client**
  "If you don't stop Tippy's barking, it will turn into biting and you'll end up in a lawsuit."

- **Judging, Criticizing, Blaming**
  "Well, it's apparent at a glance that you started Tippy out badly as a puppy."

- **Interrogating, Probing**
  "What in the world made you do such a thing with Tippy?"

- **Abrupt Ordering, Directing, Commanding**
  "NOW! Do it NOW! You must make a loud noise, NOW, to stop Tippy's behavior."

- **Confrontation**
  "Slapping Tippy for barking at dogs is wrong; it's ineffective, stupid, and cruel."

*Chapter 6   People Skills*

When people's attitudes are attacked, they are likely to defend those attitudes, and in the process, reinforce them. If comments like the above come to mind while you are speaking with a dog owner, keep them there—in your mind. If spoken, they could put up an immediate barrier between you and your client. A blunt, blame-laden confrontation is apt to be met in one of three ways:

1. **"YES BUT"**
   Client acknowledges the information, but counters with his own argument.
   "Yes, but my dog is of a breed that is supposed to bark. It's genetic."

2. **WHAT DOES SHE KNOW?**
   Client attacks the messenger in hope of destroying the credibility of the message.
   "Are you sure? You've never owned Tippy's breed. Besides I've heard your dog barking."

3. **IT DOESN'T APPLY TO ME**
   Client is tuning you out.
   "That's the way I was doing it, the teacher must be talking to someone else."

Your comments can be made in a way that will not alienate the dog owner. As an effective teacher, accept the feelings of the client, however different they may be from your own. A good instructor realizes that while genuine, the owner's current opinion may be transient and influenced by the stress of the moment. The client's information base might be weak. His conclusions, based on a weak foundation of knowledge, are naturally apt to be deficient. The owner is doing the best he can with his current skills. Our job, therefore, is to build a rapport with the owner and add to his information base. We need to break down human communication into its basic components.

## It's Not What You Say, It's What They Hear

It's not what our message does to the listener, but what the listener does with our message that determines our success as communicators. An instructor might assume that as long as the message does something to the audience, communication will take place. The instructor wants to acknowledge and praise the dog's and owner's progress at an exercise:

| | |
|---|---|
| **MESSAGE SENT:** | "Your dog's 'Sit-Stay' is great this week!" |
| **STUDENT A RECEIVES:** | Instructor thinks we're doing great. |
| **STUDENT B RECEIVES:** | I'd better work harder. I must have been awful last week. |
| **STUDENT C RECEIVES:** | I'm there! I can relax now. |
| **STUDENT D RECEIVES:** | Instructor is being kind because our 'Down' is always terrible. |

**BETTER MESSAGE:** "Your dog's 'Sit-Stay' is great! Spot is right where he needs to be for this week's goals on that exercise. You must be following the training schedule carefully! Keep up the good work! How do you feel about your progress?"

Listeners generally interpret messages in ways that make them feel comfortable and secure. Each of us has a protective filter around us, built up of life's experiences. The filter will allow information that is "safe and normal" to pass through, but when something is new, different from the ordinary or perhaps scary, we screen it out or only let in the "safe" aspects of it. People learn best with repetition. Craft your repetitions by using different words and formats to be sure your true meaning comes across. Our message is at the mercy of the receiver's protective screen. Your communication should include cross-checks to be sure the receiver understood.

## *The Telephone Game*

This activity is an illustration of the effectiveness and/or limitations of speaking and listening as the only means of communication. It will make a person think twice before giving instructions over the phone where you have to paint a verbal picture without the help of facial expression, gestures, or anything else! We often do this demo at instructor courses, making sure the volunteer has a good self-image and high threshold for stress.

The volunteer "instructor" sits in a chair with her back to you, the "student." No peeking! You then phone up the instructor. Report that you have forgotten how to do one of the basic, important lessons learned in class. Pick a simple, non-dog-training task, like opening a bottle of of soda. Have a bottle at hand, ready to follow instructions. Are the instructors' words alone good enough to get the message across successfully? Video the interactions so that later you can prove to the "instructor" that you, the student, did "exactly" what you were told but did not accomplish the task!

Here are some honest mistakes that can be made if the instructor assumes too much:

| | |
|---|---|
| **INSTRUCTOR:** | "Hold the bottle in one hand." |
| **STUDENT:** | Holds it sideways, (horizontal) in one hand. |
| **INSTRUCTOR:** | "Grab the top with the other hand." |
| **STUDENT:** | Grabs the top (side) of the bottle. |
| **INSTRUCTOR:** | "Twist the top." |
| **STUDENT:** | Tries to twist the side of the bottle |

OR

| | |
|---|---|
| **INSTRUCTOR:** | "Put the bottle on the table, pointy side up." |
| **STUDENT:** | "I don't have a table." |

OR

| INSTRUCTOR: | "Put the bottle on the table pointy side up." |
| --- | --- |
| STUDENT: | Does so. |
| INSTRUCTOR: | "Now grab the cap and twist." |
| STUDENT: | Does so, but nothing happens because the bottle is not held with the other hand. |

**OR**

| INSTRUCTOR: | "Grasping the bottle firmly in one hand, twist the top counterclockwise." |
| --- | --- |
| STUDENT: | Does so but didn't bother to hold the bottle right side up. . . . What a mess! |

**OR**

| INSTRUCTOR: | "Grasping the bottle firmly in one hand, twist the top counterclockwise." |
| --- | --- |
| STUDENT: | "Ouch!" (It wasn't a twist-off cap, but one that needed a bottle opener!) |

We could go on and on with examples of how easily the simple act of opening a bottle can become confusing when the instructor can ONLY use words and doesn't choose them properly!

We quickly see it's not what the message is, but what the listener does with the message. Our verbal communication can be refined by exercises like the above—no help with feedback, no demonstrations. If we try very hard for our verbal information to be effective on its own, then when we add demonstrations and other aids, it will make our communication very, very effective!

The follow-up activity would be to make a lesson plan for teaching bottle opening over the phone.

## Cross-checks for Comprehension—Was Your Message Received Properly?

In dog training class, make sure the message you send is the message received. Here are some ideas:

- Do you have any questions?
- Watch this demonstration.
- Please tell me the steps you will take to perform this exercise.
- Will you show me how you will practice this week?
- At home this week the handout (video, tape cassette) will help you stay clear on this.
- If you have a question this week, contact us. We return all calls and e-mails promptly.

With experience, instructors begin to get a feel for the different ways in which their student might interpret their instructions.

## Make the Exercise Valuable to the Student

"This is the Figure 8. It's what we do in obedience trials." The following might be more relevant and attention getting. "Ever been downtown and encounter a phone pole? You go one way, your dog goes the other way and your leash does this." (Make appropriate gesture!) This exercise will help with that problem.

## Common Verbal Communication Problems in Class

| | |
|---|---|
| INSTRUCTOR: | "Keep a loose leash." |
| STUDENT: | "If I hold it any looser, I'll drop it." |
| BETTER WAY? | "There should be no tension in the leash." |
| | |
| INSTRUCTOR: | "Use only one cue for 'Sit'" |
| STUDENT: | "I am!" (As the student repeats the one word: "Sit," "Sit," "Sit") |
| BETTER WAY? | "One cue, one response." |

If you think this is tough, try teaching a dog class in a foreign language. Some concepts, much less words, just do not interpret well. Here are some true-life (honest!) examples from my experiences teaching in Japan.

| | |
|---|---|
| ENGLISH-SPEAKING TEACHER: | We're going to use counter conditioning to help this problem. |
| JAPANESE INTERPRETER: | bla bla bla |
| STUDENT'S REPLY: | bla bla bla |
| JAPANESE INTERPRETER: | She said her dog doesn't steal from the counter any more. |
| | |
| ENGLISH-SPEAKING TEACHER: | Oh! A Golden Retriever! We have an awful lot of Goldens in the U.S. |
| JAPANESE INTERPRETER: | bla bla bla |
| STUDENT'S REPLY: | bla bla bla |
| JAPANESE INTERPRETER: | She said Goldens are really nice in Japan, not many awful ones. |
| | |
| ENGLISH-SPEAKING TEACHER: | . . . and so Pavlov's dogs salivated . . . |
| JAPANESE INTERPRETER: | (with a straight face) bla bla bla |
| STUDENT HAND UP: | bla bla bla? |
| JAPANESE INTERPRETER: | She wants to know why Pavlov made all the dogs vomit. |
| | |
| ENGLISH-SPEAKING TEACHER: | This week, smear a bit of peanut butter inside a hollow rubber Kong toy and give it to Momo when she's in her crate. |
| JAPANESE INTERPRETER: | bla bla bla |
| STUDENT LATER REPORTS: | bla bla bla |
| JAPANESE INTERPRETER: | He's complaining that Momo's coat gets all sticky when he smears the inside of her crate with peanut butter. |

| | |
|---|---|
| ENGLISH-SPEAKING TEACHER: | (Seeing cloudy eyes on a student dog): "Cataract?" |
| JAPANESE INTERPRETER: | (Quizzical expression) bla bla bla |
| STUDENT REPLY: | (Also a quizzical expression) bla bla bla |
| JAPANESE INTERPRETER: | No, she says she drives a Mitsubishi. Why do you ask? |

And the all-time best one from my first trip to Japan:

| | |
|---|---|
| ME AT HOTEL ROOM DOOR TO LITTLE MAN IN A WHITE COAT: | Hello? |
| LITTLE MAN IN WHITE COAT: | Bla, bla, bla, smile, bow, bow, smile (. . . much body language later . . .) |
| ME, TO SELF: | "How do I get rid of this guy, I asked for my messages not for a massage . . ." |

# THIS IS NEW STUFF—FROM OUR STUDENTS' POINT OF VIEW

After you've been instructing for a while, you will begin hearing the same questions over and over again. You will see the same mistakes being made. Patience! Remember back to when YOU were attending your first training class. Some concepts are now very basic to you, but keep in mind that it's all new for the student. Turn your boredom around to your advantage. Have some stock answers or remarks ready for these times.

### EXAMPLES:

"Teacher, you won't believe this, but he does it perfectly at home."

| | |
|---|---|
| *Poor reply:* | "Everybody says that. But that doesn't do you any good here." |
| *Better reply:* | "Hey, dog class is a strange place! It's common for the dog to fall apart under distractions. But now we know he understands it if he'll do it at home. It's just a matter of time before it will carry over to other situations." |

"Teacher, my dog is stupid."

| | |
|---|---|
| *Poor reply:* | "There are no stupid dogs, just stupid owners." |
| *Better reply:* | "I don't think so. I think he's very clever and has found an easy way around it." |

## The Left Brain/Right Brain Paradigm

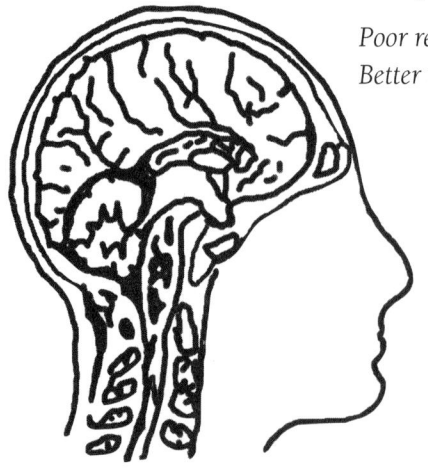

Each person processes, uses, and stores information differently. There are many different explanations for this. I prefer the left-brain, right-brain paradigm which is old, but Roger Sperry won a Nobel Prize for his work on brain dominancy in 1981, and I'm still impressed with its helpfulness. In most individuals, one side of the brain is dominant over the other. Actually the left and right hemispheres operate together as a team. Messages are sent back and forth so that both hemispheres are somewhat involved in most of the neurological activity of the human brain. Among other things, brain dominancy can influence personality and learning styles. Talking to a left-brained person with a left-brain message will appeal to that individual. We can use slightly different words with each repetition, but we can pitch those words to left-brained people one time and right-brained people the next. Here's a very simple list from the works of Sperry and his associate Paul Torrance (*Your Style of Learning and Thinking,* 1980, University of Georgia Press). It describes the characteristics each hemisphere deals with:

| Left Side Brain Dominancy | Right Side Brain Dominancy |
|---|---|
| Intellectual | Intuitive |
| Remembers names | Remembers faces |
| Responds to verbal instruction | Responds to illustrations and demonstrations |
| Experiments systematically | Experiments randomly |
| Makes objective judgments | Makes subjective judgments |
| Planned and structured | Fluid and spontaneous |
| Prefers facts | Prefers hypotheses |
| Prefers talking and writing | Prefers drawing and manipulating objects |
| Prefers multiple choice questions | Prefers open-ended questions |
| Controls feelings | More free with feelings |
| Poor at interpreting body language | Better at interpreting body language |
| Rarely uses metaphors | Frequently uses metaphors |
| Serious nature | Playful nature |
| Good ability to focus | Poor ability to focus |
| Sense of time | Sense of humor |
| Conformity | Flexibility |
| Organization and common sense | Creativeness |
| Attracted to math and science | Attracted to art and music |

## *Possible Profile of a Left-Brained Person*

Liking rules and order to life, she is organized and focused. She has a serious work ethic, one to get the job done and done well with no nonsense. She is comfortable and good with verbal skills, including writing. Using common sense, she is logical and analytical, liking to put things in sequential order. She is always looking for the bottom line. She is a responsible person who is prompt, neat, and efficient. In class, this type of person is on time, has done the homework, has called during the week, asks questions, carefully evaluates each step in an exercise, and enjoys handouts.

## Possible Profile of a Right-Brained Person

She is creative, spontaneous, and flexible. She has a great imagination, is able to visualize abstract concepts, and enjoys art and music. Playful and humorous in nature, but also emotional and reactive, she will be more apt to openly show enjoyment, fear, anger, or sadness. She laughs and cries easily. She is intuitive, is often successful at playing hunches. She might have difficulty staying within limits set by others. In class, she and her dog might have reached the homework goal, but not by following the steps you have outlined. She's apt to be working with her dog, but inattentive to the instructor. She might be late for class, and she'll make a joke about it.

## A Basic Message: "Hand Signals Are Better Than Verbal Cues"

It's fun to practice crafting the same message to appeal to right-brain students and then craft the same message to appeal to left-brain students. Here is an example:

### Left Brained—Appeal for Hand Signals:

- Useful alternative to calling if you have laryngitis
  Common sense

- Research shows that successful obedience trial competitors use signals
  Work ethic (the experts do it that way)

- The signal catches the attention faster than the human voice
  Sense of time

- This is an advanced exercise
  We left-brained people like that stuff!

- Signals are 2.5 times more predictably consistent than the voice
  Math

- This is state-of-the-art stuff
  Conformity

### Right Brained—Appeal for Hand Signals:

- Gestures appeal to the free spirit of the dog
  Emotional

- Less demanding
  Flexible

- Can experiment to see which gestures your dog prefers
  Arty, creative

- Sweeping gesture is like a magnet drawing your dog to you
  Visual

# Turning Negative Instructions into Positive Instructions

Negatives aren't very helpful teaching tools. Most of the time they just point out what NOT to do. Negatives also run the risk of alienating your student. Compare the negative remarks below with the more positive, instructional ones that follow.

**"You can't EVER let Ginger run free in the neighborhood again."**
"For Ginger's safety and everyone else's, you can increase your supervision and control of Ginger by _____."

**"Make Jimmy stop teasing Ginger!"**
"We'll need to limit Jimmy's interactions with Ginger unless there is supervision. At those times Jimmy may play one of the following three games with Ginger _____."

**"Please stop Ginger from barking so we can go on with our conversation."**
"Great! This is an excellent time to deal with Ginger's barking—right now while it's happening! This is what I want you to do _____."

# Improving Your Listening Skills

Listening is considered by many educators to be the most valuable teaching tool. Instructors should not let their enthusiasm for teaching get in the way of taking time to listen to dog owners. People are more likely to listen to us if we also listen to them. Others learn by our example. When I was a child, my mother told me there was a reason I had two ears but only one mouth! In a teacher-student relationship, how can we discover what's going on with our students if we don't allow them time to tell us?

Be aware of two common roadblocks to effective listening.

- **THE NEXT-ONE-UP-TO-BAT SYNDROME**
  You are listening, but too busy planning your reply to be paying close attention.

- **THE FAULT FINDER**
  Rather than listening attentively, you are busy trying to find points of disagreement or mistakes so you can clobber the speaker later.

## Teacher Effectiveness Training

The following concepts will help you improve your listening skills. These points were taken from the works of Dr. Thomas Gordon. Dr. Gordon began his series of effectiveness training more than 40 years ago with his classics: *Parent Effectiveness Training (PET)*, and *Teacher Effectiveness Training (TET)*.

**Passive Listening (Silence).** It may be difficult for clients to talk to you if you are doing all of the talking. Silence in itself communicates acceptance of the message, conveys trust that the client will share what is important in the matter, and gives the client a feeling of being in charge of his problem. Silence safely avoids communication roadblocks of saying the wrong thing; however, some clients will feel you are not interested if you are completely silent.

**Acknowledgment Responses.** These responses can be used to let your client know you are paying attention. When your client pauses, use verbal or nonverbal cues to indicate that you are listening:

| *Nonverbal Cues* | *Verbal Cues* |
|---|---|
| Nodding | "I see" |
| Leaning forward | "Uh-huh" |
| Smiling | "Oh!" |
| Frowning | "I understand" |
| Arching eyebrows | "Is that right?" |
| Pursing lips | "Really?" |
| Taking notes | "That's interesting" |

**Door-Opening Messages.** Sometimes our clients need additional encouragement to talk to us. Become comfortable with using phrases such as these:

"That's interesting; then what happened?"
"Would you like to say more about that?"
"Sounds like you have strong feelings about that."

Notice that these are open questions and statements, which contain no evaluation about what is being said and in no way influence the client's response. These phrases create an opportunity for the client to begin talking. That's your cue to be silent and listen.

**Active Listening.** Active listening is a method often used by professional counselors. Active listening contains no actual message but mirrors or feeds back the client's message. By repeating in your own words what the client has told you, the client feels that you understand and are interested in what he is saying. It involves interaction between the client and the consultant.

*Examples of Active Listening:*

STUDENT: My dog is too dumb to "Come" when called.
TEACHER: You think Toby is not intelligent?

STUDENT: Maybe he's deaf or something.
TEACHER: You think he has a physical problem that prevents learning?

| | |
|---|---|
| STUDENT: | I wonder if he'd be better off in a home in the country. |
| TEACHER: | You think he would respond better in a different environment? |
| | |
| STUDENT: | My family is disgusted with Toby. |
| TEACHER: | Is there a problem in the relationship? |
| | |
| STUDENT: | I'd be lonely without him |
| TEACHER: | You're worried about the possibility of giving Toby up? |

We went from the statement that Toby is mentally and physically defective to the probable issue that the client wasn't able to verbalize: fear of giving up his dog.

It's important that you gain the trust of your client immediately. Active listening helps you accept the feelings of the client, and conveys a message of caring and understanding. It encourages the client to listen to you later because you listened to him. To hear you verbalize his thoughts in different terms might encourage him to think more critically when making assumptions about his dog.

Be careful when you use active listening. If you become too automatic with your responses, it will seem as though you are insincere and patronizing.

# TURNING "YOU" MESSAGES INTO "I" MESSAGES

Clients are not there to be blamed. If things are going poorly between the family and the dog, they already know it. They have come to you to get your opinion and help. If you alienate the client by the way in which you communicate information, he will not be receptive to your advice.

Here are some poorly worded messages, followed by one that might be better received:

**You** have spoiled Buffy.
**I'm** glad you enjoy each other so. I can help you teach Buffy a few simple house rules.

**You** never taught Buffy the correct behavior.
**I can** show you and Buffy a few basic exercises.

Buffy doesn't listen to **you.**
**I see** a good starting point. Let's teach Buffy to check in with you when you call his name.

Do **you** really want to help Buffy?
**I'd** like to show you how to teach Buffy a few appropriate behaviors.

# Dealing with Emotional Students

Every once in a while, a client will become angry or have his feelings hurt. Usually these situations are not a reflection of how a client feels about us personally. We just happen to be handy when emotions run high. Here are some ideas of how to handle the situation.

The letters in the word **STOP** can remind you of steps that will help you remain calm and work through the problem:

**S = Signal.**
Understand and recognize your body's early warning signals for becoming upset. Do you clench your fist, scowl, raise an eyebrow, clench your jaw, sigh, or raise your voice? Have someone you know help you identify these signals in yourself.

**T = Take Control of Your Own Emotions.**
Use self-talk, such as "I'm not going to let this person ruin my day. I just need to let them vent. Boy, they must have had a terrible day themselves to be in this kind of a state." Do whatever makes you feel good or calm. Look at a picture of a pleasant scene, think of your best friend, use your sense of humor, or think of a favorite saying, such as this one by Eleanor Roosevelt: "No one can make you feel inferior without your consent."

**O = Opposite.**
Do the opposite of whatever your "signals" are: Unclench your fist/jaw, take some deep breaths, and relax your face. Concentrate on keeping your voice lowered.

**P = Practice.**
You have to practice this STOP technique to get good at it!

# The Talkers in Class

If the owners are talking to each other, they are not listening to you or watching you and your assistants. This makes you repeat instructions or makes them miss something important. Talking to each other also draws the owners' attention from their own dogs, increasing the chances that their dogs will get into trouble. The usual reason for talking is that they are enthusiastic and enjoying themselves and sharing goodwill! Make sure the reason is not that your class is dull, the instructor lacks animation, spends too much time with one individual, or takes too long talking with no activity for the class!

# LATE ARRIVALS

The best policy is to ignore latecomers. They already know they are late. If they have missed something critical to their success, ask an assistant to work with them for a few minutes after class. Most instructors teach in little segments. If the latecomer missed the first "Sit" exercise, hopefully, the instructor has several other "Sit" exercises scattered throughout the duration of the class. Consider taking roll mid-session. You won't mark a late person absent, and it allows you to get the dogs started right away.

# PET LOSS

We are pet professionals. When our clients come to us, they are entrusting us with a creature that is very special to them. When they lose that animal they may rely on us for support because they know we are interested and care about them. Help if you can.

## What Are Grief and Mourning?

Grief is an intense emotional suffering caused by loss. Mourning is the expression of grief, the act of working through the pain. Grief and mourning, as well as death, are inevitable parts of pet ownership.

Common reasons for pet loss are death due to accident, illness, or old age. Pet owners also mourn if their companion animal is lost, stolen, given up for adoption, or euthanized due to an unresolved behavior problem.

Many humans form strong emotional bonds with their pets. Some individuals have an extra special attachment. In getting to know your clients, be on the lookout for people with unusually strong attachments to their pets, when the pet dies, these people might have a particularly hard time. Respect all relationships. Dr. James Harris, at a pet loss workshop in the early 1990s, listed these factors as contributing to very special bonds:

- Pets that got owners through a "hard time" in life
- Pets that were rescued from death or near-death
- Pets that were childhood companions
- Pets that are their owner's most significant sources of support
- Pets that have been anthropomorphized (given human qualities)
- Assistance animal
- Pets who are symbolic of a significant person who has passed away

*Chapter 6  People Skills*  147

People around us may trivialize pet loss. Consequently, your client's feelings may be covered up and denied. Your client's true feelings may not be apparent to you. All people should realize that

- Grieving is the healing process necessary for recovery from loss.
- Grieving is the normal way to cope with loss.
- Grieving takes time and is not over in a matter of days or weeks.

When grief is allowed free expression, the healing time is reduced; when grief is restricted, its manifestations last much longer. It's helpful to be able to identify grief in stages. Most human and animal grief counselors divide the stages into these categories:

1. **DENIAL**
   "This can't be happening. The mass is not cancer. The lab must have made a mistake."

2. **GUILT**
   "Why did I leave the door unlatched? I should never have been so careless to allow Ginger to get into the street!"

3. **ANGER**
   "What's wrong with my veterinarian? He should have found this problem last year when I took Ginger in for her inoculations!"

4. **BARGAINING**
   "Please, please let the lab test come back negative. If it does, I will spare no expense and time at giving Ginger a good life. I will volunteer every Saturday morning at the shelter, I will . . ."

5. **DEPRESSION**
   "I can't go on without Ginger. I miss her too much. I cannot think clearly, I don't even want to get out of bed."

6. **ACCEPTANCE**
   "I loved Ginger. We enriched each other's lives. I'm glad that we had each other. She'll always have a special place in my heart."

## What You Can Do to Help Your Client

Unless you are a human health professional, as well as a training class instructor, do not go beyond being a good listener and friend. Mental health professionals can help. Do some research now—ahead of time—to find out who in your area accepts pet loss clients. Make a personal contact stating who you are and what you do. Explain that you would like to refer clients who ask for help to a specialist. When you make an appropriate contact, ask if you can stop by to pick up a few of their business cards to share with clients who request help.

Here are some thoughtful ways to get through the situation:

- Don't belittle the loss.
- Don't encourage or discourage the acquisition of another pet.
- Don't scoff at the idea of a ceremony—people need closure and a chance to say goodbye.
- Allow your client time to grieve.
- Don't say, "It was just an animal."
- Allow for individual differences in grieving.
- Be a good listener.
- Should the client blame someone for the loss of her pet, do not try to reason with the grieving person at this time. Just remain passive and continue to support the grief.
- If asked about acquiring a new pet, don't use the word *replacement*.
- Avoid the terminology "put to sleep"; parents put their children to sleep every night.
- Send a card or note. Several companies have pet sympathy cards.
- Make a donation to a charity in memory of the dog, and tell your client about it in a card.

For information and help on the appropriate way to respond to clients experiencing a loss, contact the Delta Society, 875 124th Avenue NE, Suite 101, Bellevue, WA 98005-2531, (425) 679-5500, *info@deltasociety.org*. Their extensive resources on pet loss include up-to-date publications, a free state-by-state referral list of professional pet loss counselors, plus information on hotlines and support groups.

# HUMAN PERSONALITY DIFFERENCES

Understanding a bit about your client's personality can help you to tailor your approach to fit the learning style of that individual. There are many references for identifying and dealing with various personality types. Nichole Wilde has authored an insightful book entitled *It's Not the Dogs, It's the People!* (Phantom Publishing, 2003) written especially for dog trainers wanting to improve their skills with clients.

As with dogs, it's difficult and perhaps not even helpful to put people into categories. Concentrate on communication rather than evaluation. You are the teacher. Communication between you and your students should be relevant, polite, but to the point. You have a job to do and that job requires that you communicate with the student. A method I've used successfully in getting my students, regardless of their personality types, in tune with me is to "wear different hats."

# Edward De Bono's Six Thinking Hats™ Method for Dog People

The Six Thinking Hats™ fact-gathering technique is the work of human psychologist and medical doctor Edward de Bono who coined the term *lateral thinking* in the 1960s. His original work was designed to help individuals and corporations solve problems by being more creative. I've adapted and applied these concepts to issues involving dogs and their people. The Six Hats method will help keep you and your client on task. As the problem solvers put on each of the Six Hats, they separate their own biases, emotions, and knowledge and deal with issues one at a time. With the Six Hats technique, you have a strategy for smoothly changing gears. You are able to get out of a rut and to turn up more options for behavior and training problems.

In his book, *Serious Creativity* (Harper, 1992, London), de Bono teaches that gathering the information is like drawing a map. Developing the information into a program for your client is choosing the best route on that map.

Mrs. Smith needs your help. Let's use the Six Hats Method for helping to take her profile. This is what she has to say: "My dog Spot is a three-year-old male Border Collie. He hasn't been neutered. I got him at five weeks of age at a pet shop. Spot barks aggressively at cats. He barks all day long. It must be stopped immediately. My neighbors are threatening to call the police. I'm really mad at Spot. He must have had a bad experience with cats as a puppy. I've tried every kind of punishment, and I've tried bringing him in and distracting him. . . . He must be too old to train. I'm at wit's end."

## *The White Hat Style of Thinking*

White, the absence of color, indicates purity and neutrality. White Hat thinking uses only facts and figures. It is computer-like thinking. White Hat thinking is neutral and objective, relying on facts only and is not open for interpretation.

As Mrs. Smith's instructor, you should phrase your questions and answers to obtain facts. Now is not the time to rely on personal opinion, hearsay, or anecdotal information.

There are two categories of facts:

1. *True:* Checked and proven to be true facts
2. *Maybe:* Facts believed to be true, but not checked

*True* —Documented proof that Spot is a Border Collie.

*Maybe*—It's a generalization (and maybe wishful thinking) that has people calling any black and white dog a Border Collie.

*True*—Spot barks. (Mrs. Smith has heard him.)
*Maybe*—Spot barks all day. Who said so? The neighbor? Is there proof?

*True*—Spot barks. (Mrs. Smith has heard him.)
*Maybe*—Spot barks aggressively. (Does Mrs. Smith have the ability to classify the barking as aggressive? What is her definition of aggression?)

## The Red Hat Style of Thinking

Red implies anger, as in "seeing red." It also means red, as in blushing with excitement. Red Hat thinking is based on emotions and feelings. The person is not thinking objectively. A Red Hat thinker uses hunches, intuitions, and impressions. Red Hat wearing relieves us of the need to give reasons. Red is simply how a person feels about something.

If emotions and feelings are not permitted as input to the thinking process, they will lurk in the background and affect thinking. Red Hat thinking acknowledges emotions and brings them out in the open where they can be dealt with.

Is Mrs. Smith really mad at Spot? If so, can she be rational when training? Or, does she admire Spot's spunkiness even though she knows his barking is a problem. Red Hat thinking allows these less-than-logical feelings to be brought out and considered in the planning of the behavior modification program.

There is no need to justify Red Hat thinking. For example, if Mrs. Smith has a hunch that a certain part of your program just won't work for Spot, allow her to state that and keep it in mind. She might be right, even though neither of you can defend the position. More importantly, if she THINKS she's right that might influence her ability to carry out the program successfully.

## The Black Hat Style of Thinking

A Black Hat thinker will be looking at the dark or black side of issues. He sees a cloudy day, overcast and dark.

Black Hat thinkers stay within their own knowledge and range of experience. They can be logical but not necessarily objective. They are negative but not emotional. Black Hat people dwell on why it won't work. They use critical judgment. They hold a pessimistic view and frequently play the devil's advocate.

Most western cultures feel comfortable wearing a Black Hat. It's an important part of thinking through a problem, but it leaves out the creative and constructive aspects of thinking.

Black Hat thinking might occur in Mrs. Smith: "Spot must be stopped immediately, I've tried everything. He's too old to train now."

Possible Black Hat thinking on the part of the consultant: "Mrs. Smith is stupid. This problem has gone too far to help. Spot is a Border Collie. They all like to bark. Well, I'll try to help her with my usual stuff."

Typical statements by Black Hat thinkers:

- "My neighbor tried that with his dog and it didn't work."
- "My husband won't let me spend all that money on new fencing."
- "What if I put in all this time and Spot doesn't improve?"

Chapter 6   People Skills

## The Yellow Hat Style of Thinking

Yellow Hat thinkers exude brightness and sunshine. They are positive, optimistic, have vision and hope. They focus on benefits and are constructive. Yellow Hat people are speculative and look to the future.

Yellow Hat thinking is the opposite of Black Hat thinking. They search for benefits. Yellow Hat thinking will ask "what if." They are not being creative, just optimistic.

If the people involved with Spot were using a Yellow Hat attitude, the thought process would be: "I'm really glad Spot's never attacked a cat. It's a good thing that Spot doesn't dig under the fence and get out. At least there are only three cats in the neighborhood. I've experienced lots of success with barking dogs of other clients. He's scheduled for neutering; this may calm him down a bit. Is he barking aggressively or does he simply want the cat's attention? Well, all the thieves know you have a dog."

## The Green Hat Style of Thinking

Each new growing season, the fertile earth awakens to new life, and the earth is green with new growth. Green Hat thinkers are creative and find new ideas and concepts. They are perceptive and deliberate in the creation of new ideas. Green Hat people are comfortable with change and they constantly strive for alternatives.

For effective Green Hat thinking, both client and instructor should be wearing Green Hats at the same time. Green Hat thinkers move from one idea to discover another. If a person only uses the established methods of dealing with training and behavior problems, new solutions are unlikely to occur. To help be a better Green Hat thinker, practice random word association. It's a good exercise to do at trainer's meetings.

**Random Word Stimulus—A Green Hat Exercise:** The leader selects any word from a dictionary by choosing two random numbers: one number is between one and the number of pages in the dictionary; the other is between one and twenty. The first number selects the page; the second number counts down to the word. Don't simply skim the dictionary looking for likely words. That's cheating! You can get any magazine (dog magazines are also a form of cheating). Close your eyes, open to any page and point. Open your eyes. That's your word! You can, however, end up with an embarrassing or rude word this way. (I have a story . . . it's best not written down . . . ) Anyway, you can find nice, safe random word lists on the Internet. There is also a list in the Appendix: INSTRUCTRandomword.doc, "Random Word List." Let's say the word that turned up is *TABLE*. Set a timer for 30 seconds. Forget about dogs and training; just think of the word. *TABLE*. Each person shouts out the first thing that pops into his mind when thinking of the word *TABLE*. The word can be used to prompt you into an opposite meaning or a word that rhymes. There are no wrong or silly ideas in this exercise. The leader is jotting these down on a white board or flip chart. The list might say: "Table makes me think of cloth, stable, chair, label, setting, leg, coffee, and so on. Time's up! Or time can be up when you run out of paper.

Now forget about the word table and think of the problem at hand. As a group, see where that word leads you in your problem solving.

| | |
|---|---|
| **Cloth:** | Is there some sort of muzzle we could try? |
| **Stable:** | Let's train Spot to be less reactive, more stable, in general. |
| **Chair:** | Sit in your chair, get out the phone book, and call a behavior consultant. |
| **Label:** | Can't think of anything. |
| **Setting:** | How about setting out (planting) some new bushes to screen Spot's view? |

Not all of these ideas will prove useful, but that's okay in Green Hat thinking!

## *The Blue Hat Style of Thinking*

A Blue Hat person is the one who oversees everything from beginning to end. A blue sky is passive, but it is all encompassing. In a client/instructor relationship, you need to be the one that wears a Blue Hat. You will tell yourself or the client which of the other five hats to wear, and when, during your session. A Blue Hat person asks the right questions. He or she is calm, calculated, and in control. You remain detached, as the conductor of an orchestra is detached but in tune with the others. You define the problem and choreograph the work to be done. A Blue Hat person is the one who oversees everything from beginning to end.

The other hats have given you a road map, but the Blue Hat selects the route to take on that map. Wearing the Blue Hat is your ultimate job as instructor, consultant, and problem solver. Wearing your Blue Hat, you now prepare an instructional format based on the ideas, a practical step-by-step, user-friendly method to apply the results of your lateral thinking.

Dr. de Bono's Six Hats method of lateral thinking allows us to get out of the usual rut. It gets us out of dead ends. Further, it allows us to get away from arguments or adversarial situations with our clients because we can ask our clients to wear the same hat we are wearing at the same point in the discussion. It allows us to be more productive and useful to our clients.

There is a one-page illustrated summary of the Six Hats method in the Appendix. It's listed as INSTRUCTSIXHats.doc, "Six Hats: Lateral Thinking for Dog Training."

# Demonstrations and Other Visual Aids

To increase the success of what we say to our students, various visual aids can be used. The most obvious visual aid in dog training is a demonstration by a dog and trainer! This section of the book will discuss the pros and cons of dog demonstrations, as well as various other visual aids such as interactive demonstrations, meaningful word pictures, and impromptu graphics. An important rule for demonstrations is the K.I.S.S. rule: Keep it short and simple. Small bits of information are best. A good goal is to get your point across to clients in 60 seconds or less.

## Demonstrations with Dogs

Demonstrations during class need to be very short. The student's dog will be easily distracted if not kept busy. However, if you do an orientation without dogs, you can spend a bit more time. A demonstration of the goals of the class would be in order on orientation night. Be honest in what you show. If your class doesn't get to precision off-leash heeling, don't bother to show it as a demonstration. If you want to spend a minute or two showing the steps and the increments you teach to reach the class goals, that's fine, but don't expect your class to remember them.

## Demonstrations with the Head Instructor's Dog

Should you, the head instructor, bring your own dog to class for demonstrations? Your own dog might be the best choice for demonstrations because your dog is trained and predictable. You know your dog will do the behaviors needed. Your dog's reliability will be time efficient. You won't have to worry about reminding someone to bring a demo dog. No worries about which class dog to select for a demonstration. You can show off the accomplishments of your dog and raise the credibility of your instruction. You can show the attitude and personality you believe is important for dog trainers. The way in which your dog responds can be a defined goal for the students. The performance could be motivating for the class.

There are possible drawbacks to class demonstrations using your own dog. It is difficult to talk to your class and handle a dog at the same time. If you use your own dog, have an assistant talk you through the demonstration. Students might think: "But, of course, your dog looks great. You're a professional trainer." Or, "Your dog was raised properly; I just adopted my pet from the shelter." (A good point!) The instructor's dog probably won't wiggle and be inattentive like the students' dogs. By the time you set up, teach one or more classes and clean up, your dog might have to wait around for several hours. Your mind will be (and should be) on the well-being of your own dog. This will naturally distract some of your attention from the class. And, of course, there's always the chance your dog will completely blow it! It's most important to show a happy, under control dog that likes people and other dogs on one end of the leash and a happy, positive handler on the other end. A dog that is perfect, technically, but seems intimidated or afraid of the environment does not make a good demo dog.

## Demonstrations with a Dog from Class

Should the head instructor borrow a dog from the class to use as a demonstration? Benefits of using a class dog for demonstration include showing how to deal with a wide variety of responses. You can be a role model for dealing with unexpected behaviors. A student who sees his dog perform the behavior realizes that his dog is capable of learning the exercise. Handling a class dog shows the owners that you are gentle and enjoy the company of all dogs, not just your own dog. You might be able to demonstrate that you have a variety of methods to teach the same behavior.

There are possible drawbacks of borrowing a student's dog. The owner may feel embarrassed at being singled out, or resentful if you handle his dog, especially if you are pushy about it and do not give the owner a chance to decline. A borrowed dog may place an inexperienced instructor in a greater position for failure. The dog might be ill at ease with you, not only making a bad demo, but showing that you cannot read stress in a dog or don't care. You have a greater chance of putting the dog at ease if you ask the owner to bring the dog over to you, rather than going into the dog's established safety zone and taking the dog away from the owner. If you ever handle a student's dog and the dog is showing signs of becoming afraid or aroused, simply admit that the dog is stressed and you don't want to stress him further. Ask the owner to take the dog back.

## Demonstrations with an Assistant's Dog

Having your assistant provide the dog is a good compromise between the head instructor's dog and a student's dog. Your demonstration dog and handler both need to have appropriate temperaments. The demo could well be the highlight of the class, so make sure your assistant knows exactly what you want demonstrated. It's always good to show the finished goal, but especially when doing demonstrations during class when the students' dogs are present, your assistant should know exactly what parts of the exercise and sequence you want demonstrated. This will mean the dog will have to perform at basic levels of the pet curriculum no matter how accomplished the dog might be now. Where will your assistant's dog be when not demonstrating? Either he will be in a crate in the training area or in a car if the temperature is appropriate. Having a demo dog that barks for attention is counterproductive. Unless you have an excess of assistants, the demo dog's handler must concentrate on the students when not demonstrating.

You might invite a dog and owner from a recently concluded class. Prepare them ahead of time by telling them exactly what you want and when you plan to do it. Then, talk them through it again as part of the demonstration. Having more than one demo dog is also a good idea. Students can relate to different sizes and personalities. Demos can be done from different angles. Because of problems perceiving left and right, if positioning is critical to the exercise, the demonstration team should have their BACKS to the students. As the head instructor is explaining what the demo is showing, be sure to point out or demonstrate the usual things that go wrong. For example, it's common for an owner using lures for the first time to position the lure incorrectly. It's instructive to show what happens in the demo, but try to keep the demonstration geared to positives.

### *Puppets and Toys*

Effective demonstrations can be done with a child's stuffed toy dog that is big enough to be seen. The toy dog is always there when you need him and you don't have to worry about his well-being. A toy dog that can stand, sit, and lie down is best. You might have to shop around or perhaps do "orthopedic surgery" on a toy dog by inserting wires in the legs to make the dog more compliant! Your toy dog might arouse some looks from dogs in class. Be ready to make your toy dog turn away, allow his tail to be sniffed, or otherwise put the interested dog at ease.

Even more convenient is a puppet dog that can be kept in your pocket. Demos are limited because this dog won't have legs. He can have a back—your arm, and even a hind end—your elbow. You can demonstrate "Sit" with a lure. Remember: "Control the head, control the dog." When the dog's nose goes up, his rear (your elbow) goes down on a table into the "Sit" position.

## MORE DEMONSTRATIONS—WITHOUT DOGS

Be creative! Sometimes it's better not to use a dog at all. There are several good demonstrations that can be done with a prop that is small enough to place in your pocket. Sometimes it's effective for the owners to help in demonstrations. Be very sure the person you've asked to help demonstrate has VOLUNTEERED. Don't put anyone in a position of embarrassment. You are accustomed to standing in front of a group, others may not be. At the very least, give a brief idea of what will be needed without giving away the punch line, if there is one.

### *Demo Dog—Your Hand*

This is a simplified version of the puppet and it's always available. Make sure the students get the picture of this impromptu dog by opening and closing the dog's mouth (moving your fingers like a dog's mouth). The "dog" can even bark. Have fun and shorten the muzzle by closing your fingers into a fist. Tell them it's a Pug.

### *Control the Head, Control the Dog—The 2″ × 4″ Dog*

Have in plain sight a piece of lumber approximately 2″ × 4″ by 18 inches long. Be sure the ends are square so that you can balance the piece of wood on end. This prop needs to be able to stand by itself on the floor or a table. Students will wonder how you will use this piece of wood for dog training.

Coaching People to Train Their Dogs

**The Demo:** Quickly draw eyes and mouth on one end of the wood and a tail on the other end. Show the students how easy it is to help the wooden dog sit. "Sit" means to balance the wooden dog on end so that it can sit by itself. This is "control the head, control the dog." With one hand, grasp the head end very near the top of the lumber. You will easily be able to balance the wooden dog into a "Sit." Take your hand away for the "Stay." Then start over but try to help the wooden dog into a "Sit" by controlling the rear (holding the 2″ × 4″ with one hand very close to the "tail" end of the lumber). Ask the students which method seems easiest to get the wooden dog to sit. In fact it's much more difficult to balance the wooden dog while holding the bottom than it is while holding the top. Next ask for a volunteer to try and report which feels easier. Be careful that they don't hurt themselves!

### Control the Head, Control the Dog—What Moves First?

Ask for a volunteer to sit in a chair in front of the class. Ask the class to observe the volunteer's body. An instructor in the back will cue the volunteer to rise. The class must say, "Stay," to the volunteer when they first realize the "dog" is getting up. When the "dog" hears, "Stay," he must freeze. Let's see how far into standing position the dog got before he heard and responded to the "Stay" cue. It usually takes a few tries before the class prevents the "dog" from getting at least halfway into the standing position. Have a discussion on body language. All other things being equal—legs not crossed, for example—it's the head that moves first. Ask your volunteer to get up one more time. (The class doesn't need to say "Stay" anymore!) Most will agree it's the head. Some will claim to read the eyes or the tensing of the muscles. Good! They can read their dogs that way also.

### Control the Head, Control the Dog—A Client on a Chair as a Dog

A volunteer sits in a chair and focuses on a squeaker or food held over her head. Ask her to get up. Help her so she doesn't fall. She can do it, but it's really hard. Then ask the rest of the class to look at a spot directly overhead—ask them if they can get up out of their chairs. It can be done, but with difficulty. We can help dogs to remain sitting the same way. Control the head UP. How? Lure, Gentle Leader®, eye contact, or get really close to the dog. Gravity usually wins and "Sit" happens.

### Control the Head, Control the Dog—Client on Hands and Knees as a Dog

Pick a young and enthusiastic owner for this one. Tell her that the cookie you have in your hand is like Velcro to the dog's nose. Allow the owner to experience luring the head into a "Sit" and a "Down."

### Control the Head, Control the Dog—All Owners Stand

First, show how you can get a dog to flop over on his hip to relax in the "Down" position. A piece of cheese is the magnet to the dog's nose. The dog is in the "Down-sphinx" position. With the magnet, pull the dog's nose over to his rib cage. The pelvis will turn and the dog is very apt to flop its hindquarters over. Ask all owners to stand up. Tell them a magnet is on their nose, bring the magnet to look over one shoulder, then down toward their ribs. They will feel what the dog feels.

## Opposition Reflex

These demonstrations show that a dog will naturally resist (oppose) pressure. It's one reason that pushing a dog's bottom toward the floor is not a good way to teach "Sit." It's one reason that pulling back on the leash is not the best way to get a dog to walk on a loose lead.

Show this with your own demo dog first. Your dog can be sitting or standing. Without speaking to the dog, push him slightly on the shoulder. Most likely he will lean into the push instead of the direction you are pushing. Stand your dog on all fours, gently grasp the base of his tail and exert a little backward pull. Does the dog back up or pull forward? The same thing happens when a dog feels the pull of a leash on his neck or a hand on his rear. Show dog handlers know how to use the tail tug to good advantage. Just before the judge looks at the dog, the handler gently tugs at the base of the dog's tail. The backward pull makes the dog's front come forward into a proud, alert stance.

## Test and Punish versus Lure and Reward

Don't fall into the habit of testing to see if the dog knows what a cue means. To set the dog up for failure is counterproductive and tempts a trainer to use aversives. Here's a demo to illustrate how unfair testing can be in dog training. Place a chair a few feet in front of you, facing your way. Ask for a volunteer to sit in a chair. The instructor makes eye contact and says, "Yackety yack," distinctly. The volunteer will probably look confused. Say it again, pretending to get a little mad.

The points to make include:

- **Ask your class if they heard you and if they think the volunteer heard your verbal cue.**
  They'll have to say yes.

- **Ask the class if you should jerk the dog's chain now because she didn't obey?**
  They'll have to say no.
  (Sometimes if a family member or friend is present, he will say yes.)

- **What might the dog learn if I punish now?**
  To be afraid of the owner.
  To worry about being in the room.
  To dislike the words *Yackety yack*.
  Never to sit in your presence again.
  Any number of things are learned, but chances are one of them isn't what *Yackety yack* means.

- **Ask why the volunteer dog didn't respond to that verbal cue.**
  What we just discussed is the test-and-punish method of dog training. We still don't know what *Yackety yack* means. Let's go on with the demo. Face the volunteer dog (who is still sitting) again. Flash a peek at a candy bar, which is in your pocket. With the candy in view, say "Yackety yack," give a beckoning gesture, and guide her up to you. Immediately give her the candy.

- **Ask the "dog" what she learned.**
  This is where the second lesson comes in. Don't assume that your dog will say "Yackety yack" means to come to you. She might say, "You have candy in your pockets" in which case, you point out that's a great thing for her to learn.

  She might say, "I'm not sure"—a good time to talk about how much repetition is needed in training.

  She might say, "It means for me to stand." Admit that you can see how she might have learned that. Talk about how better timing might have prevented it. Next time you call your dog, and he gets up and stands, looking at you, ask yourself if you didn't train him to do just that.

# THE TRAINING GAME—WHAT THIS INTERACTIVE EXERCISE CAN TEACH STUDENTS

I first learned about this animal trainer's classic from Karen Pryor, author of *Don't Shoot the Dog,* at a seminar in New Jersey in the 1980s. The idea of the exercise is to teach shaping skills. When Karen first taught us this game, she used a whistle for the bridge. Now, most people use a clicker for the exercise. Chapter 3 describes shaping in detail.

*LESSON:* It helps people learn the idea of rewarding the good behavior and to ignore the unwanted behavior. Mark out a training area. This can be done with chairs, a few leashes, or with a verbal description of the boundaries.

*LESSON:* We want to cut down on the distractions when we first train a new behavior. A small, boring area helps the dog focus on the trainer. Ask for a volunteer training subject who is not shy! Tell the class the subject is a curious, high-energy dog. The subject's high activity level helps speed up the demonstration! In a few minutes you will shape the subject to perform a behavior that the rest of the class secretly decides upon. Condition that volunteer to the clicker. Click/Treat. What kind of treat? For this game it can be a pretend treat, but ask her what she loves.

*LESSON:* What YOU think is good, the dog might think is boring. Click/Treat, Click/Treat. "What does the click mean?" Perhaps the subject will say, "I'm doing something good." Tell the class that you will set a timer for six minutes. If the subject is not trained in six minutes, the game is over, and we will talk about the training to that point.

*LESSON:* This can lead into a discussion of short and sweet training sessions. It will also take the pressure off of the subject! Ask the audience to please be quiet and observe because we will be discussing what they see. When the shaping starts, the subject should not ask questions, but like an animal, she will repeat behaviors she is rewarded for. Tell her the behavior will be something she can easily do. It will not require touching any of the dogs or people in the room. (Please remember this rule. You can avoid lots of problems this way!) The subject leaves the area and a simple, one-step task is chosen.

*LESSON:* Talk about chunking complex exercises into smaller bits. The task is to pick up the teacher's pen.

*LESSON:* Talk about criteria setting: Does it matter which end of the pen he picks up? How long he holds it? What he does with it? Subject returns. You shape. Did your subject "get it"? If not, the exercise is over in six minutes! (Set a timer!) Ask the subject what he was thinking. Ask the rest of the class what they observed. A late click? Oh well, you're only human. The subject got an extra goody is all. You clicked for being close to the pen, but his eyes were focused on the chair.

*LESSON:* Can we read the dog's mind? See how easily it is for the dog to make the wrong association? Oh well, the subject got an extra goody is all. You clicked when the subject turned toward the pencil; now you are getting turning behavior. Was the subject inhibited from touching the teacher's stuff?

*LESSON:* Do we ask dogs to do things, especially in a class setting, that are socially inappropriate from the dog's point of view? An example would be to force dogs in a beginners' class that don't know each other to lie down shoulder to shoulder. This can provoke a discussion of personal space and greeting rituals.

# OTHER TRAINING AIDS

## Video

I'm not in favor of showing videos in class. Your students want personal, hands-on attention from you and your assistants. They could rent or buy a video and watch it at home. Video can be used effectively as an aid to personal class time.

Here are some ways I have used videos:

- After a brief introduction to the Gentle Leader® headcollar at orientation, we offer to loan a video for home viewing.
- Brief 30-second or less video clips on canine body language are embedded in our PowerPoint® orientation.
- We direct students to Legacy's resource library of books and videos.
- For competition classes videos of the student at work and also videos of others in the sport are helpful.

## Slides, PowerPoint®, and Overhead Projector (OHP)

Computer PowerPoint®, conventional slide projectors, or overhead projectors can be especially helpful for orientation. They can be used passively during class to show a training progression or the class's time schedule. The software comes with a good tutorial on how to create your own presentation.

## Motivational Messages

Keywords, catchy phrases, or motivational slogans can be prepared ahead of time as a computer-generated banner, a slide, an overhead projection, or just written on the board. Have a new one up each week or after every break. It's good to put an assistant in charge of this job. Be on the lookout for motivational or instructional sayings or quotes. It keeps things interesting. Ask students to be on the lookout for appropriate material. When someone turns in a contribution, they get an extra bonus bone for the end-of-class lottery. There are plenty of examples throughout the textbook. Here are some others:

"Train, don't complain."—Bob Self
"Every handler gets the dog he deserves."—U.S. Army
"Do unto others as you would have others do unto you."—Holy Bible
"Your dog is running for higher office"—Erich Klinghammer
"What's in it for the dawg?"—Herb Morrison
"Compassion, our last great hope."—Leo Bustad

## Spontaneous White Board Visuals

Spontaneous notes, simple diagrams, or jotting down a key word as you teach can be helpful. It's quite obvious when the person conducting the class walks away and writes something. A blackboard, whiteboard, or flip chart can be ready and available for a quick demonstration or key word during the hands-on section. K.I.S.S. (Keep it Short and Simple). Write large enough for all to see, or don't do it at all. With the availability of computer-generated PowerPoint® slides, there are a lot of overhead projectors sitting around gathering dust. Having one in the corner already focused on a screen or white wall is a good aid. Keep a supply of blank transparencies and pens on hand. It's easier for you—you have a lot more practice writing on paper than on a board. It is a time saver—you can write more quickly on the overhead than on the board, and you don't have to waste time erasing. Just have lots of blanks ready—you can rub them all out at the end of class. Here are some examples:

- If you are working on limited hold and you want the dogs to respond to a cue within three seconds, write a big "3" on the board.
- If you are working on a sequence, put key words or an acronym on the board as you describe each step.
- If someone has a point to make or a question that's not immediately appropriate, put a key word on the board, so you don't forget to respond before class is over.
- If you need to further explain a certain handler position in relation to the dog, tell them to imagine a bird's-eye view (from above) and draw a circle for the owner and an oval with a "D" in it for the dog. Draw arrows to illustrate position.

### Bulletin Boards

You can find decorative cork boards with frames at an office supply store. Cork tiles purchased at a home center could be glued to a wall. The sky is the limit here. Have the staff be on the lookout for interesting articles. It's a good place to post emergency numbers and facility rules. How about one board for "student of the month"? Take a quick digital photo and write a paragraph about family and dog. Put up group photos of each class and call it a "Wall of Fame." People have fun looking back and finding themselves and friends in the pictures.

### Giant Post-Its® or Plastic Write/Erase Sheets

This is an alternative "board" when you are at a borrowed facility. The plastic sheets cling to a smooth wall by static electricity. Giant Post-It sheets are expensive and you can only use them once. However, you can tear individual sheets off and put them around the room. You can list the steps of a complex exercise, or put up game rules! You can put up the agenda for the evening, but there's a drawback to doing so; if you outline the night's lessons on the wall, how will you or your students feel if you can't keep within the schedule?

### Handouts

Handouts are an excellent aid to communication. There are different ways to think about handouts! If they are too long, will the student read them? If they are too short, can you get enough useful information across? Make sure your handout is serving the purpose for which it is intended.

Is a particular handout meant to be complete enough so that almost anyone, whether in class or not, would be successful at carrying out the instructions? Handouts like this make a good insurance policy—if the instructor has forgotten to mention a detail, it's right there on the handout. This more complete handout is also good for answering questions you don't have time for. "Jane, the next class is starting in a few minutes. Neutering is an important topic, please speak to your vet about it; meanwhile, I have a handout on it that will answer a few of your questions. You might want to take it home and share it with your family before you contact your vet."

Some handouts are just a list of key words—for example reminding students what to practice during the week. You might consider having these printed on Post-It notes and encourage the students to stick them up where it will remind them to practice—like on the bathroom mirror or refrigerator door.

You might want to print handouts on colored paper. They are easier to refer to if the student has more than one handout. Example: "If you want to review the steps in our "Sit" sequence, look in your notebooks for the green handout."

Another idea is to have an identifying logo or picture on each handout. It's a quick cross-check that they have found the correct title. You might help students make certain they have the correct handout by saying something like, "You said you need help with home-alone barking. The resource shelf has a stack of handouts. Look for the one with the howling dog on the front."

Good handouts have these characteristics:

- Use the same terminology used in class
- Are concise
- Cover only one topic
- Use illustrations to make them appealing and easy to identify
- Have adequate "white space" provided so information does not appear so daunting
- Are prepared with margins large enough to punch for a ring binder
- Include enough blank space for note taking
- Have instructor's (or school's) name, date, and phone number on it
- Include a written invitation to contact your school for clarification or additional help
- Give credit to source if not written by your school (Did you have permission to copy?)

## INVOLVE ME AND I'LL UNDERSTAND

In Chapter 2 we learned about engrams and the importance of "training the brain" in the mechanical skill of dog training. After explaining and demonstrating the exercise, it's time for action. Help your students go through the motions of each exercise. You may choose to do this without dogs at first. Stand in front of your class, with your back to the students, so that they can easily identify right and

*Chapter 6   People Skills*

left as you demonstrate. Talk them through motions as you do the same motions. The instructor's lesson plans in the Appendix give details on ways to coach your students in the actual mechanical skills of each exercise.

## Spouses and Friends

If you are welcoming friends and family into class, think about your policy before you do so. It's very easy for relatives to want to call out advice to your student! Don't let it happen. It will only put your client under stress and be generally disruptive. You can reduce this by asking that family members to take a seat ACROSS from the dog and handler. Explain (truthfully!) that if they sit across the room, their dog is able to see them without having to look behind or around the room. If they sit still, the dog will know just where to check on them. The advantage to the person handling the dog is that their family members will be unable to put their hands on the dog or bother the dog's handler! Visiting friends and family can be observers or, if planned ahead of time, take turns handling the dog. If this is the case, everyone planning to participate needs to attend every class to reduce confusion and provide the dog with consistency. I recommend one handler for one class session, but at times we switch in the middle of the class. If observers seem to be starting their own conversation, just walk over there and conduct the class from there. They will usually quiet down.

## The Children in the Family

Training should be a family event, but in our enthusiasm to make it such, it's easy to reduce the quality of the training. Most instructors make the entire family welcome. The social dynamics of a family include the dog.

In puppy classes we group the families together, usually on the floor. Children actively participate in their puppy's training, but need to be very carefully supervised. It doesn't take much for an enthusiastic child to drop or otherwise injure a puppy. It is your ultimate responsibility to make sure everything goes well in class. Do you have enough help to supervise, supervise, supervise?

When children are present we like to include a "How to Meet a Dog" exercise. It's brief and worthwhile. The dog met should be an appropriate staff dog. Possibly the children can meet each family's puppy also. It depends on the temperaments of the children and the dogs! Do not be tempted to practice "How to Meet a Dog" involving the dogs in a beginners' class. It's prudent to use staff dogs only for this.

In more structured classes that include an assortment of untrained older dogs, children need to be supervised even more carefully. There is no way we can trust a beginning class dog to be appropriate with children, especially when children leap off their chairs and skip in front of the dogs and owners on their way to the toilet. Therefore, our rule is that children must remain in their seats. If they have to get up, they should raise their hands. I make the statement on orientation night, and the rule is also in the class notebooks. It's up to the parents if they want to bring the younger children or not. Their parents know if their children can follow these simple rules. The majority of children who end up in class as observers are just fine. If the child does get up, I simply stop the class and wait for the parent to do whatever is needed. I don't resume class until the child is settled. Those actions usually show that we are serious about the rules.

Here are some other ideas to keep things running smoothly when children are present.

- **ASSIGN A SEAT:** You might want to have some puppy pictures and place them on the backs of chairs. The children have to remain in the "puppy chairs." Use regular adult-sized chairs. Kids can't pop out of them as easily as small ones.

- **ART CENTER:** Have a supply of clipboards. The type that is attached to a thin plastic box is very easily managed. Most shelters have educational coloring sheets or paper and pencil activity books for children. Better yet, make your own! If your handouts are illustrated, blow some of those up to make the child feel like a real part of the class. Some of mine are in the Appendix under Misc KidsColorSheets.doc. When the family dog is working on "Sit," the child can be coloring the blow-up with the word "Sit" across the top! Oops, that's the teacher coming out again. Blank paper, however, allows the child more creativity. Ask them to draw a picture of their dogs. Amazing results can occur! Try it! When class is over, place the drawings on your school bulletin board.

- **CREATE A KIDS' READING CORNER:** You can do this with expandable baby gates. It doesn't have to be too big. The parents can see in and the children can see out. But the boundaries are distinctly visible. If you want, you can make a double boundary to be sure little arms don't stick out to pet unsuspecting passing dogs. Many children's books have dogs as a theme. Find a few extra large toy dogs posing in a "Down" position. Garage sales are good for this. The children can use them as pillows and read stories to the dog. Perhaps a soft roll up carpet in the kids' corner would be nice. A small doghouse to crawl in and out of or for reading is also fun.

- **ASSIGN AN ASSISTANT:** If you have the luxury of an extra assistant instructor, you could provide an actual learning experience for the children. One activity might be to role play how to meet a dog. Find some toy dogs from garage sales and fit them with collars and leashes. Your assistant can help the children play "dog class." Play the shaping game. Children know it as the Hot and Cold Game. Take turns. Decide on a behavior, like "Sit" on a certain chair. Ask the child to think of a funny word as a bridge. Talk about positive reinforcement. Stickers make a good reinforcement. Don't use candy unless you clear it with the parents.

- **PLAY DESK:** Toy stores have little school desks, usually plastic. The seat and the desk are connected, and the desktop lifts up. There are all kinds of busy work toys in the desk. All are appropriate for a child sitting in the seat, never getting up. These are small, inexpensive, and a very good way to help children stay put. They don't fold up, so you are stuck with them in your center, but they are lightweight and can be kept on a high shelf.

- **KIDS' NIGHT:** You might designate one class where the kids do some training for a few minutes, right out on the floor like mom and dad. Double-leash the dog—child has a leash; parent has a leash. If space is at all limited, I suggest having half the class sit out to give you double the room. Dogs regard children differently. We want plenty of space and no problems. Do one or two stationary exercises only, and then have the child return to his seat.

- **KIDS' LESSON:** If you have plenty of time, room and helpers, after class an assistant could coach child and parent together in some basic exercises. This should be done in a separate area from the main flow of traffic. The dog should be doubled-leashed—parent has one leash, child the other. *Caution:* Between classes there is always a high risk of a conflict between dogs. People aren't as diligent coming and going as they are in class. And the movement or the thought of going somewhere is stimulating to the dog.

Don't miss this opportunity to nurture good relations between dogs and children. Children are the world's future dog owners, trainers, and instructors. They are the ones who will be setting dog policies in communities, becoming lawyers on bite cases, or teachers of children. We are missing an opportunity to make an impact on dog ownership in the future if we aren't friendly to children today. Think strongly about offering a "Kids and Kanines" class as described in Chapter 7. Information for parents appears in the Appendix as INFO Kids&Kanines.doc, "Kids and Kanines."

## Handlers with Disabilities

You will know ahead of time through the registration or profiling procedure if you will have a disabled person in your class. You may need to speak to an occupational therapist or physical therapist for help in adapting your program for the individual. The same disability affects individuals differently, so you will need a new plan each time you help a disabled person train his dog.

Help, but don't do it for them. If the individual can't do the exercise himself, he won't be able to practice at home. You need to be a lateral thinker and come up with a technique that works for that individual.

Perhaps you need a more extensive pre-class profile on both the dog and owner. If you are not experienced with the ramifications of various disabilities, consult with the appropriate health care professionals.

Ann Howie, a social worker and dog trainer, has challenged me with these questions.

- *Is the client physically able to do the work?*

    Can the client reach the dog?

    Can the client give hand signals?

    Is the client able to speak or make sounds?

    Will the client come alone with his dog?

Will the client come with an attendant?

Will you need a translator?

What about sign language?

- *Is your client intellectually able to learn?*

    Is your client developmentally disabled?

    Is the person able to learn at the same pace as others in the class?

- *Environment*

    Will extra space be needed because of mobility equipment or attendants?

    An instructor might need to be in a position to
    —Touch the person
    —Have the person read his lips
    —Best allow the person to hear or see

    Acoustics are more important with some disabilities.

    Will static on your sound system be a problem?

    Are your training area, restrooms, and surrounding areas accessible to a person with a mobility deficit?

- *Curriculum*

    Do not build false expectations. Unless you are actually doing so, make it clear from the beginning that you are not teaching service dog behaviors. Your school teaches pet manners.

- *Equipment*

    Can your client hold a leash?

    Can your client adjust a collar?

    Can your client dispense treats?

    Can your client use a clicker?

You probably know some of the answers to these questions or have good resources to find out. A shorter leash might be easier to control. Adapt a leash with a thick foam handle for people with a poor grip. Making the leash rigid by slipping it through a piece of pvc pipe might make things easier for some folks. And of course there's the target stick and laser pointer to extend reach. Would the client be less apt to trip with a quad cane than a regular cane? The best resource is the person coming to class. Politely ask for their help in designing the best possible learning experience for them. There's got to be a dog loving physical or occupational therapist to give you ideas. Service dog trainers are overflowing with adaptive ideas. At our training location we have a bench with steps leading up and down. Although it is good for teaching puppies to maneuver steps, it was designed as a raised dog training platform for students having trouble reaching their dogs.

# Using Music as an Aid to Communication

I use music in my classes to help communicate a variety of messages. Everyone has his own preference. I use '60s music. If anyone groans, I smile and invite them to bring a CD of their choice with the same beat next week. They usually don't take me up on it! I condition the owners to various cues early, and they know just what to do with very little reminding when they hear the music:

- **We're Starting Class Within One Minute**—I use it as my one-minute warning. When the song is done, I expect people in their places and ready to begin. Happy, fast rock and roll works nicely for this. You can have fun with hidden messages in the songs you choose. I like 60's music and Golden Oldies. Recently our starting music has been "Wild Thing" by the Troggs or "Run Around" by the Beach Boys. Of course, there is the classic, "Ain't Nothin' But A Hound Dog" by Elvis.

- *Instant "Down" and Relax*—I have this one keyed to play at a second's notice when I need immediate control. Often I'll use it when things get a bit too stimulating for the dogs. Sometimes this happens when we play an active game. By the time I can say, "Down position, please," the music will be on and my assistants know to help spread the word that we are doing a relaxed (hips over) "macaroni" Down. We do quiet, slow doggy massage at this time. The arousal level comes right down, and you can soon resume what you were doing. Slow music is important. Many of my students enjoy Japanese taiko drum music, which resembles a heartbeat. I have run across a few (American!) dogs that react aversely to taiko drumming. Another of my favorites is "Silence Is Golden" by the Tremeloes.

- *Heeling*—Music for leash work tends to keep the handlers moving quickly and the dogs attentive with tails wagging. The CD "Hooked on Classics" can be found in almost all shops. It has lots of music with a good beat for heeling. Marches, such as football team fight songs, are terrific, also. Be sure to alternate the school songs of any local universities or you'll get a bad time from the students. I encourage students to find their own music, one that has a good tempo for them and their dog.

- *Stationary Exercises*—Music can bring a smile to the owners' faces and help them remain positive during the long wait for a "Sit" or "Down" duration exercise. Or you can change the music to something that has a calming effect on the owners. Favorite choices are "Stay . . . just a little bit longer" by Maurice Williams and the Zodiacs and "Stop in the Name of Love" by Diana Ross and the Supremes.

- *Class Is Over*—Make sure that you have asked for questions and all announcements have been made. When the music plays, the class is officially over. The head instructor can make the message clearer by saying, "Good night," or, "Have a good week," while stepping away from "center stage." Assistants can say a good night to whoever is close to them and move away to other tasks. Often the head and assistant instructors are speaking to or helping students, but this clear message of goodbye allows all the others to go home and not stand around being polite because they are not sure if the class is really over or not. The song I most often use is the Nylons' "Kiss Him Goodbye." ("Na na na-na, Na na na-na, Hey, Hey-A; Go-od-bye.) My husband, Bill, teaches most classes with me. He's a John Denver fan, so if Bill is present, the goodbye music ends up being "Country Roads."

# REMEMBERING NAMES

Your student will be flattered if you can remember his name. It will make him feel that he's special and important, not just part of the crowd. Often it's easier to remember the dog's name. Some instructors refer to the owner as "Fluffy's Dad" or "Fluffy's Person." Personally, I think that's better than not remembering either name, but this may offend some people.

One way to help you learn names is to call roll aloud each class. Call the person and the dog's name. It will also help the class members get to know each other's names.

Name badges might be helpful. Some instructors make permanent badges that are kept on a bulletin board in the entry way of the training room. Others will ask students to make a new disposable name badge for each class.

Name cards on the back of chairs or on traffic cones will show the client where to go and will help instructors remember names.

Using mnemonic tricks, rhymes, and associations can help you remember names. For example, you might take note that Mrs. HYATT has a HIGH-energy dog. Carol, has a hairstyle just like your mother. Your mother's neighbor is named Carol. By the time the Carol in your class has a chance to change her hairstyle, you will have remembered her name anyway!

# IMPARTIALITY

Everyone in class paid for an equal amount of your time. Avoid the tendency to give more time and attention to

- the very good student
- the student who seems to agree with you
- the student with the same breed of dog you have
- the pleasant student
- the youngster
- the student with the cutest puppy
- EVEN the student having the most difficulty

If attention is given to just one student during class, the others in the class are not only left out, but also probably bored. There's nothing worse than a class that drags on. If you want to give extra time to these students, do it after class, after the students are formally excused. If you have more than one class back to back, schedule adequate time between classes. Another approach is to assign one assistant to help this student, but that can be distracting for the other students, and unless your assistant is keeping right up with you, the student will miss the next points the head instructor is making.

# ABSENT STUDENTS

I overheard a conversation at a dog training workshop once. The instructor said she always registers at least 20 dogs because, within a few weeks, attrition reduces the class to a more manageable 12 or so!

If we can't keep the owners in class, we can't train the dogs. If your classes have more than a 10% dropout rate, take a close look at your instructional format, your methods, and your attitude. Is your facility friendly and comfortable? Can students hear your instructions? Is a person having a particularly difficult time? Are you teaching your students what they want to learn? It's not realistic to expect 100% attendance during the span of a dog-training course, but be concerned about every owner who doesn't finish your class.

Absentees fall roughly into two categories:

**MOTIVATED**—A student wants to come to class, but an obstacle prevents attendance: Illness or unexpected conflicts are legitimate reasons not to attend. An instructor should be concerned about such students and offer alternatives quickly. When one class is missed, it becomes easier and easier to miss the next class, especially if the client feels he is behind.

**UNMOTIVATED**—A student does not want to return to class. There had to be a degree of motivation or the student would not have signed up for class in the first place. An instructor can enhance the client's initial motivation for dog training or be responsible for diminishing that motivation. Frustration, embarrassment, inability to understand the exercises, unrealistic goals, instructor alienation, and sense of failure can be the source of a drop out. Once this has occurred, it's difficult to motivate the student to return to class. An experienced instructor will consider these factors in planning the class curriculum.

Be sure you have stated your make-up policy at orientation and that it is written in your registration materials so that there are no misunderstandings or surprises. Keep clients wanting to come back by previewing the next class. Pick out one exercise of particular interest to the students. Tell them just enough about the benefits that they will be anxious for the next lesson.

Some examples include:

- "Those who came early saw the advanced class doing agility. Those students have agreed to stay late next week and do a demonstration for you. As soon as your dogs are working reliably off leash, you will have a chance to try out this sport.

- "Next week we're going to have surprise visitors." (Have your advanced class do a fly ball or drill team demonstration.) Point out to the students how the basics they are learning are the foundation for these fun activities.
- "The newspaper will be here next week to do a story on us."
- "Have you ever played Revenge of Godzilla? We're all going to give it a go next week."
- "The pet shop people will be here next week to give out free gifts."

## "Come Back" Cards

We tell our students at Legacy that if they don't come to class and we don't know the reason why, we will be getting in touch with them. We usually don't call. I feel it's an interruption and a bit pushy. We send a postcard. You might not want to put your student on the spot and ask why she wasn't in class. Politely acknowledge her absence and give her options for help in making up the material. This card shows that you really do care. Don't give your student the impression that he is way behind because of the missed class. That might make him give up the class entirely!

At Legacy, the assistant who takes roll will automatically fill out a funny cartoon postcard for the absent student. This is quick and easy because the addresses of the students are right on the roster. The stamps are already on the postcards. We simply hand write a personalized "We Missed You" note. It's the assistant's responsibility to drop the card off on her way home. In our area, most people will get them within a day. Our phone number and e-mail address are on the card.

# EVALUATIONS

Most schools do the evaluation at the end of class. Here are some of the common questions on evaluation forms. This is not a true evaluation because those who did not have their needs met may have already dropped out.

1. In what areas is your dog most improved?
2. What areas important to you need more improvement?
3. What areas of interest to you have we failed to address?
4. Have you gotten enough individual attention?
5. What exercises confused you the most?
6. What exercise is least helpful for you?
7. What exercise is most helpful for you?

## Other Ways to Measure Your Effectiveness

Monitor the dog's progress. It's best not to do this with a formal test because testing makes most owners nervous. Besides, the dog can be quite good, but simply not pass the test at the moment.

A suggestion box and pad of paper in the training area is an inconspicuous way for students to tell how they feel. Check it each week, and hopefully, you can implement appropriate suggestions before the session is over.

Instructors' meetings or brief critiques after each class give instructors and assistants a chance to exchange opinions and information before it's forgotten.

**Mid-Course Evaluation:** The profile filled out at orientation by each student should include questions as to what the student wants to accomplish in class. Check to see if the student feels adequate progress is being made. I favor a mid-course evaluation. We might pass out paper and pencils and have people respond to three simple questions while we wait:

1. What can we cover in the upcoming weeks to help you?
2. What class subjects are of least help/interest to you?
3. Do you have a suggestion that will make your experience in class better?

Papers are then folded and collected so that the writer can remain anonymous, if so desired. In this way we can tweak an individual's program to do our best to help them. There is a sample evaluation form in the Appendix listed as PDM4 MidCourseEval.doc, "We're Halfway Through Classes—How Are You Doing?"

# PRIVATE LESSONS—SPECIAL CONSIDERATIONS

Perhaps you offer private lessons on a regular basis or as a make-up session. Perhaps a client's dog is not appropriate to have in class for one reason or another. Teaching one-on-one lessons is often the route taken for a behavior problem. Lots of your group class skills will apply to private lessons, but there are other considerations as well. For one thing, private lessons can be more stressful for the student than a class setting. Extra precautions can be taken to put your client at ease and make the session as productive as possible. Unless it's a make-up session, a bit more preparation might be necessary to customize the best lesson for the dog and owner's particular needs.

Here are some brief points to consider:

- **THE LESSON AREA:**
    Where will you conduct the lesson?
        The client's home?
        Your training center?
        Your office or public place?

    Will the lesson area be escape-proof for safety and for an off-leash evaluation if desired? Can you ensure that your session will not be interrupted? Can you lock the door or put up an "in-session" sign?
    Client's records and handout materials should be readily available

- **AT THE TIME THE APPOINTMENT IS MADE:**
  Ask the client to begin a list of concerns and a to-do list and bring it to the session
  Invite the family to attend the appointment
  Bring paper and pen or tape recorder to the consultation or tell them you'll tape or video the session for them
  Don't give training advice over the phone

- **BEGINNING OF THE SESSION:**
  Be on time for your appointment
  Be sure the client knows the time schedule; stick to it
  If this is a new student, take the profile yourself; don't have the client fill out the form
  Politely keep client on track

- **DURING THE SESSION:**
  Keep an eye on the dog. Try to politely catch inappropriate actions and talk about them. Find something good and comment on it.
  Give the client a chance to repeat what you've said
  Be sure to give the client a chance to practice what you've taught

- **END OF SESSION:**
  Don't make promises or guarantees
  Be sure policy is clear on payment, homework, and follow-up
  Give them exercises that will be successful immediately
  Refer to upcoming classes
  Leave the client with the impression that both the dog and he are important to you

- **AFTER THE SESSION:**
  Write up your notes for the file you will keep on this client
  With permission of the client, send a copy of the report to the referring veterinarian
  Fill out two "how are you doing" postcards with the client's address. Send one immediately, and another the following week.
  Remember the ethics of privacy and confidentiality

# EVOLUTION OF CHANGE

When you teach a person something new to her, you are attempting to change that person. Change can sometimes be difficult. As your own classes evolve, people will react in various ways.

Karen Pryor, a marine mammal trainer and expert in operant conditioning, has greatly influenced change in dog training methods. At a workshop Karen taught the various ways people react to change and how instructors might respond effectively to their concerns.

Here are my notes from her presentation:

- *Ignore the issue.* For example:
  - THEY: Change the subject
  - You: Keep doing and demonstrating

- *Pretend to agree, but don't understand or do it.* For example:
  - THEY: Nod and smile and do it the same old way
  - You: Use new examples and demonstrations

- *Resist idea and attack your opinion.* For example:
  - THEY: "It won't work because . . ."
  - You: Don't take it personally. You can say "I thought about that too, and . . ."

- *Start to absorb but tentative.* For example:
  - THEY: "That works well in the USA, but not in Japan."
  - You: Continue with more examples

- *Start to use it.* For example:
  - THEY: Especially if no one is looking
  - THEY: Method is okay for some things
  - You: Notice, keep up the good examples

- *Say they've done it all along.* For example:
  - THEY: Say they invented it, forgot you taught them.
  - You: Let them take credit. Be happy, you have allies now.

Another excellent reference on change is *Who Moved My Cheese?* by Spencer Johnson (Putnam, 2001). It is a simple parable, less than 100 pages, that reveals profound truths about change. It is an amusing story of four characters who live in a maze and look for cheese to nourish them and make them happy. They are faced with unexpected change. As you go through the trials and tribulations of these characters, you can reflect on your own change or that of your students.

## USING THE CHINESE WISDOM PUZZLE TO PRACTICE TEACHING SKILLS

This puzzle, called the "ch'i ch'iao tu" (seven piece wisdom board), originated in ancient China. Legend says that a workman dropped a porcelain tile that broke into seven pieces. As he tried to reconstruct the square, he created various shapes.

It's known as a popular brainteaser for children and adults. This toy is known as a tangram in the United States. The seven pieces include five triangles of various sizes, a square, and a parallelogram. There are hundreds of abstract designs and identifiable objects you can create with the seven pieces. I've adapted the game as a teaching tool for dog training class instructors.

We use the puzzle to practice a variety of teaching skills in Legacy's Instructor's courses. I like my students to practice on pieces of paper at first, rather than people and dogs. The basic exercise calls for at least four people in addition to you, the leader. Ask for a volunteer "instructor," a "student," and a "scribe." People left over are observers. Several instructing groups can participate simultaneously. In fact, the game is better that way. Warn your volunteers that the instructors will be subject to a critique, and the students will be questioned. The scribe has minimal work but will need paper and pen. The observers will be interviewed. Make sure your volunteers are comfortable in these roles.

## The Basic Exercise

The objective of this three-minute exercise is to give a starting point for subsequent discussion of instructing skills. It works best if the leader only has the solution to the puzzle at first. Be prepared, however. All of the participating instructors will need to see the solution. Make a large visual for them. This can be done in PowerPoint®, or you can lay the pieces on an overhead projector. You can sketch it ahead of time on a large piece of paper, but don't put the paper up until needed.

Each group will need a flat surface to construct the puzzle. Floors work, but depending on the participants, you may need to arrange tables for this. The designated student sits at the table with her back to the front of the room—where you will eventually be showing the puzzle solution.

**Rules for the Students:** Keep your back to the front of the room, no peeking! You can't ask questions. Fold your hands until the buzzer goes off.

**Rules for the Instructors:** You must coach your student to use all seven pieces to construct the shape requested by the leader. You can see the student, you can talk to the student, you can describe the shape, and you can tell the student step by step what to do. Your hands must remain folded, and you cannot touch the student or use your hands in any way. You must use all seven pieces, you can't stack the pieces on top of each other, and they must all be used flat on the table.

**Rules for the Scribes:** Shhh. This is a secret. Designated scribes come up and form a huddle to receive your directions! The secret directions given by the leader to those in the huddle are: "You will need paper and a pen. Create two columns on the paper. The heading of one is POSITIVE COMMENTS. The heading of the other column is NEGATIVE COMMENTS. The scribe can decide what comments are nice and helpful and which are not so nice or helpful. The scribe simply tallies those comments on the paper. In addition, the scribe selects one unhelpful comment and writes it down. When time is up, don't say anything and don't let anyone know what you were doing or see your paper. We are going to have two attempts at this, your job is to document only the first trial." Give each scribe a set of puzzle pieces.

**Rules for the Observers:** No talking, watch quietly. Be ready to give constructive comments later about any aspect of the teaching, the learning, or anything else of interest.

**Leader Begins the Game:** He says, "Okay, when I say 'go,' the scribe will place the puzzle pieces on the table. You will then have three minutes, instructors, to coach your student to form a perfect square. When your puzzle is solved, start cheering so I know you are done. Ready? Go!"

At this point someone will point out that they don't know the solution. Tell them it's just a common square and to do their best. The leader can walk around the room and stare at the instructors. The leader can call out times: "This is a 30 second warning." BUZZER! Time is up! (You will need to remind the student that time is really up, most want to continue working on the puzzle.) How many solved the puzzle? None of them. Time out for discussion. What do the instructors have to say? What do the students have to say? Spectators?

The leader should then bring up these points if they haven't been made by the others:

- A teacher needs to **KNOW THE SKILL** well to teach it.
  —Your teacher did not know what he was doing.
  —In dog class you will be well-prepared.

- Communicate **LEFT/RIGHT WHILE FACING** the students.
  —In class it might work better if the demonstration or instruction is oriented in the same direction the students are facing.

- Make certain that students are **FAMILIAR WITH THE LANGUAGE** being used.
  —Teach the needed vocabulary: is that funny shape a quadrilateral, a squished rectangle, or a parallelogram?
  —Establish a common language in class.
  —Don't assume that a familiar word to you is familiar to students.

- There must be **STUDENT OWNERSHIP** in the task.
  —Were there statements like, "Let's try" instead of, "Do this"?

- Students need to feel free to **ASK A QUESTION.**

- Teachers need verbal **FEEDBACK** from your students.

- Teachers need to check if students are **UNDER PRESSURE.**

Tell the participants that you purposefully set them up for a less than positive experience. It's not a good feeling. We can make our classes a lot less stressful with some planning. For one thing, instructors must know the material they are teaching inside and out.

Just to make everyone feel better, do the exercise again. Same players, except say, "Scribes, you are off duty now, but keep your secrets! You are plain old observers now, but thanks for your help. We'll hear from you later."

Let's do it again. Same time limit, same rules. There is one rule change for the instructor. The instructor gets to see the solution. This time, when the students' backs are turned and everyone is settled, put up the solution so the teacher can see it. GO!

More than half and often all of the groups finish their puzzles. I sort of fudge on the timing until everyone finishes. There is usually more discussion and then it's a good time for a break.

After the break, reconvene in the normal sitting arrangement, not the work groups. Ask the scribes to deliver their papers to the leader. The leader then reads off the tallies and also reads the one negative statement on the paper (if any). It's less embarrassing if the report is done this way, no one has to own up to his negative statement, but they usually do!

This is the starting point for a drill on turning negative, unhelpful comments into the same message only in a more positive, instructional way.

The leader should be prepared with some canned negative comments and be prepared to brainstorm with the students for substitutes that are more helpful.

The variations to the Chinese puzzle exercise are endless. Make up your own. One of my favorites is to have the groups pull a card. On the card is a common disability, such as a handler who is hard of hearing. Have the group come up with an adaptive plan to teach the puzzle to a hard of hearing student.

A template of the puzzle appears in the Appendix as INSTRUCT Chinese Puzzle.doc, "The Chinese Wisdom Puzzle." If you get tired of the plain square puzzle, call a toy shop to see if they carry the game. These websites have many interesting configurations of the same seven pieces:

*www.ex.ac.uk/cimt/puzzles/tangrams/tangint.htm*
*www.strongmuseum.org/kids/images/tangrid.print.gif*

## CROSS-TRAINING FOR TRAINING TRAINERS!

We're not so different from other trainers training other skills. There's a wealth of published information on adult learning. One of my favorite authors is Gary Kroehnert. His book, *Basic Training for Trainers,* starts out by warning the reader (the student instructor) not to be a NINCOMPOOP. Then he goes on to explain the Top 10 bloopers new trainers (read instructors) can make:

| | |
|---|---|
| **N** | Not being prepared |
| **I** | Inadequate content |
| **N** | Not delivering the goods |
| **C** | Constantly boring the trainees |
| **O** | Overload of information |
| **M** | Misreading the group |
| **P** | Poor pacing |
| **O** | Omission of practice |
| **O** | Odd or distracting visuals or verbals |
| **P** | Poor handling of questions |

# CHAPTER 6 REVIEW QUESTIONS

1. List three silent acknowledgement signals.
   a.
   b.
   c.

2. Make up three positive comments for when everything is going wrong for a student.
   a.
   b.
   c.

3. List three things that have made you angry in class in the past.
   a.
   b.
   c.

4. List three different strategies for diffusing your anger over the points listed in Number 3.
   a.
   b.
   c.

5. Make an analogy (a comparison to illustrate a concept, using different subject matter) for an important lesson you teach in class.

6. Make a plan to politely ask two students to stop talking during your demonstrations.

7. When listening to the radio or TV, take note of a negative, unhelpful statement. Think of ways to convey the necessary information in a more positive tone.

8. Which is an example of Thomas Gordon's "active listening technique"?
   a. While you speak, move around a lot to keep your student's attention on you.
   b. Repeating in your own words what the client has told you.
   c. Ask for more details after every point the student makes.

9. Direct warnings, interrogation, and probing is
   a. apt to be a roadblock to further communication.
   b. the best way to let the student know you are very serious about your job.
   c. the only way to make a distinction between right and wrong.

Answers: 8. b  9. a

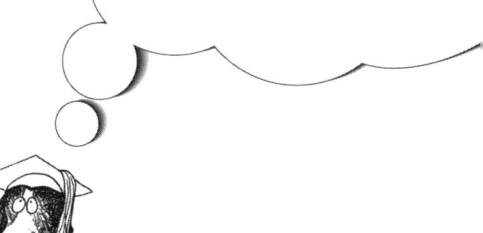

Chapter 6  People Skills

## ADDITIONAL READING/RESOURCES

De Bono, E. (1990). *Lateral Thinking.* New York: Penguin.

Gordon, T. (2003). *Teacher Effectiveness Training.* New York: Three Rivers Press.

Gordon, T. (2003). *Parent Effectiveness Training.* New York: Three Rivers Press.

Keirsey, D. and Bates, M. (1984). *Please Understand Me: Character and Temperament Types.* Del Mar, California: Prometheus Nemesis Book Company.

Krames, L., Graham, J., Alloway, T. (1995). *Sniffy the Virtual Rat.* Pacific Grove, CA: Brooks Cole Publishing.

Kroehnert, G. (1999). *Basic Training for Trainers.* Australia: Synergy Books International.

Mackay, H. (1994). *Why Don't People Listen? Solving the Communication Problem* (Dolly Fiction). Sydney: Pan Macmillan Australia Pty Ltd.

Miller, P. (2001). *The Power of Positive Pet Dog Training.* New York: Howell Book House.

Tawzer Dog Videos and DVDs, P.O. Box 423, Meridian, Idaho 83680, 1(888)566-3003, *Tawzer2@msn.com* (Videos and DVD's of Terry's programs and others).

Von Oech, R. (1990). *A Whack on the Side of the Head.* New York: Warner Books.

# CHAPTER 7

# CLASS ORGANIZATION

*"The goal of education is to create people who are capable of doing new things, not simply repeating what other generations have done."*

—Jean Piaget

# DEFINITION OF A GOOD TRAINING CLASS

A good training class does not fit into a certain mold. What is working well for Legacy's students and staff might not be right for another community. A good class is the result of carefully evaluating what your students really need. The way you successfully meet your goals is an expression of your own personality and aptitudes.

In my opinion, a successful instructor will:

- Conduct the majority of the exercises by reinforcing good behavior rather than waiting for a mistake and then punishing the inappropriate behavior.

- Give owners a measure of individual attention and coaching rather than simply calling out general directions. We don't want students to feel lost in the crowd.

- Keep the ratio of five students or less to one instructor to ensure some one-on-one time for each student. If larger classes are a must, recruit and train associate instructors.

- Offer skills that fit the lifestyle of your students. You can determine the exercises to include based on your experience, an overview of past student profiles, student feedback, and evaluation forms.

- Have a pre-planned curriculum and advertise accordingly. Use a few words of definition in even the shortest ad. For example "basic obedience" could mean almost anything. "Pet dog manners" is a bit more specific.

- Stick to the general advertised lesson plan but be flexible to a certain extent. Build in time to add to or change your lessons a little to meet the requests or needs of individuals while keeping within the planned class objectives.

- Will have the class under reasonable control. It should be clear to any stranger walking into the training area who the instructor is and what is happening in the class. However, don't confuse enthusiasm and animation with lack of order! A good class can have both.

- Provide the most humane and effective training for the particular needs of those involved. A good class doesn't stop at teaching cue/response. A good class has a positive influence on the relationship between the dog and the dog's family, and their impact on their community.

# The Site and Equipment for Your Class

The business chapter has information on site selection and a list of the common equipment needs. Tap into your network to get the very best ideas on this subject. Before construction began at our current location, I made contact with other class instructors and asked them a few questions:

1. What do you dislike most about your current location?

2. What do you like best about your location?

3. If you had unlimited power and money, what would be the number one change you would make in your training site? (It's fun to dream!)

With expert information from your peers, go out there and find a place! Set no limitations. Desperate for an indoor location, I once asked the mayor of our town if we could use city hall! After looking at me as if I were from Mars . . . or Venus, she said, "Why not! Let's try it. But if anything goes wrong, you're out on your ear" (and she didn't define "anything"). Legacy held classes for 16 years in city hall without being thrown out. It doesn't hurt to ask! We've held classes in the church basement, in a parking garage, in the vet's waiting room, in the park, in the American Legion Hall, in the foyer of a university building, in the national guard armory, in the nursing home parking lot (with lots of entertained spectators looking out the windows), and in The Boys' and Girls' Club building (compete with boys and girls in the next room). We even held classes in a condemned school building once!

# The People in Class

Chapters 5 and 6 include ways to best serve your clients. Always seek feedback to continually improve your service to the humans on the other end of the leash. Your job is not about dogs, it's about dogs and their people. Without gaining the people's compliance, you can't train the dogs.

# The Dogs in Class

## Fearful Dogs

Fearful dogs cannot focus on learning. Dogs that are just a little apprehensive can usually be put at ease. If you are lucky, you will know about the dog before class starts. If you conduct a people-only orientation, ask that dog to attend as a special guest. Assign one associate to do nothing but supervise, coach, and otherwise monitor that dog and his family. Don't make a big issue of the dog's presence with the others. Thank the class for leaving their dogs home and mention that there are some staff dogs here for demo and other special reasons. The dog can get used to the room and people with only a couple of polite staff demo dogs present. If you think this might be disruptive or will prevent the family from concentrating on the orientation information, ask them to visit an advanced class. Advanced classes are often quieter; the owners understand more about interacting with fearful dogs than the beginners' class. They should attend under the supervision and coaching of one of your associates. Perhaps the dog will only stay for a few minutes. If the dog is accepting matters well, the associate should usher him out and send him home happy and ready to start in with a regular class. If the dog needs more work, ask the owners only to come to beginners' classes to learn the lessons. Invite the owners AND the dog to a couple more advanced classes, just to sit and watch. These situations are a good opportunity to observe the dog and a great learning opportunity for your associates.

Here are some ideas to help nervous dogs. You might consider a private session to assess the dog. You might assign counter conditioning and desensitization homework. "Dog Training Class Sounds" is one of the selections in Legacy's "Sounds Good" CD series. At our center, we have a stack of washable rugs and towels. Send a towel home to help a nervous dog get used to the smell of class before class starts. Refer to the handout "MISC TapeNTowel.doc in the Appendix for more details. In Chapter 2 we referred to dogs sensitive about space as "yellow light" or cautious dogs. Putting a yellow bandana on a worried dog will remind others in class to give him plenty of space.

## Dogs That Act Out Offensively or Defensively

These dogs can be disruptive in a beginner's class. Even if they are kept under control, the other students and their dogs might be concerned. It is not the type of training environment you want for your students. If your screening procedure doesn't catch these dogs before the first night dogs are present, put an associate full time with them for the evening. The associate will keep the dog at a safe distance where he is less reactive and explain why class is not a good idea for the dog. The associate might even take the owner and dog to a completely different area, give a thirty-minute private lesson, and ask them to go home. Follow up the very next day. Set a time when they can be called before they go home. Talk with them about various alternatives for their dog, such as private lessons or slow integration into class if appropriate. Some schools have classes that group reactive dogs together. Some instructors specialize in reactive dogs.

## Disabled Dogs

Be sure the owner has approval from the dog's veterinarian to attend class. If you have been networking, the vets in your area know what you are doing in class. Offer to call the vet and explain the exercises in class before the vet makes a determination. Since there are so many variables with disabilities it really should be the decision of the vet and owner, with input from the instructor. Dogs adapt amazingly well to the little glitches life sends their way. We need to be creative and adaptive to help them out. Legacy hosts interns from the field of occupational and/or physical therapy. While the interns are here learning about dogs in general and service dogs in particular, they give me ideas about adapting human lifestyles for disabled dogs! Networking with those in different but related fields can be very helpful.

**The "Safe Home Base" in Class.** Dogs that are overly nervous or challenged physically should be given a safe place to call their own in your class. Understandably, they might be more sensitive to their personal space than normal dogs. In class select a home base with no traffic behind it. This could be a corner, or a stall you create with tables turned on end as partitions. The idea is for the dog never to be surprised in his area. Be sure to leave enough room for the dog to back up.

## Deaf or Blind Dogs

The most usual time for an instructor to notice deafness or blindness is in puppy class where a dog disabled from birth may not have had enough time with her owners for them to realize she is different. When there is an aged dog in class, be alert for loss of sight or hearing. The onset may have been gradual and the dog has adapted so far without the owners catching on. There are breeds that come to mind when you think of deafness, but don't overreact. Not ALL Dalmatians are deaf! Make sure your staff does not throw scares into people, but do make observations and refer the owner to his vet. These dogs may or may not be suitable for class training. A blind or deaf dog is often more reactive to her environment, therefore more excitable or easily frightened.

Deaf dogs seem to scan their area even more than others dogs. They are quick to pick up hand signals. A few years ago I met an entire family, including young children, who communicated successfully with their dog using standard American Sign Language (ASL) cues. Remember Clever Hans from Chapter Two? One clever dog came to class already knowing a smile was a good thing and a frown, a bad thing. Help owners elaborate on that. With a private lesson or two, we have successfully mainstreamed deaf dogs into our classes. Our protocol now is to have a private evaluation lesson and see what communication has already been established. Then we give general advice about keeping the dog safely on leash and not allowing folks to surprise their dog by touching him suddenly if the dog doesn't know they are there. The first thing we teach is a cue for "look at me." If you can give your client that one tool, the rest is standard dog training. We've used foot stomping, light flashing, but most recently we have employed a remote control vibration collar to help teach "check in." It feels like a pager. Pair a brief but consistent tap of the pager with a food lure from the dog's nose to the owner. Help them with timing. When eye contact is made, even a glance, the treat is given along with anything else the owners devise to tell the dog that he's brilliant. And so he is. The rest is simply regular reward-based dog training.

There are several recent books on living with or training deaf dogs, some from the owner's perspective. Another excellent resource is The Deaf Dog Education Action Fund, P.O. Box 369 Boonville, CA 95415, *www.deafdog.org*. Their website can direct you to Internet chat groups and a wide variety of resources including where to obtain or how to make a vibration collar.

If contacted by the owner of a blind dog, first-aid management should stress the use of fences and leashes. Owners should decide on a furniture arrangement and stick to it. Perhaps they should blindfold the children in the family (under close supervision, of course!) and allow them to experience life without vision. It might help them to remember to put their chairs back under the dining room table, place their backpacks on the hook, and, in general, to be tidier people! Mark the edges of upright surfaces with any handy odor. Roll-on or spray deodorant, lavender, balm, and disinfectant have been used. Alcohol-based products tend to evaporate and need to be refreshed once in a while. If there are steps, they can be made more negotiable in the same way, with a thin line of scent on the edge of the step that will indicate the drop off. Children are usually heard before seen anyway, but adults in the family might want to wear slippers with bells on them. Place a bell on the collar of other pets. A "check in" behavior can be taught with rewards similar to the vibrating-collar-on-deaf-dog method. An initial word, such as the dog's name, is given, then the owner can start humming a favorite tune as a beacon the dog can follow to make his way over for the treat.

Be sure grooming doesn't include removing fur or whiskers from the dog's head and mouth. They are good feelers for the dog. Many years ago I was trying to help a friend with a blind cocker create a collar with "feelers" so the dog could sense what was directly ahead of her. We went to the auto parts shop and got the old fashioned "curb feeler" springs. We tried to attach them to a variety of collars and harnesses. We failed miserably as engineers, but the dog had a great time with all the extra attention we paid to her. Enter Dave! He did it successfully and shares his skill with the world: *http:// www.btinternet.com/ ~dave.higham/buildaharness.htm*. A good first Internet resource is *www.eyevet.org* or *http://groups.yahoo.com/group/blinddogs/*. Books, chat groups, and other references can be found there.

### *Female in Estrus*

Most instructors I know allow females in season into their classes. Most pet dog classes don't encounter that many intact animals anyway. In our classes we state at orientation to call our instructors if a female comes into heat to receive instructions about what to do about class. Most of the time, the instructions are come to class and to act normally. Do not draw attention to the fact that your dog is in heat. If there is a chance the dog will be messy, you might ask that she wear absorbent panties made for that purpose. Either have them available at your training site or know just what pet shops carry them. Some instructors request the dog in season be left at home while owners attend class to learn the lessons. The dog is welcomed back in two or three weeks when she is out of season.

## Two Handlers and Two Dogs from the Same Household

Even though it might be more trouble for the owners, it's usually best if you ask that both of them not be in the same class. The dogs may look to each other for comfort when the idea is to build the relationship between the dog and his person.

## Preventing Dog Fights

A physical conflict between dogs will be almost nonexistent if you run your classes thoughtfully with proper profiling and class management. Continual reading of the dogs and proper spacing will prevent problems. If one dog is eyeballing another, walking between the dogs is often enough to prevent a potential problem for the moment, but then take the time to reposition the two, increasing the space between them. Our training room has PVC pipe dividers, about three feet high and four feet long. A fabric panel is suspended between the upper and lower bars, making a lightweight visual barrier.

If a couple of dogs have a noisy exchange of words, most of the time it's just that—noise, with no real contact. However, it's upsetting for everyone, so increase space and get back to work as normal. Don't dwell on it. The class looks to you for composure, much as I look to the flight attendants when the airplane makes a big lurch! If a contact, hang-on type of fight should break out, it needs to be stopped immediately, dogs separated, and for the sake of the rest of the people and dogs in class, the class must go on to help calm everyone's nerves. I believe the ultimate responsibility lies with the lead instructor. Don't depend on owners or even associates to help, even if you do have a game plan for such occasions. It's not easy to break up a fight without help. My first course of action would be to make a very loud, startling noise—not yelling. Yelling could seem to the dogs as if you are cheering them on. There is probably a metal dog pan close by. If not, put one where you can find it. Banging a pan on a wall might separate them long enough to grab one. Unless you have help or one dog is small enough for you to lift away, the dog you grab is at risk of continued attack from the other dog. Therefore, the standard how-to-break-up-a-dog-fight advice of grabbing one dog by the hind legs doesn't work unless there are two people working in synchrony. There is probably a chair nearby. I know this conjures up the old lion tamer image, but a chair inserted between two engaged dogs is safer than a hand. There is probably a coat or dog blanket nearby to throw over and separate one of the dogs from the other. The next-to-the-bottom line is that you are in charge and you are apt to be bitten. The bottom line is that you are in charge, so prevent dog fights.

# Associate Instructors for Your Classes

**From the Lead Instructor's Point of View**—Training class associates can make your job less demanding, allow your class to flow more smoothly, and ensure a greater measure of individual attention for students. It's an extra set of ears, eyes, and hands to make sure nothing helpful for your student is overlooked. Team teaching allows you to accomplish details that, while not urgent, are the little things that make your class special.

**From the Student's Point of View**—More than one instructor allows time for special attention should a student need or desire a bit of one-on-one coaching. It is a message to your students that the quality of their training experience is taken seriously.

**From the Associate's Point of View**—Assisting is one of the safest and most successful ways to gain skills needed to become a lead instructor. A person can gain experience without jeopardizing the education of the people and dogs in class. It reduces the stress that comes with the total responsibility of being a lead class instructor. In the early days there were very few actual instructor education courses. Helping was the common way to gain experience. In the last few years, more and more excellent opportunities have become available for instructor education.

When I was an obedience trial judge, I had very enthusiastic ring stewards, many of whom did not know exactly what to do to help. After a few shows like that, I made up a one-page "to do" list for each class I judged. Most stewards were appreciative of the direction provided by the list. Helpers are a great attribute to a training class, but clear instructions can maximize the benefits for all concerned.

The first step to become a Legacy class associate is to take a Legacy class with his or her own dog. Then, before they begin to help with class in any way, they take a look at the "to do" list on page 189.

## *Nurturing New Class Instructors*

There are books, workshops, seminars, camps, and courses designed to nurture dog training class instructors. Since I have been doing instructors' courses, I have required prospective Legacy associate instructors to attend one of those courses. I might waive the tuition and have them join a course as a work-study participant. Not every associate aspires to go on to become a lead instructor. Some people are happy and comfortable with the role of assistant. One of my best associates never, ever wanted to be a lead instructor, but was a truly effective and appreciated assistant.

# Class Associate To Do List

- ☑ Please Do attend orientation so the students know we are a team and can start to become comfortable with us. The Lead Instructor may ask you to bring your well-groomed dog for demonstrations. You will be given a part of the orientation to present.

- ☑ Please Do use the locker area assigned to you for your coat, and any other personal belongings. Let's try to keep the training area uncluttered.

- ☑ Please Do wear your Legacy shirt or vest and name tag. You might want to leave them at the training site. No problem with forgetting to bring or wear them! Set a good example by wearing appropriate shoes.

- ☑ Please Do arrive to each class at least ten minutes before class is scheduled to begin so that you can help me greet the students. Please Do provide a crate (not an x-pen) for your own dog if you choose to bring your dog to class. The first responsibility of associates is to the class. You will be too busy to be able to supervise your dog properly. It is not appropriate for associates to have dogs in the building or parking lot that are noisy or showing symptoms of stress. If your dog will be doing a demonstration, you will know ahead of time so you can be ready.

- ☑ Please Do refer to the lesson plan for each class so you know exactly where the students are in their training.

- ☑ Please Do be prepared to take over the class should the instructor have to help an individual. This will be a rare occasion.

- ☑ Please Do be pleasant and visit with the students before and after class and during breaks. If the instructors stand together during breaks, students do not feel free to come up and ask questions. Be impartial if you have personal friends in class. Be accessible, please!

- ☑ Please Do let the students know you are interested in them. Try to remember names. Make a positive remark to each individual student at least once during class. The needy student gets attention and the adept student often receives a comment. Let's not forget the average student.

- ☑ Please Do make sure your actions and words make each student think his or her dog is the neatest dog in class.

- ☑ Please Do not remark about a dog or owner, roll your eyes, or shake your head when you think no one is looking!! If you must say something to the student that could possibly be taken wrong, couple it with several positive remarks.

- ☑ Please Do help the Lead Instructor keep an eye on the observers.

- ☑ Please Do not take over a client's dog to demonstrate. The Lead Instructor will decide if such a demonstration is needed.

- ☑ Please Do remember if you are "Specifically Assigned" or "Freelancing" during the lead instructor's lesson. Freelancing means to jump in and help where needed. Examples of specific assignments:
  - Coaching one individual during the entire session
  - Watching the entire group for one particular aspect of handling

- ☑ Please Do make practice rotations smoothly. After each step of each lesson, the Lead Instructor will tell you with which student to begin. Please try to be through coaching your group at the same time as the others. (It's still a class, not a private lesson!) If there is a backlog, the lead instructor will jump in and take a few students.

- ☑ Please Do not talk to students while the Lead Instructor is talking. They will just get that much more behind. If they try to talk to you, politely hold up a shushing finger and point to the lead instructor. We'll remember to give that person attention when appropriate.

- ☑ Please Do feel free to make suggestions or corrections you know the Lead Instructor would make. If you have a different idea, if it's practical, let's talk about it first (but don't interrupt the class to do so). If, because of the safety or effectiveness of the class you MUST do something different, be sure to let the Lead Instructor know before the night is over! Different approaches are usually okay but we need to give the impression to our students that we are together.

- ☑ Please Do take action right away, without asking questions first, if you see imminent danger to a person or dog.

- ☑ Please Do plan to stay after class for our class critique. If you notice anything different about a handler or dog that you think the Lead Instructor should know, let's talk about it before you leave for the night.

- ☑ Please Do try to watch as class is dismissed and single out each client to wish him or her a good week on the way out.

- ☑ Please Do know that we appreciate your help!

**Thank You!**

When an associate is ready to accept more responsibility, the transition to Lead Instructor can be gradual. Have your associate lead an exercise the students already understand. This does not require any new instructions but the associate gets a feeling of class control. Next allow the associate to teach one new exercise. Plan this well in advance to be sure your associate is comfortable with the lesson and knows exactly how to do it. You might have your associate do a mental run through as you teach the exercise. If your associate is okay with that dry run, he or she can be the Lead Instructor for that exercise the next time it is taught. This is especially effective if you are running two classes back to back.

## Jobs for Class Helpers

There are others ways for volunteers to help you and gain experience that don't even involve team or assistant teaching. Job assignments depend on the desires and expertise of the individual helper:

- Bringing activities for children on sidelines
- Taking roll
- Fitting collars
- Equipment inventory
- Librarian
- Sending postcards to absent students
- Acquiring door prizes
- Organizing the games' equipment
- Duplicating and distributing handouts
- Maintaining a bulletin board
- Organizing name tags
- Refreshments
- Recordkeeping
- Making out certificates
- Taking photos, videos
- Returning calls
- Planning field trips
- Notifying newspapers of special events
- Planning events for last class festivities

## Perks for Associates

The vast majority of training class assistants in this world are doing it for the fun and/or experience. Here are some ideas to show your appreciation:

- A holiday season gift
- Gift certificate for a restaurant, bookshop, or pet shop
- Tuition waivers for your school's programs
- Dues paid to a special interest association
- A subscription to a training magazine
- Paid tuition for an out-of-town workshop

# ORIENTATION

Most training programs include an orientation of some sort. In the briefest form it's a chat over the phone or written information mailed before the class begins. The other extreme is an orientation that spans a couple of weeks, with homework in between. Over the years I have tried many different orientation models. Once I was asked why I conducted the first pet dog class without dogs. My answer was, "I want my students to be successful." Another instructor I respect was asked why she always had dogs attend the first session. Her answer was "I want my students to be successful."

I believe owners need a bit of knowledge before they train their dogs. I use the analogy of the horse and rider. If a horse isn't trained and a rider doesn't know how to ride, the rider will probably get into trouble. A few lucky ones will ride off into the sunset and live happily ever after, but the majority will experience a rough ride. It's the same thing with dog training. Orientation can help owners avoid sometimes irreversible mistakes.

For years Legacy has offered some kind of combination behavior and training class. Our curriculum evolved slowly and has taken many different forms. At first we had separate behavior and obedience classes. Only a few students signed up for the behavior option. I began to notice that when there was a question or someone stayed after class for extra help, it would be someone who hadn't taken the optional behavior class. The minority who got the theory first went home happy and successful after each class. I eventually decided that there would be no option. It was one class, a behavior and training class. Period. I called the behavior portion orientation.

The first models of this combined class met for seven or eight consecutive weeks. The first and second meetings were two hours each for people only. Learning theory and its practical application were presented, and students were given a background on reading dogs and a workshop, "The Toolbox" based on the book "The Toolbox for Remodeling Your Problem Dog" (Howell, New York, 1998). Although the book is currently out of print, you'll find a very condensed version of the eight remodeling tools from the Toolbox in Chapter 8. Students did homework on their leadership skills and some basic training exercises, such as establishing a reinforcer and beginning to teach a "check in" cue when the dog's name was called. The remaining five or six weeks were 50-minute sessions with the dogs. Currently Legacy is doing only the first session without dogs, but it's a two-hour session.

To be effective, orientation needs to be relevant, immediately useful, and somewhat entertaining. Theory can be hidden behind interactive exercises, visuals, demonstrations, and handouts. Our orientation is held as the first week of each new Pet Dog Manners and KinderPuppy class, the two entry level classes in our program. Owners from PuppyHeadstart, our drop-in puppy class, are encouraged to come, but they may start attending the drop-in class without going to the orientation. Students enrolled in a Legacy continuing education class are welcome to attend again. Any community member who would like to attend, whether registered for a class or not, is welcome to attend for a small fee. Allowing them to attend serves as a good introduction to Legacy classes and our training philosophy. Orientation includes live dog demonstrations, owner-interactive demonstrations, and a PowerPoint® presentation with short video clips embedded in the presentation. The PowerPoint® slides serve mainly as instructor notes and are used as a background to the live activities. When the instructor refers to a handout, that handout appears on the PowerPoint® screen. Each handout topic is identified with a unique drawing. There is time to interact with clients during several breaks scheduled throughout the orientation. Every attempt is made to keep orientation interesting and interactive.

Students attending orientation have pre-registered by completing a profile form and paying for their class. We meet our students at the door or at the edge of the parking lot and direct them to the seminar area. An associate stationed at a desk at the entry greets the family. That person also checks the name against the roster and takes care of any outstanding business, such as checking immunization records. Students are offered refreshments, given their notebook, and invited to choose seats at a table. Most of the instructors will have their dogs present, in crates, until needed for demonstrations, or entertainment! Sometimes the instructors and their dogs will mill around with the students chatting and introducing themselves. The session ends with a review and demonstration of the homework for the following week. At the end of orientation, our usual end-of-class goodbye music is played and an announcement is made that the orientation is formally over. The students are invited to visit with our dogs. Instructors then spread out and informally start performing some tricks and fun behaviors.

## *Orientation Topics*

Here is a list of the topics covered during the evening:

> Introductions
> Contact Information
> How to Use Our Facility
> Evolution of Legacy Behavior and Training Classes
> Humane Guidelines for Training
> Training Theory
> Relationship—How to Gain Attention and Leadership
> How Dogs Communicate
> How Dogs Learn
> Handouts—Three Types
> Dog Demo (Live) of Final Goals
> Use of Food Rewards, Feeding, and Nutrition
> ABC's of Training
> Law of Effect/Rewards Drive Behavior
> Use of Toys and Play as Rewards
> Live Dog Demo of Magnet Game

Equipment
Gentle Leader® Video Clip
Bonus Bones
Yellow Light Dogs—Yellow Bandanas
Laws, Health Issues
Aversives
Toolbox for Changing Unwanted Behavior
Stress Identification
Reactive Dogs
The First Class with Your Dog
Review Week 2 Homework Goals
Demonstration of Specific Exercises

## *The Orientation Notebook*

Participants in our classes receive a notebook at orientation with the materials they will need for their class. These class materials are listed in the appendix under the "PDM" heading for students enrolled in Pet Dog Manners Class. Students enrolled in our puppy classes receive the handouts listed under the heading "PUPPY" in the appendix. Students are also offered additional handouts on specific topics such as barking, digging, eating poop, and several others. These handouts are listed in the appendix under "INFO."

## *Class Time Scheduling—The Entire Course*

It's an exciting time to be a training class instructor. Access to new and different ideas is becoming easier and easier. Standards are getting higher. In general, dog training classes are following the trend of most adult education courses, which means there are fewer number of meetings in a course. A greater variety of skill levels and subject matter are also being offered. The typical dog training class meets once a week for about an hour, for a set number of weeks. Once underway, new students are not accepted into that particular course. Upon completion, the students can sign up for an advanced class. Other possible formats are listed below.

- **TWICE A WEEK** is possible with carefully guided homework and motivated owners and instructors. About 20 years ago I ran twice-a-week classes every summer for several years. It started because I tried to accommodate the schedules of my clients. In our town, most of my clients were students or in some way connected to the university. People rarely stayed in town for more than a few weeks in the summer. The classes met for four consecutive weeks and the curriculum

*Chapter 7   Class Organization*   **193**

was the same as our regular once-a-week classes that lasted seven weeks. There is pressure to do homework when you don't have a whole week to put it off. Our nice, long, warm daylight hours lent themselves nicely to twice-a-week classes.

- **TRAINING WEEKENDS OR FIVE-DAY CAMPS** are good for busy people who can't devote consecutive weeks, but can put aside a weekend for training. A lot can be accomplished in a two-day camp, but care must be taken to give both owners and dogs some down time. I found this schedule to work well: Start at 10:00 on Saturday—this allows people driving in from a distance to take their time. We quit for the day at 4:00, but would meet again from 7:00 to 9:00. On Sunday we began at 8:30 or 9:00 and finished by 4:00, giving people extra time to get home

- **PET DOG BEHAVIOR AND TRAINING PACKAGE** is a concept Legacy has been pilot testing for a couple of years. It's the regular Pet Dog Manners format plus one private or semi-private lesson. I have seen great results with some clients receiving just one extra lesson during the course. I believe it has made the difference to some people between happily continuing with their classmates to the end of the course or becoming frustrated and perhaps dropping out of class.

- **ROLLING CLASSES** are ongoing classes that people can join at any time. The teacher of such classes must have several associates and subgroups to make good progress for the students, or be satisfied with mediocrity. The very good dogs run the risk of not progressing if the teacher spends more time with the out-of-control dogs. This is a good format for people who enjoy getting together and socializing with other doggy friends and doing a little training as well. Some groups will eventually divide, splitting into higher and lower skill levels. Legacy's Puppy HeadStart is conducted as a rolling class.

- **LEVEL-ORIENTED PROGRESSIVE CLASSES** are similar to rolling classes. People can join at any time. In order for this to work, several specific skill levels are offered as separate mini-classes, either consecutively or periodically throughout a day or weekend. People can move up at their own speed and can challenge the test for a level and skip it altogether. This plan is good for people who live far away and like to devote a weekend at your school to progress with their training. The level format is good for people with sporadic schedules; it encourages people not to worry if they are absent because they won't fall behind as they would in a traditionally structured class. Their current level is always being offered. However, offering level-oriented classes use up lots of space and instructors and might not be economically feasible unless you have a large client base.

# CONSIDERATIONS WHEN CHOOSING TRAINING METHODS

## Owner Aptitude

When teaching inexperienced owners, ask yourself this question, "Can the majority of students in class use this method successfully with their dogs?" It makes no difference if it's not YOUR favorite method. Select techniques that do not place a premium on timing or athletic ability, or plan to have enough time and exercises included in your course for the owners to develop the skills needed.

## Owner Acceptance

It's human nature to be enthusiastic about things that you like, are your idea, or make total sense as the best way. Pet owners will be more successful if they fully buy into your program. Their heart needs to be in it for it to work well. Many people refuse to accept any degree of compulsion. Some people are totally against food. Be prepared to objectively spell out the pros and cons of what you are teaching and the alternatives acceptable to your school.

## The Impact on the Dog

Plan for your standard technique to work well for the majority of dogs. Expect that there will be some dogs in your class that will benefit from a different approach. Most dogs work well for food lures and rewards. Some dogs become overly reactive to a high value food treat in the hands of an inexperienced trainer. A burst of cheering for success is fine for most dogs. Some dogs will find that frightening. Most dogs don't seem to mind music in the classroom. Some dogs worry about the percussion instruments.

## Ethical, Legal, Successful, Safe, and Humane

Instructors should put the student in a position of success using methods that are safe and humane. Both the American Humane Association and the Delta Society have documents outlining humane and professional standards for dog trainers and instructors.

## Attitude of the Instructor

Last but not least, you must be fully comfortable with any method that you teach. Let your experience and knowledge show through as confidence and poise. Don't do something just because every other instructor is doing it. If your heart isn't in it, you will not be able to do a good job.

# Entry Level Classes

What classes will be the backbone of your school? How can you best serve the dogs and people in your community? Currently, Legacy offers three different entry-level classes. Two are variations on puppy classes, and the other is open to any beginner over the age of four months. In order to attend any of our advanced classes, the owner and dog must have attended a Legacy entry-level class.

## Puppy Classes—In General

"As the twig is bent . . . so grows the tree." This saying has been used to describe the ancient Japanese art of Bonsai (dwarfed trees). The same could be said of raising human children or training puppies. A review of the literature reveals the value of early childhood education in humans. The words of Robert Fulghum were inspiring to Bill and me when we were raising our children. I believe his words ring true for puppy raising as well, not to mention our own lives as adults.

Fulghum's book is entitled *All I Really Need To Know, I Learned in Kindergarten* (1990, New York, Villard Books). He says, "All I really need to know about how to live and what to do and how to be I learned in kindergarten. Wisdom was not at the top of the graduate-school mountain, but there in the sand pile . . . These are the things I learned:

- Share everything.
- Play fair.
- Don't hit people.
- Put things back where you found them.
- Clean up your own mess.
- Don't take things that aren't yours.
- Say you're sorry when you hurt somebody.
- Wash your hands before you eat.
- Flush.
- Warm cookies and cold milk are good for you.
- Learn some, think some, draw, paint, sing, dance, play and work some every day.
- Take a nap every afternoon.
- When you go out into the world, watch out for traffic, hold hands, and stick together."

Milo Pearsall, a founding member of the National Association of Dog Obedience Instructors, pioneered Kindergarten Puppy Training classes in the 1960s. Since then, a lot of thought has gone into puppy training. Dr. Ian Dunbar, founder of The Association of Pet Dog Trainers, should take a bow for getting the idea of puppy training into the mainstream.

Unfortunately, some training organizations tend to put their least experienced staff in charge of puppy classes. The thought is that the goals are less rigid, the dogs tend to get along without serious altercations, and the owners can control the pups without much skill. It takes just one adverse experience to form a hang-up that will continue to haunt the pup and her family long after they leave your class. In my experience:

- There should be a very tight window as to age grouping. Young puppies, regardless of size, can be set back by the brashness of an older pup.
- Families should be welcome, but the class should not turn into a wild, free-for-all party. Children especially should be carefully supervised, or pups could learn the wrong things about kids.
- Free play among small groups of carefully selected puppies can be beneficial to their social skills. Care must be taken not to allow bully dogs to overly dominate the quiet ones.

The ethology chapter of the book pointed out some mechanics of early learning. Instructors need to turn that science into an art form called Puppy Class.

## *Puppy HeadStart—For Very Young Puppies*

The objective of Puppy HeadStart is to provide an immediately available class for the youngest of pups. The instant availability takes advantage of the puppy "honeymoon" period when interest in the pup is high in the entire family. It also considers the importance of the onset and ending of optimal windows of training opportunity described (see Chapter 2).

HeadStart classes are held at least once a week all year long. Offering two classes a week on different days and times provides more flexible scheduling for busy families and gives puppies twice the experience. The first time a puppy participates, the family is given a suitable chew toy as a baby gift and a package of fancy poop bags. They receive a Legacy magnet for their refrigerator door that says, "Catch Them in the Act of Doing Something Good." They receive our "Crate and Housetraining" handout. Classes are about 30 minutes long. Puppies are accepted as young as veterinary approval can be obtained (see Chapter 4). We view HeadStart as a place to begin dog/owner relationship training and canine social skills while they are waiting for our more structured KinderPuppy class to start. It's free. The average stay in Puppy HeadStart is two to three visits. Depending on age, the puppy will go into either the next scheduled KinderPuppy or Pet Dog Manners class.

In class, collars are checked for proper fit. To prevent tripping, we are on the lookout for dangling leashes. This is especially important when owners are carrying puppies. We help owners read body language and judge when their pup is approaching a fear/anxiety threshold or becoming overly stimulated. If there is a play session, it is very short and it is ended before the puppies become overly aroused and before it turns into a free-for-all. At Legacy classes, we introduce pups to specifically chosen adult dogs with good manners and body language. Then, thoughtful introduction and brief play is allowed in small, carefully chosen groups of puppies, taking care that the pup does not receive or deliver bullying behaviors.

The exercises presented are spontaneous, instructor's choice. Because it's an ongoing class there will be a variety of instructors teaching over the year. The class takes on a life of its own and is guided by owner questions and whatever inspires the instructor on a given night observing the puppies. If an instructor wants some guidance on what to do on a given night, they refer to the Puppy Training Menu and choose an unchecked item. A copy of that menu is in the Appendix, INSTRUCT PuppyMenu.doc. The instructor chooses an activity from different categories of the menu and then puts a check by it to indicate the puppies in this class have completed the activity. Each week, new exercises are chosen from the different categories. It makes no difference how far the class gets on the menu. This check-off menu ensures that, regardless of who is teaching, the students are continually getting different exercises from as many different categories as possible. The same menu system is continued in KinderPuppy Class.

## *KinderPuppy Class—For Young Puppies*

The objective of KinderPuppy is to provide ongoing assistance to puppy owners during the critical period of development, up to about 16 weeks of age. It provides many novel, but positive life experiences, builds self-confidence, teaches a few basic skills, and establishes a foundation for further training.

KinderPuppy is scheduled at the same time that at least one Pet Dog Manners class begins. KinderPuppy students attend that two-hour orientation without their puppies. Students are provided with a notebook with illustrated information sheets addressing typical pet-owner concerns and some special puppy information. General information about the use of the facility is included as are community and regional pet ownership laws.

We provide several short exercises rather than spend a longer time on one activity. We are ready to change exercises to a lower key activity should the puppies become too rambunctious or overly stimulated. We coach good handling by owners.

## *Pet Dog Manners—Four Months and Older*

The objective of Pet Dog Manners is to help families and their dogs live together happily in their neighborhoods. Pet Dog Manners is Legacy's name and the format for what is generically known as a basic or beginners' class. The objectives are to:

- Provide timely and relevant information for people with dogs of any age.
- Enhance dog/owner relationship training, attention, and trust.
- Offer a flexible program to suit the behavior and training needs of the individuals.
- Make help available to clients on an ongoing basis via private lessons, phone, or e-mail consultations, specific handouts, and/or continuing education classes

In Pet Dog Manners, families learn to understand their dogs and to develop communication channels with them. Appropriate social relationships between pet and family, plus pet and other community members are taught. Many of the exercises are presented as noncompetitive games. It is a goal-oriented course, with easily reached weekly goals and a clearly defined ending goal. There is flexibility to modify the program for each individual.

The class usually consists of eight students and their dogs, a head instructor, and at least one associate instructor or trainee. In week two, the first lesson with dogs present, we try to have at least three staff members in attendance. The normal ratio is one instructor to four to five dogs. Student to teacher ratios are adjusted as the weeks go on depending on the needs of the class.

The Appendix has the information you will need to organize this class. Materials for the Pet Dog Manners class are identified with the letters PDM or INSTRUCT. You will find:

- Lesson plans and instructor's notes for each class including suggested games for each week and supplemental informational handouts appropriate for that week.

- A student handout showing the step-by-step progression of each exercise taught in PDM class.

- A student homework reminder sheet for each week. This is a page that concisely tells them where we are on the more detailed exercise sheets. The one-page handout has become known as "the yellow sheet" because it is the only yellow paper ever to appear in the student notebooks.

## INSTRUCTIONAL FORMAT FOR THE INDIVIDUAL EXERCISES

Some people are naturals at organization. Others need help remembering what comes next so as not to forget anything important. Class format eventually comes down to exactly what you will teach and how you will structure the minute-by-minute progression of each class.

I carry a clipboard with the lesson plan attached to it. Often I'll be lead instructor for several sessions of the same class. It's easy to lose track when I am doing so many classes, so the clipboard is good for me. However, sometimes I'll put the clipboard down in the middle of class to help someone, and then I can't find it when I want to refer to it!

Some instructors will keep a pack of index cards in their pockets with a segment of the class on each one. If you decide to use this method, number them in case you drop them.

There have been times when I've put my outline on PowerPoint® and I have run the outline in the background.

Other instructors will have a flip chart or overhead projector in the training room with the class outline on it in plain view

Personally I find flowcharts helpful in creating and following lesson plans. I use the flowchart metaphor "Building a House." You'll find this in Chapter 8.

## P.R.E.D.I.C.T.O.R.

Some instructors rely on acronyms to remember all the steps that are needed in teaching an exercise. The acronym **EDICT** has been borrowed and used by dog training class instructors. I first ran across it in a seminar presented by Glen Johnson, author of the book *Tracking Dog: Theory and Methods*. **E**—Explain, **D**—Demonstrate, **I**—Instruct, **C**—Correct and **T**—Train! It prompted me to expand on a good idea. Over the years I changed the C from Correct to Coach. I now use the word PREDICTOR to help remind me how to plan for, carry out, and improve each exercise. I think of it as "A PREDICTOR of a good class."

**PREDICTOR** = **P**LAN

This is the instructor's homework! What is your goal for the class and for each exercise? What methods will you use and what alternatives will you have available? Do you need more information or materials to feel comfortable with your plan? How will you break down big tasks into easy steps and sequences? Will you need help, handouts, or equipment?

**PREDICTOR** = **R**EVISE

Is there a better way to do this? What are others doing? Check with other dog training instructors, but don't stop at dog training. Teaching is teaching. For example, I learned about breaking down tasks into smaller parts from a juggling instructor— yes a clown taught me valuable dog training lessons! I got good ideas on how to orient my body for demonstrations from an aerobics instructor. Can you borrow and adapt something new from a different discipline? Refer to evaluations! Comments from past students are invaluable for class revision; they can help you decide which direction to take, or not to take!

**PREDICTOR** = **E**XPLAIN

Now you have the students in front of you in class. The first thing you want to do for each exercise is to paint a word picture of the exercise. Give them the name of the exercise and the practical reason for teaching it. What does it lead to? What is the foundation? How can students apply the exercise to their daily lives? What cue will eventually be used in conjunction with that behavior? And then, of course, explain the first step to teach the exercise.

**PREDICTOR** = **D**EMONSTRATE

People learn best with lots of repetition. Talk the students through the exercise again. This time show them as you go, step-by-step. How will you show them? Draw a picture? Do it yourself with a dog? Use a puppet? Chapter 6 gives lots of ideas on how to make demonstrations more effective for your students.

### PRED**I**CTOR = **I**NSTRUCT

This step is hands on for the students, but with coaching. Don't turn them loose to make mistakes. Get it right the first time. Sometimes an instructor will stand in front of the group facing in the same direction as the students. We ask the students to think their way through what the instructor is doing in front of them. No dogs. Students just watch and imagine they are doing it with their dogs. In our classes we have a small student-to-teacher ratio. We are able to give each student and dog individual attention as they perform the exercise. When each student has had an individual turn with an instructor, we might do more repetitions as a class. Training is a physical skill requiring coordination. Make sure your students have the moves before you send them home.

### PREDI**C**TOR = **C**OACH

You can never learn enough about teaching others. Read some books on coaching sports. Dog training is a mechanical skill just like hitting a baseball. Before you comment, ask yourself: Is this instructive? Or am I just reporting what I'm seeing? Pinpoint proper actions and praise the students for their expertise. A well timed, "That's it!" will make your client smile. If you see a mistake or omission, point it out to the student in a positive way. Be clear and specific. "Correct your dog" is not positive or instructive. "Let's try it this way" is more instructive than, "That won't work." Careful coaching of each student is important. Unless the owner does it correctly in class, he will not be able to practice correctly at home. In every class there will be one or two students who will require extra help. It should not, however, be given at the expense of the other students. In coaching, remembering the four I's is helpful. Let's use the problem of the dog that trips the owner while walking: Identify the specific problem: The dog is leaping around instead of sitting when the owner stops while heeling. Isolate the weak link. It's because the owner is holding the lure too high. Make a plan to Improve on just that segment. Go back to the "magnet game" with the food lure held closer to the dog's nose. Integrate the improved bit back into the exercise. Put the improved lured sit back into the walking on leash.

### PREDIC**T**OR = **T**RAIN

Student's homework! Don't send them home with the recommendation, "Practice!" Tell them how to practice. Have them show you what they will do before they go home. Tell them how long to practice. Give them reasonable goals. Give them handouts to remind them what to do and how to do it, and what to do when it doesn't work.

### PREDICT**O**R = **O**BSERVE

Observe students during class to think of ways to help or improve. Get observations and opinions from your associate instructors. How are the students doing compared to last week? How are they doing compared to other classes at this stage?

Are the people and dogs successful, or are they struggling? Is it time to try a different approach?

**PREDICTO**R = **R**EVIEW

Review your program to be sure you are meeting your class goals. Do you have measures in place to evaluate student progress? On the last week of class do the dogs look like your demo dog from orientation? If not, break the exercises down more. Rethink the homework assignments. What do your associates think? In the Appendix is a graph that allows you to see at a glance the steps needed to teach any one exercise. It's listed as INSTRUCT PREDICTOR.doc, "P.R.E.D.I.C.T.O.R. An Acronym Aid for Instructional Formatting." I find it helpful for working out program revisions.

# TRAFFIC CONTROL STRATEGIES FOR STATIONARY EXERCISES

## Individual or Group Exercises in Class?

A class instructor always has this dilemma: giving individual attention to one student at the risk of boring or alienating the others. Neither the people nor the dogs like to stand around. If working with one person is a useful (but short!) demonstration for all, there is not a problem. Many instructors without assistants have the class perform each exercise together on the instructor's command and stand in a place where he can see all of the class. For this to work well, you need very small classes and students who are at comparable levels. The problem is that some students forget to follow your directions carefully, and they move ahead—return to their dogs on a Sit-Stay without being told to, for example. This compounds the problem of the instructor being able to see all things at all times.

A workable compromise is to introduce and demonstrate the exercise that is to take place. Ask for a volunteer to demonstrate the exercise again. Then, split up the associate instructors so that they rotate through the class giving each student one time to perform the exercise and receive some coaching. This creates some stand-around time, but you can stress that the students WATCH the others because their turn is coming up in a minute or two. When each student has received individual attention at least once, do the exercise again as a group. Their questions and difficulties will have been addressed individually.

## Positioning the Dogs and People within the Training Area

It's best not to do active, moving exercises in the first few classes. Give the dogs a chance to settle down. Each owner should have a chair that will be the focal point and a means of controlling how close the dogs get to each other. A "U" shape for arranging the chairs, with the lead instructor at the opening of the "U," is a very useful set up.

Try to place the shy dogs where other dogs don't have to move past them—in other words, far away from the entry door. For reactive dogs—either place them as far away from the door as possible or position an associate nearby.

# TRAFFIC CONTROL PATTERNS FOR MOVING EXERCISES

Space-wise, one of the more difficult exercises to manage in a class is leash work. The big mistake is to do too much, too close, too fast. In my opinion, just a few minutes here and there throughout the session is much more effective. Often I'll start a heeling session by saying, "Walk your dog 1, 2, 3; you're done." That's right—only 3 seconds of heeling. End the exercise before the rowdy dogs lose composure, before the herding dogs want to chase, and before the anxious dogs cave in. K.I.S.S.—once again, keep it short and simple.

Consider having only a few dogs work at a time to keep arousal levels low. Don't bore the others; have an associate work with them on a stationary exercise. Practicing a variety of safe heeling patterns will not only teach the dog to be more fluent at leash work, it will also be less boring for the owners (and instructors!). Lots of heeling can take place in the form of games, but if you really want to do a bit of a drill, here are some patterns to consider (O = Owner, D = Dog).

## *Perimeter Heeling*

Many instructors rely on the perimeter pattern. Often a circle or an oval shape is used. Squares and rectangles are common for indoor training areas. Expect the perimeter to get smaller and smaller when owners cut corners! It's also common for an owner to "get lost" and go the wrong way. To keep the owners walking in the right direction, mark the path with powdered chalk on the grass, tape on a hard surface, or draw a line in the dirt. You can also mark the perimeter with cones or another highly visible object. Direct the people to walk OUTSIDE of those markers. The lead instructor should NOT stand in the middle of the perimeter as she should have all of her class in sight at all times. Stand to one side and back a little, and position associates where they can be most useful.

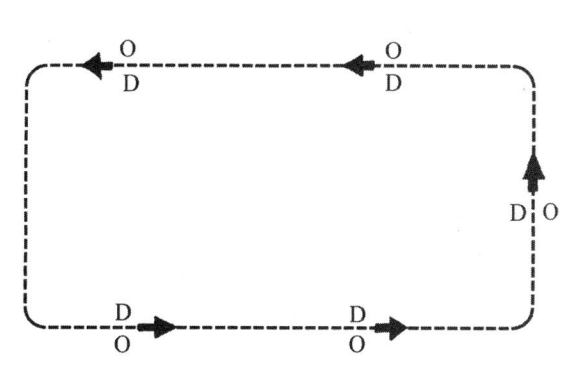

Perimeters are not the best choice for beginners. There's always a dog to chase or sniff in front and always a dog to distract or frighten from behind. Rarely do people in class walk at the same speed, which also creates a traffic jam and violates "space" issues.

## Double Perimeter Heeling

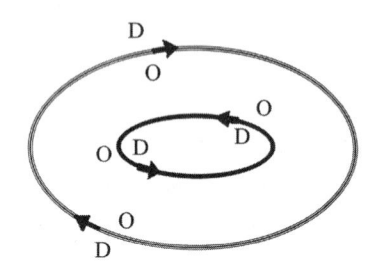

To save space, use an oval (square, rectangle, circle) within another. Large dogs use the outside because they walk faster and small dogs are on the inside. Changing the direction each group travels changes the difficulty of the heeling pattern. Dogs to the inside (or left) gives the owners a bit more control because they are walking into their dogs and helping them turn inward with their own bodies. Use maximum separation to increase safety and reduce distraction.

## Heeling in a Row

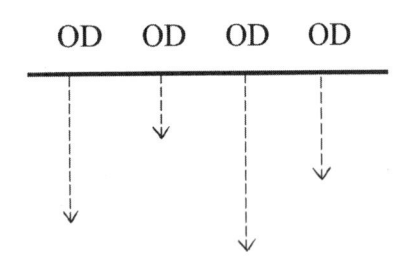

Heeling in a row is a good one if you have plenty of space. If the instructor stands at one end and toward the front or back, it's easy to see all of the students. Rather than all starting out at the same time, you can tell each row to start three seconds after the next. This puts more separation between the students and their dogs. You can direct them to another line in the distance and tell them to about turn there or simply call out an about turn before they get too far away.

## Heeling between Targets

Each student has two specific targets to walk toward such as posters on opposing walls, two chairs, or two marks on the floor. You might be able to do away with targets and simply put lines on the floor for each to follow. In this way, no dog has a dog in front of him (to chase!); no dog has one behind him (to be afraid of). Each team can do about turns independently of the others, whenever they reach their own target.

## Tracing Alphabet Letters

Students take turns tracing letters that have been drawn on the floor with chalk or masking tape. Some letters are more difficult than others. For letters with intersecting lines, like A, students stop and "Sit" their dogs before proceeding.

## Block Heeling

This is a good advanced pattern. The instructor calls, "Walk your dog, turn left, turn right, about turn, sit your dog, go fast, go slowly" in various order. Dogs must perform with others working closely around them.

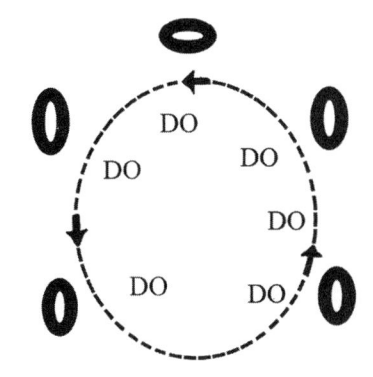

## Chairs as Targets

Dog and owner can do left, right, and about turns in place, using their chair as a target. Students might be asked to circle their chair—left circle, then right circle. They might be asked to progress to the next chair (tell them clockwise or counterclockwise) and "Sit" their dogs.

# INSTRUCTIONAL FORMAT FOR HOMEWORK ASSIGNMENTS

All of Legacy's Pet Dog Manners homework assignments are in the appendix. Use them as guides to formulate your own assignments. You will have to decide how you will assign homework. Here are some popular plans:

1. **Goal Oriented**
   This format describes WHAT the dog should look like on each exercise by the next class. "Practice the Sit-Stay exercise until your dog can do it without moving, without your help, for 30 seconds." Be sure you teach the skills during the class to allow the client to accomplish the goal. Most instructors rely on this format to help keep the class at a somewhat even level.

2. **Time Oriented**
   Tell the students to "practice the Sit-Stay exercise—15 minutes a day." Unfortunately, dogs are not uniform in the amount of time it takes them to become proficient at an exercise.

3. **Rep Oriented**
   "Do a Sit-Stay exercise 10 times per day." There is too big a risk of under training or over training a dog with this strategy.

4. **Personal Best**
   Have your students set personal challenges. They can measure their progress from week to week, regardless of what the rest of the class is doing. See the Appendix for Legacy's personal best homework ideas.

5. **Resource Room Option**
   Consider having a shelf or closet set aside as a resource room/space. If you don't have the luxury of a permanent facility, you could have a resource box. Books and videos that support your lessons are made available to loan to students.

# Continuing Education Classes

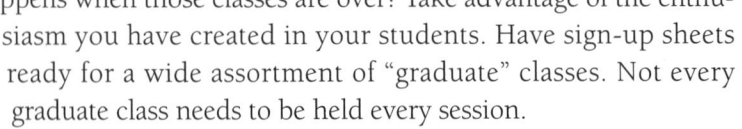

Puppy classes are so fun! Basic training of pet manners is so rewarding! But what happens when those classes are over? Take advantage of the enthusiasm you have created in your students. Have sign-up sheets ready for a wide assortment of "graduate" classes. Not every graduate class needs to be held every session.

Here are some of my favorite continuing education classes and some class ideas from other schools I have visited:

## Pet Dog Manners II

*Objective:* Provide an immediate, familiar setting in which to continue training the basics. Less structured than PDM, the exercises are planned to help dogs gain fluency in basic skills including social graces. PDM II gives people and their dogs more confidence in each other and it's a prerequisite for taking part in other specialized continuing education classes.

## Fun and Games Class 101

*Objective:* Have a good time while continuing to train the dog in a structured and supervised environment. All of the basics learned in the entry level class will be covered and a few more will be taught. The exercises are all presented as games. Examples of games are in the Appendix.

## Fun and Games Class 102

*Objective:* Continue the good times while playing training games in a structured, supervised environment. Participants must have completed Games 101.

## Drama Dogs

*Objective:* Provide fun and training practice . . . to a theme. Well-known plays are selected and dogs are cast for parts. Play practice and costuming is ongoing and the class concludes with a public performance.

## Run, Jump, and Fetch Classes

*Objective:* Promote fun and exercise and try out new skills. A motivationally shaped retrieve is taught. Practice on low level jumps will be offered. We will teach a front paw target touch and dog-to-dog manners. Fast, reliable recalls are stressed. Flyball for fun is the end goal of this class.

## Click a Trick Class

*Objective:* Practice catching and shaping a behavior while improving your skills at using timing and rewards. Review the basics and put them together into trick formats. All students use a clicker. The instructor will work with owners to develop safe tricks that appeal to the owner and are appropriate for the dog. Safety and fun will be stressed.

## Kids and Canines

*Objective:* Help children from 7–12 years of age understand and have a good relationship with the family dog and all dogs in their future. The dogs attending must have completed Pet Dog Manners I and II before the child can enroll. Skill games, dog appreciation, lots of fun, and safety around dogs will be covered.

## Dancing with Dogs

*Objective:* Folks of all ages can continue to work with and enjoy their dogs in a supervised training environment. As a class, everyone will do various square dances, reels, and line dancing. No dance experience is needed. Individuals can work on their own dance routine, selecting music, speed, and steps to match their personalities and ability. For some ideas on individual moves, Sandra Davis has an excellent book on freestyle basics called *Dancing with Your Dog*. You can order it via her website: *www.caninefreestyle.com*. For square dancing, ask around. There is probably a club in your area. Mike King has a good website on square dance basics, the information is also on CD. His website is *www.squaredancecd.com*.

## Let's Get Ready To . . . Rally

*Objective:* Provide a class that ends in a structured competition event where students can demonstrate the skills they learned. Rally (or Rally-O for Rally Obedience) is a sport in which the dog and handler complete a designated course. It can be an on-leash or off-leash event, timed or not timed, scored or not scored. The dog and handler proceed through a course of 10 to 20 stations. A sign at each station announces what skill is to be performed.

## Demonstration Team

*Objective:* Promote motivational training to the public while getting together for a fun time. Games, drill team routines, tricks, and dances can be presented for specific occasions such as community parades, school assemblies, community markets, half-time entertainment at athletic events, or Sunday afternoons at an animal shelter. The team can perform in roped off sections at a mall, train station, or grocery parking lot. Free handouts for the observers will provide information about motivational dog training and useful tips for pet dog owners.

## Animal-Assisted Activity Classes

*Objective:* Work with health care and dog training professionals to select dogs suitable for visiting nursing homes and other health care facilities. Strict guidelines for the initial screening of both dog and handler will be followed. Owners must understand the animal-assisted activity concept and be willing to meet the special requirements for a handler of such dogs. Only stable dogs with reliable manners are selected. Both dog and handler attend regular classes to refresh the basic training, learn dependable special behaviors suitable for facility visiting, and learn about the various aspects of the populations to be visited.

## Agility Foundation Class

*Objective:* Introduce dogs and owners to the sport of agility. Fitness, safety, and control are stressed. The class focuses on communication techniques important for agility, building teamwork and motivation, canine conditioning, and proper jumping techniques.

## Obedience Competition

*Objective:* Prepare dogs and handlers for high scores and good attitude in AKC obedience trials. We will define and refine the mandatory Novice exercises. We'll provide lots of distraction training. We'll cover the AKC regulations and judging procedures, work on handling and ring presence, and go through mock trials.

## Supervised Floor Time

*Objective:* Provide a climate-controlled safe area in which owners and competitors can practice. At least one instructor will be present at all times to help owners solve problems or to run through obedience trial exercises—anything that the owner needs.

## Game Night

*Objective:* Provide a family evening out with the dog for fun and for a little practice and socialization for everyone—humans and dogs. Groups sit at card tables and play board or card games. A good board game to use for this event is the game "My Dog Can Do That." Owners select an activity card. Their dog must perform the basic training task on the card. If the dog successfully performs the task, the token is moved on the game board. If you can't find a copy of this out-of-print game, buy a package of index cards and make up your own. You can also use this method to modify basic card games. Identify a particular suit. Whenever a card in that suit is drawn, the owner must select an index card and perform the exercise for extra points. Refreshments, breaks, and training tips are furnished during the exercises. This class can be a series of meetings, or a one-time event.

### The Nose Knows Class

*Objective:* Allow dogs the natural pleasure and stimulation of using their noses. Provide new and interesting things for owners to do with their dogs. Depending on the season, scent discrimination (touch or retrieve), hide-and-seek, the three-cup game, and tracking are a few of the activities possible. This can be an indoor or outdoor event.

### Feisty Fidos

*Objective:* Teach dog-reactive dogs to get along better with each other. Some instructors organize special small classes to help overcome dog-to-dog issues. Both operant and classical conditioning techniques are used. For tips from the experts: *Feisty Fidos—A Training Manual* by Pia Silvani and *Feisty Fido: Help for the Leash Aggressive Dog* by Patricia McConnell and Karen London.

### Good Citizen Prep Class

*Objective:* Become fluent in the skills necessary to pass the American Kennel Club Good Citizen test. It's not difficult to become an evaluator and this class is fun to train. The AKC gives certificates for the performance of ten everyday trained behaviors. Contact information for the AKC is listed at the end of this chapter.

### Local or Regional Good Dog Organizations Class

*Objective:* Grant special privileges for people and dogs that put in extra time at training. How about a Good Dog Club for your city or county? Perhaps you could work with your local shelter on a training and testing program. Dogs and owners who complete the program receive special recognition. A laminated card may be given that allows dogs into local hotels and restaurants and any other public place that will cooperate with the program. The program I helped develop in Japan, "The Japanese Canine Good Citizen Program," is a national program. It's not associated with a kennel club. Those who pass the test get a leather passport with photos of the dog and owner and special privileges at public places in the country of Japan. The test must be taken every two years for recertification.

## ONE-SKILL, ONE-TIME SEMINARS

*Objective:* Give a crash course for those with little spare time. The idea is to give a quick head start for creating or changing some of the most important pet behaviors. The class will devote approximately 90–120 minutes to training one behavior. Dogs may or may not attend. The seminar will be supplemented with PowerPoint® slides, interactive exercises, and live demonstrations. The course includes detailed, illustrated information about the topic. Loaner books and videos from our resource room are made available.

Topics that have been successfully presented as one-skill seminars are:

## Leadership Headstart

*Objective:* Describe the theory of leadership and provide take-home exercises to help owners establish communication channels and an appropriate relationship with their dog. This is not a behavior or training class. The seminar helps structure everyday interactions with the family pet. Each participant is given Legacy's pocket-sized pamphlet *"TAKE THE L.E.A.D." Leadership Education for Anyone with a Dog.*

## Dog Selection

*Objective:* Provide a pre-ownership workshop to help people make informed decisions about bringing a new dog into the family. What type of dog is suitable for your family's lifestyle? What are some basic characteristics to look for in a puppy or in an adult dog? What are some good questions for breeders and shelters? Several dogs from the local foster home group will be present for evaluation. Sue Sternberg is an especially good resource for screening dogs. Her website is *www.suesternberg.com*.

## The Toolbox for Remodeling Your Problem Dog

*Objective:* Give a short, convenient, and affordable overview of motivational training to change unwanted behavior. The pros and cons of each method will be discussed. Information about how to determine the dog's motivation for the behavior will be shared. The session ends with an interactive workshop to suggest possible tools appropriate for a particular dog's behavior.

## The Bark Stops Here

*Objective:* Help owners figure out why their dog is barking. Determine reasonable quiet-dog goals and give management ideas as first aid. This workshop is a good follow-up to a "Toolbox" workshop, but it stands alone nicely as help for the barking dog. The workshop includes Legacy's book, *The Bark Stops Here*.

## Stress Reduction and the Latchkey Dog

*Objective:* Identify and reduce stress, especially in dogs left home alone. Management techniques, home alone hobbies, and many enrichment ideas will be shared as well as an explanation of counter conditioning.

## Come When Called

*Objective:* Help owners realize that the word "Come" is not a substitute for a leash or fenced yard. Owners will learn how to establish an emergency "Come" cue, how to avoid bad habits, and how to manage a dog that doesn't come when called. Owners will be encouraged to think about the behavior from the dog's point of view.

# SPECIAL EVENTS

*Objective:* Find an excuse to get together with other dogs and their people to have some fun.

**Birthday Parties.** Once a month, open your school for a party, which includes all the dogs with birthdays in that month. Invitations are sent out to former students. A birth month is assigned to dogs of unknown background! You can even out the numbers in that way. Show off tricks, play games, eat cake (dog food cake for dogs), and work through some basics as a refresher. This event could be offered free of charge.

**Guest Workshop.** This is a half-day to two-day workshop on a special topic. Dogs, and their owners, will have the opportunity to learn about topics not offered by your school. The workshop can provide continuing education opportunities for instructors. Some topics might include massage therapy, tracking, nutrition, pet first aid, or holistic animal care.

**January—New Year's Resolution Workshop.** Offer a free, 50-minute general class to get folks back in the habit of training their dogs. These can be scheduled throughout the month or on a designated day. Owners and dogs still pre-register for this workshop, so groups can be kept to a manageable size.

**February—Valentines for Animals.** People and dogs play heart, love, and valentine theme games. Everyone brings a different kind of homemade or purchased dog cookie. The participants decorate and assemble bags of assorted cookies to be delivered to the elderly with pets or to shelter dogs.

**March—Spring Cleaning.** Recruit appropriate students from your dog classes to donate a few hours bathing and grooming dogs at the local shelter under the supervision of shelter staff.

**April—Nature Walk.** Go to a park, beach, or woods. People and their dogs split up to look for something interesting to show the others. Give the group a clearly defined area and a time limit. For example: "The area is the beach from the edge of the water to the beginning of the cliffs. The northern boundary is the giant dead tree over there and the southern limit is where the stream comes out to meet the ocean. Your time limit is 20 minutes. Let's synchronize our watches! Please come back to our meeting place here by the big rock when 20 minutes are up." Items of interest you might discover: a pretty shell, a starfish, a beach agate, some unusually shaped driftwood, perhaps even an eagle feather. Take turns leading tours to the items of interest.

**May—Help Your Vet Month.** In many areas, veterinarians give free rabies shots and parasite dips. Your students could assist with this by entertaining the dogs and owners gathered with tricks and games or they might teach some basic training skills, too.

**June—Old-Fashioned Picnic.** Families gather for a potluck picnic at a place where there is water for people and dogs to play. Games such as baseball and scavenger hunts are organized for the dogs and owners.

**July—Walk in the Woods.** Find a nice, cool wooded area, perhaps a park. Play "Go Find." Set clearly defined area limits. You might want to go out ahead of time and tie some bright yarn around trees to form the boundary of the area you've chosen. Remove the yarn when done. We don't want to turn this into a search and rescue party. Within the area hide a variety of biodegradable items—walnuts, for example. Ahead of time the leader has put a number between 1 and 5 on each walnut. People, with their dogs on leash, search for and gather the nuts. Everyone must return to the starting point at a designated time. The scores are tallied. The participants don't know the formula for tallying the scores. For example, add up the walnuts numbered 1, 2, 4 and 5, and then deduct any walnuts numbered 3 from that total. The day can end by playing a game of on-leash hide and seek. Leaders take turns holding the dogs behind a blind. The dog's owner says goodbye and goes a short distance to hide behind a tree or rock. The leader then goes with the dog on leash to find his owner for a happy reunion.

**August—Water Play Party.** The best place for this party is probably outdoors. Enjoy a cool afternoon playing games with dogs. Invent games such as: Who can retrieve a tennis ball from the tub? Who can retrieve a sunken Kong from a tub? Who can retrieve a water balloon? Form two teams: Owners must weave through five poles and pass the cup on to the next person with their dogs on leash, holding a cup of water in the same hand holding the leash. The team that ends up with the most water in the cup wins. Go surfing. Dogs wear a visor and sunglasses. They must do a Stand-Stay on a surfboard (on dry ground please!) while listening to 30 seconds of a Beach Boy's tune. Another activity—who can dig the best hole in the sand in the allotted time?

**September—Back To School Night.** Just like the New Year's resolution workshop, invite past students to come in for a free lesson.

**October—Halloween Party.** Host a costume contest with various categories for judging costumes. For example, best dog and owner combo, most scary, most original, etc. Play a trick and treat game. While still in costume, each dog and owner visits the other participants for a trick or treat. The dog must perform a behavior for a treat, such as Sit, Down, or Stand.

**November—Make Holiday Gifts.** Work on Christmas gifts for shelter or other needy dogs. Ask people to collect clean unmatched socks. Many people have lots of mismatched socks, but the leader should be collecting socks throughout the year from relatives and places like Goodwill or garage sales. A production line will be set up for stuffing the socks with batting and creating "tubes." The tubes are then sewn together in a spiral to form a dog cushion. Meanwhile the dogs are doing supervised Down Stays or quiet crate time (whichever the dog needs practice on) with staff members. Other arts and crafts activities might include decorating dog collars and leashes, and making dog themed Christmas ornaments. At intervals from 5 to 10 minutes each, music is played. That's the cue to go get your dog. It's time for a training game before we resume arts and crafts.

**December—Christmas Carols.** Gather at someone's house. Pass out song sheets. Bring flashlights. As you take your dogs for a nice winter's walk, spend a few minutes caroling. Return to the house for hot chocolate—no, not for the dogs! Have a gift grab for the dogs. Each person brings one wrapped dog gift. All the gifts are piled in the center of the room. One at a time, each dog has a chance to choose a gift from the pile.

## OPTIONS FOR THE LAST CLASS

Most schools do something special for the last night of class. Sometimes it is some type of evaluation test. A one-time test is not always the best gauge of success. Testing puts some owners under so much stress that they don't show up on the last night of class. Some schools still do a pass or fail test. I have mixed emotions about that. I opt not to do a test at all. However, some owners do better with a goal or a bit of pressure to excel. I've compromised by giving challenge tests throughout the course. They are optional. One of Legacy's challenge tests is called the Leader of the Pack Figure 8. It's described in the appendix, PDM 4 LeaderOfThePackFig8.doc, "Leader of the Pack Loose Leash Figure 8 Challenge." Other challenges can be found in INSTRUCT BonusBones/Challenges, "Class Challenges and Bonus Bones."

For Legacy graduations, we have refreshments, including gourmet dog biscuits, and everyone gets a very nice Certificate of Completion. Sometimes we roll the certificates and place them in the arms of a small stuffed dog that is wearing a traditional mortarboard graduation hat. Alternately, we give ribbons of participation—red, white, and blue—and everyone gets one. Some schools give certificates with photos of the dogs on them. Some take a class photo and put an 8½" × 11" print up on a "Wall of Fame." Another important part of the last class—the students perform their tricks! Everyone in KinderPuppy or Pet Dog Manners is asked to teach their dog a trick during the course. Showing off the tricks is optional, but I am always pleased that the majority of dogs have something to show off. We pull more names for Bonus Bone gifts on the last night even if we have done it during the class. We also announce the winners of the special challenge awards.

In addition to the traditional activities, I ask each associate to take a turn planning a part of the class activities. Since we play games every week anyway, we have a list of special games or activities reserved for the last class. One of those is always a lateral thinking game. I want the students to go home realizing how great they are at solving problems! You can find GAMES PUP&PDM.doc, "Training Games for KinderPuppy & Pet Dog Manners Class" in the Appendix, but often our creative associates come up with something totally new.

# CHAPTER 7 REVIEW QUESTIONS

1. List five points that come to mind should a handicapped dog be in your class.

2. Write two different job descriptions for two future class associates.

3. Think of your current training location. Make a list of the good features and the bad features of your location. How can you improve the way you use your facilities?

4. You have been asked to teach a community class, with dogs, on the skill of "Come-When-Called." Your facility is a public room measuring 10′ × 20′. Using some of the resources in this book, make an outline of your lesson plan.

# ADDITIONAL READING/RESOURCES

American Kennel Club, 5580 Centerview Drive, Raleigh, NC 27606 or *www.akc.org.*

Becker, Susan. (1997). *Living with a Deaf Dog.* Susan Cope Becker, Cincinatti, OH, 45244.

Guertin, Joan. (2003). Classes by Levels, Common Sense Dog Training. Branson, MO 65616.

Johnson, Glen. (1975). *Tracking Dog: Theory and Methods.* Rome, NY, Arner Publications.

Legacy Canine Behavior and Training, Inc., *www.LegacyCanine.com* or 360-683-1522: Camps, DogSense & Instructor Workshops, E-tips, What's New.

McConnell, P. and London, K. (2003). *Feisty Fido—Help for the Leash Aggressive Dog.* Black Earth, Wisconsin, Dog's Best Friend, Ltd., *www.dogsbestfriendtraining.com.*

Miller, P. (2001). *The Power of Positive Pet Dog Training.* New York: Howell.

The following books and CDs can be purchased from: *www.LegacyCanine.com* or 360-683-1522:

Ryan, T. (1994). *Games People Play . . . To Train Their Dogs. Volume I.*

Ryan, T. (1996). *Games People Play . . . Volume II—"Life Beyond Block Heeling."*

Ryan, T. (2002). *The Bark Stops Here.*

Ryan, T. (2003). *L.E.A.D. (Leadership Education for Anyone with a Dog).*

Ryan, T. (2004). Sounds Good, CD Series for Sound Desensitization.

Ryan, T. and Mortensen, K. (2004). *Outwitting Dogs.* Guilford, CT: The Lyons Press.

Silvani, P. *Feisty Fidos—A Training Manual.* Mail order: St. Hubert's Dog Training School, 22 Prospect Street, Madison, New Jersey 07940. Telephone Order 1-973-377-0116, *www.sthuberts.org.*

Sue Sternberg, Community Animal Shelter Association, 4628 Route 209, Accord, NY 12404. Telephone: 1-845-687-7619; Fax: 1-845-687-0802.

Tawzer Dog Videos and DVDs, P.O. Box 423, Meridian, Idaho 83680, 1(888)566-3003, *Tawzer2@msn.com* (Videos and DVD's of Terry's programs and others).

# CHAPTER 8

# A TOOLBOX
## FOR REMODELING PROBLEM BEHAVIOR

*"Training teaches how; education teaches why."*
—Nido Qubein

# REMODELING PROBLEM BEHAVIOR

There are very few problem dogs. Some dogs are living in problem environments. Dogs engage in natural doggy behaviors like barking, digging, and protecting themselves. Humans deem these behaviors as inappropriate. When the canine and human lifestyles get out of sync, and when dogs and humans don't see eye to eye on appropriate behavior, it's time to get busy and see if a change or a compromise is possible. Finding out what's really going on is a challenge. Sometimes owners can't see the forest for the trees, or the other way around. Sometimes it takes a different and neutral person to analyze the situation. It at least takes an objective owner that can exercise critical and lateral thinking.

The ethology, learning theory, and training chapters have given you some of the background needed to help your clients untrain behaviors. To that foundation, add the "Hippocratic Oath" and "The Law of Parsimony" in your quest to help owners have better behaved pets.

## "First Do No Harm"

You may be anxious to try to help a dog overcome some bad habits, but take the time to think and consider carefully your training options and how each will affect the dog—right now and for the long haul.

The familiar dictum "First, do no harm," comes from Hippocrates' work, *Epidemics, Book I:* "Declare the past, diagnose the present, foretell the future; practice these acts. As to diseases, make a habit of two things—to help, or at least to do no harm." Hippocrates' recommendation should also serve as a caution to enthusiastic and well-meaning trainers. We shouldn't rush ahead in an attempt to solve a problem behavior without thinking through the possible results of the training. Taking the time to think and consider does not mean that we won't make mistakes. There are so many variables in dog training; we might not get the best recipe (set of tools) on our first try. That's not failure. It's diagnostic! It's information we can use to evaluate and alter our approach to the training. With careful planning, anything we try that doesn't work, will at least not make matters worse.

## The Law of Parsimony

The Law of Parsimony is an edict that dog trainers should keep in mind while problem solving. The question about this law is often one that stumps students at Legacy Instructors courses! What is the Law of Parsimony? The short answer is that "when two competing theories make the same predictions, the one that is simpler is more likely to be accurate." Here's the long answer: Occam (alternate spelling Ockham) was an English monk and philosopher circa the 1300s. He said the simplest of two or more competing theories is preferable and that explanation for unknown phenomena should first be attempted in terms of what is already known. The Law of Parsimony is sometimes referred to as Occam's razor, the law of simplicity, or the law of economy.

## THINKING OUTSIDE OF THE BOX

You can increase your success at problem solving if you think outside of the box. Instructor Donna Duford gave me these problems to solve. They can help you begin to think outside of the box:

1. A man is found lying dead in a field. Next to him there is an unopened package. No other creature is in the field. How did he die?
2. An astronaut had a brother named Tim. What relation was the astronaut to Tim? "Brother" is not the answer.
3. A man in Africa marries 20 women in his village, but isn't charged with bigamy (which is a crime in his village). Why not?
4. Jason is lying dead. He has an iron bar across his back and food in front of him. Where is Jason lying?
5. A man pushed his car. He stopped when he reached a hotel where he immediately realized he was bankrupt. Explain.

The answers are at the end of this chapter!

## DOCUMENT THE PROBLEM—WHAT'S REALLY GOING ON?

The best experts on dog behavior are dogs themselves. Let them tell you what is going on. Start by having the family document the behavior concerning them. Ask them to place a notepad in a convenient, obvious location. Get all family members to help by observing and documenting details of the problem behavior for several days. Perhaps a friend or neighbor could help observe the dog when the family is not home. Try setting up a tape recorder or video camera in a safe place to gather information while the family is gone. Jot down the details of the behavior. As an example, let's use barking as the problem. Answer these pertinent questions:

• **When does the behavior occur?**

Is there any pattern to when the dog barks?

Does she bark in the morning, on the weekends, or only after the family leaves for work or school?

- **What is the duration of the behavior?**

    How long at a time will she bark?

    Are there breaks between barking sessions?

    How long are the breaks and how long does the barking go on?

- **What is the intensity of the behavior?**

    Is it loud or soft? Strong or weak?

    Six barks per minute or sixty barks per minute?

- **What is the quality of the behavior?**

    Is it an excited bark? A casual bark? A worried bark? A furious bark?

    Does it have a boring and repetitious sound to it?

- **Where does the behavior occur?**

    Is the dog in the backyard when she barks or is she inside?

    Is there a certain room in which she barks? A certain side of the house?

    Does she bark like that in the car? While it's parked? While it's moving?

- **Who is present when the behavior occurs?**

    Does the dog only bark when she's alone?

    Does it make any difference who is with her?

    Are there other pets in the home?

    Can you determine if people, automobiles, or other animals are present when the barking occurs?

- **Was the dog rewarded in any way for the behavior either by the people or the environment?**

    What did the dog want? For example, did the dog want the children to leave? Did the children leave after she barked?

- **Which methods of behavior modification have been tried so far?**

# "Build a House"—A Metaphor for Instructional Formatting

The "build a house" metaphor below is a good model to share with students, as together you carefully select appropriate goals and plan a program to reach that goal.

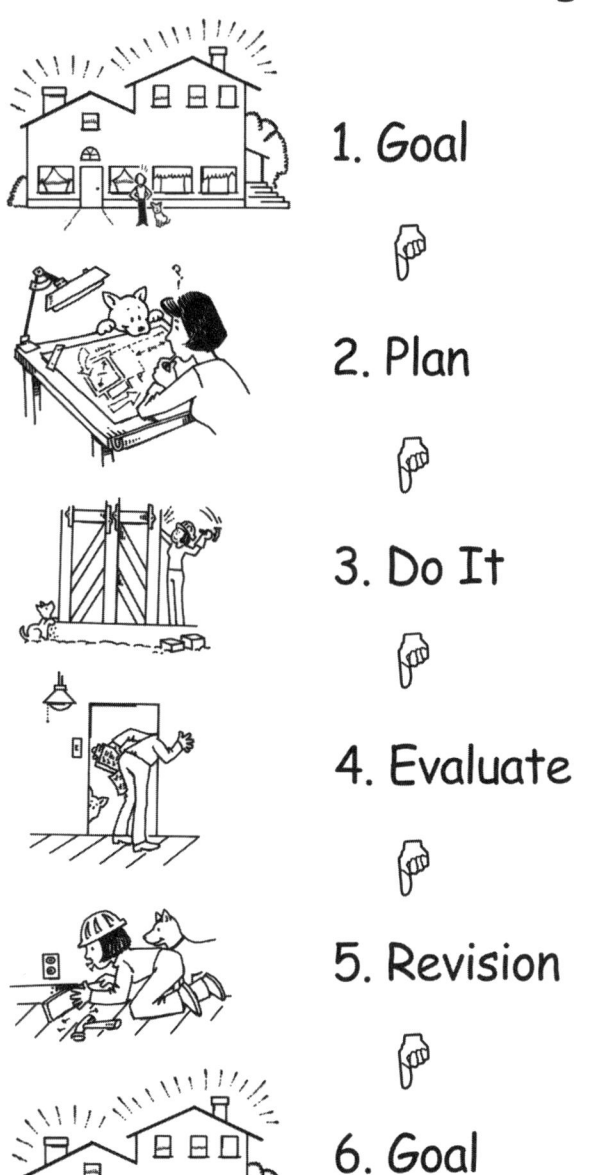

## Instructional Formatting

1. Goal

2. Plan

3. Do It

4. Evaluate

5. Revision

6. Goal Achieved?

*Chapter 8   A Toolbox: Remodeling Problem Behavior*

# Decide Upon Clear Goals—What Do You Really Want?

Having a clearly defined plan of action is necessary to remodel a dog effectively. Setting goals and formulating a course of action will avoid confusing the dog.

Make sure your dog training goals are clear. The carpenter knows he needs to roof the house, but hasn't thought through the problem: Will he use shake shingles or ceramic tiles? Should the roof be pitched or flat? Should he put in a solar panel? How about a skylight? At times dog training goals will be obvious, but at other times, they will be vague. For instance, do you want the dog to stop barking, or is it okay if she barks at a strange noise in the middle of the night. Is it okay if she whines? How about just one bark? Each goal has a different game plan. Take a look at the illustration, which compares canine behavior modification to building a house. When working with dogs, people tend to jump right in with training the dog, and then evaluate, only to find they have to go back and consider their goals and techniques.

Deciding which combination of principles to use to train or untrain a dog is an art, and we will try to assist you with that art in this chapter.

Behaviorist Dr. Pam Reid categorizes canine behaviors into four categories: useful, critical, nuisance, and dangerous.

**USEFUL**—a behavior we want, such as "Sit" or "Stand," which helps make the dog an enjoyable companion.

**CRITICAL**—a behavior we want and need, such as "Come" or "Stop," whose lack may endanger the dog.

**NUISANCE**—a behavior we don't want, such as chewing up shoes, or begging for food while people are eating, that can be avoided by environmental management.

**DANGEROUS**—a behavior we don't want and can't have, such as biting to hurt others, or chasing cars, that could end in harm to another animal, to a human, or to the dog herself.

Desired behaviors can be trained with reward-based methods. Only if such training fails after a fair trial should other means be considered. In fact, the humane trainer always uses a carefully considered approach before deciding that aversives are warranted. Even then, the least aversive alternative with a realistic expectation of success should be chosen.

This chart shows a logical and humane progression in selecting training techniques for the four categories of behavior described previously:

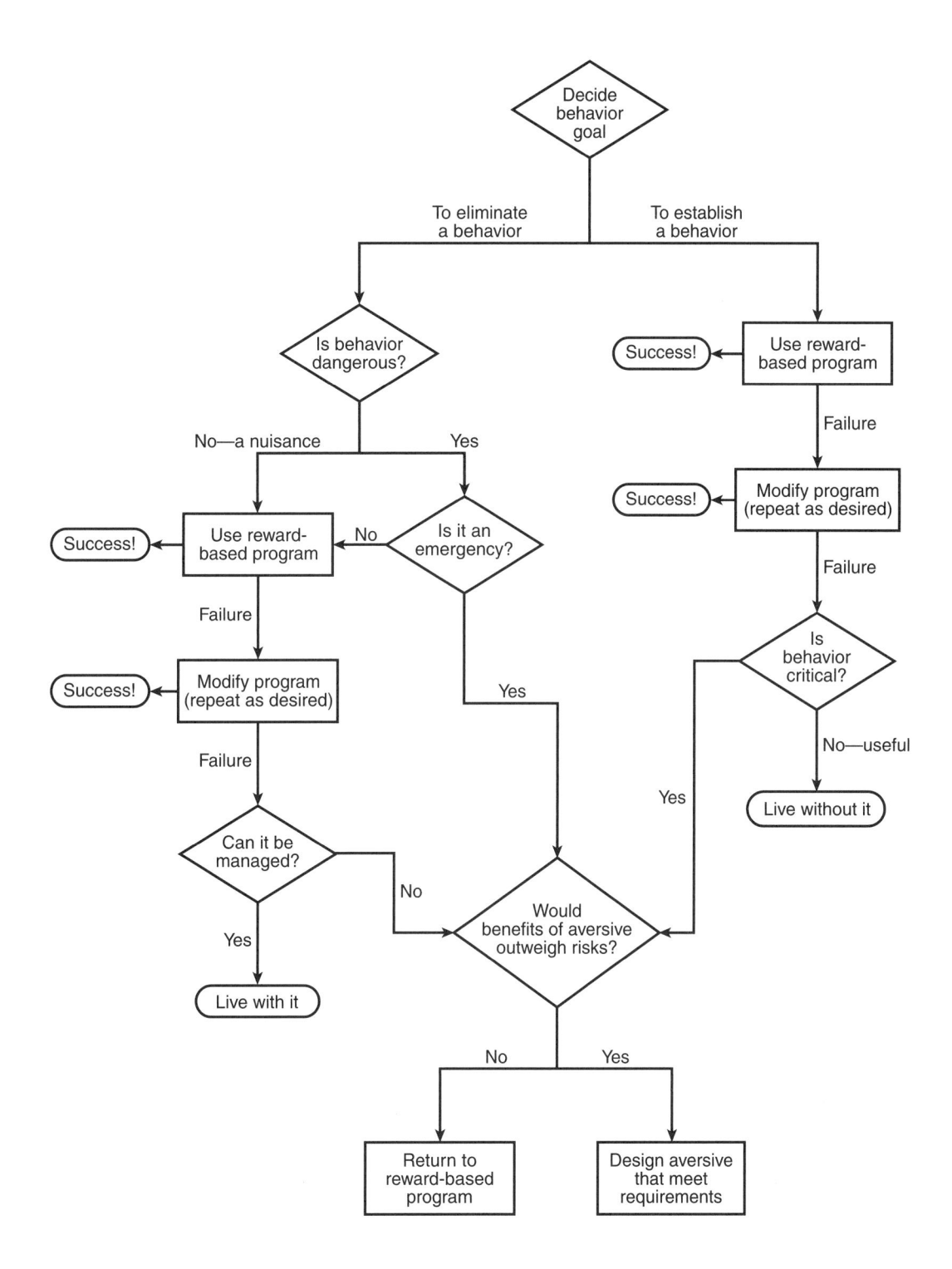

```
                         Decide
                        behavior
                          goal
              To eliminate        To establish
               a behavior          a behavior

              Is behavior                    Use reward-
              dangerous?      Success! ←    based program
                                                 ↓
         No—a nuisance    Yes                 Failure
                                                 ↓
         Use reward-    No    Is it an       Modify program
         based program ←     emergency?  Success! ←  (repeat as desired)
  Success! ←                                     ↓
              ↓                               Failure
            Failure                              ↓
              ↓                                  Is
         Modify program                       behavior
  Success! ← (repeat as desired)              critical?
              ↓                       Yes
            Failure                          No—useful
              ↓                                  ↓
           Can it be                         Live without it
           managed?         No
                              ↘
         Yes                   Would
          ↓              benefits of aversive
       Live with it     outweigh risks?
                         No          Yes
                          ↓           ↓
                      Return to    Design aversive
                     reward-based    that meet
                       program      requirements
```

From the Delta Society's August 2001 Document entitled "Professional Standards for Dog Trainers: Effective, Humane Principles." Contributors are S. Hetts, T. King, P. Reid, P. Silvani, M. Nitschke, T. Ryan (and their committees).

*Chapter 8  A Toolbox: Remodeling Problem Behavior*

# The Language of "Punishment"

To understand why non-aversive training is so effective, popular, and long lasting, it's good to fully understand aversive training. And then compare. Then choose your options. Over the years, punishment has become associated with behavior modification. It is appropriate to explore aversive training before we go on. The language of the harsh and punitive things we do in the name of training is complicated. Behaviorists work with positive and negative punishment as well as positive and negative reinforcement. Refer back to the operant conditioning graph in Chapter 3, "Learning Theory." For the purposes of this book, punishment means positive punishment.

Dog trainers talk about correcting a dog, but that term is fuzzy and difficult to interpret. It means different things to different people. This book will use the term aversives as a universal, general term. All specific labels like correction, punishment, or "nasty stuff" will fall under the umbrella term aversive.

Clients might have had experience with the harsh handling of dogs. They might believe slapping, jerking on the leash, hollering, threatening stares, shaking, or pinning the dog to the floor is the norm. On the surface these actions might seem to work. If you holler or make a loud noise, the dog's natural orienting reflex causes him to pause and turn toward the sound. Some trainers call this an "interrupter." This does not mean the dog has learned to stop the behavior. It does not mean the dog has learned what to do instead. If the dog turns away from a threatening stare, this is a response to the owner's social cues. It doesn't mean the dog is sorry or has learned anything about the behavior that caused this interaction in the first place. Instead of criticizing these harsh handling methods, quickly show how effectively your reward-based method changes their dog's behavior.

Punishment has the ability to stop behavior or, at least, to stun or diminish behavior dramatically, but only if complex criteria are met. For example, not many dogs display the combination of behaviors that makes punishment an appropriate option or even the first choice. More importantly, an even smaller percentage of dog owners possess the judgment, timing, or desire to do what is necessary for punishment to work effectively. Legacy's student handout on punishment can be found in the Appendix as PDMI Aversives.doc.

# The Four-Piece Dog Training Puzzle

Helping dogs and people live together happily is like putting together a puzzle. In brief, four important dimensions to consider before you start working out a training program are:

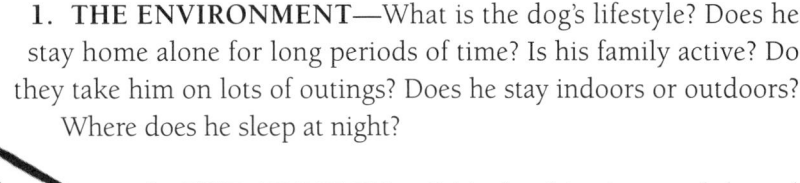

1. **THE ENVIRONMENT**—What is the dog's lifestyle? Does he stay home alone for long periods of time? Is his family active? Do they take him on lots of outings? Does he stay indoors or outdoors? Where does he sleep at night?

2. **THE PROBLEM**—Critical, objective, and lateral thinking is needed to clearly identify the cause of the problem. Sometimes the owner can get a more objective opinion from a neighbor or friend who knows the dog and the dog's environment.

3. **THE DOG**—What size? What breed type? High energy or low energy? What is the relationship with the owner and family?

4. **THE OWNER**—What are the humans capable of doing with the dog? If they have poor timing, consider a method that doesn't require great timing. If they are totally against food in training, be a lateral thinker and come up with other rewards. The humans have to have their heart in the program or even the best of advice will not help the dog.

You have read information in the first few chapters of this book that might help you sort through the four puzzle pieces. It's important to continue to expand your network, critically gathering information as you go. There are many variables to consider and there is usually more than one correct answer for any question.

# Legacy's "Toolbox" Concept for Changing Behavior

Here are two concepts to use when attempting to change behaviors that are commonly described as problems. The use of acronyms "HELM" and "YES TRAIN" are used as prompts to make sure no stone is left unturned during the process of building a behavior modification plan. Legacy client handouts pertaining to problem behaviors apply both the HELM and YES TRAIN concepts.

## H.E.L.M.

To set the stage for success, always check that you will be building on a strong foundation. The acronym HELM represents four foundation blocks. Life with your dog is like a pleasant cruise and you are at the HELM! Helm stands for **H**ealth, **E**nvironmental Enrichment, **L**eadership, and **M**anagement.

*Chapter 8   A Toolbox: Remodeling Problem Behavior*

## HEALTH

As an instructor, keep in mind that some physical problems manifest themselves first as a change in behavior. Your training and behavior program should include cooperation with and referral to appropriate veterinarians. A hormonal imbalance might first show up in class as sluggishness or refusal to comply. Neurological problems can be at the root of some unusual behavior. Orthopedic disorders might first show themselves as grumpiness due to pain, or refusal to do an otherwise simple request such as "Sit" and "Stay." A fine line exists between doing your job as advocate for the dog and her family . . . and giving veterinary advice. Do not practice veterinary medicine without a license!

## ENVIRONMENT

Consider the impact that family members, including children and other pets, may have on the dog. Are there social interactions or hierarchies influencing behavior? Being home alone is a common source of behavior problems. An instructor should be politely attentive to opportunities to improve a dog's environment. A client handout on enrichment appears in the Appendix as INFO HomeAlone/Enrichment.doc, "Home Alone and Enrichment Ideas."

## LEADERSHIP

An appropriate relationship between dog and owner is paramount in training. Care must be taken to explain the difference between leadership and unnecessary harshness. The leadership program entitled "Leadership Education for Anyone with a Dog" is described in a client handout in the Appendix, PDM 1 LEADership.doc, "Take the LEAD."

## MANAGEMENT

It's up to owners to help their dogs live problem-free lives. Sometimes a band-aid intervention is the owner's first appropriate course of action. Find methods to keep the dog and those around the dog safe and happy during the weeks training takes place. Options like a fence, a leash, more supervision, or even a temporary change in lifestyle are appropriate first aid measures.

# TOOLS FOR CHANGING UNWANTED BEHAVIOR

After checking and making suggestions for the foundation blocks represented by H.E.L.M. it's time to become more specific. A carpenter doesn't arrive at a remodeling job with just a couple of tools. He brings an entire toolbox full of them. He'll use one or two a lot, most of them occasionally, and some may never make it out of the box. Each job requires a different assortment of tools. Your toolbox for remodeling problem dogs is a collection of ideas and concepts that will help create your own approach to behavior modification. Here are some tools, in no specific order. Once again, an acronym might help: "Yes, Train!"

**Y** ield a Little
**E** liminate the Trigger
**S** ystematic Desensitization

**T** ake Away the Reward
**R** eward an Incompatible Behavior
**A** cclimate the Dog
**I** mprove the Dog's Association
**N** ot Much Nasty Stuff

## Using the Y.E.S. T.R.A.I.N. Tools

**Y Is for Yield.** Don't give in completely to the dog, but sometimes give in a little. This helps make an equitable living arrangement. Often overlooked as an option in dog training, a compromise can be an easy and effective solution. "Yield a Little" appeals to owners with little time, talent, or inclination to train. "Yield a Little" allows the dog's preferred activity, where punishment might simply encourage the dog to pick another annoying habit. "Yield a Little" works well in combination with other tools. The main drawback is there might not be a suitable compromise available. Yielding a Little is never appropriate for problems that might endanger the dog or those around the dog.

### Examples of "Yield a Little"

- "You can bark to announce the arrival of the delivery truck, but only three times and you have to be quiet when told to hush."
- "On days we can't walk you, we'll hire a dog walker."
- "You can't dig in the lawn or flower bed, but it's okay to dig in this corner."
- "You can get on the bed only when invited, and you have to get off when asked."

**E Is for Eliminate the Trigger.** Keep things simple. We might be overlooking a simple solution to the problem: taking away the cause (trigger) of an unwanted behavior. You have to be sure, however, to correctly identify the cause. There may be a combination of causes or cues that provoke the behavior and you'll need to peel them away like layers of an onion. "Eliminate the Trigger" is quick and, when used appropriately, solves the problem forever and without stress to the owner or dog. Bear in mind, however, that eliminating the trigger may resolve one specific issue, but may not change the dog's attitude toward other similar situations. If we put shoes away at home, are we eliminating the cause of chewing shoes, or will the dog be tempted to chew something else? It's better to dig deeper for what may be the real cause of the chewing.

*Examples of "Eliminate the Trigger"*

- "We can't stop the children from walking past your fence, so we will build a second inner fence to prevent you from seeing people on the sidewalk."
- "You don't like the sound of fireworks? Let's get your owner to keep you indoors and play classical music on the 4th of July.
- "The garbage container is now in a closet so you won't be tempted to get into it."
- "You're barking at the mailman? Guess we'll cancel home delivery and get a box at the post office."

**S Is for Systematic Desensitization.** Systematic Desensitization is a technique frequently used for fear responses. The problem-producing situation is presented to the dog at gradually increasing intensities.

Systematic Desensitization and counter conditioning are terms found in every psychology textbook. For pet dog training, adding counter conditioning to systematic desensitization is successful in changing a dog's mind about worrisome events. In the YES TRAIN acronym, counter conditioning is represented by the generic term "Improve the Association." Critical to success is the owner's ability to control the dog's environment. Care must be taken not to proceed too quickly and overwhelm the dog. It's especially helpful if improving the association is used in conjunction with systematic desensitization.

*Examples of Systematic Desensitization*

- "Dog, we're sorry you're afraid of the vacuum cleaner. We're going to play a tape of the vacuum sound. We'll play it for just a little while, so low you'll barely hear it. Tomorrow we'll turn it up just a tad. Then up a bit more, waiting to be sure you're okay with each step."

To use the combination of systematic desensitization and improve the association it would be: "Dog, we're sorry you're afraid of the vacuum. We know you love your food. We will make a tape of the vacuum running and we'll start with it very low, but each meal we'll play the tape a bit louder if you are coping well.

- "Dog, we don't want you to worry about walking on a leash, so we'll use systematic desensitization. First we'll just snap it on your collar, and take it right off. Then will keep it on for a few seconds. Then we'll walk around the room and take it off. After that we'll go for a brief walk around the backyard.

To use the combination of systematic desensitization and improve the association would be: "Dog, we don't want you to worry about walking on a leash. First, we'll just snap it on your collar. You'll get a food treat and then the leash will come right off. Then we'll keep it on for a few seconds while you receive lots of kind words. In the next step we'll walk around the room, go over to your food bowl and after you've finished your meal, off it comes. In another session we'll snap the leash on just before the door is opened. We'll go for a brief walk around the backyard, and I'll toss the ball for you a little before I take the leash off."

**T Is for Take Away the Reward (Extinction).** Almost all behaviors are sustained by a reward of some type. Sometimes the reward is subtle, and clients will need help in figuring out appropriate rewards. If the reward can be identified with certainty and eliminated, the behavior will decrease eventually and go into extinction.

Extinction is the scientific term for taking away the reward for a previously rewarded behavior. "Take Away the Reward" is easy and takes little time or effort. Sometimes the reward is not identified or impossible to remove. Often there is more than one reward sustaining the behavior.

With extinction, the behavior will often increase immediately after the reward is withdrawn, which is known as an extinction burst. In plain words, sometimes it gets worse before it gets better. Warn clients that this will occur, and then congratulate them—extinction is working! The dog says, "Huh? What happened? I want that back. Let me try harder for a little bit." If the owner gives in and the dog is rewarded during this transient increase in the behavior, that teaches the dog to play the lottery! Now the behavior will be even more difficult to extinguish.

Another feature of extinction is the spontaneous recovery of the behavior. In one session, you can greatly decrease a behavior by eliminating the reward. The next time the dog is in that same situation, the behavior most often shows itself again, even if briefly. Remind your client not to reward this spontaneous recovery. It's a natural occurrence and part of the extinction process. The behavior will again decrease, probably more quickly than the previous time.

### Examples of Take Away the Reward

- "When you jump on Jimmy, he's going to ignore you rather than yelling and pushing at you. You're looking for attention, and Jimmy is not going to give it to you."
- "If we really want the begging to stop, everyone has to stop slipping the dog tidbits from the table."
- "Dog, I'll bet you think pulling on the leash is what gets you to the park sooner. From now on, when you pull, your people are just going to plant their feet and stand still until the leash goes slack."
- "Okay, Dog, from now on, we are going to leave the old, broken TV remote on the coffee table. No one in the family is going to pay attention to you when you steal it."

**R Is for Reward an Incompatible Behavior.** Help your client select, train, and reward his dog for a good behavior that can be performed instead of the bad behavior. This is a very positive method because in the very same situation, the dog can now be rewarded for being good rather than being punished for being bad.

Instead of pushing the dog off for jumping up, have him sit and hear "Good Boy!"

Instead of "No!" for chewing the shoe, it's "Yes!" for chewing the toy bone.

Rather than a smack for barking, it's "Good Job!" on the retrieve.

Replace "Shame on you!" for begging with "Have a tidbit for Down-Stay on the mat."

Rewarding an incompatible behavior reduces stress for all concerned. It does take time to train the good behavior and preparedness to be ready to reward it when it's offered. Then it's simply a matter of repetition until the dog knows when and where that behavior is expected.

### Examples of Reward an Incompatible Behavior

- "You can't bark and bother Dad when he's on the phone if you are busy getting a snack out of a food dispensing toy."
- "You can't grab Jimmy's pant leg if you're carrying your squeaky hedgehog."
- "Instead of pacing back and forth in the station wagon, how about using the time to lie down and lick the peanut butter out of your Kong toy?"
- "Instead of barking for joy when the kids come home, go over to the toy box and pick up a ball. They'll throw it for you."

**A Is for Acclimation (Habituation).** Acclimation is especially helpful to fearful, excitable, or over-reactive dogs. In the scientific world, it is referred to as habituation. Simply, habituation or acclimation means "getting used to it." The dog is exposed to the problem-producing situation in a safe and controlled manner. The dog should not be presented with a reward or punishment. In a calm and neutral environment, the frightened dog discovers there's nothing to fear. The excited dog learns his antics will not be rewarded.

Acclimation (habituation) is simple and requires little skill, but it can be time consuming. This technique may yield poor results with reflexive or instinctual behaviors. Monitor the situation and stop if the dog is showing signs of stress.

*Examples of Acclimation (Habituation)*

- **THE LOCATION:** "Your family is going to take you to the veterinary clinic. If you have lots of these visits to the hospital where nothing dramatic happens, you will be used to the clinic when you have to go for treatment."

- **THE LOOK:** "You don't like people with hats? Your entire family is going to be wearing hats this week. You'll soon be bored with hats."

- **THE FEEL:** "Dog, wear this collar. Get used to it. Nothing bad will happen, nothing good will happen. Period."

- **THE SOUND:** "Dog, we're going to be going to dog shows, so I'm going to let you listen to this tape of dog show sounds every day."

- **THE SMELL:** "Worried about the vet? Here's a carpet square from the office. It smells just like the clinic. Get used to it. Your family is going to put it in the hallway where you have to walk over it each day."

**I Is for Improve the Association (Counter Conditioning).** The correct term for Improve the Association is counter conditioning. It is one of the most widely used and successful behavior modification concepts for overcoming fear. It can work in two slightly different, but effective, ways:

"Improve the Association" is useful when you can't change the problem environment. Pair something of high value to the dog—a walk, a chance to play ball, presentation of the food bowl—with the problem situation. The reward must be strong enough to overcome the problem, or else you might get the reverse effect: the reward becomes a cue for something bad.

Behaviorists categorize these two different types of counter conditioning as:

***Classical counter conditioning***—The dog's original emotion is changed to another emotion.

- The dog worries about seeing the mailman. The dog sees the mailman and barks. The hungry dog is engaged in delivery of treat after treat from her owner. The dog now associates the mailman with pleasure and reward.

*Operant counter conditioning*—The dog is conditioned to perform a behavior physically incompatible with the problem behavior.

- The dog worries about seeing the mailman. The dog sees the mailman and barks. Dog is taught to hold a ball in her mouth in preparation for a game of fetch when she sees the mailman. The dog no longer barks when she sees the mailman. The dog has a choice to bark or play and chooses to play.

**N Is for Not Much Nasty Stuff.** For purposes of simplicity, the Toolbox acronym uses the word Nasty. Nasty means something the dog does not like that has the power to decrease or stop behavior.

So far we've given lots of thought to choosing meaningful rewards from the dog's point of view. It's the same with "nasty stuff." A squirt of water in the face may be unpleasant for one dog, while a Labrador Retriever might just ask for more. The best nasty state of affairs is one that the dog perceives as a direct result of his own actions regardless of where the owner is or what the owner does. In other words, if the dog realizes you are involved, you become a "conditioned punisher" and the threat is only of value if you are present—your absence signals all clear. If the "nasty stuff" comes from the environment rather than you, the dog is less apt to break down the trust in you. Therefore, carefully crafted "remote control" set ups must be employed.

There are times when a nasty state of affairs can be the best way to go. Following are some typical aversives that have been used successfully to stop behavior.

### *Examples of Nasty State of Affairs*

- **SOUND:** "The next time you try to steal dirty laundry from the hamper, the motion sensitive alarm will go off!"
- **TASTE:** "You'll teach yourself not to chew up magazines because all the magazine covers now have a bitter taste."
- **SMELL:** "Each time you bark, a little device in your collar will release a yucky smell."
- **SIGHT:** "Last time you were digging and scratching that spot in the carpet you got sprayed with a plant mister. Maybe your family will put the mister near that spot on the carpet as a reminder."
- **FEEL:** "Dad's easy chair is not as comfortable for you now. When the family leaves home, they place a metal cookie sheet on it."
- **COMFORT:** "If you jump up on Mom, she's going to grasp your paws and not let go. You will be trapped! It's uncomfortable to stand on your hind legs for more than a few seconds."

Coaching People to Train Their Dogs

# CHAPTER 8 REVIEW QUESTIONS

1. The following is true about extinction (Take Away the Reward):
   a. It's an immediate fix.
   b. The behavior most likely will get worse before it gets better.
   c. It's appropriate mostly for small dogs.

2. Habituation (Acclimate the Dog) is used with the sense of
   a. smell.
   b. touch.
   c. Can be used with several different senses.

3. In working with a problem behavior, positive punishment alone
   a. doesn't teach the dog what behavior is appropriate.
   b. is the best way to help a fearful dog overcome the fear.
   c. can be used regularly with any adult dog, but not with puppies.

4. Your client's dog bit the mailman. You should tell the client to:
   a. call a vet, all unexplained aggression is due to epilepsy.
   b. begin a strict management program . . . TODAY.
   c. call the post office because your dog must have been abused by the mailman.

5. Training an incompatible behavior to compete with the bad behavior
   a. takes time, so it is not an immediate fix.
   b. almost never works.
   c. requires the dog to be boarded with a professional trainer.

6. What is the Law of Parsimony?
   a. Dogs should have only one spouse.
   b. It is the best way to grow parsnips.
   c. The simplest, obvious answer is usually the best.

**Answers:** 1. b  2. c  3. a  4. b  5. a  6. c

*Chapter 8  A Toolbox: Remodeling Problem Behavior*

# ADDITIONAL READING/RESOURCES

Dogwise, A Direct Book Service, 701 B Poplar, Wenatchee, WA 98801, 1(800)776-2665, mail@dogwise.com (Terry's books and others).

Donaldson, J. (1997). *The Culture Clash.* Berkeley, California: James and Kenneth Publishers.

Donaldson, J. (2002). *Mine!—A Guide to Resource Guarding in Dogs.* San Francisco, California: Kinship Communications/SF-SPCA.

Dunbar, I. (2003). *Doctor Dunbar's Good Little Dog Book.* Berkeley, California: James and Kenneth Publishers.

Estep, D. and Hetts, S. *Pet Behavior One Piece at a Time.* Animal Behavior Associates, ezine@AnimalBehaviorAsssociates.com.

Hetts, S. and Estep, D. (2000). *Canine Behavior: Body Postures and Evaluating Behavioral Health.* Animal Care Training, Humane Society of the United States.

Hetts, S. (1999). *Pet Behavior Protocols.* Lakewood, California: American Animal Hospital Association Press.

Hippocrates (c. 460–c. 370 B.C.) *Epidemics, Book 1, Section 11.* Hippocrates, trans. W. H. S. Jones, Vol. 1, p. 165 (1923).

Landsberg, G., Hunthausen, W., and Ackerman, L. (1997). *Handbook of Behavior Problems of the Dog and Cat.* Boston, Massachusetts: Butterworth-Heinemann Medical.

Overall, K. (1997). *Clinical Behavioral Medicine for Small Animals.* St. Louis, Missouri: Mosby.

Ryan, T. (2000). *The Bark Stops Here.* Sequim, Washington: Legacy Canine Behavior and Training, Inc.

Ryan, T. (1998). *The Toolbox for Remodeling Your Problem Dog.* New York: Hungry Minds, Inc.

Ryan, T. (2002). *Leadership Education for Anyone with a Dog.* Sequim, Washington: Legacy Canine Behavior and Training.

Ryan, T. (2004). Sounds Good, CD Series for Sound Desensitization. *www.LegacyCanine.com,* 360-683-1522, P.O. Box 3909, Sequim, WA 98382.

Tawzer Dog Videos and DVDs, P.O. Box 423, Meridian, Idaho 83680, 1(888)566-3003, Tawzer2@msn.com (Videos and DVD's of Terry's programs and others).

*The answers to the lateral thinking questions on page 219:*

1. His parachute didn't open
2. His sister
3. The man was a priest
4. Jason is a mouse, and he's lying in a mousetrap
5. He was playing Monopoly

# APPENDIX

# CONTENTS

This Appendix is made up of actual materials currently used in Legacy's programs. They are divided into categories by their document name. Capitalized prefix letters of the document name are listed below.

| | |
|---|---|
| **PDM** | Entry Level Pet Dog Manners Handouts |
| **PUPPY** | For Puppies Specifically |
| **INFO** | Various Topics of Help for Clients |
| **CONT ED** | Some Intermediate/Advanced Handouts |
| **GAMES** | Training Games Mentioned in This Book |
| **INSTRUCT** | Material Helpful for Instructors |
| **MISC** | Anything Else! |

## PDM—Pet Dog Manners Class

These are the class materials for the student notebooks. They are organized in this Appendix by week and then alphabetically.

| | | |
|---|---|---|
| PDM 1 Aversives.doc | About Punishment (Aversives) in Training | 239 |
| PDM 1 EyeContact.doc | Eye Contact—Attention to Name Using a Toy/Play Reward | 241 |
| PDM 1 FocusingExercise.doc | Focusing Exercise—Trick Training | 243 |
| PDM 1 Homework.doc | Be Ready for Week 2 | 245 |
| PDM 1 LEADership.doc | Take the L.E.A.D. | 247 |
| PDM 1 Select/UseRewards.doc | The Selection and Use of Training Rewards | 251 |
| PDM 1 SitHappens.doc | Sit Happens! Using a Lure: The Magnetic Sit Exercise | 255 |
| PDM 1 StressSigCalmSig.doc | Stress Signals, Calming Signals | 259 |
| PDM 1 Toolbox.doc | The Toolbox for Remodeling Problem Dogs | 261 |
| PDM 1 YesCommunication.doc | "YES!" as a Reward Marker—Communication Homework | 263 |
| PDM 2 Come.doc | Come-When-Called | 265 |
| PDM 2 FourD's.doc | The Four D's To Help Your Dog Gain Fluency | 269 |
| PDM 2 Homework.doc | Be Ready for Week 3 | 271 |
| PDM 2 LeashWork.doc | Leash Work | 273 |
| PDM 2 PersBestWalkABout.doc | The Personal Best Walk-About Route | 277 |
| PDM 3 Down | Down | 279 |
| PDM 3 Homework.doc | Be Ready for Week 4 | 283 |
| PDM 4 Homework.doc | Be Ready for Week 5 | 285 |
| PDM 4 LeaderOfThePackFig8.doc | Leader of the Pack—Figure 8 Challenge | 287 |
| PDM 4 MidCourseEval.doc | We're Halfway Through Classes!—How Are You Doing? | 289 |
| PDM 5 Homework.doc | Be Ready for Week 6 | 291 |
| PDM 6 Homework.doc | Be Ready for Week 7 | 293 |

## PUPPY—Specifically for Puppy Classes

Puppies also receive some of the Pet Dog Manners (PDM) information as appropriate.

| | |
|---|---|
| PUPPY Chewing&Mouthing.doc | Chewing—On You, On Your Stuff   295 |
| PUPPY Crate&Housetrain.doc | Crate Training and Housetraining   297 |
| PUPPY PupHeadStartIntro.doc | Introduction to Puppy Headstart   301 |
| PUPPY HeadStartHomework.doc | Participation In Class Is Not Enough   303 |

## INFO—Helpful Supplementary Topics for Clients

This material addresses the common questions asked by pet dog owners about care, training and problem behavior. These topics may or may not be addressed in class.

| | |
|---|---|
| INFO Barking.doc | The Bark Stops Here   305 |
| INFO Digging.doc | Digging   313 |
| INFO EatingPoop.doc | My Dog is Eating Poop!   315 |
| INFO Escaping.doc | Escaping—The Houdini Hound   317 |
| INFO HomeAlone/Enrichment.doc | Home Alone and Enrichment Ideas   319 |
| INFO Jumping.doc | Jumping on People   321 |
| INFO Kids&Canines.doc | Kids and Canines   323 |
| INFO OffFurniture.doc | Staying Off Furniture   329 |
| INFO Spay&Neuter.doc | Neutering Your Male Dog/Spaying Your Female Dog   331 |

## CONT ED—Graduate Level Handouts

Legacy's various Graduate Level classes don't rely as heavily on handouts and supportive material as beginner classes. Here are a few we've found useful.

| | |
|---|---|
| CONT ED ClickBasics.doc | Click! Clicker Basics   333 |
| CONT ED Clicks&Sticks.doc | How to Start Target Stick Training with a Clicker   335 |
| CONT ED Fetch.doc | Fetch!   337 |
| CONT ED ScentDiscrim.doc | Scent Discrimination   339 |
| CONT ED Stand.doc | Four on the Floor—Stand   341 |

# GAMES—Why, When, and How to Play Games in Class

This section contains information about the games mentioned in the book, and some special end-of-class activities.

GAMES Decathlon.doc  The Decathlon Event  343
GAMES PUP&PDM.doc  Training Games for KinderPuppy and Pet Dog Manners Class  345

# INSTRUCT—For Use of Instructors

INSTRUCT 2 LessonPlan—Do In Class Week 2 Dogs Debut  353
INSTRUCT 3 LessonPlan—Do In Class Week 3  355
INSTRUCT 4 LessonPlan—Do In Class Week 4  357
INSTRUCT 5 LessonPlan—Do in Class Week 5  359
INSTRUCT 6 LessonPlan—Do In Class Week 6  361
INSTRUCT 7 LessonPlan—Do In Class Week 7 Last Class!  363
INSTRUCT BonusBones&Challenges.doc  365
INSTRUCT ChinesePuzzle.doc  369
INSTRUCT PREDICTOR.doc  371
INSTRUCT PuppyMenu.doc  373
INSTRUCT Randomword.doc  381
INSTRUCT SixHats.doc  383

# MISC—Any Other Stuff!

MISC StudentProfileForm.doc  385
MISC TapeNTowel.doc  387
MISC KidsColorSheets.doc  389

The illustrations and text in this Appendix are copyrighted by Terry Ryan, Legacy Canine Behavior and Training, Inc. unless otherwise noted. Limited excerpts of the appendix of this book may only be reproduced with prior written permission. For permission, send an e-mail to info@LegacyCanine.com with your name and the name and address of your school, phone numbers and e-mail addresses. You can also contact us at Legacy Canine Behavior and Training, Inc., P.O. Box 3909, Sequim, WA 98382. Thank you!

# About Punishment (Aversives) in Training

**PUNISHMENT MUST BE DO-ABLE BY THE OWNER**
Few owners have the ability or desire to select and administer punishment effectively.

**PUNISHMENT ONLY SUPPRESSES BEHAVIOR**
Owners hope that punishment will stop a behavior. There is evidence to believe that adding an aversive after an unwanted behavior may just "stun" a behavior temporarily.

**PUNISHMENT IS INAPPROPRIATE FOR FEAR OR ANGER RESPONSES**
Angry or fearful dogs can be made worse. Harsh correction (punishment) can easily frustrate the dog and escalate the dog's aggression or fear.

**INEFFECTIVE ATTEMPTS AT PUNISHMENT CAN BE A REWARD**
Your dog is in the backyard, barking. You open the door and say, "Bad dog! No!" Regardless of the shouting, he may have gotten a reward: He saw your face, heard your voice . . . you are paying attention to him. Barking can become an "Owner Interact with Me" cue!

**PUNISHMENT IS AN INCOMPLETE PROGRAM**
Punishment only teaches the dog what NOT to do. The dog might stop the punished behavior, but begin doing something else wrong. An example is that a dog leaps about and mugs visitors at the door. Mugging is bad, but what do you WANT the dog to do? Sit is good because it is incompatible with jumping. Now you can reward at times when you would otherwise be punishing. Doorbell rings, it's the dog's cue to sit quietly on a mat within sight of the door. When the guest is seated and things calm down, the dog can earn the further reward of being released to visit the guest.

**PUNISHMENT MIGHT DAMAGE YOUR RELATIONSHIP**
Punishment often causes confusion and reduces the trust that is so important between you and your dog. It's best to earn your dog's respect by consistency in leadership and good training, not to demand it through intimidation, force, or physical abuse.

**PUNISHMENT NEEDS TO BE CONSISTENT**
Punishment should be administered at the FIRST sign of the unwanted behavior and every single time that behavior occurs thereafter. If you miss some of the behaviors and do not punish them, your dog will learn to take his chances and play the lottery.

**PUNISHMENT MIGHT NOT GENERALIZE**
If your dog is sniffing while you've asked him to Heel on leash and you jerk the lead, you are hoping the dog will understand that he shouldn't sniff while in formal Heel position. Even if it works as a communication of "no sniff"—and it's always questionable just what the dog is learning—he might interpret it as he shouldn't sniff in that location. It's okay to sniff further along. Or he might learn that he shouldn't sniff on concrete, but sniffing on grass is okay.

CONTACT US IF YOU NEED HELP   info@legacycanine.com   360-683-1522

*PDM 1 Aversives.doc*   *Coaching People to Train Their Dogs* © Terry Ryan 2005

## PUNISHMENT NEEDS TO WORK THE FIRST TIME APPLIED
Actions are not having the proper effect if they need to be repeated more than once or twice. After that, punishment constitutes abuse.

## GOOD TIMING FOR CORRECT CONCLUSION
The aversive should be delivered within two seconds for it to be associated with the specific behavior. We do not live in a sterile environment. Many things are happening at once in real life. The dog might not make the association you had in mind. "Was I bad for chasing the squirrel?" "Are you angry because I did not catch the squirrel?" "Should I not like the child who was standing there as I was being punished for chasing the squirrel?"

## PUNISHMENT CAN LEAD TO THE LEARNED HELPLESSNESS SYNDROME
The dog shuts down. She decides that nothing she can do is good and so she does nothing, she just takes the punishment. The dog doesn't learn, she just endures punishment.

## PUNISHMENT AND THE SUBSTITUTION SYNDROME
Repetitive actions, such as barking, digging, chewing, and licking calm a dog, much like rocking a baby settles the child. You might be able to interrupt or temporarily stop them, but the dog might engage in a substitute behavior even more annoying or dangerous. If you stop a dog from barking, he may begin digging holes, chewing the furniture, or licking his paw until it's sore. The calming effect of these repetitive behaviors is a natural reward for the dog.

## PUNISHMENT NEEDS TO BE AS SEVERE AS NECESSARY
The punishment should be aversive and intense enough to stop the behavior right away. The FIRST TIME! If not, you will end up escalating the punishment until it is much stronger and harsher than if you had started with the appropriate level in the beginning.

## DOG CAN THINK PUNISHMENT IS CONTINGENT ON OWNER'S PRESENCE
The dog should experience the aversive as independent of the owner's presence, or else you will only get results if the owner is present.

## PUNISHMENT SHOULD BE TO CHANGE THE DOG'S BEHAVIOR
The goal of an aversive is to quickly and permanently change the unwanted behavior, not to let the owner feel better because he's "punished" the dog.

## *There are Humane and Effective Alternatives*

For the purposes of this handout, the words *punishment* and *aversive* mean "adding something the dog considers yukky or nasty" with the intent of stopping the behavior. No attempt is made at categorizing the examples into formal learning theory.

The information contained in this handout is supported by facts and research by M. and K. Breland, R. Bailey, B.F. Skinner, K. Pryor, M. Sidman, M. Burch, B. Schwartz and others.

# EYE CONTACT:
# ATTENTION TO NAME USING A TOY/PLAY REWARD

**YOUR GOAL FOR EYE CONTACT—SEVEN WEEKS OF TRAINING**
Your dog willingly turns away from a distraction to make eye contact with you.

Attention is a basic element of your relationship and your communication with your dog. Some people use the dog's name indiscriminately. For example, they expect the dog to come to them if they say the name or they expect the dog to stop doing something bad when they say the name in a threatening way. Let's teach the dog that his name means "Make Happy Eye Contact with Your Owner." Starting now, don't use your dog's name in conjunction with punishment. Don't call his name to take him away from fun. We want to retrain your dog to love it when you call him. Perhaps your dog has a bad association with his name. Does he sink down or turn away when you call his name? Perhaps that's because you have been saying things like, "Buffy, BAD!" In extreme cases like this, it will be helpful to give Buffy a new name! Here is an easy step-by-step program that results in happy eye contact when you call the dog's name. It's also the foundation for "Come-When-Called."

### STEP 1: ORIENTATION
You watched our demonstration dog focus on a small toy and follow the toy with his eyes to a position under the owner's chin. Now it's time for you to try it. Follow the instructions in Step 2.

### STEP 2: LURE WITH TOY, TRACE, SAY NAME, PLAY
Five times a day help your dog make eye contact by tracing a line between his face and yours with a toy. Do 3 to 5 repetitions per session, 3 to 5 sessions per day. To avoid confusion, food is not used in this particular exercise. Food will work just fine for attention but we want your dog to be as excited about you as he is for a food treat. Therefore, for the first few steps of the attention exercise, we won't use food as reward. We will use a toy. Make the toy interesting by moving it from side to side, or toward the floor, or behind your dog until he is excited. Once your dog is focusing on the toy, quickly bring the toy (and with it, your dog's attention) to a spot just below your chin. As soon as that eye-to-eye lock is made with your dog, even if its just for one second, say your dog's name in a normal but happy voice and launch into lots of praise and games with the toy. Having fun when making eye contact for hearing his name is the beginning of a communication channel between you and your dog. It's an important step in future training. When your dog hears you say his name, it should mean "pay attention, something great is going to happen." Be sure something great does happen. Throw the ball, give lots of pats, snap on the lead and take him for a walk. **GOAL:** Success at 5 out of 5 repetitions, 4 out of 5 sessions. A *repetition* is each time you practice a single behavior. A *session* is the time you set aside to work with your dog.

### STEP 3: NO LURE, SAY DOG'S NAME, REWARD
Do this in a distraction-free place. Keep your hands still and toy hidden. Say your dog's name: "Buffy!" If he makes eye contact, praise him and make something great happen. Making eye contact is your "on" button. Get excited, praise lavishly. **GOAL:** Success at 5 out of 5 repetitions, 4 out of 5 sessions.

CONTACT US IF YOU NEED HELP    info@legacycanine.com    360-683-1522

PDM 1 EyeContact.doc    *Coaching People to Train Their Dogs* © Terry Ryan 2005

## STEP 4: DISTRACTIONS

Luring is okay here since distractions are difficult. We'll start phasing the lure out in the next step. Although you established eye contact and attention with toys and interaction, now it's okay to surprise your dog from time to time with his food bowl. Here are some sample set-ups.

| | | |
|---|---|---|
| **A.** | HELPER: | Bounces a ball in the same room as you and your dog |
| | YOU: | Call, "Buffy" |
| | HELPER: | Puts ball in jacket and turns away |
| | BUFFY: | Looks at you |
| | YOU: | Bring out your own ball and play with your dog |
| | BUFFY: | "WOW, MY OWNER HAS A BETTER BALL!" |
| **B.** | HELPER: | Has a packet of food on a leash and rests it on the floor |
| | YOU: | Walk Buffy past the packet within a few inches of it. |
| | HELPER: | If Buffy looks at the food, pull the food to your chest and turn away |
| | YOU: | Call "Buffy!" |
| | BUFFY: | Looks at you. |
| | YOU: | Get his food bowl with BETTER food in it from a shelf behind you. |
| | BUFFY: | "HOW DOES MY OWNER DO THAT? IT'S MAGIC. MY OWNER IS REALLY POWERFUL." |
| **C.** | Helper: | None. Take advantage of naturally occurring distractions |
| | YOU: | Call your dog's name |
| | BUFFY: | Looks at you |
| | YOU: | High value reward! |
| | BUFFY: | "YOU ARE SUCH AN INTERESTING OWNER!" |

## STEP 5: YOUR DOG CHOOSES TO MAKE EYE CONTACT

The dog has more responsibility to voluntarily check in with you. Similar to A, B, and C above, only now WAIT for your dog to choose to look at you. Don't call his name. Make him do the work now. Eye contact makes the fun begin. This might mean a wait of several seconds until your dog finally checks in. It's always fun to wait and see just how long it takes to figure out what they need to do. This is a good cognitive exercise for your dog. When he makes the contact, explode with praise and play. Use rewards better than your helper had! The dog learns that his decision to turn away from the distraction and look to you was worthwhile. Your helper might need to withdraw the distraction to help your dog decide to look to you for fun. If no eye contact within 5 or 6 seconds, call his name and play or praise. Go back to Steps 2 and 3.

## STEP 6: RANDOM REWARD: VARY DELIVERY AND VARY TYPE OF REWARD

**Vary Delivery of Reward**—This is a variable schedule of reinforcement. Mix it up. Sometimes your dog has to make eye contact three times before he gets the reward, sometimes two times, sometimes he gets three rewards in a row for making eye contact once.

**Vary Type of Reward**—Sometimes the reward is running away and playing tug of war, sometimes the reward is throwing the ball. Sometimes it's the presentation of his food bowl with dinner in it. Sometimes you get attention and give no more than a smile. Mix it up.

## STEP 7: USE RANDOM, DELAYED REWARDS NOW

Sometimes you should not have your rewards with you. Be sneaky. Be prepared by hiding a reward somewhere ahead of time. For example, before you take your dog for a walk, go out and hide a ball in a hedge. If you are training in the living room, hide a toy there when the dog's not looking. Make your dog think you can perform miracles. You will see lots of progress toward the end of these steps. Even without your friend helping with set-ups, when Buffy sees something interesting on a walk, he might glance at it, but quickly look at you. You will know the training is working. Because of Steps 5 and 6 your dog thinks that you can find rewards anytime, anywhere and he will be willing to play the lottery with you.

# FOCUSING EXERCISE (TRICK TRAINING!)

Pick a fun behavior that's fairly easy but requires your dog's undivided attention. The behavior will be used to redirect the dog's energy and engage her mind. Train this behavior when both you and your dog are upbeat and enthusiastic. The strategy is to make this special focusing behavior produce really great rewards and jackpots. It can then be used as a means to keep the dog's attention in a distracting situation.

Some suggestions are:

**SPIN**—Encourage your dog to do a tight 360 degree circle at your side. You can start this by using a food magnet on the dog's nose. Lure her head in a circular pattern in whichever direction seems easiest for your dog. Once the head gets going, the body is apt to follow. Don't say anything. If she doesn't make the full turn, just stop for a few seconds and try again. Be sure to follow through and bring the food completely around in a circle. Be ready with your, "YES!" and food treat the first time she does a 360. When it becomes easy for you to get the behavior, start giving a spin hand signal or verbal cue. Do not reinforce the behavior if the dog spins spontaneously without the cue.

**SHAKE OR HIGH FIVE**—Get down low with your dog and show her you are hiding a piece of food in your closed right hand. Tease her a little. She's apt to put her nose on your hand. Ignore that. Tease some more. Sooner or later she will try to use her foot to make you give up the food. As soon as her foot moves, even a little, say "YES!" and open your hand to give the treat. Shape this into a distinct lifting of the foot toward your extended fist. Then start with an empty fist but produce the food from the other hand or your pocket.

For a shake, grab her paw when she extends it and say "YES!" and give a food treat. For a high five, open the hand and reward the paw on the palm of your hand. Slowly move your hand upward with each repetition until you get into a high five position. Go for duration, style, whatever, but make sure to reinforce the behavior with a high-ranking reward. When it becomes easy for you to get the behavior, start giving a hand signal or verbal cue. Do not reinforce the behavior if the dog offers it spontaneously without the cue.

**TAKE A BOW**—The dog puts his front legs and chest against the floor while holding his rear end up. Use your lure (food magnet) to get his nose to the floor. The path of your lure should be directly down and then in toward his stomach a little. At the same time, place your other hand in front of his rear legs or under his belly to hold his rear up. No cue until you a get the action easily. It's a good warm-up stretch and makes your dog appear friendly, too.

## YOUR HOMEWORK GOALS
## BE READY FOR WEEK 2

Practice about 3–5 sessions a day, 3–5 repetitions per session.
This week's goal is to achieve about an 80% success rate at Step 2 in the exercises below.
Your notebook has details on each exercise. If you need help: info@legacycanine.com, 360-683-1522.

**REWARDS (pg. 251)**
Read and follow instructions in the **Select & Use Rewards** handout!

**"YES"/TREAT (pg. 263)**
Read the **"YES!"/Treat** handout.
Complete the exercises

**SIT HAPPENS!—READ THE HANDOUT, DO STEPS 1 & 2 (pg. 255)**
Warm-up: Food magnet on nose—nod head up and down, shake left and right, then move magnet (still on nose) up and back between ears. When dog's bottom makes contact with floor, "YES!"/Treat. No words! Don't say "Sit" yet! Dog leaps around or doesn't sit? The handout has the solutions.

**EYE CONTACT—READ THE HANDOUT, DO STEPS 1 & 2 (pg. 241)**
Get your dog focused on a toy then use the toy to lure eye contact up to your face. Say your dog's name cheerfully, play 3–5 seconds. (Do not say "YES!," do not give food.

### DON'T FORGET! (pg. 247)
The **L.E.A.D.** Program: Leadership Education for Anyone with a Dog
Important! Read the **L.E.A.D.** Handout.
Implement two or more **L.E.A.D.** exercises—your choice.

### BEFORE YOU COME TO CLASS NEXT WEEK:
- Obtain appropriate collar. Bring a 6-foot leash and mark the 3-foot point with a pen, or a knot.
- Wear clothes with pockets or get a waist pouch for rewards.
- Toilet your dog at home before you come to class or use our designated toilet area.
- We will escort you in via the entry (right side) door—please respect the personal space of other dogs.
- We'll assist you in making your dog comfortable and happy.

CONTACT US IF YOU NEED HELP    info@legacycanine.com    360-683-1522

*PDM 1 Homework.doc*    *Coaching People to Train Their Dogs* © Terry Ryan 2005

# Take the L.E.A.D.

## Leadership Education for Anyone with a Dog

Like humans, dogs are social creatures. When individuals live in a social group, regardless of species, they need skills for getting along successfully. A respected leader is important to the survival of the group. Families have parent figures, towns have mayors, corporations have CEOs, wolf packs have alphas. Your dog has you. Dogs are different from wolves and different from people. Dogs are a unique and important part of your family. Understanding your pet's social needs can enhance your relationship and provide a strong foundation for future training.

The L.E.A.D. program is about communication between you and your dog. It's not about the training exercises, it's about the way you structure daily interactions with your dog. Your dog is learning all the time from the world around him. Puppies benefit from a head start that helps them avoid inappropriate habits that will be more difficult for you to deal with at a later age. Adolescents readily accept your guidance if they perceive it as in their best interest. Nervous or shy dogs of any age need assurance that they are not alone to cope with the scary world. Pushy or untrained dogs will be less likely to be assertive if you demonstrate, in terms the dog understands, that you are a more capable leader.

Leadership is an attitude, a state of mind. It has nothing to do with size, age, gender, or seniority. It's not about strength or harshness. A good leader needs to be intelligent, confident, have empathy, and be responsible for those trusting to follow his lead. Dogs can sense leadership in a person by observation. Being mostly nonverbal communicators, dogs are good at observing and interpreting the actions of their humans. L.E.A.D. is written to take advantage of this fact and to help you provide clear non-verbal cues for your dog, paving the way for a good relationship.

## Collar and Leash

Choke collars are not necessary for training. A buckle collar (belt type) or martingale (limited restriction) is recommended. A six-foot leather or cloth leash works well for training.

For some extra control for heeling, you may want to try the Gentle Leader® head collar. This collar controls the dog's head like a halter. Where the head goes, the dog will follow. The muzzle strap mimics the control signal of a dog gripping another's muzzle. Ask to borrow the informational video. An instructor will assist you in fitting and using the Gentle Leader® head collar.

> THE L.E.A.D. Program is not a rehabilitation program for dogs that threaten or are aggressive toward people or dogs. Your pet will benefit from a behavior modification program designed for the specific problem. L.E.A.D. should be implemented by the adults in the family.

# HOW THE L.E.A.D. PROGRAM WORKS

L.E.A.D. is more of a relationship program than a training program. A good foundation for further training, L.E.A.D. will outline some important concepts about everyday actions such as eating, playing, and personal space. Individual dogs have varying concerns. Some dogs don't worry about resting places. Some dogs couldn't care less if you take a toy from them. Therefore, some exercises might seem difficult, others too easy! Start with the easy ones that appeal to you. Here are the leadership exercises, as taught to an imaginary dog named Fuzz:

1. **THE ATTENTION EXERCISE—USE A TOY**
   Attention is a communication channel that will stay open for the rest of your dog's life, once it's established and reinforced. Several times a day, help Fuzz make eye contact with you and then play. A separate, detailed handout on the steps to take to gain reliable eye contact is provided in your orientation notebook.

2. **IS YOUR DOG POLITE?**
   Fuzz probably loves games and attention from you. Interact with her more, not less. However, "obeying" her demands EVERY time gives the message that she's always in charge. If she is attention seeking, she may try annoying you—that often works to get you to talk to her, doesn't it? ("Fuzz quit it!") If this bothers you, try ignoring Fuzz when she noses and paws at you for attention. Continue to ignore her even if she barks. When Fuzz is quiet and still, wait 5–15 seconds, then initiate play. Play by your rules. You can wait until Fuzz spontaneously offers a "Sit" or quiet behavior. Reward that with the attention she deserves.

3. **SOME POINTS CONCERNING FOOD**
   It's okay to feed Fuzz from a bowl, but don't allow the bowl to be down at all times. Save some food to be *FED BY HAND,* keeping your hand still so Fuzz doesn't learn to be grabby. Dogs fed by hand or from a bowl held in the hand learn to associate hands with good things. Sometimes put the empty bowl on the floor first, then place the food into it with your hand. Scheduled meals also help regulate potty breaks—what goes in on schedule comes out on schedule. For health reasons, avoid strenuous activity after a meal. Some of Fuzz's food can be given in special food-dispensing toys to give her something fun to do while you're not home.

   With scheduled meals, you'll know when Fuzz is hungry. Practice training exercises such as the *MAGNET GAME.* A few times a day, take a pinch of her food, no more than a pea-sized portion, and put it in front of her nose. Her snout will attach to your fingers like a magnet. Don't say anything, just move your "magnet" two inches here and there and see if her head follows. After two slight head movements, say "YES!" and give the treat. The exercise is over! Do it again in a few seconds. This time you might try luring her head far enough that she also has to move her feet to keep her nose on the magnet. After these two slight moves, say "YES!" and give the pinch of food. That's all! Exercise over. Your dog understands the game. In class we will turn, "YES!" into a clear message of approval and reward.

   **NOTE:** *From now on, only use the word "YES!" during specific training exercises such as the magnet game. "YES!" is a promise. Don't break promises! Always follow the "YES!" by giving the pinch of food or "YES!" will loose its power!*

### 4. CONCERNING RESTING PLACES

Fuzz should have a place of her own where she can relax without worry. If she is allowed on the furniture, she should be willing to give up her comfy place without reluctance at your request. At first, lure Fuzz off with a food treat—food makes getting off happen. Then you can switch to rewarding her as soon as she gets off; getting off makes the food treat happen.

### 5. CONCERNING SPACE

Dogs take notice of the personal space around their bodies. You can use this to move your dog around. For example, if she's lying across a hallway, gently walk toward and into her body. As you get closer to the space right next to the dog, she will learn to yield space.

### 6. GREETING MANNERS

A knock on the door is great excitement for a dog. Fuzz can practice a "Sit Stay" while you open the door. Tie her leash to some immovable object in sight of the door or get a helper. Don't close her in a back room—it will only make her worse.

When you're out for a walk, Fuzz might want to run up to greet other dogs or people. You, her leader, can ask for a "Sit Stay." You can then decide if and when it is appropriate to release her to go say hello.

### 7. WHEN PLAYING TUG OR FETCH

Keep special tug or retrieve toys out of her reach. Bring them down once in a while, invite her to play with you for a little bit, then put the toy back. This keeps her special interactive toys new and interesting. Games can also be timed to reward good behavior during a training session. Use toys with a handle, like a ball attached to a rope or inserted into a nylon stocking. Should Fuzz not want to give up the toy, just stop playing. Hold the toy tightly, close to your body, and don't say anything. Just wait. You are no fun if you don't pull. She will find that in order for you to resume tugging or throwing, she will have to give up the toy temporarily. Fuzz should have other toys, especially chew toys, available on the floor at all times to play with when she wants.

### 8. RELAX FOR GROOMING

Fuzz should cooperate when you brush, bathe, or wipe her muddy feet. If she is worried about grooming or can't stay still, try some peanut butter therapy. Smear a little peanut butter (or squeeze cheese—some dogs have peanut allergies) at her nose level on a washable surface such as a glass door or side of the bathtub. While Fuzz is licking it off, get in a few strokes with the brush. Be alert for parasites, bumps, cuts, or anything out of the ordinary. Eventually you want her to be calm on a low table or bench for grooming. It's easier on your back and helps her accept being out of her territory and at ease in yours, or the vet's, territory.

---

## LEADERS ARE FAIR, KIND & CONSISTENT TEACHERS

Dog training is like a savings account. Time invested now will pay off dividends—years of good companionship. Stick with the program.

# THE SELECTION AND USE OF TRAINING REWARDS

## Taking Food Gently
## Giving Toys Back Willingly

Experiment and see what reward your dog likes best. A good reward will catch and maintain interest even if slight distractions are taking place. Be sure to consider these rewards from your dog's point of view, not yours! You may be attracted to a cute squeaky toy, when in fact your dog prefers the plain old gummy tennis ball. You might decide a bite of cheese is best; your dog might place higher value on a bite of chicken. Some exercises are best done with toys; others are best done with food. Active exercises like "Come-When-Called" might best be served by an active game. Quiet exercises like "Down" might be better reinforced by a quiet bite of food. When timing is critical, food is best because it's faster. Food is also good for chaining and shaping—techniques we will use later on in class. Play takes longer and you'll have to settle the dog down for the next step. It's important to have a variety of rewards: food, toys, and games.

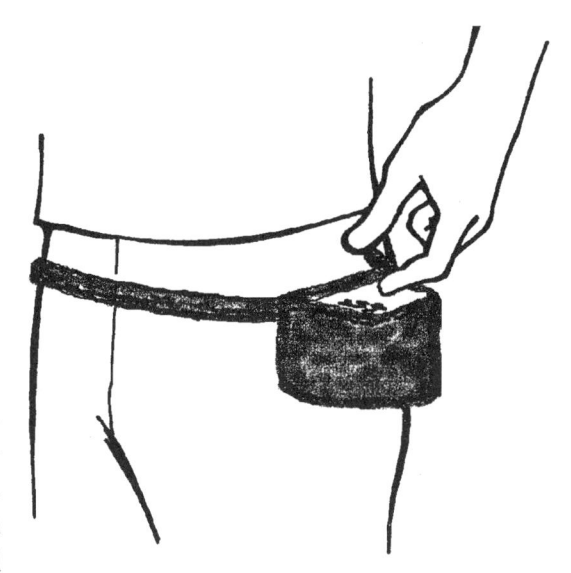

## FOOD AS A REINFORCER

For the vast majority of dogs, the reward of choice is food. It's a primary reinforcer. To eat is to live. Survival dictates an animal to be highly receptive to information associated with the acquisition of food. We can use some of the dog's intrinsic survival instincts to help us in training. Dogs evolved from predators. Dogs no longer need to figure out how to find and catch their own dinner, but they are still programmed to be alert and responsive when food is available. Let's take advantage of it. The food need not be special. In fact some dogs consume their everyday ration of food as training rewards distributed at certain times throughout the day. Schedule a training session around meal time. Soft foods don't need much chewing and are less apt to crumble, fall to the floor, and distract your dog from the task at hand. Dog food companies are doing a good job of making a variety of yummy, appropriate and in most cases, well-balanced training treats. Sometimes a special food treat is preferred. Some owners enjoy preparing homemade goodies.

A few examples of food rewards:

- LOWFAT PROCESSED CHEESE cut into ⅛" cubes. It comes in stick form (string cheese, mozzarella). Simply slice off little circles, or hold it in your hand and pinch it off as needed.
- LIVER TREATS can be made by boiling sliced calves' liver and drying it on a grate in the oven at 300 degrees. Turn your oven off after 30 minutes, but leave the liver in for another 30 minutes, then cut into ⅛" cubes.
- TURKEY FRANKS are a favorite. After you slice them into thin little coins, microwave until firm, or use as is or hold half a frank in your hand, and pinch off little bits as needed.
- SQUEEZE CHEESE is handy. Dogs learn to take little bits right from the nozzle.

If you use human food for training treats, common sense prevails. Refrigerate all perishable foods. If your dog has a food allergy, remember that when choosing training treats. Some dog breeds have an intolerance to high protein levels. Care must be taken not to unbalance ANY dog's diet. Let your veterinarian know what you wish to do! Cheese, liver, hot dogs and the like are not nutritionally complete. Too much of these treats can cause upset stomach, obesity, or other serious problems. A respected veterinarian, Christine Zink, says that human-food treats should not comprise more than 10% of the dog's daily ration. If you are using a prepared dog food for your treat, you can see how many calories your dog is eating. Look on the back of the dog food package, and then compute the calories in the food treat to determine how much your dog should have each day. If you are making your own dog food, you are probably under the guidance of a veterinarian. Ask your veterinarian for advice.

Whatever you decide to use, put each day's quota into a package. You can make each package last twice as long by cutting the pieces in half. In fact, it seems most dog prefer two little bites rather than one big bite. It's possible that the anticipation and act of taking the food may be a big part of the reward for the dog. If you are using factory-prepared kibble as a training treat, you might make it seem special by sealing it up overnight in a baggy with a piece of cheese or liver in it.

## TEACH YOUR DOG TO TAKE FOOD TREATS GENTLY

Often dogs have learned to be grabby because of less-than-confident people who try to hand feed dogs but pull away when they feel the dog's lips on their fingers. Don't let that happen to your dog. Some dogs are naturally enthusiastic about receiving food, anytime, including from your hands. To overcome that habit, feed your dog only very small pieces of food, so he always has to make contact with your fingers. If he's rough, don't take your hand away, simply keep it there and hold on tighter to the piece of food. Wait until he becomes gentle with you and then release the food. If he barks or paws at your hand, remain still and quiet and hang on tightly to the food until you feel him becoming gentle. For overly ambitious dogs or for people with tender fingers, I learned about this method from trainer Dawn Jecs. Place the tidbit into the bowl of a spoon. Direct the handle of the spoon over your wrist so that only the bowl and food are in your hand. Put your thumb over the food. Now if the dog bites too hard, he makes contact with the metal, which is not very pleasant. Take your thumb off the food when your dog's lips become gentle. You need not say a thing. Your dog will learn to accept food nicely.

## HOW ABOUT USING TOYS AS A REWARD?

For many dogs, the best reward is to receive a toy or to have social interaction with the owner. The choice of toy is up to the dog! Different dogs enjoy different games. Some like the chase game, some like the tug of war games, some like to make a toy squeak, and some like chewing on things. Use of toys is more time-consuming than use of small food rewards—so fewer repetitions of behavior will be possible within a limited amount of time. When training with toys, you eventually have to get them back. Giving up the toy could be seen as an aversive state of affairs by the dog. With interactions, you eventually have to stop. Toys are especially appropriate as rewards for active exercises like "Heeling" or "Come." Toys used as training rewards should be put away after use. They should not join the other toys on the floor that are available to your dog all the time.

Here are some ideas to try out on your dog:

- **BALLS**—If you have a ball-crazy dog, you have a great reward opportunity! Hollow rubber balls collapse and hide in your hand, pocket or nearby furniture, and can be popped into view when the dog least expects it for a quick game of catch or chase. Balls that squeak are especially interesting.
- **BALL WITH A HANDLE**—A ball with a rope or a nylon tail is fun. The tail makes it easy to control the dog and the ball at the same time! Make your own by knotting a ball into the toe of an old nylon sock. Hide it in your jacket or up your sleeve, and whip it out by the tail to launch for your dog. The tail fluttering excites dogs. A ball with a tail doesn't roll as far when thrown.
- **SQUEAKERS**—Some dogs just cannot resist a squeak toy. My favorites are 3-inch discs that can slip easily in and out of your pocket. Your hand can fold over it so your dog never knows if you have the squeak toy or not.

## MAKING TOYS SPECIAL AND INTERESTING TRAINING REWARDS

Broaden your reward base by getting your dog interested in a special interactive toy. In life, one of the critical aspects of survival is food acquisition. Behaviors we might consider play could be thought of as practice for food acquisition. The prey chase chain of events in canids is stalking, chasing, grabbing, shaking, mouthing, and bringing food items back to the den. What part of this sequence does your dog enjoy most? Chasing a flying disc? Making a toy squeak? Retrieving a ball? Select a few toys for special training rewards. All you really need is an old sock or hose. Knot into the toe the item your dog would be most attracted to, attach a strong string to it, about three feet long, so you can pull it along the ground.

Choose a soft toy that doesn't roll too much. If you have a food-crazy dog, select a toy that snaps open or has a Velcro pocket so you can include a delectable treat. Trainer Susan Garret would advise you to keep these toys in a drawer or high on a shelf. You and your dog will visit this place before each meal for the next week. Just walk over acting very excited. He will want to be with you to see what is happening. Make a funny noise, one you don't usually make, like a sudden intake of breath. Turn quickly toward the shelf, stare at it, and stalk up to it slowly with exaggerated motions to keep your dog's attention. You might even talk excitedly to yourself. Open the drawer or reach up on the shelf, get the toy and get really, really excited with the toy, but ignore the dog and don't let him have the toy. For 30 seconds, go wild with the toy in view of your dog, but don't let him have it! Pretend the toy is alive and is getting away, exclaim, laugh, whisper, stop and stare at the toy, then start over again. Put the toy away after 30 seconds. Don't say anything to your dog, but go ahead and feed him then. Be creative!

## PLEASE GIVE THE TOY BACK WILLINGLY

### THE BASIC GIVE-FOR-A-TREAT EXERCISE

This exercise is important for all dogs of any age. It should be taught in every puppy class. You never know what a dog might pick up, and the worse it is for them to have, the more they seem to want to keep it. Teach your dog early on the release for a treat exercise. Do this as a completely different exercise, not when he is racing around the room daring you to take the remote out of his mouth and not at the end of a game of tug of war when the dog is fully aroused.

Start by sitting down with a pocket of goodies and a low-ranking, somewhat boring toy. Choose a toy that allows you a good grip on the toy outside of the dog's mouth, perhaps a ball on a rope. Your dog is on a leash. You may have to show him a treat or otherwise get his attention. If all goes well, he'll open his mouth for the treat and you take the toy. Say, "Give" and as soon as he releases the toy, then say "YES!" and give a treat ("YES!"/Treat). As soon as the dog swallows the food, give the toy back. You might even give a better toy that you have hidden in your shirt, or you might toss the toy if she likes to retrieve. Since you have the leash on, she can't play keep away this time. Three or five sessions a day, three or five reps in each session, for a week or so should give you and your dog a good foundation. When you can do these exchanges smoothly nine out of ten times, you can start using the word without showing the food. The food comes out of hiding when you get the toy. Then you can start putting the reward on a random schedule with 1-fers and 3-fers.

### TAKE TOY THEN GIVE A TREAT

While you're at #1, start using the verbal cue "take" when your dog grabs the toy. You can even have little sit down sessions of Take/Give/Yes/Treat. It's really a good first step in breaking down reliable retrieving.

### DEAD TOY (BACK UP PLAN "JUST IN CASE")

Tug toys are no fun when they don't tug back. If your dog becomes overly stimulated or won't "give" when asked, stop playing, plant your feet, turn your head, put your hands and the object close to your body and wait. The dog might continue tugging while you hold. Slowly, hand over hand, work up the toy until you are holding it right against his mouth. Now the dog's nose is against your hands and your hands are tight against your body. Very little tug action can take place. Not much fun. After you get the toy, do some calm Take/Give/Treat sequences and play again. If you don't play again, the dog may just try harder to retain possession of the toy next time. So keep him engaged somehow. In order for him to settle down, you might want to do a few focusing exercises first, then the Take/Give/Treat and then try another tug game. If your dog is the type that might mouth your hand before giving in, apply a little Bitter Apple before you play. Any time the dog does put teeth on human flesh, even if it was an accident, the game stops immediately.

### DRASTIC LAST DITCH MEASURES

Your dog's nose is against your hand, and your hand is tight against your body. You are not tugging and your dog is not letting go of the toy. It seems like a stalemate. Drop your end and walk out of the room, say nothing. He got the toy, but he lost you and the tugging action. It works for some dogs.

*Following is a sample list of Food, Toy, and Social Interaction Rewards. Encourage the whole family to help in filling in your own list with things your dog considers a reward! Then put the rewards in rank order. We like to save the top-ranking rewards for jackpots or really earth-shattering accomplishments. Some of Legacy's class exercises will suggest a certain reward category (food, toy, or interaction) as especially appropriate for a particular exercise. In the end, YOU are the ultimate reward. Food and toys are just temporary tools to make you more attractive.*

| Food | Toys | Social Interactions |
|---|---|---|
| 1. Low fat cheese | 1. Food-stuffed toy | 1. Tug of war game |
| 2. Boiled chicken breast | 2. Chew stick | 2. Fetch |
| 3. Commercial training treats | 3. Squeaker ball | 3. Go for a walk |
| 4. Hot dog slices | 4. Nylon bone | 4. Pats and praise |
| 5. Regular dog food | 5. Fleece toy | 5. Car ride |

# SIT HAPPENS!

# USING A LURE: THE MAGNETIC SIT EXERCISE

### YOUR GOAL FOR SIT—SEVEN WEEKS OF TRAINING
With one cue, your dog will sit within three seconds. With minor distractions, and no further help, your dog will stay in that position, quietly for one minute until released.

**STEP 1: DURING ORIENTATION**
You watched our demonstration dog nod his head up and down and back and forth using a piece of food as a "magnet" directly on his nose. Warm up by trying that exercise two or three times with your dog. "YES"/Treat every couple of moves. No words, except "YES!" followed by the treat.

**STEP 2: THE MAGNETIC SIT EXERCISE: PLAY AT LURING AND REWARDING SITS**
Begin your session when your dog is alert, but not overly excited. You will do 5 repetitions of this exercise. A *repetition* is each time you practice a single behavior. A *session* is the time you set aside to work with your dog. Hold 5 pea-sized pieces of food in your hand ready to feed one by one to your dog. Hold the food within a fraction of an inch of or directly on your dog's nose. When she is focused on the food, move your hand holding the treat back over her head, between her ears. See the illustration. Her nose should be like a magnet following the food. As her head goes backward, her balance will shift. Gravity! The dog's rear drops into a sitting position. "YES!"/Treat.

Note: You haven't said "Sit" yet. For now, don't say the word "Sit" until you are able to play this luring game and can get the dog to sit 5 out of 5 tries, almost (4 out of 5) every session. Just remember: get the Sit before you name it. Dogs learn by association. Getting the behavior before you name it is the best way to help her make the correct association. (If you say "Sit" when your dog is standing in front of you, wagging her tail, she might assume Sit means "stand in front of owner and wag tail!")

If your dog tries to get the food with her mouth or paw before she is sitting, just hold the food to your chest and turn your head away until she settles. Once she settles you can try again. You may want to use a less delicious food treat! If your dog backs up instead of sitting, train her against a wall or in a corner. If Sit doesn't happen, don't worry! You haven't given her a command, so she hasn't done anything wrong—just try again. It's only a game. Is your dog jumping up for the food? She's doing her job and the treat is doing its job. YOUR job is to hold the treat low enough, right in front of her nose, so she doesn't have to jump up. The treat should act as Velcro to the dog's nose. Step 2 should go quickly. You can probably get 5 out of 5 in the first few tries of this game.

**STEP 3: NOW NAME THE SIT**
When you can consistently get 5 out of 5 reps in 4 out of 5 sessions, add the word "Sit" immediately before (not during or after) you put the lure in front of the dog's nose and use it to guide the dog's head back. Say your dog's name to get his attention. Say "Sit." Keep your luring hand still until the T in SIT is out of your mouth, then use the lure if you need to. When your dog's rear reaches the floor, immediately say "YES!" and give a treat. Be quick with your "YES!"/Treat. You might want to set up a mirror at home to help you know just when your dog's rear makes contact! Practice this a few times a day, no more than 3 to 5 Sits per session.

CONTACT US IF YOU NEED HELP   info@legacycanine.com   360-683-1522

To review, the sequence is:

*SAY YOUR DOG'S NAME (OPTIONAL)*

*SAY THE WORD "SIT"—KEEP STILL, DON'T FORECAST THE LURE WITH BODY LANGUAGE*

*USE THE LURE WHEN "T" IN "SIT" IS OUT OF YOUR MOUTH, IF NEEDED*

*SAY "YES!" AND GIVE THE TREAT WHEN DOG SITS*

## STEP 4: MAINTAIN THE SIT / RELEASE THE SIT

### A. Delayed Rewards Instead of Immediate Rewards

When your dog sits, don't immediately "YES!"/Treat. Now we will wait a little. (In technical terms, we are going for short, variable durations.) Alternate between a range of 3–10 seconds of maintaining the sit before you "YES!"/Treat. Your dog might need help to stay sitting for these few seconds. Hold the treat still in a position to allow her to sniff and even nibble a bit. "Control the Head, Control the Dog." Your Goal: When the dog consistently stays sitting for short, variable durations, 5 out of 5 reps in 4 out of 5 sessions, it's time to go on.

### B. Starting the Stay Cue

When your dog is performing a stationary exercise like "Sit," or "Down," "Stay" is implied. During "Sit" for example, the dog can't be moving and sitting at the same time. However, an additional cue for "Stay" can be comforting to you. It's also comforting to some dogs. The dog associates the word "Stay" as a "keep going, you're doing great" cue, and "Stay" should be said in this encouraging tone of voice.

To help your dog understand the new cue "Stay," ask your dog to "Sit," . . . then say "Stay" . . . and turn your head away and break eye contact. That's a good first step at leaving a dog that is attentive. Or, after you say "Stay," shift your position slightly, as if you are going to move, or try moving away only one step. It's usually the initial change in your body language that tells the dog you are leaving. Be sure you are close to your dog so you can help her stay by having her focus on the lure. Tell your dog she's good while she's staying by giving some quiet, generalized praise and smiles. When your dog can maintain 3–10 second Stays at least 4 out of 5 sessions, it's time to go to the next step.

### C. The Release Cue Instead of "YES!"/Treat

Until now, your dog has only been asked to sit for a very short interval before we ended the exercise with a "YES!"/Treat. We now want to teach the dog to stay in the sit position for longer durations. To do so, we are going to replace the "YES!/Treat with a release word. Legacy uses the word "Okay"* to tell a dog that she's done, the sit is over, she can do whatever she wants now. Note: when you say "okay" she might decide to keep on sitting or she might decide to go off and be a dog. Either is fine. She's been released to do whatever she wants. To start teaching your dog to stay until released: Tell your dog to "Sit." At a time predetermined by you (a range of 3–10 seconds), say your release word. The exercise is over! You can play with her or give her a reward or do nothing. There will be many times now when we recommend that you give your release cue and do nothing—no reward. That's because we will start giving rewards DURING the Sit. We get what we pay for and we want the dog to be rewarded for a long Sit. We don't want her rewarded for being released from a Sit. Release and reward are two different things; however, until that is perfectly clear to your dog, you can accompany your release with animated praise, a food reward, or a game.

*Many trainers use "Okay" as a release term. You might want to choose a word that's not used much in your everyday conversation. Some popular release terms are "Free" or "Done."

**STEP 5: GET RID OF THE LURING HAND**
Most dogs associate your moving hand, whether it contains food or not, as a signal to sit. That's fine: silent hand signals are useful. But let's be sure your dog has caught on to the verbal cue to sit as well. Keep your hand perfectly still, even if you are holding food, and say, "Sit." If you get the Sit, give the treat and/or lots of praise. Don't fall into the habit of repeating the word "Sit" if your dog doesn't respond. If you don't get a sit, give the dog a peek of the food without moving your hand as a signal. Or move your hand only slightly. That's usually enough of a jump-start to get the sit.

**STEP 6: THE ALL-IMPORTANT SIT LOTTERY**
During your practice, start getting at least one, but no more than two, free Sits from your dog. That means ask for Sit once, release, then ask for Sit and this time treat when your dog Sits. Sometimes get three Sits, sometimes get two Sits, before the dog earns a reward. Sometimes you will reward each Sit. Keep your dog guessing and mix it up—two-fers, three-fers, one-fers. This teaches you not to rely on food, and before long, your dog will learn to enjoy playing the lottery game.

At this point you can sometimes keep the pieces of food in your pocket or pouch. The food is out of sight and will be brought out when you are ready to reward the behavior. This step is the beginning of weaning off food. We are phasing out luring and phasing in the true concept of reward. Before long your dog will be able to Sit and Stay and not expect a treat each time.

---

**THINK ABOUT THIS IMPORTANT DIFFERENCE:**

a. AT THE START OF TRAINING: Dog sees food (lure)—the food makes Sit happen. This is luring. Luring is okay for a jump-start. Luring is a training aid, but . . .

b. QUICKLY PROGRESS TO: Dog hears "Sit" (or sees Sit signal)—Sit makes reward (food) happen. This is the real meaning of reward in training.

---

**STEP 7: SIT LOTTERY WITH REMOTE REWARDS**
Now we'll vary the delivery of rewards even more. (At this stage, you and your dog will not be depending on continuous rewards for good behavior.) When you are successful at Step 6, begin training sessions by hiding your food or toys somewhere else in the room. You should not have any food or toys on you. After your dog responds to your cue, and at random times, go to the spot where you hid the food (or toy) and go back to your dog and reward him. (Before long your dog thinks you're magic—always able to produce rewards from the strangest places!) Now, say your release cue, you're done, generalized praise is okay.

*Optional Hand Signals:* When we first taught the "Sit," "Down," and "Stay" exercises, we helped the dog learn with lures. Lures are similar to hand signals. Next we clearly and distinctly taught verbal only cues to avoid any possible overshadowing. If you would like to teach a hand signal so that your dog will respond to either verbal or hand signals, simply present the signal before (not after and not during) the verbal cue. The dog will soon get the association.

### *Work on the Four D's: Distance, Duration, Different Environment, Delivery of Reward*
This concept is the same for all exercises. If you raise one criterion (for example, distance on the Sit), lower the other criteria (duration, distractions). When things become potentially more difficult, increase your rewards and lower your expectations until your dog makes the breakthrough. Your dog doesn't need as many sessions or repetitions now if he is performing perfectly. Each session should be highly variable in location and distractions. For more details, see the Four D's handout.

# MORE ABOUT SITS

## *Alternative Method: Folding*

### (PHYSICALLY MODELING THE DOG INTO A SIT)

The "control the head, control the dog" method works with the vast majority of dogs, but not all. That's what makes dog training interesting. Some dogs will back up instead of sit, and you might find it helpful to work in front of a wall or piece of furniture as a stopper. You can also use one hand to hold the lure and the other to fold the dog's hind legs into a sitting position. A gentle tuck behind her knees is a physical prompt that works much better than pushing her rear. Most dogs simply brace against pressure when you push on the rear. We want to go WITH the dog, not against the dog. It's important to establish happy compliance to sit. It will be used again and again as a foundation on which to build advanced exercises.

## *Alternative Method: Gentle Leader® for Sit*

The Gentle Leader® works very well for Sit. It's especially helpful if you use the Gentle Leader® in conjunction with a food lure. If the Gentle Leader® becomes tight and the dog sits, quickly release the tension and give the dog a slack leash for sitting. Don't forget to check your Gentle Leader® periodically to make sure you have a good fit.

## *Practical Applications for Sit*

### SIT AT YOUR SIDE WHEN YOU STOP ON WALKS

We want your dog to be a well-mannered, accepted member of your community. If you ask her to "Sit" each time you stop while walking in Heel position, it will help keep her under control and out of the way of other pedestrians. The obvious application is for the dog to Sit during walks when you stop. During walks, when you need to cross a street, make it a point to stop at each curb, even if there is no traffic. Teach your dog to Sit before you start across. This keeps your dog under better control in busy traffic and safer if a car gets too close to the curb.

### SUBSTITUTE FOR A PROBLEM BEHAVIOR

Once Sit is established as a rewarding behavior, it can be used as a substitute for problem behavior. In the following example you can see how Sit-Stay competes with and takes the place of an irritating habit! Great! Now you can praise your dog in situations where you previously felt like punishing!

### BEFORE PASSING THROUGH DOORS

Dogs get excited about coming and going. The L.E.A.D. program suggests that when it's time to go outside, you make it a habit for your dog to sit by the door until it's opened and not go through until invited. In addition to making things easier, it will prevent the dog from dashing outdoors unexpectedly and getting into the street. You will also find it very convenient to ask your dog to "Sit" at the door before you enter.

# Stress Signals, Calming Signals

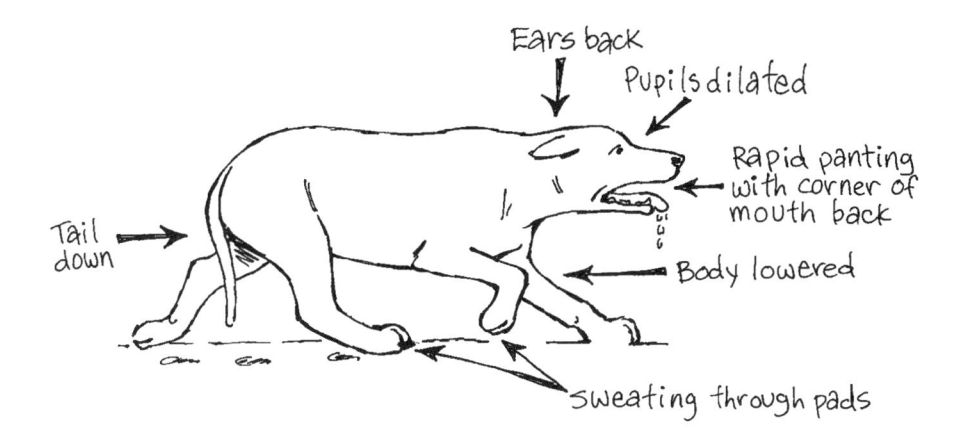

*Ears back*
*Pupils dilated*
*Rapid panting with corner of mouth back*
*Tail down*
*Body lowered*
*Sweating through pads*

The dog in the drawing above is showing signs of stress. Stress is abstract and subjective. What's terribly stressful for one dog could be neutral or enjoyable for another. Some stress is good and increases productivity in both dogs and humans. Too much stress immediately inhibits the learning process because of chemical influences on the brain. Stressors, which lead to fear and anxiety, activate the dog's flight or fight impulses. These behaviors are essentially out of the dog's control. To make matters worse, stress is cumulative and can produce a variety of illnesses, some of which may not become apparent until years later.

The signs shown below are often associated with an attempt to resolve a social conflict. Known as displacement activities or calming signals, these behaviors seem out of place for the context. One or two alone are not necessarily signs of a conflicted dog. Clusters of calming signals will alert you (and the Legacy staff) that all is not well with your dog. Adjustments to the environment will be made according to the individual.

**Sniffing**      **Yawning**      **Blinking**

**Licking**      **Turning Away**

CONTACT US IF YOU NEED HELP   info@legacycanine.com   360-683-1522

*PDM 1 StressSigCalmSig.doc*   *Coaching People to Train Their Dogs* © Terry Ryan 2005

# THE TOOLBOX
## FOR
## REMODELING PROBLEM DOGS

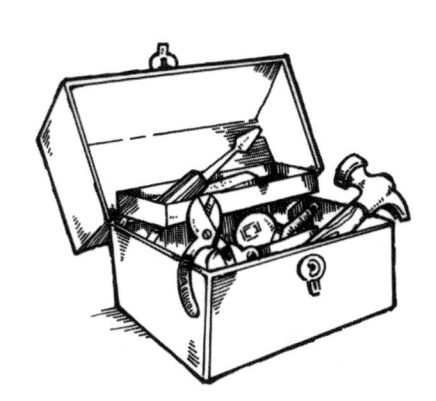

### FOUNDATION BLOCKS . . .

Life with your dog is like a pleasant cruise . . . and you are at the **HELM.**

**H** ealth—*Vet Check, Stress Reduction, Exercise*

**E** nvironmental Enrichment—*Home-Alone Hobbies, Social Time*

**L** eadership—*Consistency, Train Appropriate Behavior*

**M** anagement in General—*Common Sense: Supervise, Confine, Control*

### SELECT SPECIFIC REMODELING TOOLS . . .

The **"Yes"/Train** acronym might help you remember your options:

**Y** ield a Little—*Compromise*

**E** liminate the Trigger—*Remove the Reason for the Problem*

**S** ystematic Desensitization—*Little by Little*

**T** ake Away the Reward—*Identify and Remove the Reinforcer*

**R** eward an Incompatible Behavior—*Train a Competing Behavior*

**A** cclimate the Dog—*Habituation*

**I** mprove the Dog's Association—*Counter conditioning*

**N** ot Much Nasty Stuff—*Association With an Unpleasant Condition*

**Selection Considerations:** Dog's Temperament, Environment, and Ability of Dog and Owner

**Regarding the Problem:** Ask—"Where, When, What, Who . . .?"

CONTACT US IF YOU NEED HELP   info@legacycanine.com   360-683-1522

# "YES" AS A REWARD MARKER
## Communication Homework

This exercise is for the first week only. The word "yes" is a tool we'll use to start each new behavior. "YES!" will turn gray areas into black and white for your dog. You may have heard of clicker training or seen some of the Legacy staff with clickers. "YES!," is used instead of a clicker for Legacy's entry level training. Your dog will learn that "YES!" predicts a food reward. Here's how: Three to five times a day, hold three to five pieces of food in your hand. Say "YES!" and immediately give the food to your dog. Your dog can be doing ANY neutral, acceptable, or good behavior. Best not to "YES!"/Treat if your dog is doing something you consider unacceptable such as barking, jumping on you, or mouthing your hand. (You get what you pay for!)

**IMPORTANT:** "YES!" followed immediately by food should occur at random time intervals. Example:

| | |
|---|---|
| "YES!"/Treat | (Wait 5 seconds before doing again.) |
| "YES!"/Treat | (Wait 15 seconds before next repetition) |
| "YES!"/Treat | (Wait 2 seconds before next repetition) |
| "YES!"/Treat | (Wait 10 seconds before next repetition) |
| "YES!"/Treat | That's five! you're done for now! |

**IMPORTANT:** You and/or your dog should be doing something different each time you "YES!"/Treat. Just wait: something will change. If the dog doesn't change, **YOU** can change! Example:

| | | |
|---|---|---|
| Dog walks across floor: | "YES!"/Treat | (a few seconds later . . . ) |
| Dog looks at you: | "YES!"/Treat | (30 seconds later) |
| Dog lies down: | "YES!"/Treat | (a minute later) |
| Dog still down, you turn | "YES!"/Treat | (a few seconds later) |
| Dog stands | "YES!"/Treat | That's five! you're done for now! |

You are not training your dog to **DO** anything. You are simply building power (value) into the word "YES!" by immediately following it with a delectable treat. You will find that you have your dog's complete attention after just a few repetitions. We're not working on attention particularly, but that's a nice side benefit. "YES!" is a promise that food will follow. Try not to say "YES!" to your dog at any other time. "YES!" predicts a treat and is now a special word for training.

Save some of your dog's daily ration for the "YES!" exercise. Non-dog food should be less than 10% of your dog's daily caloric intake! Consider allergies when feeding non-dog food. Read the "Selecting Rewards" handout.

---

### TIMING IS IMPORTANT

As you progress in your training, "YES!" will indicate the exact behavior you want to reward. To be sure you can say "YES!" at the right time, here are some exercises to practice your timing.

Drop a book on the floor. See if you can say "YES!" just as the bang occurs. Toss a tennis ball into the air. See if you can say "YES!" at the highest point of the toss. Watch a TV weather report. See if you can say "YES!" to coincide with the reporter touching the map.

# COME-WHEN-CALLED

---

**YOUR GOAL FOR COME-WHEN-CALLED—SEVEN WEEKS OF TRAINING**
With one call, your dog runs to you, past minor distractions, close enough to snap on a leash.
This should be done in a safe enclosed area, or with your dog on a long line.

---

Some dogs have learned a poor association with the word, "Come." Think back over the last few days. When did you say, "Come" to your dog? Did the dog's coming to you result in good or bad consequences for your dog? Make a list and look it over to decide if you would give the situation a plus or minus. Below is a typical list. The odds of this dog wanting to come the next time he's called are not favorable.

- "Come"   He was jumping up to get Granny's ice cream cone (–)
- "Come"   The kids left the door open and he was in the neighbor's trash (–)
- "Come"   It's time for your bath (–)
- "Come"   I had to get the Kleenex out of his mouth (–)
- "Come"   It's time to go for a walk (+)

Come is not a substitution for a leash or a fenced yard, but is an exercise that could save your dog's life some day. It's important to motivate your dog to want to come to you. Chances are she's figured out that you are in no position to make her come unless she's on leash. Threats won't work. She knows you're not able to carry them out.

## THE ELEMENTS OF COME-WHEN-CALLED

Come-When-Called has several components: attention, motivation, timing of the reward, set-ups to get the behavior, and alternatives to come, to name a few. Work on the individual components as separate exercises before you put them together for a Come. If you are diligent with foundation work, your path to a good Come-When-Called will be smoother. Use the strategies we've learned for training so far: a clear cue, move quickly from lure to reward, and a clear release. The Four D's are important when teaching Come. (See the Four D's handout.)

## SAFETY MANAGEMENT WHILE TRAINING

Make up your mind that your Come-When-Called training will take place in a safe, enclosed area or on leash. If there is no safe area, keep the leash on when outdoors. All of the following exercises assume you are indoors, in an fenced area outside, or using a leash. The information that follows will help you and your dog get into the correct mindset for training Come-When-Called. No amount of training will make your dog 100% reliable. Please read the entire handout before you begin.

## STEP ONE:

**THE "GOTCHA" EXERCISE** —This is to condition your dog to anticipate good things when you grab his collar. Some dogs tend to shy away when you grab for them, knowing that something good ends: she doesn't get the garbage she was about to scarf up, she is hauled out of the park and away from a good time, etc.

- a. Several different times in your day, when your dog is up and about, grab her collar and give a "YES!"/Treat. No name, no word "Come." Do it slowly, do it quickly, do it while you're walking, do it when the dog comes up to you for attention. Do it in lots of situations.

- b. Once in a while, grab the collar, put the leash on and give the "YES!"/Treat, but take the leash right off again. This teaches the dog not to duck or play "keep away" when someone wants to put a leash on her. Is your dog reactive to your hand? Go very slowly. Take every opportunity to make collar grabs a good thing. Don't use the word "Come." Some ideas are: grab the dog's collar—when she's resting on your lap, when you put her food bowl down, when she is jumping up into the car.

**ATTENTION IS THE FOUNDATION OF COME-WHEN-CALLED**—Continue to work on attention separately from the Come. Do this in lots of different areas with distractions. It's not a test, but a training exercise. In other words, make your dog think eye contact with you is the best choice when she has competing motivations, such as garbage on the ground! Let her win the rewards in this game by looking at YOU. For details refer to the Eye Contact handout.

## STEP TWO:

**FOOD BOWL COME**—By now, you are probably using a great deal of your dog's food for hand feeding to establish a bond. You may also be putting food in toys as enrichment and using food as training treats. There may not be a lot of food left over to feed in a bowl, but use your remaining food for twice daily feedings. As you prepare her food bowl, your dog will probably be right there with you, having heard all the cues that means food is coming: closet opens, bag rattling, can opener, etc. Even if she is right there by your feet when you're ready to put the food down, quickly step backwards a few paces and say, "Come" as she reaches you and the bowl. Then, stand still and say, "Yes!" and give her the bowl of food instead of giving her a treat. Sometimes say her name first "Maggie," then say "Come." Other times, just say "Come" as she reaches the food bowl.

**OPPORTUNITY COMES**—Watch for other times during the day when your dog is already focused on you and coming to you in a highly motivated way. For example, when you reach for the leash to take your dog for a walk. Say, "Come" or "Maggie, Come" as she rushes up to you. If your dog sees you take her favorite tug toy off the shelf, say "Come" as she runs up for the game. Stand still, say, "YES!," and then play.

## STEP THREE:

**SURPRISE, CONTROLLED COMES ON LEASH**—Most dogs cannot resist investigating when you quickly move away. While on a walk, at a point when your dog seems least engaged in her environment, stop suddenly. Become dramatic and make some sort of exclamation, such as "Oh! Wow!" and either back up quickly or turn around and run away a few steps. If training outdoors in an unfenced area, use your leash to keep your dog safe. Your dog will wonder what's up and will turn to see, perhaps even begin to run up to you. When you see that she is highly motivated and moving toward you, call your dog's name, "Come," and pull something wonderful out of your pocket such as her dinner in a baggie or her favorite tug toy for a game.

# STEP FOUR:

**TAKE IT "ON LOCATION"**—Same exercise as Step Three, only now find new and interesting places to practice. Pull over at a park during a drive. If your dog does not respond to your call, make a show of eating the food treats yourself or playing with the ball . . . solo. Better yet, have another dog or person to share the fun. Convince your dog that no matter what, coming to you is a better choice than investigating a distraction.

*You were asked to read the entire Come-When-Called handout before you started Step One. Please read it again before you begin working on Steps Five, Six, and Seven.*

**POSTURE WHEN CALLING**—Don't bend over or stretch your hands out to your dog. If you have a small or shy dog, stoop down. Bending over might prevent the dog from coming in close enough for you to grab her collar.

**DIFFERENT CUES FOR DIFFERENT SITUATIONS**—Decide what Come really means, and stick to it. If it's going to eventually mean "come and sit in front," make that the eventual goal for the word Come. You can have a different term for a casual, "come over here closer to me."

**CHOOSE A NEW WORD FOR COME**—You may have to choose a new word for the Come cue. More than likely your dog is used to ignoring the old word, or she's learned that it cues a game of chase. But, don't use the new cue until you have a very good training plan in place! Be sure your dog will come. This means you have to be a superb second-guesser, you will only use the new word when you know she'll come. Make up your mind that you will never use the old word for Come again.

**HAND SIGNAL FOR COME**—Remember the principle of overshadowing. If you nod your head, extend your hands, and say "Come" at the same time, the dog may be attending to only one of those cues. Hand signals are very useful in noisy areas, but they should be taught separately, not simultaneously, with other cues. A common signal for Come is to extend an arm out away from your side at shoulder height, then bring it down into normal position. This shows your arm in contrast to the background so the dog can see it more easily.

**NO MORE BAD ASSOCIATIONS**—Don't call your dog away from fun. Don't call her and then punish her. Don't ruin the effectiveness of the new word. This means good management by not allowing her to get into trouble. If need be, go get the dog, but don't call her to you. Don't abuse the word Come by expecting results before the dog is trustworthy.

**THE L.E.A.D. PROGRAM**—The leadership program (L.E.A.D.) provides a strong foundation for Come. It provides good opportunities for your dog to learn to respect you without using force or punishment.

**CALLING FROM A SIT**—It's not very often that a dog is called from a boring Sit-Stay. In real life she is called when she's in the trash or when she's about to mug a child for his ice cream cone. Make it a habit of calling your dog from different situations, but be careful, you need to win this game.

**TONE OF VOICE**—People tend to raise their voices when training Down and Come. Train your dog to Come on a medium voice. If he's paying attention, he'll hear you.

**SIT WHEN DOG COMES?**—Keep in mind that you are working on Come, not Sit. I've seen many enthusiastic comes go badly because the dog is forced into a Sit, corrected to sit straight, and helped to sit quickly. Get a happy Come-When-Called. Period. Get a happy Sit and put them together later in the program. Instead of Sit, have a party once your dog allows you to touch his collar. Eventually you will want the dog to sit when she comes. It's another way to control those "keep away" games.

**STEP FIVE:** Select two exercises from the list below. Add them to your Come practice this week.

**STEP SIX:** Select two different exercises from the list below. Add them to your Come practice this week.

**STEP SEVEN:** Try two more options from the list below this week.

- **KEEP HER GUESSING**—Coming to you shouldn't be boring. Keep your dog guessing as to what will happen next when she gets to you. At times you should touch her collar, sometimes you won't. Sometimes put the leash on, other times release her to go back to what she was doing. It is wise to call, snap a leash on, then immediately take it off and release her again. This way she will learn that coming when called and the presence of the leash won't always mean the end of a good time.

- **MY HUMAN DOES MAGIC**—Before you go on a walk, hide something great in your jacket or sneak out without your dog and hide something in a tree or on a fence: a ball on a rope, or a portion of the dog's dinner. Periodically call your dog for a game or for part of her supper. This helps you maintain your appeal even with new and interesting things to explore.

- **REAL-LIFE DISTRACTION**—If you train alone, you are tempted to leave your dog in a Sit-Stay, then walk away and call her to you. In real life, you rarely call a dog from a Sit. Get some help. Have a friend hold your dog by the collar and talk or play with her. Then call. If the dog decided to stay with the friend, the friend should turn neutral (not mean, just not fun).

- **A CHALLENGE—CAN YOU DO IT?**—Place a coin under each of your arms. Practice calling your dog! No reaching! If the dog doesn't come close enough so that you can put your hands on the dog's collar without dropping the coins, work at rewarding only close Comes.

- **COME AND RELEASE TO TREAT**—This works indoors or in a fenced area. Have a handful of goodies. Call your dog to you. Give a treat. Release her and throw a treat several yards away. When she eats it, call her to you. Give her a treat. Release her again and throw a treat in another direction. Move on to two-fers right away. Sometimes there is no treat when she runs up close to you, but you'll throw one for her to go get. Sometimes ask her to sit before you throw a treat. Sometimes touch her collar before the treat.

- **RESTRAINED DOG**—An adult family member holds your dog by the collar. The dog should be on leash, but the helper must hold the dog close by the collar. Say goodbye. Bounce a ball as you go, or pretend to munch on some liver. Tell your helper not to let go right away when you call. A delay of a second or two will increase the dog's enthusiasm to get to you. This can't be done with a spooky dog that will be upset by being handled by someone else.

- **IGNORING THE DISTRACTIONS**—Your helper has something great on a leash—a toy, a ball, and bounces or wiggles it on the floor near the dog's path to you. If the dog pays attention to the distraction, it's retracted quickly by your helper. Out comes something even better from your pocket. Play with the dog when he gets to you, or have your helper toss YOU the toy.

---

### STRATEGIES FOR EMERGENCIES

Train a positive Come with high value, but random rewards. Practice good mangement with leashes and fences. What if she gets loose accidentally? In an emergency: Run away from her, she will think she's missing something! Be dramatic and convincing and she might follow to see what's going on. Try opening a car door. If your dog loves to ride, she might come over and hop right in. Pretend there is something good on the ground! Pick up a piece of grass and talk to it. Your neighbors will think you're crazy. These measures will probably only work once, if at all, until your dog becomes wise.

# THE FOUR D'S
# TO HELP YOUR DOG GAIN FLUENCY

*Trainers strive for fluency in every exercise. A dog is fluent when she can perform by herself, on cue, no matter what the circumstances. For example if she learned "Sit" indoors by the couch, she might not understand what "Sit" means outdoors next to another dog. Dogs don't seem to generalize well. You will see below that the common criteria for most basic dog training exercises all start with the letter "D." Change only one "D" at a time. As you're making one aspect of an exercise more difficult, relax the other criteria. Doing so will reduce the possibility of failure and increase the probability for reward. Reward drives behavior! For example: If you are working among Distractions, decrease the Distance you are from your dog and the Duration, or length, of the exercise.*

### DISTANCE
Sit and Down are often practiced at a distance from the trainer. If the dog will sit and stay reliably 80% of the time when she is very close to you, start moving away a little farther. Are you in a safe area to be so far from your dog in training? Use a fenced area or a long leash.

### DURATION
After the dog is steady on Sit-Stay for 15 seconds, it's time to try extending the exercise a little. Ping-pong back and forth on duration. One time it might be 25 seconds, the next time 10 seconds, the next time 40 seconds, and then 15 seconds.

### DIFFERENT ENVIRONMENT
If your dog performs well in her usual, calm training environment (home, yard, training class), it's now time to complicate matters a little by introducing distractions or taking her to different training sites. Will your dog sit and stay in your living room if you walk to the closet and put on your overcoat? Will she come if called while the doorbell is ringing? Don't overwhelm the dog with unfair distractions. We are trying to train, not test. Little by little is the policy.

### DELIVERY OF REWARD
Legacy classes begin with a continuous rate of reinforcement (rewarding every try), then within weeks rewarding at random, asking for perhaps two or three behaviors for one reward. We will ping-pong back and forth at random (2-fers, 3-fers, 1-fers, 3-fers). Soon we will watch for the very best of the behaviors and reward them. We might decide to work on speedy responses. If you're stepping up one level of difficulty you may want to go back temporarily to delivering the rewards more frequently. This helps make it easy for the dog to earn rewards and to keep her attention focused on you.

## IN OTHER WORDS:
When you add a new aspect to an old exercise, temporarily loosen up your expectations on the old criteria. This increases the rate of reward, hence success!

CONTACT US IF YOU NEED HELP   info@legacycanine.com   360-683-1522

# YOUR HOMEWORK GOALS
## BE READY FOR WEEK 3

Practice about 3–5 sessions a day, 3–5 repetitions per session.
This week's goal is to achieve about an 80% success rate at Step 3 in the exercises below.
Your notebook has details on each exercise. If you need help: info@legacycanine.com, 360-683-1522.

**EYE CONTACT—READ THE HANDOUT, DO STEP 3 (pg. 241)**
Work in a distraction-free area.
No lure! Keep still, say your dog's name cheerfully.
The instant your dog makes eye contact you should play enthusiastically for 3–5 seconds (no "YES!," no food)

**SIT HAPPENS!—READ THE HANDOUT, DO STEP 3 (pg. 255)**
Keep still (no lure). Say your dog's name, then say "Sit."
If your dog doesn't Sit, use the lure (bet you won't need it).
When Sit happens, "YES!"/Treat.

**NEW: COME—DO STEPS 1, 2, & 3 IN HANDOUT (pg. 265)**
Gotcha exercise
Food bowl and other "opportunity" Comes
Surprise while walking on leash—engage dog for 3–5 seconds

**NEW: LEASH WORK—HEEL——DO STEPS 1, 2, & 3 IN HANDOUT (pg. 273)**
Sit dog in Heel position by using a lure or curb. "YES!"/Treat
Lure a couple of steps in Heel position, then sit your dog. "YES!"/Treat
When the luring becomes smooth, say "Heel" an instant before you lure. *Note:* Your dog will eventually learn to Sit automatically when you stop walking.

### DON'T FORGET!
Continue to work on the **LET'S GO** exercise—be specific—it doesn't mean "Heel."
The **L.E.A.D.** Program: Add two more different exercises. (pg. 247)
**TRICK** (Focusing Exercise): Ask for help if you need it. (pg. 243)
Read the **PERSONAL BEST** Walk-About handout. Try it out. Time it. (pg. 277)

CONTACT US IF YOU NEED HELP  info@legacycanine.com  360-683-1522

# LEASH WORK

## DIFFERENT EXERCISES FOR DIFFERENT NEEDS

*One of the biggest annoyances is the dog that pulls ahead during a walk. There are two concept—"**Let's Go**" and "**Heel.**" Until you perfect your skills at training your dog to heel, read about **Let's Go** and start using it on your walks.*

---

**GOAL FOR "LETS GO"—SEVEN WEEKS OF TRAINING**
You will be able to walk your dog on a loose leash past minor distractions.

---

## TRAINING THE "LET'S GO"

"Let's Go" means that you don't care much what happens on walks as long as the dog doesn't pull on the leash and make you both uncomfortable. The cue for this, "Let's Go," is used when no one is around who can be bothered by a less-than-perfect dog. You determine the requirements for "Let's Go." It depends on your lifestyle. Perhaps you want the dog to be in any position on a Flexi-leash. Allow the dog to enjoy life, sniff, and explore—just be a dog. It makes no difference which side of the owner the dog is on. The dog can be slightly ahead or behind. You have minimal rules for appropriate behavior except: Don't Pull on the Leash!

If your dog forges ahead and creates tension on the leash, stop. She'll soon learn she's not going anywhere if the leash is tight. Act as if she was tied to a post—you're the post. Don't say or do anything. If you don't follow, she will eventually slacken the leash—probably to look around and see what's wrong. Mark and reward instantly with "YES!"/Treat. That's when the post comes to life—you are the most interesting thing on the walk. Continue walking.

You can help release the tension on the leash by calling your dog's name. When she looks up, the leash will slacken—change directions slightly and encourage her to walk with you. Try stepping to one side, then jiggle the leash. This will give her a sense of unbalance. If she adjusts her feet for balance, it will cause the leash to slacken. Trying too hard to get her attention back on you when she's pulling could be a reward for pulling. Make yourself unpredictably more interesting than the environment. If the leash gets tight, suddenly start walking backwards. Careful! Don't trip. It's just as effective to turn around and walk the other way. Most dogs give up and want to see why you changed directions. Your dog will wonder if she missed something important! Any time she spontaneously slackens the leash or turns to look at you, pull out a toy, or food treat, and be animated in your play and reward. Do something more fun for her than pulling and getting nowhere.

Put your dog's favorite toy or tug rope in a paper bag. Get a friend to help by holding the leash. Cross the room and sit down on the floor well beyond her reach. Rattle the toy inside. Let the toy peek out of the top of the bag for a second. The dog will be keen to investigate. Your friend starts walking toward you, but if the dog pulls, walking stops. The only way she gets to you and the bag is on a slack leash. If your friend doesn't have good timing, give him the bag and you work with the leash! If you don't have a helper, put your dog's food bowl on the floor on the other side of the room. Same thing. She can approach it as long as she doesn't pull. It might take a while, but she will learn the only way to get there is if the leash is not tight.

CONTACT US IF YOU NEED HELP   info@legacycanine.com   360-683-1522

---

**GOAL FOR HEELING—SEVEN WEEKS OF TRAINING**

You and your dog will be able to weave in and out of a set of three markers spaced six feet apart.
Your dog will be able to navigate this course in Heel position on a loose leash.
The leash will be loosely draped around your shoulder.

---

# TRAINING THE HEEL POSITION

This cue means for the dog to stay very close to your side and give complete, polite attention. Heel is a more formal and precise style of walking, which is appropriate when you need more control to keep up her image as good citizen; for instance, when pedestrians are about or you are forced to walk on the shoulder of a road. Say you are walking your dog with the Let's Go concept. All of a sudden you see the entire kindergarten class walking toward you. They're talking and skipping and they all have ice cream cones. Ask your dog to Heel and you'll be able to get past the kids without her mugging them for the ice cream. When they're gone, go back to Let's Go, and she can now safely revert back to being a dog.

**DEFINITION OF HEEL POSITION:** Heel means to walk in the same direction as the owner, to stay very close to the owner's leg, giving the owner complete, polite attention. The dog should not notice with more than a glance any distractions and should never pull on the leash. Imagine that you are wearing a pair of trousers. The dog's nose shouldn't fall behind the seam of your pant leg, and his shoulder shouldn't be ahead of the seam. He should be as close as possible to you without touching. This position is in force while walking, sitting, or lying down. It's in force at a normal pace, slow and fast. Think of Heel position as an imaginary little oval by your side. Some trainers teach the dog that to travel anywhere outside of the Heel position is bad and subject to punishment. This is often done with a choke chain and a jerk of the leash without even trying to develop attention and teamwork. We prefer to teach the dog that being inside the oval is a great place to choose to be, and nothing better can happen outside of the oval. We teach the dog to start at the owner's side and choose to remain there because it's a great place to be. When the owner moves forward, no matter the speed, the dog hurries to maintain that position because there is something in it for the dog! Most dogs are taught to walk on the left side of their owners and most tests require left-side walking. Regardless of the method used, heeling sessions should be very short, only a few seconds at first and with random rewards.

**ALTERNATE SIDE HEELING:** You also might want to train your dog to Heel by your right side for a number of reasons: (1) The dog is blind in his left eye; keep the seeing eye on the outside. (2) Owner is handicapped and can work with the dog more easily on the right. (3) Owner wants to change sides, depending on traffic. (4) Control from both sides is a requirement in some competitive training events. (5) Owner has two dogs and prefers one on each side. (6) To keep the dog's neck muscles symmetrically exercised—for dogs that look at their handler lots. (7) Owner is left-handed and wants his right hand free for other activities.

Much of the time it doesn't make much difference if the dog is right next to your leg during walks. In fact, it's good to allow your dog to sniff, look around, and enjoy the walk. As long as he's not bothering other people or dogs, is safe and is not pulling or making it difficult for you, NO PROBLEM! There will be times, such as around people or other pets, crossing the street, negotiating obstacles, or avoiding distractions that you will need more precise control on a walk. This is called Heel position.

*Note on the Opposition Reflex:* Dogs naturally pull against (oppose) pressure. This is why constant pressure on your end of the lead is not effective. The more you pull, the more the dog will pull in the opposite direction!

## HEEL TAUGHT AS A VARIATION OF SIT

**STEP 1: Begin with the dog sitting in Heel position.** If your dog is not in the habit of sitting at your left side, facing the same direction you are, find a stopper. The woman in the illustration at the bottom of the page is using a wall. Look around. Any vertical surface will work. Depending on the habit your dog has fallen into for sitting, you may need to go back to the luring game to get her in position against the stopper. Start with five pieces of food in your hand. Don't do any more than five reps at a time before you give your dog a break. A *repetition* is each time you practice a single behavior. A *session* is the time you set aside to work with your dog. When you are 80% successful at luring the dog into a tight sit against a stopper, you can move on to Step 2.

**STEP 2: The *Luring Game* while adding a cue.** Show the dog your food and walk forward a step or two. It's the same old luring game with five pieces of food. No cues yet, just see if you can use the magnet lure to take his nose where you want him to go. As this becomes smooth and successful, say, "Heel" an instant before you lure your dog to walk by your side. Only a step or two at first! Sit the dog again. "YES!"/Treat. You may find that you will need to say, "Sit" for a few sessions, but very quickly (clever dogs!) they figure out that "Sit" means sit no matter what. And "Heel" means stick close to the owner's side and if she stops, sit automatically. You can now see one of the most important applications of our motivational sit. The time spent on that foundation exercise is about to pay off! The frequent, happy sit will control the dog and prevent him from forging ahead. Don't forget to use your bridge "YES!" and also the reward.

**STEP 3: Different directions.** Have five pieces of food available. Sit your dog and pivot a little to the left or to the right, luring your dog around with you, rewarding him for a sit if she keeps up in good heel position. Pretty soon you and your dog will look like a smooth team, almost like dancing! Then you can start full about turns, one way and then the other, until your dog unmistakably moves as if Velcro attached her to your leg. This should only take a minute or so. Three 30-second repetitions are better than a minute and a half straight.

**STEP 4: Treat for walking instead of sitting.** So far you have been giving the treat when the dog sits. Now begin to give the treat once in awhile as the dog is moving along with you nicely. Still get the Sit, but don't reward it. Ping-pong back and forth between treats for the sit and treats while walking. Remember how we varied the rewards for attention with 2-fers, 3-fers, back to 1-fers? It's time for the variable schedule of reinforcement. Build up slowly to giving your five treats at random during about 15 steps of heeling.

CONTACT US IF YOU NEED HELP   info@legacycanine.com   360-683-1522

**STEP 5: Vary the type of reward.** Very short, positive, and perfect heeling sessions will keep your dog motivated. Quit while he is still enthusiastic! Heeling can be ended with "Okay," (or whatever release word you've chosen to use) and a quick tug of war game. Other times it's "Okay" and throw the ball. Sometimes the dog gets a smile and praise while heeling; other times, you play a quick game of tug before resuming your heeling practice. Reserve Heel for really specific and short occasions. Your usual long walk for exercise is the time to use "Let's Go." With this alternative to Heel, the dog is able to enjoy his walk, sniff, take potty breaks, and do almost anything except pull on the leash. Clearly release the dog from the Heel position. This will help your dog understand the difference between relaxed Let's Go behavior and strict Heeling behavior.

**STEP 6: Random, delayed, remote rewards.** Before you work with your dog, hide a treat or a toy along your practice path (the limb of a tree, on top of your car, on a picture frame in the hall). At some point when your dog is heeling nicely, release your dog and use lots of praise as you run together to get the reward. Your dog will think you are magical. It's a fun way to continue the idea of random reward in dog training.

**STEP 7: Distractions.** Practice heeling around various distractions. Plan big rewards when your dog maintains the heel position past a big distraction.

# MORE TIPS FOR TEACHING HEELING

**CURB YOUR DOG WHILE HEELING**—Use fences, curbs, and walls to help control the dog. Pull the couch into the middle of your living room and heel around it. Whatever method you choose to teach heeling, using a curb will be very helpful in getting your dog to sit and walk in heel position.

**HEEL TAUGHT WITH THE GENTLE LEADER®**—Because it is so quick and easy, many Legacy students use a Gentle Leader®. People and dogs benefit from this tool for all training, but I find it especially helpful for heeling. It is designed to take advantage of the opposition reflex. For more information, borrow a Gentle Leader® video from us. All students using a Gentle Leader® in class are entitled to a free private lesson on the fit and use of this helpful tool.

**TARGET HEELING: THE EZ CHAIR GAME**—Using your fist as a target to prompt and reward good Heel position works well with or without the Gentle Leader®. Sit in a chair with your dog nearby. Relax, this is fun. Conceal five pieces of food in your left hand (right hand if you are teaching your dog to walk on your right). Let your dog watch! She will naturally try to sniff your hand. When she makes contact, let her have a piece. You're down to four. Touch, treat, touch treat. Once presented, your hand stays still and the dog moves her head to do the touching! The dog is hooked! Put your fist behind your back or tuck it under your arm and bring it out only when you are ready for your dog to touch. If she doesn't touch within two seconds, take your hand away! She's missed her chance. This will make her more attentive! Can you get two touches for one treat? Can you move your hand slightly and have her head follow to touch your hand? Make sure your hand always appears the same. We want her to remember what the target looks like. Just three simple steps: (1) present fist, (2) dog touches fist, and (3) dog gets treat. All of this and you still haven't gotten out of your chair! Now the fun part begins. No food in your hand! Same hand, same picture, but your hand is empty. The food is in your pouch, shirt pocket, or on a table behind you. The dog touches the same, but now you deliver the treat from your other hand. Don't say anything. The dog will understand. When she is doing this reliably 80% of the time, it's time to move it from an easy chair game to a walking game!

# The Personal Best "Walk-About Route"

Does your dog leap around at the front door when someone knocks? Does he push into the refrigerator when you open the door? Does he tangle you in the leash on the way down the steps for a walk? You enrolled in class to improve your dog's manners. The goal of Legacy classes isn't to impress the instructors during class or to look better than the other dogs in class. Gauge your success on the amount of improvement you make with your dog from week to week. Coaches often speak to athletes about their *personal best*.

Here's an exercise for you with that thought in mind:

Plan a walking route in and around your home that includes locations associated with a control problem. During class you have been learning a variety of substitute, appropriate behaviors to replace the bad habits. Things like Sit, Down, and Heel are a few behaviors you can use to replace the inappropriate behaviors. As an example, what follows is a typical Walk-About-Route planned by Judy for her dog Shane. You can set up a similar exercise at your house.

- It's Monday night at your house. Judy takes note of the time. She gets the leash and walks to the door. Shane's there, bouncing around, ready for his walk.

- Shane must remain sitting at the front door while Judy attaches the leash to his collar.

- Judy opens the door. Shane remains sitting until they walk out together in heel position. Shane sits again while Judy closes the door and reopens it.

> BY THE WAY, ONE MORE RULE! JUST LIKE A BOARD GAME, IF SHANE IS UNSUCCESSFUL AT ONE OF THE STATIONS HE AND JUDY MUST GO BACK ONE STATION AND THEN GO ON WITH THEIR COURSE!

- Judy goes through the doorway and back into the house while Shane sits. She then calls the dog in and closes the door. Shane stays sitting while Judy knocks on the door. The Sit-Stay lasts 10 seconds after the knock ends. Then Shane is released and has at least 10 seconds of playtime with Judy.

- Judy must settle the dog into a Sit after the 10 second play session.

- From the door, they walk through the living room, with no pulling! If Shane's leash becomes tight, Judy simply takes him back to the start to work with him. Alternately, she can simply stand still and not go forward to give him the idea he's not going anywhere! When the leash is slack again, they proceed.

- Now Shane must remain on a Down-Stay at the threshold between the living room and kitchen while Judy opens the refrigerator and rattles some food around. If Shane is successful, Judy will call him to her. If not, Judy starts over. Judy plays the reward lottery with Shane. Judy sometimes gives a treat after she closes the door and after he comes when she calls him, but **not** if Shane hasn't stayed in position, and only *sometimes* if he's been good. Shane enjoys playing the lottery.

- With the leash loose, they walk to the coat closet. Shane has to sit and stay (no cheating . . . or you must start over!) while Judy puts her jacket on and takes it off again.

- Now Shane has to lie down by the closet while Judy walks over to wherever her car keys are kept. Maybe you're lucky and they're in the same place as your coat! Shane STAYS DOWN while Judy gets the keys out, rattles them and puts them back. This helps desensitize Shane to the departure cues that excite him.

- Exercise finished! Judy notes the time and plays some inside games with Shane.

---

### GOAL FOR YOUR PERSONAL BEST WALK-ABOUT-ROUTE

The Walk-About-Route is a **training** exercise, not a **test** course. Judy will take time at any point during the route to communicate with and help Shane be successful. Judy and Shane will try the route again every Monday. If she and Shane do their class homework, Shane's time will most likely improve when they run the course again next Monday night. Maybe not, but over several weeks there will be a marked improvement.

**We'll be asking for brags the last night of class. Report your progress!
We reward braggers!**

---

This information has also been published in the (8-7-98) *American Kennel Club Gazette.* Copyright © Terry Ryan.

# DOWN

**YOUR GOAL FOR DOWN—SEVEN WEEKS OF TRAINING**
On one cue, your dog will lie down within three seconds and your dog will quietly stay in that position with minor distractions for three minutes with no further help from you, until released.

## Using a Food Lure to Teach Down

The principles for teaching the dog to lie down on cue are the same as we learned in the Sit exercise. Down is a vulnerable position. Fearful dogs might worry about doing Down in class. Unruly dogs might object to the position because they are not used to doing as their owner suggests in a distracting situation. Some people have used Down as punishment—it's not. Don't confuse your dog by saying "Down" when you should be saying "Off." Off is the word to use to get the dog off the furniture or to stop jumping up on a person. It means "remove yourself from this surface."

**STEP 1: THE MAGNETIC DOWN GAME—PLAY AT LURING AND REWARDING DOWNS**
Begin with three to five pieces of food in your hand. It may be easier for your dog if this is done on a smooth surface so that he can easily slip into the Down position. Get the dog's attention on your luring hand. Drop your hand suddenly to the floor in front of him. The path of your hand makes an "L" shape. If your dog is attentive, his head will drop to see what's going on. Then pull your hand along the floor out in front of his nose. In most cases, the dog's body will follow his nose and slip into a Down position. Just at the daylight disappears under your dog, say "YES!" and give a treat. You're doing great when you are successful five out of five repetitions in four out of five sessions. A *repetition* is each time you practice a single behavior. A *session* is the time you set aside to work with your dog. Don't bore your dog by training one exercise any more than five times in a row.

### *Luring Aid: Alternative Method I—Chair*
The rung of a sturdy chair can be used as an aid. Show the dog the motivator on the opposite side of the obstacle. He will have to get down low to follow the treat under the obstacle. "YES!"/Treat.

### *Luring Aid: Alternative Method II—Leg*
You can sit on the floor and use your own bent leg as an obstacle! As soon as he lies down, "YES!"/Treat.

## STEP 2: THE RELAX POSITION (MACARONI DOWN)

If a dog is relaxed in the Down position, he's less apt to want to pop up. Some dogs naturally and quickly roll to one side. If your dog is the type that wants to lie in the sphinx position with belly down and legs under him, you can get him to roll onto his hip with a tidbit of food or an interesting squeak toy. Put it on his nose—it's the magnet game again! When he's focused on it, draw it along the floor toward his hip. His nose will follow it like a magnet and his hips will turn, flopping his rear over into a relaxed position. "YES!"/Treat.

## STEP 3: NOW NAME THE DOWN

When, you can reliably lure a Down five out of five Reps, four out of five Sessions, you can begin using the word "Down" before you start moving the luring hand. Be sure to follow the verbal "Down" with the lure. Your hand motion is an assumed signal by the dog. Don't use the word "Down" and the hand signal simultaneously or overshadowing (a mental blocking out one or the other cue) may occur. To review, the sequence is: Say the word, "Down," use the lure; dog lies down, you mark the position with, "YES!" and give one food treat. Be sure to use a normal tone of voice when saying, "Down." Down is not a punishment; it's just another position. Don't advance to the next step until you are successful 5 out of 5 repetitions, 4 out of 5 sessions.

## STEP 4: MAINTAIN THE DOWN/ RELEASE THE DOWN

### A. *Delayed Rewards Instead of Immediate Rewards*

When your dog goes into the Down position don't immediately "YES!"/Treat. Now we will wait a little. (In technical terms, we are going for short, variable durations.) Alternate back and forth between a range of 3–10 seconds of maintaining the Down before you "YES!"/Treat. Your dog might need help staying down for these few seconds. Hold the treat at nose level in a position where he can sniff and even nibble a bit. "Control the Head, Control the Dog." **Your goal:** When the dog consistently stays down for short, variable durations, 5 out of 5 reps in 4 out of 5 sessions, it's time to move on.

### B. *Starting the "Stay" Cue*

When your dog is performing a stationary exercise like Down, "Stay" is implied. During Down for example, your dog can't be in the Down position and moving at the same time. However, an additional cue for Stay can be comforting to you. It's also comforting to some dogs. The dog associates Stay with "keep going, you're doing great" and Stay should be said in this encouraging tone of voice.

To help your dog understand the new cue "Stay," ask your dog to "Down," then say "Stay" and turn your head away and break eye contact. This is a good first step at leaving a dog that is attentive. Or, after you say "Stay," shift your position slightly, as if you are going to move, or try moving only one step away. It's usually the initial change in your body language that tells the dog you are leaving. Be sure you are close to your dog so you can help him stay. Tell your dog he's good while he's staying by giving some quiet, generalized praise and smiles, or some massage and petting, or the opportunity to nibble on a treat in your hand held down low, close to the floor. When your dog can maintain 3–10 second stays at least 80% of the time, it's time to go to the next step.

### C. The Release Cue Instead of "YES!"/Treat

Until now, your dog has only been asked to Down for a very short interval before we ended the exercise with a "YES!"/Treat. We now want to teach the dog to stay in the Down position for longer durations. To do so, we are going to replace the "YES!/Treat with a release word. Legacy uses the word "Okay"* to tell a dog that she's done, the Down is over, she can do whatever she wants now. Note: when you say "okay" she might decide to stay down or she might decide to go off and be a dog. Either is fine. She's been released to do whatever she wants. To start teaching your dog to stay until released: Tell your dog to "Down." At a time predetermined by you (a range of 3–10 seconds), say your release word. The exercise is over! You can play with her or give her a reward or do nothing. There will be many times now when we recommend that you give your release cue and do nothing—no reward. That's because we will start giving rewards DURING the Down. We get what we pay for and we want the dog to be rewarded for a long down. We don't want her rewarded for being released for a Down. Release and reward are two different things; however, until that is perfectly clear to your dog, you can accompany your release with animated praise, a food reward, or a game.

*Many trainers use "Okay" as a release term. You might want to choose a word that's not used much in your everyday conversation. Some popular release terms are "Free" or "Done."

## STEP 5: GET RID OF THE LURING HAND

Does your dog know the verbal cue alone? Someday you might have your arms full of packages. Keep your hand perfectly still, even if there is food in it, and say, "Down." If you get the Down, pay for it with a "YES!/Treat. Don't fall into the habit of repeating the word, "Down." If he doesn't go down, give a jump-start by showing a peek of the food with as little hand movement as possible.

## STEP 6: THE DOWN LOTTERY

During your practice, start getting at least one, but no more than two, free Downs from your dog. That means ask for Down once, release, then ask for Down again and this time treat when your dog goes down. Sometimes get three Downs, sometimes get two Downs, before the dog earns a reward. Sometimes you will reward each Down. Keep your dog guessing and mix it up: two-fers, three-fers, one-fers. This teaches owners not to rely on food, and before long, your dog will learn to enjoy playing the lottery game.

At this point you can sometimes keep the five pieces of food in your pocket or pouch. The food is out of sight and will be brought out when you are ready to mark and reward the behavior. This step is the beginning of weaning off food. We are phasing out luring and phasing in the true concept of reward. Before long your dog will be able to work for longer and longer durations and not expect a treat each time.

## STEP 7: DOWN LOTTERY WITH REMOTE REWARDS

### A. Remote and Random Rewards

Now we'll vary the delivery of rewards even more. (At this stage, you and your dog will not be depending on continuous rewards for good behavior.) When you are successful at Step 6, begin training sessions by hiding your food or toys somewhere else in the room. You should not have any food or toys on you. After your dog responds to your cue, and at random times, run to the spot where you hid the food (or toy) and go back to your dog and reward him. (Before long your dog thinks you're magic—always able to produce rewards from the strangest places!) Now, say your release cue. You're done. Generalized praise is okay.

## *Optional Hand Signals:* When we first taught the "Sit," "Down," and "Stay" exercises, we helped the dog learn with lures. Lures are similar to hand signals. Next, we clearly and distinctly taught verbal only cues to avoid any possible overshadowing. If you would like to teach a hand signal so that your dog will respond to either verbal or hand signals, simply present the signal before (not after and not during) the verbal cue. The dog will soon get the association.

## *Work on the Four D's: Distance, Duration, Different Environment, Delivery of Reward*

This concept is the same for all exercises. If you raise one criterion (for example, distance on the Down), lower the other criteria (duration, distractions). When things become potentially more difficult, increase your rewards and lower your expectations until your dog makes the breakthrough. Your dog doesn't need as many sessions or repetitions now if he is performing perfectly. Each session should be highly variable in location and distractions. (For more information, see the Four D's handout.)

# YOUR HOMEWORK GOALS
## BE READY FOR WEEK 4

Practice about 3–5 sessions a day, 3–5 repetitions per session.
This week's goal is to achieve about an 80% success rate at Step 4 in the exercises below.
Your notebook has details on each exercise. If you need help: info@legacycanine.com, 360-683-1522.

**EYE CONTACT—READ THE HANDOUT, DO STEP 4 (pg. 241)**
Find an area with distractions. Okay to go back to luring if needed.
When dog makes eye contact (with or without the toy lure) . . . Play!

***NOTE:*** *Starting This Week—Important for Sit, Down, and Heel:*
*Start using Stay and Release cues in place of "YES!"/Treat*
*Read the Four D's handout (pg. 269). Vary them in your practice sessions.*

**SIT HAPPENS!—READ THE HANDOUT, DO STEP 4 (pg. 255)**
Sit, Stay, Release. Vary the Four D's, no "YES!," no treat

***NEW EXERICSE: DOWN—DO STEPS 1, 2, 3, & 4 (pg. 279)***
Like the Sit, we start by luring Down position with a magnet.
Roll hips into the macaroni position. Next say "Down." No lure!
If your dog doesn't comply, jump-start or lure.
Begin Stay. Reward the position. Clear release. Vary Four D's.

**COME—REFER TO HANDOUT, DO STEP 4 (pg. 265)**
Your handout has lots of ideas. Please read it again.
Pay attention to your body position.
Make your reward better than anything out there.

**LEASH WORK—HEEL——REFER TO HANDOUT, DO STEP 4 (pg. 273)**
Sometimes reward and release from the Sit.
Sometimes reward and relase while you are walking along.

### DON'T FORGET!
Stick with the **L.E.A.D.** Program!! (pg. 247)
How is your **TRICK** (Focusing Exercise) coming along? (pg. 243)
Do the **PERSONAL BEST** Walk-About. Time it! (pg. 277)
Remember, **LET'S GO** is a different cue and
different behavior than Heeling. (pg. 273)

CONTACT US IF YOU NEED HELP   info@legacycanine.com   360-683-1522

*Coaching People to Train Their Dogs* © Terry Ryan 2005

# YOUR HOMEWORK GOALS
## BE READY FOR WEEK 5

**LEGACY**
Canine Behavior & Training

Practice about 3–5 sessions a day, 3–5 repetitions per session.
This week's goal is to achieve about an 80% success rate at Step 5 in the exercises below.
Your notebook has details on each exercise. If you need help: info@legacycanine.com, 360-683-1522.

**EYE CONTACT—READ THE HANDOUT, DO STEP 5 (pg. 241)**
Distraction—No lure unless absolutely necessary!
Wait for your dog to check in with eye contact.
Lots of praise! Your dog made the right decision!

**SIT HAPPENS!—READ THE HANDOUT, DO STEP 5 (pg. 255)**
Say dog's name, then say "Sit" (**but say it only once!**)
If your dog doesn't Sit, jump-start as described in handout.
Use the Four D's. Use Stay and Release cues.

**COME—REFER TO HANDOUT, DO STEP 5 (pg. 265)**
Select at least two exercises from the Come list.

**LEASH WORK—HEEL——REFER TO HANDOUT, DO STEP 5 (pg. 273)**
Heel is a precise position.
Remember to use clear releases from Heel position.
Conduct short, fun sessions. Vary and randomize rewards.

**DOWN—DO STEP 5 (pg. 279)**
Say dog's name, then say "Down" (**but say it only once!**)
If your dog doesn't go Down, jump-start as described in handout.
Use the Four D's. Use a variety of rewards.
Use Stay and Release cues.

## DON'T FORGET!
L.E.A.D. Program • TRICK • PERSONAL BEST • LET'S GO
(pg. 247) (pg. 243) (pg. 277) (pg. 273)
FIND THE MID-COURSE EVALUATION SHEET IN YOUR NOTEBOOK.
FILL IT OUT AND EXCHANGE IT THIS WEEK FOR A BONUS BONE.

CONTACT US IF YOU NEED HELP   info@legacycanine.com   360-683-1522

# "LEADER OF THE PACK"

## FIGURE 8 CHALLENGE

## Rules:

Dear Dog:

This challenge is OPTIONAL. Your instructor and owner won't make you do this! However, if your owner is the competitive type, you will probably end up trying this challenge! In the upcoming weeks, a few minutes will be reserved after class officially ends. The challenge will take place then. Any assistant instructor can "test" you and your owner.

Two cones will be placed about eight feet apart. You must follow your human around the cones, in Heel Position, in a Figure 8 pattern. Your leash MUST BE SLACK! No food, no toys—by then your human will be more charming than food or toys. You can try the challenge only *once* a week.

If you make it all the way around without tightening the leash, your name goes into a special drawing. The prize? A 50% discount on your next Legacy pet dog class.* Everyone completing the challenge will receive a beautiful *Leader of the Pack* challenge certificate.

*The fine print! Non transferable. No cash value. Prize expires 12 months from date on certificate.

# WE'RE HALFWAY THROUGH CLASSES!

## *HOW ARE YOU DOING?*

We want to be sure we meet your needs before the classes are completed. Please answer these evaluation questions, then turn the paper in for a Bonus Bone.

INSTRUCTOR: _____

DATE OF CLASS: _____

1. **PLEASE TEACH US MORE ABOUT:**

   _____

   _____

2. **I NEED INDIVIDUAL HELP WITH:**

   _____

   _____

3. **MY DOG'S WEAKEST EXERCISE IS:**

   _____

   _____

4. **THE BEST PART OF THE CLASS FOR ME IS:**

   _____

   _____

**General Suggestions / Comments:**

_____

_____

### *Thanks for your input! We're listening!*

Your Name (optional): _____

CONTACT US IF YOU NEED HELP   info@legacycanine.com   360-683-1522

PDM 4 MidCourseEval.doc          *Coaching People to Train Their Dogs* © Terry Ryan 2005

# YOUR HOMEWORK GOALS
# BE READY FOR WEEK 6

Practice about 3–5 sessions a day, 3–5 repetitions per session.
This week's goal is to achieve about an 80% success rate at Step 6 in the exercises below.
Your notebook has details on each exercise. If you need help: info@legacycanine.com, 360-683-1522.

**EYE CONTACT—READ THE HANDOUT, DO STEP 6 (pg. 241)**
Your dog makes eye contact with you, ignoring distractions.
Random reward: 1-fer, 3-fers, 2-fers.
Vary rewards: toys, games, go for a ride.

**SIT HAPPENS!—READ THE HANDOUT, DO STEP 6 (pg. 255)**
No luring, no body language, don't repeat Sit cue
Use Stay and Release cues and the Four D's
Don't reward every Sit—play the "Sit Lottery"

**COME—REFER TO HANDOUT, DO STEP 6 (pg. 265)**
Go over the Come list in your handout
Select and practice at least two different Come exercises
Be safe!

**LEASH WORK—HEEL——READ HANDOUT, DO STEP 6 (pg. 273)**
Practice no more than a minute at a time
Random, remote, delayed reward

**DOWN—DO STEP 6 (pg. 279)**
No luring, no body language. Say Down cue only once.
Use Stay and Release cues and the Four D's
Don't reward every Down—play the "Down Lottery"

### DON'T FORGET!
Add more exercises to your **L.E.A.D.** (pg. 247) program.
**TRICK** (pg. 243) (Focusing Exercise): Are you working on a trick?
Ask for help if you need it.
Read the handout about **PERSONAL BEST** (pg. 277) Walk-About. Try it! Time it!
**LET'S GO** (pg. 273)—be clear to your dog on how it is different from Heel.

CONTACT US IF YOU NEED HELP   info@legacycanine.com   360-683-1522

# YOUR HOMEWORK GOALS
# BE READY FOR WEEK 7

Practice about 3–5 sessions a day, 3–5 repetitions per session.
This week's goal is to achieve about an 80% success rate at Step 7 in the exercises below.
Your notebook has details on each exercise. If you need help: info@legacycanine.com, 360-683-1522.

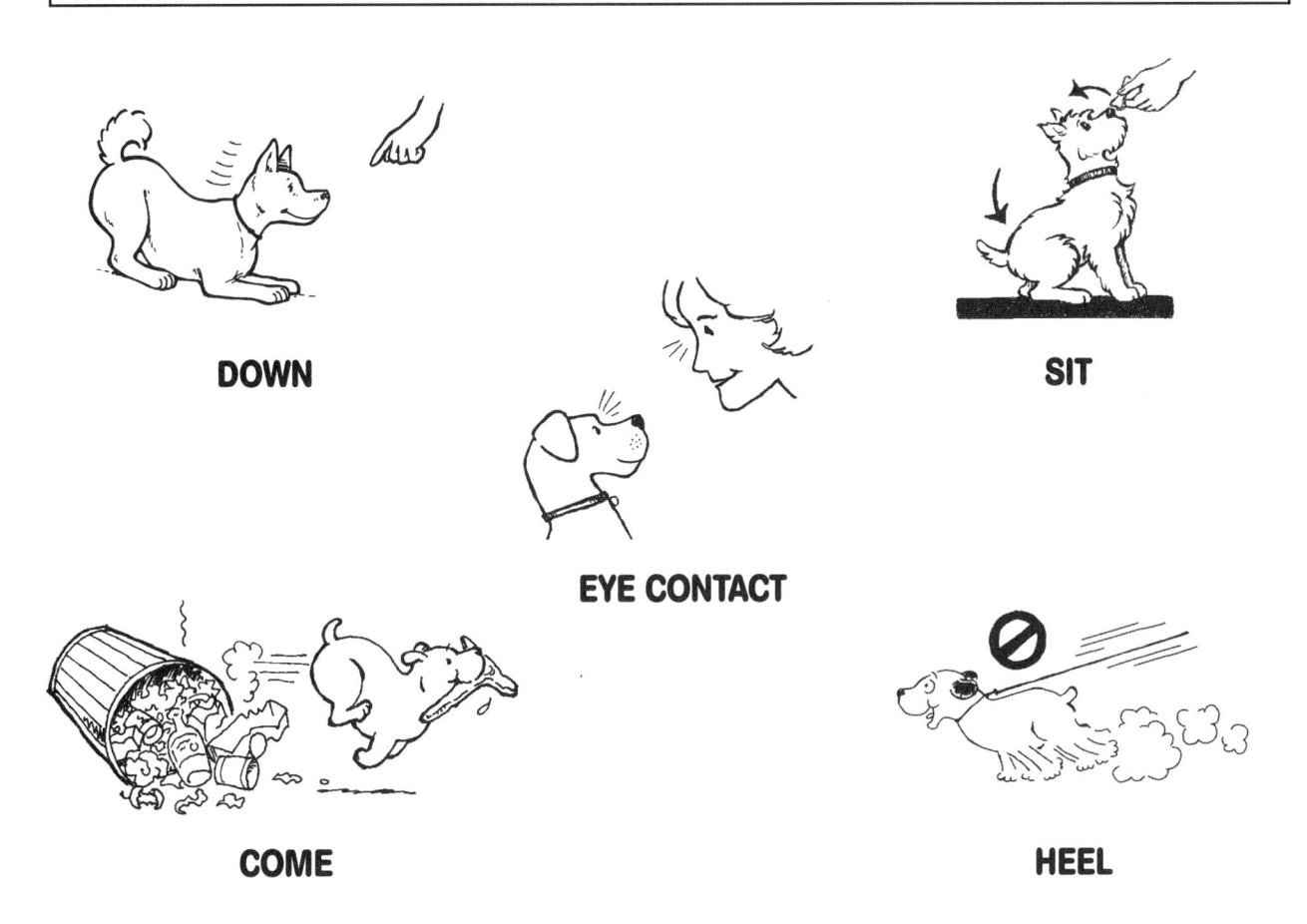

**DOWN**

**EYE CONTACT**

**SIT**

**COME**

**HEEL**

All of these exercises are at Step 7 in your handouts.
Apply these skills in your daily life with your dog.

By now you should be using only one verbal cue and random rewards.

We are looking forward to seeing your trick. Are you ready?
Next week is the last chance to try the Leader of the Pack Figure 8 Challenge.
Bring all those bonus bones for the drawing.

**Congratulations for completing seven successful weeks of training!**

This is the last Pet Dog Manners I class, but we are not done!
You've got the foundation; however, training is an ongoing process.
Register for Pet Dog Manners II. It's all downhill from here!

CONTACT US IF YOU NEED HELP    info@legacycanine.com    360-683-1522

*PDM 6 Homework.doc*    *Coaching People to Train Their Dogs* © Terry Ryan 2005

# Chewing...
# On You
# On Your Stuff!

Chewing is a great hobby. To your pup, the entire world is a chew toy. It's our job to teach chewing discrimination. Dogs throw themselves into chewing like we do when we are watching a good football game. You're lucky your dog likes to chew. Use chewing as a substitute behavior for other undesirable behaviors.

Here are some reasons why dogs chew:

- Teething puppies try to relieve pain.
- Puppies chew to explore their environment, just like babies putting everything in their mouths. Chewing can become a lifelong habit that is very pleasurable for the dog.
- The repetitious motion of chewing can be soothing to an anxious dog.
- Chewing helps remove plaque, and it's good for the health of your dog's teeth and gums, especially if you are feeding soft food. Chewing can help sweeten his breath.
- The dog is bored. Recreational chewing helps your dog release excess energy.
- It's a way to get attention from the owner if the owner is present.

The dog is not chewing your good things because he is angry with you or getting even with you. Dogs just don't operate that way. Chewing the wrong objects such as electric cords or wood covered in lead paint can be frustrating for you and dangerous or fatal for the dog. Choking, intestinal blockage, and poisoning from ingesting medicine or cleaning goods can occur. Even chocolate is bad for dogs. While you are teaching your dog to chew only approved items, make sure none of these chew hazards are within reach. Bored dogs often chew for something to do. Give them something better to do. Consider using a wire crate to safely confine your dog for short periods when you can't supervise. Keep your dog on a long line when you're home. Some owners tie the line to their belt. Others attach a bell to the line so the pup makes noise and is easier to keep track of. You might tie the line to a nearby appropriate and safe anchor, like the couch. You'll need a good tie out place in each room because your dog will want to be with you. A large piece of pegboard can be used. The dog's leash can be fastened to the middle. Keep the leash short enough so the dog doesn't get off the board. His weight will keep the board in place. It's portable. You can even put a nice soft rug over it.

Both puppies and older dogs should have lots of safe doggy chew toys. Give a teething pup something cool and hard to help him get rid of his little puppy teeth. Twist some clean pieces of old toweling, soak them in water and freeze them into interesting shapes. Rawhide chew bones can be soaked and frozen as well. Give your pup one of these when he seems to be in a chewing mood. The coldness will soothe his swollen gums. Thin vinyl toys with squeakers might be okay for games with you, but if left alone, the dog could chew it up in no time and perhaps choke. Beware of toys that are small enough to become lodged in the dog's throat. Kongs™, Nylabones™ and hollow bone toys from the pet shop can be stuffed, smeared with cheese or something else to interest the dog. Surely this is better than your shoe. Build interest in the stuffed pacifier by teasing him with it. Stuff it, but don't give it to the dog at first. Admire it, put it up on the counter. Smell it, pretend to eat it, and finally give it over.

You may want two or three of these wonderful toys. They can be washed with a bottle brush and soapy water. You can even place them in a dishwasher or clothes washer. Have enough toys that you can rotate them, putting down "new" ones every day. Stay away from real bones, raw or cooked, and be very careful with rawhide chews. Some dogs will eat too much. When it expands in their stomach they become distressed. Tennis balls can be a problem too. Some dogs are experts at peeling the covering, and then choking on it. Other dogs have been known to swallow them.

Are you paying attention to the behavior you want? If the dog is good, do you ignore her? If she starts chewing, does she get the family's attention—"Tippy, no! Bad girl. Stop it!"

Anticipate a chewing problem. As a puppy, get the dog "hooked" on appropriate chew toys. The pup must learn to discriminate.

***Chewing Things While You're Away?***
***Request a copy of our Home Alone and***
***Enrichment handout for specific information.***

| H | Health of the Dog | T |
| E | Environment Enrichment | O |
| L | Leadership and Training | O |
| M | Management Procedures | L |
| Y | Yield Compromise | O |
| E | Eliminate the Trigger | |
| S | Systematic Desensitization | B |
| T | Take Away the Reward | O |
| R | Remove the Trigger | X |
| A | Acclimate | |
| I | Improve the Association | |
| N | Not Much Nasty Stuff | |

A puppy owner's best friend is a bottle of Bitter® Apple. Apply this liquid to inappropriate items that your pup is chewing, such at the piano stool legs. A bit of special food in or on the appropriate toys and bitter apple on the inappropriate items will teach the puppy in black and white. Always try to keep gray areas out of dog training. While training your dog not to chew, you may need to restrict the area in which he lives. Make it dog proof; litter it with good chew toys.

# GOOD TOY/BAD TOY GAME FOR 7–16 WEEK-OLD PUPPIES

**STEP ONE:** Have three legal puppy toys spread out on the floor and an illegal object (your shoe, book, child's toy). If the pup investigates a legal toy, praise him and immediately have a play or retrieve session with him and his toy. If he investigates an illegal object, ignore him. Encourage him to find a legal toy. Puppy proof the floor again when the game is over. If worse comes to worse and you have to save your shoe from tiny teeth, grab it and walk away. Play again later.

**STEP TWO:** Continue the "Good Toy/Bad Toy" exercise, but make the legal toys even better by putting a tiny smear of peanut butter on them. Make the bad toys even worse by putting a taste deterrent on them. The deterrent can save other unchewables such as your furniture, shoe strings, or your good leather leash. And the best part is the "correction" doesn't come from you, so it's apt to carry over when you're not home!

# MOUTHING—WHAT IF *YOU* ARE THE CHEW TOY?

The pup's mother and littermates have done much to teach bite inhibition by immediate correction when the pup bit too hard in play. Some pups understand if you say, "Ouch" very loudly. You can also try abruptly leaving the area. The idea is to convey that you don't want to play with him anymore. At least turn your head away and tuck your hands under your crossed arms. Wait. He will probably get worse while he is figuring out that you do not respond. Be patient. Most dogs will give up and go away. If you give in and look at him, talk to him, jump, or otherwise give attention, your dog has just learned to play the lottery.

# CRATE TRAINING AND HOUSE TRAINING

*A Crate Can Be*
- *A Dog Den within Your Home,*
- *An Aid To House Training and Supervision,*
- *A Travel Safety Measure, and*
- *An Aid To Home-Alone Worries*

## A DOG DEN WITHIN YOUR HOME

Different family members have places to call their own. Adults might have a workshop, garage, or hobby room. Kids have bedrooms and family rooms. Your dog should have a place to call his own, too. I'm not talking about isolation, but a place within the family activities where he can relax and not have to be on constant lookout, a place where he can be "off duty." One of the best investments you can make is to purchase a crate before you adopt a dog. You've probably noticed that your dog likes enclosed places: under your desk, under the coffee table. We can adapt this trait and use it as a natural way to raise a dog. It's beneficial for housetraining, for safety reasons, for home-alone issues and, at times, for better co-existence between the dog, the children, and other pets in the family.

**CRATES** are the most versatile and safest enclosures. With puppies and adult dogs, the crate serves two major purposes indoors. It helps to supervise the dog while protecting your home and furnishings from curious teeth and also is an aid in teaching the proper toileting area.

Crates are available in a variety of sizes and styles: **WIRE** crates provide maximum ventilation and visibility. A blanket can be thrown over it to cut down on drafts or when your dog needs a quiet time. **PLASTIC** airline crates provide more privacy for the dog and cut down on drafts. They are good for car travel because they offer the most protection. If your dog is wet and muddy, the mess stays inside a plastic crate. **NYLON** mesh crates are see-through, very lightweight, and collapsible, but may pose a security risk. Any crate should be just large enough for the dog to lie down, turn around, and sit when full grown. If an adult-sized crate is too large for your puppy, it will be less effective because it allows room for a separate toilet area. Partition off one end with a box while the puppy is small. Better yet, invest in two crates of different sizes. Crates are important for all types of transportation, including car rides. A dog traveling in a vehicle is at risk of injuring himself and distracting the driver if he is not safely contained.

## AN AID TO HOUSE TRAINING AND SUPERVISION

Crates are good for supervision of puppies and newly adopted adult dogs. Just as parents use cribs and playpens to help them supervise their human babies, you can use a crate to confine your dog near household activities when you're too busy to supervise closely. Relaxing in a crate in the family living quarters is much

CONTACT US IF YOU NEED HELP   info@legacycanine.com   360-683-1522

*Puppy Crate/Housetrain.doc*   *Coaching People to Train Their Dogs* © Terry Ryan 2005

preferable to your dog than the isolation of being locked in the bathroom, garage, or cellar. That type of isolation is apt to make your dog miserable and will be counterproductive. A crate should never be used as a substitute for taking your dog to the toilet area, for exercise and play at regular intervals, or for training. It's a tool to aid the management and training of your dog, not a routine way of life for a dog. It is not a panacea. The crate can be used for short periods as confinement when no one is home. These portable enclosures provide peace of mind knowing your pal is safe, comfortable, and not suffering a housetraining setback. Crates are small enough to move around the house, perhaps into a bedroom at night. Crates serve as a safe place to retreat throughout your dog's life.

## GETTING USED TO THE CRATE

Most dogs need to be conditioned to the idea that a crate is a great place to be. At first, keep the door open and casually toss in a food treat or a favorite toy as you go about your business. You may want to serve meals in the crate, but don't close the door at first. Ask the dog to get in the crate, leave the door open, and sit down with a good book, keeping the dog company and petting her while you read.

A crate should be lined with an easily cleaned mat or bedding the dog is not likely to chew. It's difficult to estimate the maximum amount of time a dog should be crated. Even a casual observer knows that dogs do sleep a lot through the day. Many dogs have a way of shutting down if nothing much is happening. The effects of crating a dog should be monitored regularly. For a high-energy dog, it's boring in that crate. Your dog has lots of time and nothing to do. Make a habit of placing some time and energy consuming toys in the crate with the dog. Chew items are a good choice. These toys are only for your dog when she is alone in the crate. When you return and take the dog out of the crate, take the toy away also. Some dogs may enjoy having the radio or TV playing—it keeps them company and masks other noises that might disturb them.

## TOILET TRAINING

Dogs are inherently clean animals. As tiny infants, their mothers keep them very clean. As soon as they can wobble away, puppies seem to prefer leaving their eating, sleeping, and play areas to toilet. Folks tend to concentrate on where their dog should NOT toilet. Thought should be given to an appropriate toilet area, usually outdoors in a fenced yard. Select an area away from the general traffic pattern, but close enough to be convenient. You might set aside a small area with bark or gravel. Scooping is easier on these surfaces than on grass. If your dog will be taken to toilet on leash in a public place, it's imperative that you carry a plastic bag for prompt cleanup. Unless you want your dog to use an indoor toilet full time, it's best to skip newspaper training and teach him to toilet outside from the beginning. Exceptions to the outdoor-toilet rule might include the very young puppy left home alone for long hours, an unvaccinated puppy, apartment dwellers with small dogs, and disabled dogs or owners. These dogs might be trained to toilet on newspapers over a plastic sheet, in a litter box, or on commercially available disposable pet pads. A pup that will be left home a lot could be kept in an exercise pen. This enclosure is roomy enough to allow space on one side for his bed and toys and a place on the other side for a toilet. Made of metal or wire mesh, they are typically larger than a crate. Some have tops or bottoms, but most are simply freestanding enclosures. Called playpens or exercise pens, because of the roominess, they are not the best choice for toilet training. With no top or floor, exercise pens are not as escape-proof as a crate. They are an excellent way to confine a young dog while you are home, and simply too busy to watch the dog every moment.

While toilet training your dog, stack the deck in your favor. What goes in on schedule usually comes out on schedule. Regular meals rather than free feeding will help manage the toileting pattern. The younger the dog, the more often he needs to eliminate. Dogs usually defecate shortly after each feeding. They urinate more frequently. Very young puppies might need to urinate as often as every hour or so, especially during active periods. The dog should be taken to the toilet first thing in the morning, after a play period (or other stimulating activity), after naps, and just before going to bed at night. By 12 weeks of age, most pups should be able to make it through a seven-hour night if managed properly. Withholding food and water late in the evening will lessen the chances of a puppy needing to go out during the night. He shouldn't need water during the night, but you might feel better leaving a couple of ice cubes in the empty water bowl.

When a baby pup first comes home to live with you, set your alarm clock several hours earlier than normal so your can escort your pup to the toilet. Slowly advance the alarm to your normal wake-up time. Don't necessarily interpret whimpers in the night as a need to toilet. More than likely, he's just looking for attention. If you respond to each whimper with a midnight social hour, who's training whom? At the toilet area, stay with your dog until you get results, then heap on the praise and rewards. If you keep her on leash, slowly circle the specific toilet area to keep her focused. If she doesn't toilet within four or five minutes, try again later. When she does go in the right place, WAIT for her to finish, and praise her. If you praise at the first sight of poop or pee, you're making a mistake. Your enthusiasm might distract and interrupt the dog. Wait! And don't fall into the habit of taking her right back inside after she toilets. She probably likes to be outside with you and she may learn to take her time toileting so she doesn't have to go back in. Spend a few minutes outside with her before you go back in.

Indoors, it's easier to watch your dog in a small area, perhaps one room. Close the doors or use doorway barriers to block him from other rooms. Baby gates are see-through panels, which block off a doorway, confining the dog to a room. They are an easy way to keep a dog within supervision range in the home. Keep an eye out for sniffing and circling, which often indicate the need to toilet. When you get back inside, allow your dog the privilege of roaming the house freely while you supervise. As time goes on, he'll be able to earn access to more rooms for a longer time and eventually without supervision.

A verbal cue such as, "Go potty" or a cheerful, "Do it" can be used while he's toileting. In time, he'll associate this term with the need to go, so you can use it when you're in a hurry. I have a friend who hums his dog a little tune during such occasions! Keep an eye on your pup if he's on the move. At times when you can't give undivided attention, temporarily restrict your dog to a small area—the crate! Because we want the dog to feel safe and secure in his special place, teach children not to bother him when he's in his crate. You're apt to find that he will go into the open crate uninvited when he wants to relax and not have to worry about contact with others.

# WHAT IF YOUR DOG HAS AN ACCIDENT?

In general, don't punish accidents. Most of the time the punishment will be ill timed and not associated with the act. It will only frighten and confuse the dog. Spanking, rubbing his nose in it, or sending the dog to the cellar does nothing to help house training and does much to damage your relationship. We can never be sure the dog understands exactly what he did wrong. If he made a pile in the kitchen and you smack him with a newspaper, he has only a slim chance of associating it with the accident. Get the newspaper and smack yourself for not paying attention.

Don't allow your dog to watch you clean up. Some dogs will do anything for entertainment or attention. Finish with a commercial, enzymatic odor neutralizer and stain remover. Follow the directions and blot well. *Nature's Miracle*® is a good product. You can make your own from white vinegar. Dilute ¼ cup of it with one cup of water. Put the legs of a chair over the area until the spot is completely dry. This will help your dog avoid the spot should there be some residual scent. Vow to be more attentive and not to allow another accident to happen.

As an alternative to the crate, you could place your dog on leash and give her to a family member, or the leash could be tied to a nearby doorknob or heavy piece of furniture. Consider constructing a temporary waiting station. Here's how: Acquire a piece of plywood twice as long as your dog. Drill two holes in the middle, thread a leash through, and secure it with just enough length to allow your dog to stand and sit without tension on the leash. Place this temporary waiting station flat on the floor within view of family activities. When your dog is attached to the station, she can see what's going on, but her own weight on the plywood prevents it from moving. You can make a deluxe model by putting self-adhesive carpet squares on the top surface, or a lightweight model for very small dogs by using pegboard instead of plywood. This type of restraint should be used only for a few minutes and only when someone is supervising. Idea: How about putting a bell on your dog's collar to alert you when she's walking around? A trailing leash will also help call attention to the dog's travels and help you stop the dog in a hurry. Be careful though; the leash can become tangled easily.

## A Travel Safety Measure

A dog can travel safely with you in your automobile if she is in a crate. The crate should be attached to the seat of the car or floor of the station wagon with straps. This is important because in stop-and-go traffic, the crate can slip, making the dog uneasy or frightened, or causing an upset stomach. If there should be an accident, a loose crate flying around the car is, of course, dangerous for your dog, and also very dangerous for the driver and passengers. A dog likes to see where she is going, so if the crate can be high enough to have a view, that's good. One exception is the dog that gets carsick. That dog might be more comfortable down low or with a towel or blanket thrown over the crate. Seeing buildings, poles, and the scenery rush past the side of the car can contribute to carsickness. The motion of all that scenery rushing by could overly stimulate dogs that like to chase. This type of dog might be calmer if unable to see out the sides of the crate. It gets hot in cars VERY quickly. It gets even hotter in a plastic crate. Plan ahead; know what stops you will need to make. Don't depend on a shady place to park; there might not be one.

# LEGACY'S PUPPY HEADSTART CLASSES!

## A NEW FAMILY MEMBER!   CONGRATULATIONS!

### *You are invited to Legacy's On-Going Puppy HeadStart Class!*

**The Importance of Timely Puppy Socialization and Environmental Enrichment:**

Socialization is an enrichment process that exposes your puppy to varied elements of our environment. Think of a puppy's brain as lots of little electrical sockets and plugs floating in space. Triggers in the environment are responsible for bringing those plugs and sockets together. Most of these windows of opportunity close after the pup reaches sixteen weeks of age.

Legacy HeadStart puppy classes organize experiences to help the plugs find the sockets before the pup is sixteen weeks old. Our 40-minute "Puppy Menu" classes include exercises in:

OWNER/DOG RELATIONSHIP • MANNERS • TOILET TRAINING • DOG/DOG SOCIALIZATION
ACCEPTANCE OF HANDLING • GROOMING • HUMAN/PUPPY SOCIALIZATION
CONFIDENCE BUILDING WITH DIFFERENT OBJECTS, SURFACES, AND SOUNDS

### FEEL FREE TO STOP IN AND OBSERVE ANY OF OUR CLASSES.
252 Kitchen-Dick Road, Sequim, Washington

Puppy HeadStart class is free with a paid registration to Legacy's Pet Dog Manners I class. Call or stop by the Legacy office to register for class. At registration you will need to:
- Show proof of your puppy's inoculations.
- Bring a note from your veterinarian approving your pup's participation in class.
- Fill out our registration and profile forms.

At your first class your puppy will need to:
- Wear a buckle collar and be on a leash.
- Have her favorite food and toys along. (Regular puppy food is okay).

**LEGACY**
Canine Behavior & Training

Office Hours:   12:00–4:00 Monday–Friday
360-683-1522   www.LegacyCanine.com

CONTACT US IF YOU NEED HELP   info@legacycanine.com   360-683-1522

*Coaching People to Train Their Dogs* © Terry Ryan 2005

# Puppy Headstart Homework

## PARTICIPATION IN CLASS IS GOOD, BUT ITS NOT ENOUGH!

*If your veterinarian approves, examples of learning experiences for your puppy include:*

- Go to the beach, let your dog sniff around (On leash! Bring a poop bag!)
- Drive to your vet's office. Ask the receptionist to give your dog a treat. Leave.
- Tie a bandana on your dog! Help him keep calm as you do so.
- Give your dog a bath. Warm water! Perhaps skip puppy's head and ears at first.
- Put a hat on your head, let your pup see you. Give him a treat.
- Find a shop window display with a lifelike animal or human. Let your dog see it.
- Help your pup sit or stand on a bathroom scale.
- Find a construction site, walk up to it, but not so close that your pup is frightened.
- Invite a friend to ring your doorbell, help your pup sit quietly to greet your friend.
- Arrange for your dog to spend the night with a trusted friend - take your pup's crate.
- Learn about noisy children by walking past a school yard or play ground—at a distance.
- Clip one toenail while your dog licks peanut butter off of the refrigerator door.
- Put your pup on a low table, "play" veterinarian or groomer. Reward calm behavior.
- Play hide and seek in your living room.

## PUPPY RULE OF TWELVE*:

Before your puppy is twelve weeks old, he should experience at least twelve new and different:

| | |
|---|---|
| Surfaces to be on | wet grass, slippery tile, gravel, bark, grating, steps |
| Objects to investigate | inside a car, wind up toy, hollow paper tube, wheelchair |
| Locations to visit | if it's ok with your vet, go to a friend's home, park, busy street |
| People to meet | assorted sizes, color, gender, children under supervision |
| Sounds to hear | garage door opening, lawnmower, stove timer, various CD's |
| Moving objects | cows or horses, gates, roller blades, flag in the wind |
| Polite dogs to see or meet | ones with good manners, no bullies, only a minute or two at a time |
| Food containers | eat from food dispensing toys, a dish, your hand, hand in a dish |
| Ways for owners to handle | in lap, on table, touch inside ears, open his mouth, use a brush |
| Times alone in crate | when you're in bathroom, while you put out trash, at a friend's house |

*From Peaceable Paws

## FOR MORE EXPERIENCES:

Make a habit of placing a different novel object in your home every few days. Just put it down and let the pup investigate without your help: A mirror, ladder flat on the floor to walk through, the vacuum across a hallway so the dog has to walk over it, a big stuffed animal on the floor, a ticking alarm clock, some empty packing boxes . . . anything new and interesting.

# THE BARK STOPS HERE

It's normal for dogs to bark. Chickens cluck, cows moo, dogs bark. Barking too much, too loudly, and at the wrong times is a problem—if not for the dog, then for the people who live near the dog. Both genetic and environmental factors influence the variability of when, where, and how easily the dog is triggered to bark. Barking can be learned by experience. Perhaps the dog barked once in surprise when a person appeared suddenly. The person jumped back, also in surprise. Now the dog thinks her barking is a way to make suspicious people retreat. Or, she may have discovered that on a boring day, barking gets her owners to talk to her: "Hey you, be quiet!"

## WHY IS THE DOG BARKING?

Jot down the circumstances of the barking. A pattern might evolve that will yield some clues. If you're not home, ask your neighbors. At least they'll know you are concerned and trying to address the problem. For more accurate information, sneak back home and spy on your dog. Try leaving a tape recorder on, or even a video camera—you might at least get some good audio from it.

**When does the dog bark?** Is there any pattern to when the dog barks? Monday mornings only? Only at night while outside? Only when left alone? Only when it rains?

**When did the barking start?** Has this been occurring since puppyhood? Did the onset coincide with any type of lifestyle change? A move? Has a child left for college? After a family vacation? Do you have new neighbors?

**Where is the barking?** Inside, outside, or both? What about in the car? How about on walks?

**Who is present?** Does it make a difference if the dog is alone or with others?

**Where is the dog's focus?** On a certain person, animal, or thing? Makes no difference? Nothing at all? What solutions have been tried—how long?

## IDENTIFYING SIGNS OF STRESS IN OUR DOGS

Information about stress was included in your orientation notebook. Excessive, repetitious barking could be the dog's way of masking an unpleasant situation. Please review the information on calming signals.

## L.O.U.D.E.R.

Putting dog behavior into categories is a risky business, but for purposes of this book, an attempt to group barkers into six broad classifications has been made. The definitions are based on knowledge gained from years of observation and working with dogs by the author and others in the field of canine behavior and training. The acronym L O U D E R represents and helps us remember some of the reasons dogs bark:

**L ibby,** The "Look at Me" Barker    "Will somebody, anybody, please pay attention to me?"
**O maha,** The "Offensive" Barker    "Get out of here now. In fact, I'd like to show you the way!"
**U tah,** The "Underemployed" Barker    "I have nothing to do. Barking is my recreation."
**D allas,** The "Defensive" Barker    "I'm afraid. Please go away. I'll try to put more space between us if I can."
**E lizabeth,** The "Enthusiastic" Barker    "Do I need a reason? I'm just having a blast!"
**R eno,** The "Reduce-My-Dependence"    "Will my special person please come back?"

CONTACT US IF YOU NEED HELP   info@legacycanine.com   360-683-1522

*INFO Barking.doc*    *Coaching People to Train Their Dogs* © Terry Ryan 2005

# LIBBY, the "Look at Me" Barker

*"Will somebody, anybody, please pay attention to me?"*

This type of dog wants anyone who is handy to pay attention. The Libby-type is usually a social, pack-oriented dog. The "look at me" attention seeker could learn that digging or chewing gets attention. It just so happens that Libby favors barking instead. This dog is different from a dog that is overly bonded to an individual or a select group of favorites. The Libby-type is not picky; any kind of attention from anyone will do! The bark is somewhat high in pitch. The dog might pause and look or listen to see if anyone is interested, then start in again. During the pause the Libby-type might wag, circle, bow, or look otherwise charming. Libby is like the spoiled child in the grocery store grabbing for candy, running up and down the aisles, or yelling to get a response from Mom or the other customers.

# OMAHA, the "Offensive" Barker

*"Get out of here now. In fact, I'd like to show you the way!"*

A brave dog protecting self, territory, or possessions will growl and bark at anything or anybody perceived as a threat. The Omaha-type dog is carrying a spear, as opposed to a fearful defensive dog carrying a shield. The dog displays threatening intentions and might carry through with the threat if given the opportunity. The threshold between threat and action has a lot to do with critical distance, the imaginary circle around the dog. If a threat crosses the chalk line, the dog feels something has to be done to get rid of it. More low than high in pitch, this bark is often preceded by a growl and escalates into a bark. It's a startling bark of high intensity, but short duration that is great for the shock effect! Like Dirty Harry in the movies, Omaha dares offenders with a "make my day" attitude.

# UTAH, the "Underemployed" Barker

*"I have nothing to do. Barking is my recreation."*

The underemployed dog has lots of time and energy but nothing to do. Think of a dog's energy level as a pressure cooker. With a lack of activity, the pressure builds up and is then released by a valve. The steam comes out and the pressure cooker is okay again . . . until the next time it needs to vent. A high-energy dog with nothing to do is like a pressure cooker with a clogged valve. The Utah-type dog has no choice but to release energy in any way possible—a major bout of barking or other manifestations of his frustration. We could take the word "bark" out of this topic and insert chew, scratch, dig, or any other activity a dog discovers as a release valve.

The bark pattern of a Utah-type dog is monotonous, with repetitive intervals. It's usually of medium pitch. The bark sounds flat and boring, except some dogs embellish it with an occasional howl. The underemployed bark is directed at nothing in particular. Utah is like a bored teenager who plays the stereo too loudly.

# DALLAS, the "Defensive" Barker

*"I'm afraid, go away. Give me more space."*

A worried, fearful dog, the Dallas type might bark at anything or anybody perceived as a threat. The Dallas-type dog is carrying a shield as opposed to a bold, offensive dog like Omaha who carries a sword. The dog may try to display subordinate postures, but might carry through with a bite if there is no other choice, such as to retreat. The threshold between barking a warning and action has a lot to do with critical distance, the imaginary circle around the dog. If a threat crosses the chalk line of this imaginary circle, the dog panics. However, unlike the offensive dog, the defensive dog is more apt to increase distance by backing up than by chasing the threat away. The defensive bark is a sharp, high-pitched alarm in hopes the scary thing will go away. The dog may step forward, but then retreats to a "safe" place. Talk is cheap. Dallas would rather not put his money where his mouth is.

# ELIZABETH, the "Enthusiastic" Barker

*"Do I need a reason? I'm just having a blast!"*

This dog has uncontrolled high energy and lots of enthusiasm for life. Often self-rewarding, the Elizabeth-type dog is expressing her high spirits to the world. Things that wouldn't interest another dog arouse her curiosity. She's easily stimulated. Movement is often a trigger. Her bark is high pitched and continuous. She moves around a lot as she's barking, is alert, wags her tail, and often pants. Elizabeth is like a high-energy child at a birthday party.

# RENO, "Reduce-My-Dependence" Barker

*"Will my special person please come back?"*

Separation anxiety is quite different from the attention-seeking dog like Libby. Libby will settle for any type of interaction from any person or animal. Reno is an anxious dog who is overly bonded to one individual and suffers greatly when that person leaves. Reno can take some comfort from others, but is mainly focused on his special person. The Reduce-My-Dependence bark is usually high pitched and frantic. If you set up a video camera you might observe pacing, drooling, whining, scratching, chewing, and howling in the direction the special person was last seen or heard. The anxiety is usually at its worst right after the departure. Reno is like a homesick child at camp.

# THE BARKING 'TOOLBOX"

## H.E.L.M.—General Foundation Check

### [H]ealth, Including Veterinary Issues

If your dog is anxious or fearful, your veterinarian might suggest one of the new prescription medications to complement your training program. Extreme repetitive behaviors such as barking with no apparent purpose, circling, pacing, or licking are of special concern. Pharmacological intervention combined with behavior modification might be in order. Your veterinarian can refer you to pet professionals in complementary fields such as aromatherapy, acupuncture, touch therapy, or homeopathic remedies. Dogs can be debarked surgically. Results differ depending on the specific procedure performed and other variables. Not all veterinarians will perform this type of surgery. Not all behaviorists agree it's advisable. Do homework, ask around, and get a second opinion. Surgery may or may not be the right option for your dog.

| H | Health of the Dog | T |
| E | Environment Enrichment | O |
| L | Leadership and Training | O |
| M | Management Procedures | L |
| Y | Yield Compromise | O |
| E | Eliminate the Trigger | L |
| S | Systematic Desensitization | B |
| T | Take Away the Reward | B |
| R | Remove the Trigger | O |
| A | Acclimate | O |
| I | Improve the Association | X |
| N | Not Much Nasty Stuff | |

### [E]nvironmental Enrichment

Dogs are social creatures. The home-alone issue is a factor in some barking problems. While not a panacea for barking dogs specifically, almost any dog will benefit from an enriched environment. Unlike back on the farm with Ol' Shep, modern latchkey dogs no longer get the opportunity to tag along with their owner during the workday. From a dog's point of view, people are just not as much fun as they used to be. Even though your time may be limited, with a little creativity you can find ways to help your dog lead a fuller life. Please ask for Legacy's Home Alone/Enrichment handout.

### [L]eadership and Training

Train, Don't Complain! Focus on training good behavior, in this case quiet behavior, rather than waiting for the dog to bark and punishing the inappropriate behavior. Follow the L.E.A.D. program. It is described in a separate handout.

### [M]anagement in General

Training and behavior modification might take some time before satisfactory results can be achieved. Temporary fixes should also be considered. Determine the circumstances most likely to generate barking and determine ways to remove temptations. In some cases, temporary fixes are appropriate for use until your bark reduction program is designed, underway, and working.

# Y.E.S. T.R.A.I.N – A MORE SPECIFIC APPROACH TO BARKING

Think of yourself as a gourmet cook. You have all sorts of pots and pans and shelves of exotic ingredients. Some will be often-used standards. Some you may use infrequently, depending on the result you want. Others might never come out of the closet. Each dish requires a different assortment of utensils and ingredients. Select components in a bark reduction program the same way you select cooking ingredients. We talk about the Y.E.S. T.R.A.I.N. acronym at orientation. Now we will adapt the tools for the specific problem of barking. The concepts with an asterisk (E, S, T, R, I) are especially appropriate for barking dogs.

> Y  YIELD A LITTLE
> E  ELIMINATE THE CAUSE*
> S  SYSTEMATIC DESENSITIZATION*
>
> T  TAKE AWAY THE REWARD*
> R  REWARD AN INCOMPATIBLE BEHAVIOR*
> A  ACCLIMATE THE DOG
> I  IMPROVE THE DOG'S ASSOCIATION*
> N  NASTY STUFF

## Yield a Little

Don't give in completely to your dog, but sometimes give in a little. This helps make an equitable living arrangement. Often overlooked as an option in dog training, a compromise can be an easy and effective solution. Yield a Little appeals to owners with little time, talent, or inclination to train. This tool allows the dog's preferred activity, where punishment might simply encourage the dog to develop another annoying habit. Yield a Little works well in combination with other ingredients. The main drawback is that there might not be a suitable compromise available. Yield a Little is never appropriate for problems that might endanger the dog or those around the dog.

> *"Okay Dog, you can only bark in the side yard where there are no neighbors to hear you."*
>
> *"Dog, I'll allow two or three free barks, but then you have to be quiet."*

## Eliminate The Trigger

Why not simply eliminate the cause of the barking? You must be sure, however, to correctly identify the cause. There may be a combination of triggers or cues that provoke the behavior and you'll need to peel them away like layers of an onion. Eliminate the Trigger is quick and solves the problem forever and without stress to the owner or dog. It's good first aid. It may resolve one specific barking issue, but may not change the dog's attitude toward other similar situations. Your dog can't bark at the mail truck because he's in the kitchen with you where he can't hear it. This doesn't work with the unscheduled parcel deliveryman.

> *"Hello Mrs. Jones? Peter is pestering my dog again. Please come over and get Peter!"*
>
> *"Well Dog, our neighbor says you bark all day while I'm away at work. I guess you have too much energy. I'd better create some activity for you before, during, and after work."*

## Systematic Desensitization

Set up training sessions where the bark producing stimulus is presented at a very low level. The dog must be watched carefully for signs of impending barking. The stimulus is increased gradually, to avoid triggering the dog's reaction. Continue until the dog is able to cope with the problem situation. Systematic Desensitization works very well in conjunction with the tool "Improve the Dog's Association." If used effectively, it stands a good chance of completely eliminating the barking problem. Care must be taken not to proceed too quickly and overwhelm the dog. The owner's ability to control the dog's environment and to read the dog's reactions is critical to success. If there is no way to eliminate or at least minimize the triggering situation, Systematic Desensitization cannot be accomplished. ·

> "Dog, I'm sorry sirens get you going. Today I'll play my siren CD for a little while. The volume will be so low you'll barely hear it. Tomorrow I'll turn it up just a tad. Then up a bit more, but I'll be observing to be sure you're OK with each step. The plan is that, over time, the regular volume and the real thing won't be a big deal either."

> "Dog, I wish you wouldn't run around barking every time you see me pick up your leash for a walk. So at first I'm only going to look at your leash, then only reach for it. If you're quiet, I'm going to pick up your leash several dozen times a day. Sometimes I'll just put it back, sometimes I'll hook it to your collar and then take it off and put it back, and once in a while we'll go for a walk."

## Take Away the Reward

Almost all behaviors are sustained by a reward of some type. Sometimes the reward is subtle. You don't see it as a reward, but the dog does. If you can identify the reward with certainty and eliminate it, the barking will eventually decrease and go away. The barking behavior goes "into extinction."

Take Away the Reward is non-confrontational. It's easy and takes little time, skill, or effort. The problem is that sometimes the reward is not obvious or the reward, even if identified, is impossible to remove. Often there is more than one reward, and eliminating only one will not solve the problem. For example the reward for barking in the backyard at passersby might be

(a) Attention—the owner brings the dog in to avoid further problems and/or

(b) Satisfaction from the reaction the dog gets from the people walking by.

Be Aware. Sometimes the behavior will increase after the reward is withdrawn. This is known as an "extinction burst" and is quite normal. In plain words, sometimes it gets worse before it gets better. If the owner gives in and the barking is rewarded, the dog has learned to play the lottery. Intermittent reinforcement makes correcting the behavior much more difficult to achieve. Be Aware. Even if you don't give in, the dog might still attempt a bark the next few times the situation presents itself. Stick with it! Over time, this spontaneous recovery period of barking will also go away.

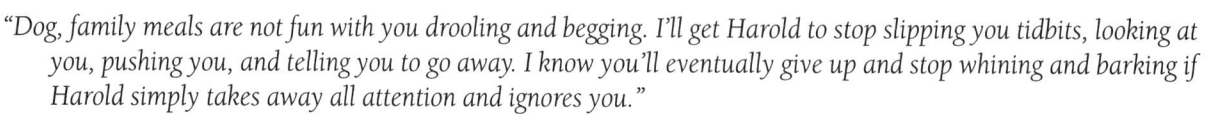

> "Dog, family meals are not fun with you drooling and begging. I'll get Harold to stop slipping you tidbits, looking at you, pushing you, and telling you to go away. I know you'll eventually give up and stop whining and barking if Harold simply takes away all attention and ignores you."

> "Dog, when I open the door and holler, "Shut up," you actually like it! You've figured out how to get me to pay attention to you. Hollering isn't punishment at all; it's a reward for a lonely dog!"

## Reward an Incompatible Behavior

In situations when the dog used to bark, give him a way to get rewarded instead of punished. It does take time to train the good behavior, and you have to be ready to reward it when it's offered. Be sure your training and the new behavior you choose are more fun than barking.

> "Here comes Joyce and Tippy walking on the other side of the street. Dog, 'Sit.' If you're sitting, making eye contact with me, and receiving a treat, you can't be barking at Tippy."

> "Dog, instead of barking for joy when I come home, go get your ball. I'll throw it for you."

## Acclimate the Dog

Acclimation is especially helpful to fearful dogs or to excitable, over reactive dogs. Often referred to as habituation, it simply means "getting used to it." The dog is exposed to the problem-producing stimulus in a safe and controlled manner. The dog is able to investigate or retreat at will, and neither reward nor punishment is presented. In a calm and neutral environment, the frightened dog finds there's nothing to fear. The excited dog learns his antics are not rewarded.

> THE LOOK: "You bark at people who wear hats? Dog, you'll acclimate to hats because the whole family will be wearing hats when we are around you."

> SOUND: "Dog, in preparation to your boarding kennel visit, this week we'll listen to the CD they play in the kennel. At least get used to how it sounds there."

> SMELL: "By the way, Dog, you have a new blanket. It's been at the boarding kennel. I don't want you to be upset and bark like the last time. This might be a way to make you feel more at home during your vacation there next week. While we're at it, I'll ask the kennel manager if I can bring some things that smell like home to keep with you during your store."

## Improve the Dog's Association

Improve the Association, formally known as counterconditioning, is one of the most widely used and successful behavior modification concepts for overcoming fear. It helps your dog establish a new, acceptable mindset and response to replace the fearful behavior. Pair something of high value to the dog—a walk, a chance to play ball, presentation of the food bowl—with the problem stimulus. Improve the Association is useful when you can't change the problem environment. It is often used with Systematic Desensitization.

> "Dog, now that I think about it, you probably don't like to ride in the car because the last three rides resulted in
> a. an upset stomach,
> b. staying at the grooming shop, and
> c. being stuck in the back seat with three-year-old Jimmy.
> Well, this month you'll ride only one block each day to the park, where we'll get out and play. I'll toss treats to you during the ride. We'll leave Jimmy home with Grandma."

The reward selected must be strong enough to overcome the problem. If not, you might get the reverse effect. For example:

> "Dog, I know you see she's wearing a white coat and stethoscope. You're suspicious. On the other hand, she's also got the best liver treats in town. Past history tells me the liver will triumph! However we're in trouble if the treat isn't worth it. Not only will your attitude toward the vet not improve, you might become wary now when liver treats are offered!"

CONTACT US IF YOU NEED HELP   info@legacycanine.com   360-683-1522

## Not Much Nasty Stuff

On the surface, punishment might seem to work. The natural orienting reflex interrupts the barking for a second or two as the dog turns to look at the new disturbance. Punishment rarely offers a permanent fix. Review the "Aversives" handout in your orientation notebook for information about possible associated problems. Aversives might be okay for a small percentage of cases, but even then, it should rarely be the first course of action. For punishment to be effective, it should be immediate and delivered as a result of the specific behavior. It should be aversive and intense enough to stop the behavior right away. The dog should see it as a direct result of the inappropriate behavior, independent of the owner's presence. Here are some aversives used for barking dogs. A quick review of the acronym YES TRAIN will show alternatives that may well have better results for these barkers. You'll notice that we always look for a chance to reward the appropriate behavior:

> SOUND: "Dog, the next time you bark and chase birds, I'm going to give you a blast from my hand held boat horn. If you see a bird and turn away, we're going to play ball."

> TASTE: "Dog, if you walk to the park quietly, I'll pop a piece of cheese into your mouth. If you start barking, I'll give you a shot of lemon juice into the corner of your mouth."

> SMELL: "Dog, we're going for a ride. Please wear this special collar. If you notice someone on the sidewalk and do ANYTHING except bark, you'll get a hearty cheer from the family. If you bark at someone on the sidewalk, the collar will release a yucky smell in your face."

> SIGHT (Avoidance): "If you remember Dog, the last time you were barking at the mouse in the wall I squirted your face with water from my plant mister. I think I'll just put the mister on the floor near that wall as a reminder."

> FEEL: "You like to jump on my chair to bark out the window? I'll leave a vinyl floor protector on the cushion, gripper side UP! It's not a comfortable barking perch anymore. I'll be sure to notice when you're in your dog bed being good and tell you so."

## Anti-Barking Devices

In general these are designed to punish a dog or to cue the dog to avoid possible punishment by remaining quiet. The device is mounted on a collar and is triggered automatically by the dog's bark. The aversives produced include vibration, shock, odor, or sound. The risk of physical and psychological side effects is great enough to warrant careful research before considering an anti-barking device. The Gentle Spray citronella spray collar is one that we have used successfully.

## Making a Recipe for a Quiet Dog

Clearly defined goals will help success. Is one bark okay, then you'd like quiet? Or do you expect total silence? Can the dog bark at strangers, but not at neighbors? You must decide these things before you choose ingredients for your recipe. If at first the recipe doesn't work out, don't assume failure. The experience can be diagnostic! Now you know what doesn't work. Try again. You have plenty of ingredients to change the recipe.

Condensed from the book, *The Bark Stops Here,* by Terry Ryan.

# DIGGING

Most dogs dig at one time or another, whether it is in the cushions on the sofa or the dirt in your flower bed. For some, it is characteristic of their breed. They are going after prey, real or imagined. Many dogs dig to bury a chew toy intending to recover it later. A dog might dig to build a den for the arrival of real or imagined puppies. Dogs also dig to keep cool—they find a shady spot and dig down to the nice cool earth. Other dogs dig to escape—they're looking for companionship or entertainment. Whatever the reason, your solution to this problem will be to eliminate your dog's motivation for digging or to redirect the digging to an appropriate place. The fact is, for lots of dogs, digging is just plain fun—you play golf, your dog digs. If the dog needs to drain his reservoir of energy, digging is probably a better choice than barking. If you absolutely have to stop the digging, be sure to provide another hobby! If he's digging, he's outside. Why? Train the dog to be good indoors. Install a dog door. As with any doggy problem, the Toolbox acronyms on the right will give you some ideas.

| H | Health of the Dog | T |
| E | Environment Enrichment | O |
| L | Leadership and Training | O |
| M | Management Procedures | O |
| Y | Yield Compromise | O |
| E | Eliminate the Trigger | L |
| S | Systematic Desensitization | L |
| T | Take Away the Reward | B |
| R | Remove the Trigger | O |
| A | Acclimate | O |
| I | Improve the Association | X |
| N | Not Much Nasty Stuff | X |

## Management

Don't let him outdoors unsupervised. Put down plastic sheeting with rocks on top to discourage him from a favorite spot. Try putting down chicken wire covered with bark or gravel. No one will know, except the dog, when he tries to dig. Maybe he'll think the entire yard is under chicken wire and will give up.

## Yield (Compromise)

Fence off a suitable area where your dog can dig. If he likes to be cool, prepare a shady area for him. You may want to replace the topsoil with heavy sand to make digging easier and to reduce mud. The miners in the goldrush of 1949 didn't dig just anywhere. Even those living in New Jersey braved hardships and RUSHED to dig holes in California—where the gold was found. Bury a toy as your dog watches. Say, "Dig!" and help him dig it up. Next take him indoors, then sneak out to bury a surprise treasure. Help him for the next few weeks. Redirect any out-of-bounds digging to the digging pit!

CONTACT US IF YOU NEED HELP    info@legacycanine.com    360-683-1522

*INFO Digging.doc*    *Coaching People to Train Their Dogs* © Terry Ryan 2005

## Take Away the Reward

If the dog is digging to escape, take away the reward by making the yard escape-proof, maybe burying a foot or more of fencing. Find out WHY the dog wants to escape and seek a remedy. Some dogs dig just for something to do. Refer to Legacy's Home Alone and Environmental Enrichment handout to offer her alternatives.

## Remove the Trigger

Some dogs engage in repetitious digging to relieve stress. You'll have to figure out what's causing the stress and do something to remedy it.

## Not Much Nasty Stuff

Try a motion sensitive alarm. Pet catalogs have them. WARNING: If you only punish the digging, without resolving the reason, your dog might try a substitute behavior for his spare energy. Do your neighbors prefer digging or barking? Additional information about possible backwash from punishment is found in the Legacy handout entitled Aversives.

# My Dog Is Eating Poop!!

Eating feces, coprophagia, is not an uncommon behavior for the canid family. Some dogs seem predisposed to coprophagia, regardless of other factors. The causes may be nutritional, metabolic, or behavioral. Dog experts suggest that while it is disgusting to us, it is relatively harmless for the dog. If your veterinarian agrees that it is harmless, one approach is to ignore the behavior.

## VET EXAM AND DIET

Tell your vet the specific problem. Some believe coprophagia may be more common in dogs fed one meal a day or fed a low quality food. It's been suggested that dogs with certain dietary deficiencies are prone to coprophagia. Malabsorption (the inability to digest food in the small intestine) could be at fault. If the food is not fully digested, feces may appear as food to the dog. Food additives, available in pet shops, are designed specifically to make the feces repulsive. Mixed results have been reported. Some people have reduced coprophagia by adding a bit of canned, crushed pineapple to the food or a sprinkle of enzymes such as meat tenderizer. Commercial or homemade remedies such as these need to be cleared by your veterinarian. Flower essence remedies might be explored. If the dog is giving stress signals (refer to Legacy's handout on stress) counter conditioning is in order.

## MANAGEMENT

Prevention is the first step in management. Don't let the dog practice eating poop. Go back to housetraining basics. We have a detailed handout on Crates & Housetraining. One recommendation is to allow access to the toilet area only under supervision. For example, take your dog outside on leash until he toilets, then bring him back into house. Go back outside without the dog and immediately clean up the feces. Make certain the dog does not watch the clean up and derive some sort of entertainment or reward from your activity. Adults should eat at least two (young dogs more) meals a day. If training with food, practice sessions can be conducted at meal times. Elimination becomes more predictable—what goes in on schedule comes out on schedule. With this type of management it will take several weeks, probably months, to see an actual behavior change. Don't test the dog too soon!

## CAN YOU CHANGE THE BEHAVIOR?

Has someone been inadvertently rewarding the behavior? Did a family member see it happen? How did that person react? The dog might be doing this to get attention! If you scold the dog or rush over to get him away from the poop, that's attention and diversion—a reward. If you have taught a cue for "Leave It" and "Take It," don't use this term for coprophagia. The dog might expect it is part of the game to eventually get the poop, too. The behavior may also be due to boredom—the dog is playing with the feces for something to do. This is particularly common in the winter months in snowy climates where frozen feces turn into a popsicle! Management is still the answer. Teach and reward a substitute behavior as a home-alone hobby.

## WILL AVERSIVES WORK?

Making the poop yucky by putting a taste deterrent on it is an aversive that has helped some dogs. Aversives can have a detrimental effect on the dog. For more specific information on punishment, request the Legacy handout "Aversives."

# ESCAPING: THE HOUDINI-HOUND

## Some Reasons Dogs Escape:

- To get to something
- To get away from something
- To find relief from boredom
- To seek attention from owner
- To challenge a passerby
- To look for a mate
- To mark an area he/she marked before
- To investigate garbage, cats, birds, a leaf, etc.

Some dogs have more than one reason for escaping, and the reasons can overlap. Some of the reasons are the same reasons dogs dig, chew, or bark! Some dogs jump the fence only to run around to the front of the house to sit on the porch—probably because they find out it's a good way to get attention. Digging, climbing, jumping, or chewing through the fence, plus dashing out an opened door are all annoying behaviors that can result in tragic consequences. Figure out why the dog is trying to escape and check The Toolbox for ideas.

Here are some suggestions to get you started:

**ELIMINATE THE TRIGGER**
Prevent fence jumping by keeping the dog inside. Hire a dog sitter or dog walker to break up the day of a home-alone dog. Get up earlier and exercise your dog. A tired dog is more apt to stay home. Do not allow your dog to urine mark on walks close to your home. When other dogs check p-mail, they might leave their own message, which in turn prompts your dog to mark again. It can become an endless cycle. If you have not done so already, consider neutering your dog.

**MANAGEMENT**
Increase the height of the fence or erect an inner, shorter fence two feet from the outside fence to interrupt a running start. Plant a three-foot hedge along the inside of the fence. Nail one-foot-long strips of vinyl flooring scraps to the fence. It will make the fence appear higher to your dog.

**TAKE AWAY THE REWARD**
Being in the wrong place is a sure way to get your attention. Prevent this from happening.

**NOT MUCH NASTY STUFF**
If you can, anticipate when a jump might occur and interrupt it with a loud noise. The goal is to let your dog think the environment, not you, gave him the surprise. Don't punish him when you catch him out of the yard. It's too late to make the right association and it might teach him to be sneaky or to be afraid of you. The result is an escape artist who is difficult to catch.

| | | |
|---|---|---|
| H | Health of the Dog | T |
| E | Environment Enrichment | O |
| L | Leadership and Training | O |
| M | Management Procedures | L |
| Y | Yield Compromise | |
| E | Eliminate the Trigger | B |
| S | Systematic Desensitization | O |
| T | Take Away the Reward | X |
| R | Remove the Trigger | |
| A | Acclimate | |
| I | Improve the Association | |
| N | Not Much Nasty Stuff | |

CONTACT US IF YOU NEED HELP   info@legacycanine.com   360-683-1522

*INFO Escaping.doc*   *Coaching People to Train Their Dogs* © Terry Ryan 2005

# HOME ALONE AND ENRICHMENT IDEAS

## I. OPTIMIZING AVAILABLE TIME

**TOURIST!**—Take your dog for a ride on short errands that don't involve waiting alone, such as driving the children to school or going for a drive-in espresso. Not much physical activity is involved, but it's a change of scenery! You could even stop off at a park for a few minutes for a brief walk or some training practice.

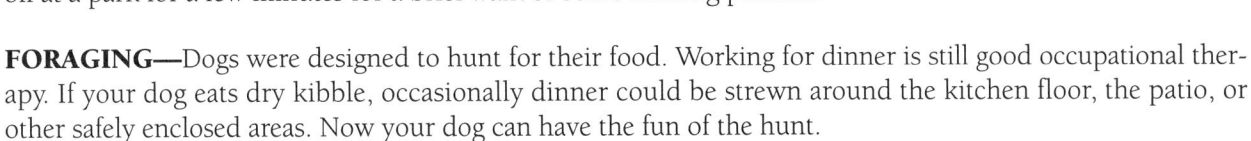

**FORAGING**—Dogs were designed to hunt for their food. Working for dinner is still good occupational therapy. If your dog eats dry kibble, occasionally dinner could be strewn around the kitchen floor, the patio, or other safely enclosed areas. Now your dog can have the fun of the hunt.

**BEGGAR!**—This is a game for dogs that enjoy food and know how to retrieve. Find a toy that's soft but heavy enough to be thrown accurately. Take some of the food from your dog's next meal. Divide it into a few tiny portions. The basic game is to toss the toy and, when it's retrieved, exchange it for a portion of food. Here are some variations to the theme: Practice training exercises by putting your dog on a Sit-Stay before throwing the toy, varying the length of the Stay each time. Increase the difficulty by throwing the toy when the dog's not looking. Pick some challenging retrieves like up on a bed, behind a chair, or out in your fenced yard! If you have more than one dog, one can practice Down-Stay while the other plays, then switch. Warning: Play this game with only a little food, not the entire meal. Too much food and too much exercise can cause medical problems for your dog.

**B.Y.O.D. BARBECUE**—Invite some friends (ones who have dogs that get along with yours) over for a "Bring Your Own Dog" backyard cook out. On a hot day you might fill a child's plastic wading pool with some water and see if the dogs want to splash around and play with some toys. Floating toys are fun, but you can stuff some heavy rubber toys with food and have them sink. The dogs can go fishing! If the dogs become too rowdy, have Time Out and ask the dogs to lie at their owner's feet for 10 minutes.

**MORE EXERCISE**—Set your alarm 15 minutes early to go for an extra long walk. Wet weather? Most of our towns have more than one park with paved walkways. Or spend time playing with or training your dog inside. For a fun activity, request Legacy's "Rainy Day Brain Exercise" handout.

## II. THE HOME ALONE ENVIRONMENT

**DOG DOOR**—If you have a fenced yard (dig proof, jump proof, chew proof, squeeze proof), install a dog door so the dog can go in or out at will. A strategically placed carpet runner can blot up much of the moisture or dirt on the way in.

**PLAY GROUPS**—Check with friends. Perhaps work schedules will allow you to take turns hosting each other's dog.

**DOGGY DAY CARE**—Are the dogs turned loose together to play? Are they rewarded for playing nicely? How are dogs corrected for inappropriate behavior? If you purchase a training option, do you approve of the techniques used by the trainers? Do those methods fit in with your idea of what's right for your dog? Do the interactions appear to be normal give-and-take, or is one dog being bullied? Does there seem to be adequate supervision? There should be rest time for the dogs as well as play time.

**COMPANIONSHIP TAPE**—When you leave your dog home alone, turn on the radio or TV. Or you might want to record a tape of your family's voices and sounds of everyday household activities. The tape might keep your dog company but, more importantly, it will help mask outside noises that can cause anxiety. One clever owner taped her husband's snoring. She reports that her dog prefers this to relaxation music.

**HOME ALONE TREASURE HUNT**—Before you leave home, hide some toys selected from the list below. Build anticipation for the hunt by getting your dog to Sit-Stay while you hide the toys. Be matter of fact when you release him and go to work. This downplays your departure and builds pleasant expectations for the treasure hunt.

## III. HOBBY TOYS

First, allow your dog to try out new toys while under supervision before leaving them down when no one is home. If the toy can break or might be small enough to get lodged in the dog's mouth or cause frustration, throw it away. If a toy seems to be a point of contention between two dogs left together, get rid of it, or use it only under supervision or with one dog separately. Try putting down several identical toys. Perhaps the value will go down and there will be no need to argue. Food-stuffed toys should be kept clean by placing them in the clothes washer or dishwashing machine. Do not leave food-stuffed toys outdoors. They attract anything from ants to coyotes.

**HOLLOW RUBBER TOYS**—Kong™ toys entertain dogs by bouncing and rolling erratically when nudged or dropped. Use a large size that won't get stuck inside your dog's mouth. Stuff Kongs™ with a portion of your dog's dinner. Mixing in a couple of *spoonfuls* of canned food will keep dry kibble from falling out too quickly, so will a piece of bread. Be creative—layer jackpots like a tiny piece of cheese or a bit of meat with the kibble. Frozen Kongs™ are a refreshing treat for a hot day, especially for a teething puppy.

**HOLLOW CHEW BONE**—Commercially prepared hollow bones from a pet supply shop are a safer bet than bones from your butcher, which can splinter and cause health problems. You can purchase these bones pre-stuffed.

**NYLON CHEW TOYS**—Bones, rings, and other interesting shapes come in all sizes. For safety, select a size bigger than recommended and check periodically for small pieces that might break off. To get the dog started, rub your toy on the sidewalk to make scratches that release the taste.

**KIBBLE DISPENSING CUBES AND BALLS**—These toys have the advantage of holding dry food. You can use your dog's regular kibble without mixing in anything. When placed on the floor, your dog will paw it, nose it, and scoot it along the floor to get the kibble out. The dog can be kept busy for a long time tracking food across the floor.

# Jumping On People

Excited, friendly jumping, not aggression, is what we are talking about in this handout. Puppies naturally jump up on people as a way of saying hello when they are excited. Your dog probably wants to get close to your face. You might inadvertently reinforce this behavior by greeting the dog. Saying no and pushing her away might be pleasant if she's happy to see you. She won't care what you say and do as long as you are paying attention! A quick trip through The Toolbox will help you come up with some ideas for jumping up.

## MANAGEMENT

Upon first seeing your dog after a long day, speak to her in a low, soft voice and get down to her level so there is no need for her to jump up to see you. Give her more exercise to help release some of that jumping energy.

## ELIMINATE THE TRIGGER

When you come home, short circuit the jumping by immediately crouching down to the dog's level for a quiet greeting. This teaches the dog how to respond to get rewarded.

| | | |
|---|---|---|
| H | Health of the Dog | T |
| E | Environment Enrichment | O |
| L | Leadership and Training | O |
| M | Management Procedures | L |
| Y | Yield Compromise | O |
| E | Eliminate the Trigger | |
| S | Systematic Desensitization | L |
| T | Take Away the Reward | B |
| R | Remove the Trigger | O |
| A | Acclimate | X |
| I | Improve the Association | |
| N | Not Much Nasty Stuff | |

## TAKE AWAY THE REWARD

Say nothing, put your face to the wall, don't peek or move. She will eventually give up because you are so boring. (She'll get worse before she gets better.) Wait her out. If you give in, she'll learn to play the lottery. Ignoring her is difficult, but not impossible!

## REWARD AN INCOMPATIBLE BEHAVIOR

Until now we have been trying to discourage the dog from jumping up, but we have not taught the desired behavior. Teach Sit. Then help the dog sit instead of jump up for attention. Get friends to help. If the dog jumps up, they turn away. Say Sit. When she does, give her attention.

---

**NOTE: The Word "Off" Is Less Confusing to Use Than "Down," "Get Off Me," or "Get Off the Couch."**

# "STATION"

Teach your dog to sit on a small mat and give lots of praise for being there. Then you can teach her to walk up to the mat and sit on her own accord. Simply place a tidbit of delicious food on the mat while you hold her back. Say, "Station" and go with her to the mat, allow her to eat the food, ask her to "Sit" and give her another tidbit. Repeat. She'll soon learn to sit on the mat when you say "Station." Say "Station" when the doorbell rings. Simply reach out and ring the bell yourself. Gradually work up to having other folks help ring the bell.

## NOT MUCH NASTY STUFF

Some people suggest putting their knee in the dog's chest and knocking her over backwards or stepping on her hind toes. There is no need to do this. It could injure your dog and it could ruin her trust in you. Would you treat a friend that way who wanted to say hello? Simply stepping into her "space" (walking into her as if she wasn't there) will help. If you insist on being nasty, try one of these:

- Say, "Ouch!" loudly and go into another room for two minutes, closing the door. The dog may decide she loses you altogether when she jumps on you.

OR:

- As she jumps up, catch her front paws and hold them. The dog is now trapped in an uncomfortable position. Say or do nothing. As she begins to struggle, allow her to do so for a few seconds, then release her. Be neutral for a few seconds. If she tries to mouth your hands in response to this trap, simply plan ahead next time and put a taste deterrent such as Bitter® Apple on your hands.

## *Catch Her in the Act of Doing Something Good!*

CONTACT US IF YOU NEED HELP    info@legacycanine.com    360-683-1522

*Coaching People to Train Their Dogs* © Terry Ryan 2005

# KIDS AND CANINES

## Families with Children and Dogs

With children of any age, parents should think of three important things when it comes to kids and dogs together:

1. **SUPERVISION**
2. **SUPERVISION**
3. **SUPERVISION**

## Introducing Your New Baby to Your Dog

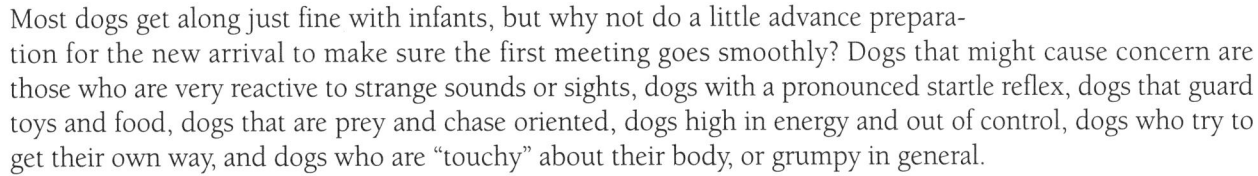

Most dogs get along just fine with infants, but why not do a little advance preparation for the new arrival to make sure the first meeting goes smoothly? Dogs that might cause concern are those who are very reactive to strange sounds or sights, dogs with a pronounced startle reflex, dogs that guard toys and food, dogs that are prey and chase oriented, dogs high in energy and out of control, dogs who try to get their own way, and dogs who are "touchy" about their body, or grumpy in general.

All family dogs should be trained. If a baby is expected, brush up on "Sit," "Down," and "Stay." Sit and Stay for greetings instead of jumping up on people should be well established. Your ability to send the dog to a specific target area, such as a special rug, and have the dog remain there until released will be helpful. Walking nicely on leash is especially important now that you will have a baby buggy to control as well as a dog. Be sure your dog realizes that you are the leader and the decision maker by implementing the concepts in the "L.E.A.D." handout.

If anything in the dog's lifestyle will change, it should change before the baby comes home. For instance, if the dog is not allowed into the baby's room, now is the time to start boundary training the dog. Go into the room, tell the dog to Sit-Stay or send him to the target area. You might simply teach the dog not to cross the threshold into the room. Make staying outside of the room very special and good. This is a time to give the dog a pacifying treat such as a chew toy or you can come out to him and load on the attention. Get the dog used to the baby before the baby comes home. Set up your crib and changing area ahead of time. Get your dog a bear or doll and place it in the crib. Choose a life-size doll that flails her arms and makes baby sounds. A few times a day, take a couple of seconds to go over to the doll. Sprinkle some powder or rub some lotion on the doll to get your dog used to these new activities and smells. Get a sound effects CD of babies crying. Play it while the dog eats, or during other times when your dog is happy. If the baby is born in a hospital, you can bring home a blanket ahead of time that has the baby's scent on it. Wrap the doll in it, and allow the dog to investigate this novel smell. Praise the dog. Give him a cookie!

When the new Mom comes home, the dog may be so glad to see her that he might forget his manners and jump up. Someone else should carry the baby just in case. Even if the dog behaves well, Mom might be nervous about the baby, and the dog might be sensitive to that and worry, too. Mom should greet the dog, but not make such a fuss that the dog becomes overly excited. Perhaps Mom should come in the house to greet the dog a few seconds before the baby. Allow the dog to sniff the baby all over unless he's too excited and out of control.

CONTACT US IF YOU NEED HELP   info@legacycanine.com   360-683-1522

In their first days together, the baby should appear, in the dog's mind, to produce attention and fun. Ideas: When anyone changes the baby, tidbits or balls can be tossed to the dog. An apron with big pockets would be handy! Or have a jar of treats or balls ready on the changing table. Parents should speak softly and lovingly to the dog while holding the baby.

Babies squeak and move like a prey animal. These sights and sounds could initiate instinctual chase and grab reactions. Some dogs might simply want to investigate. Babies and dogs should never be left alone unattended.

## After Babyhood

When your baby begins to crawl and walk, the situation changes and supervision is very important. Never leave toddlers alone with a dog even though the dog has been friendly and tolerant toward the child. A poke in the eye, a trip and fall into the dog, or a loud scream into the dog's ear could produce an orienting reflex that might make the dog whip around and knock the baby over. Worse, the child's actions might cause the dog to snap. Many a toddler has been bitten because of the natural toddler behaviors of running, screaming, throwing himself or herself at the dog, or hugging the dog, especially hugging from behind. Here's a thought provoking quote about hugging dogs from the book *The Other End of the Leash* by Dr. Patricia McConnell, a canine behavior expert:

*"I've worked with dozens of families with sweet young girls who got growled at, snapped at, or bitten on the face (usually not badly, thank heavens) when they threw their arms around their dog. . . . Yet while they were thinking warm, loving thoughts, their dog interpreted their hug as a rude, domineering threat display."*

Your dog should have an area of her own—a bed, a wire dog crate, an airline kennel, or a carpet square—any easily identifiable space. It should be accessible to the dog, close to family activities, but out of the traffic pattern. Take the dog to this area when things become chaotic. Give your dog a special treat when she's in her safety zone. Over time, she will learn to escape to this area when she wants to be left alone. Respect this. Children and their visiting friends must be kept away from the dog's "safety" zone.

## Older Children

If parents have been diligent, there is probably a mutually friendly and respectful relationship between your children and dogs. The mistake most parents make is allowing children too much freedom to interact unsupervised with the family dog. Some games might be entertaining to children, but may cause frustration or too much stimulation to the dog. When the dog finally has enough, he may decide to move away from the child, or to move the child away from him, resulting in a growl or snap or even a bite. The snapping reaction a dog gives if air is blown into his face looks comical, but this behavior can escalate into a (perhaps unintentional) snap on the face. Tug of war should be played by adults, and then by appropriate rules as outlined in Legacy's L.E.A.D. program.

**INAPPROPRIATE "GAME"**

Dogs love to chase and so do children. A little bit of chase is okay, but prolonged chasing can overstimulate the child or the dog. Another game children might play is hand teasing. The dog's reaction from chasing or hand teasing might amuse the child, but it can frustrate the dog. Just like children playing together on a playground, everyone is having fun, then all of a sudden someone is crying. The game was taken too far.

## Good Games for Kids, Dogs, and a Parent

Lecturing children about dogs is not enough. Let children learn by doing. Help children by providing good role models and by helping them play appropriate games with dogs. Instead of, "Don't do this," the child should be coached to play safe and fun games, such as:

### HIDE AND SEEK INDOORS

An adult holds the dog by the collar or helps the dog practice Sit or Down and Stay. The child makes a big deal of leaving. He says, "Good-bye dog, see ya later," and goes out of sight to hide behind a chair, under the bed, or in an open closet. The dog is then released to find the child. If the dog gets off the track, ask the child to say just the dog's name. Perhaps the child can be given a small bowl with a tidbit in it. The dog will want to find the food, and the bowl will prevent a rambunctious dog from frightening the child when he eats the food. As time goes on, teach the dog to sit when he finds the child. If he sits, the child can give the treat.

### FAMILY FETCH

For a dog that already loves to retrieve, a parent, child, and the dog are at one end of a hallway. Give the child a small, soft toy to throw. A ball on a rope, or a soft toy might be better than a regular ball because it won't bounce as much, and there is less chance that the dog will slip in his scurry to get the ball. It's easier for mom to take the ball out of the dog's mouth when he returns.

## Training as a Family

If you have too little time to spend with dogs and children, some combination time could be beneficial to all. If you are going for a walk, perhaps you can put two leashes on the dog and allow your child proudly to hold the second leash. Practicing basic exercises, under supervision, can teach your child to be kind and patient and look for the best in dogs—hopefully in humans, too!

## Card Games for Family Dog Training Fun

The entire family can play card games together. On a pack of blank index cards, write a variety of exercises within the capability of your family and your dog. It can be a reading and math lesson for your child. It can be an art lesson: have your child draw pictures on the cards or cut and paste pictures from a magazine. Make up rules appropriate for your family and remember safety at all times.

CONTACT US IF YOU NEED HELP   info@legacycanine.com   360-683-1522

Here are some sample exercise cards, some ideas for rules, and a few basic games:

### CARDS
Get a towel and wipe all four of your dog's feet
Get a chair; walk all the way around it with a slack leash
Dog in a Down-Stay; skip three circles around her
Sit-Stay while someone rings the doorbell once
Help your dog impersonate a different animal
Down-Stay in front of the refrigerator while someone removes and replaces food
Four on the floor, still, for eight strokes of the dog's brush
Sit-Stay, go about three feet from dog; dog must catch a cookie on first try

### RULES
Set the timer for three minutes. One member performs as many exercises as possible. When all cards are gone, whoever has the most cards wins. If a player or a player's parent doesn't like the card, he can put it back face down and pick up a different one. The cards can have assigned values. The player with the highest total score wins. If you have more than one dog, flip a coin to see which dog does each exercise.

### CHOOSE A CARD GAME
Shuffle the cards; students can play "Paper, Rock, Scissors" to see who goes first. Then select a running order. Take turns selecting cards and performing the exercise.

### SPIN THE BOTTLE GAME
Put the exercise cards in a big circle with a bottle in the middle. Take turns spinning the bottle and performing the activity the bottle points to when it stops spinning.

### TIC-TAC-TOE CARDS
Draw the game grid on a big piece of paper on the floor or table. Objects of any kind, in two colors, are the markers—plastic cups will do. Make teams. If a team completes the exercise within the rules, it can place a marker on the tic-tac-toe grid. The first team to get three in a row wins.

### DOMINO CARDS
Instead of making the usual cards, make index cards into dominoes. Each end has a different activity. Form two teams and take turns drawing domino cards. If the card cannot be "played" as in regular domino rules, number-to-number, that person holds on to the card. If the card can be played when it's that team's turn, they can put down their dominoes after successfully completing the exercise on their domino. First to play all "dominoes" wins.

## Being Safe Around Dogs

Appropriate interaction with the family dog is a good place for a child to practice good manners around all dogs. Here is an elementary school lesson I wrote while working for Washington State University's College of Veterinary Medicine:

*Most Dogs Like Most Children Most of the Time,*
*But There Are Some Rules.*

**Please Do** leave dogs alone while they are eating or chewing a toy. If you reach down and pet the dog, it might surprise and worry her. Do you always feel like sharing your candy bar?

**Please Do** leave the dog alone while she's sleeping. After playing all day, you like to rest. So does your dog.

**Please Do** knock on the neighbor's door and ask for help if your ball accidentally gets into their yard. If no one is home, ask your parents help. Don't go into the yard without permission. The dog might worry, just as you might if someone walked into your living room without an invitation.

**Please Do** always ask permission from an adult before going up to a dog, even if you know the dog. Ask the parents if you are visiting a friend. Dogs can't say, "I don't want to play now," but grownups are pretty good at figuring out what dogs are thinking.

**Please Do** approach the dog from the side, not from the back or front. Be sure the dog sees you. Have you ever jumped when a friend touched you when you weren't looking? It's not polite. Don't point at the dog, but show your knuckles and the back of your hand. If he wants to visit, he'll come forward for a sniff. The side of the head or under the chin is the best place to pet a dog. If the dog backs up when he sees you and looks afraid, it's best not to pet him.

# Parents

A parent should always attempt to be honest about dogs and try not to frighten a child who is otherwise not afraid of dogs. On the other hand, to do a good job, you can show a child how a dog might communicate that she doesn't want to be petted. A parent can get down on the floor on hands and knees and act like a dog. The child can go through the routine of asking an adult if she can pet the dog. Then the child can practice showing the "dog" her knuckles, the "dog" stretches forward just a little to sniff. The "dog" should wag her tail and look at the child with a soft face. This is the friendly dog's way of saying, "How about a pat?" The parent can then demonstrate two types of dog body language that say, "Don't pet me."

If the dog stands up stiff with stony eyes and a hard face, she might be angry. Don't pet the dog. It's her way of saying, "I don't feel like a pat; leave me alone." Quietly walk away. Leave her alone. Your attention may just anger her more. This body language is easy to read, even for children. The illustration of the fearful dog, as shown below is more difficult to read.

If the dog pulls back she might be afraid. Don't pet the dog. She is saying "I don't feel like a pat." Don't be tempted to comfort her. Quietly walk away. Leave her alone; your attention may just worry her more. Children more commonly get into trouble with this type of dog. Children love to role-play. Encourage them to show this body language themselves by getting on the floor with you.

**Please Do** keep walking past a dog in a parked car. Don't reach into a dog's car even if you know the dog. The dog may look like she wants to be patted, but she might worry that you might take something. Do you always feel like sharing your things with others?

If you encounter a dog that seems very angry, stand like a post. Posts don't run; they don't make any noise. They just stand still. Do the same as the post. The dog likely will sniff you and go away. If you look at the dog, move your hands, talk, or run, the dog will take more interest in you and won't go away as soon.

## IN THE LONG RUN

The family pet will influence a child's future outlook on all dogs. Your dog's opinion of children in general will be affected by your child's actions. In a few short decades, the children of today will be making and enforcing the laws regarding dogs. Hopefully your child will have a clear outlook on dogs' role in society. Children learn from adult role models and the society in which they live. Research suggests that a home with violence or abuse toward animals produces children who may pass these behaviors on to the next generations. Further, there seems to be a correlation between substantial animal abuse in childhood and later personal violence to humans. Studies show that children raised with intense coercion may imitate this behavior with animals and people.

SOURCE: *Reference "Cycle of Violence*, R. Lockwood, Humane Society of the United States, 2000.

# STAYING OFF FURNITURE

Dogs get up on furniture for a variety of reasons—it's comfortable, it elevates their position, they want to be where your scent is strongest, it allows them to see out the window.

## YIELD (COMPROMISE)

Put a towel over the dog's favorite chair. If your dog enjoys making his bed—digging and scratching around to make a nest—put some comfy blankets in that chair. Make that particular chair desirable by placing it where he can watch family activities. Invite him over to the chair for some attention. If he jumps up on the chair on his own accord, be sure to tell him how clever he is.

## ELIMINATE THE TRIGGER

If the dog is only seeking comfort, buy him a soft, plush dog bed and put it next to the chair the dog has been jumping on. Tip that chair over temporarily.

## TAKE AWAY THE REWARD

Maybe the dog is jumping up to see out the window. Close the drapes or move the chair.

## REWARD AN INCOMPATIBLE BEHAVIOR

Teach "Off." Pick one chair for training. Teach your dog to jump on it by saying "Jump Up." Tell him he's good. There will be times when you do want your dog to jump up on something: onto a bench for grooming and into the car for instance. Periodically say "Off!" and help him off. If he's reluctant, you may need to keep a collar or Gentle Leader® and a short leash on him to help guide him back to the floor. Repeat the routine. Over time the dog will know exactly what "Off" means and you can use the word even before the dog jumps up.

## NOT MUCH NASTY STUFF

Plant a surprise on the chair. Pet catalogs have vibration-sensitive dog alarms that will scream if your dog jumps up. Tip the cushions on end so there's no room. Spray underarm deodorant on the furniture. Most dogs don't like the smell. Put some aluminum foil over the seats—it's not comfortable. Put masking tape on the cushions, sticky side up. The dog won't like the sensation of being stuck. Don't do this when you're not home. The dog may panic if the tape entraps him or he could get the tape over his nose. Use the tape sticky side up while you're home and then when you leave, just put a small piece safe side up! It will still look and smell like his original sticky stuff experience. Cut a vinyl carpet protector the size of the chair seat and put it on the chair, pokey side up. Ouch! Get a large cardboard box and put it on the chair. There's no room for the dog so the dog can't practice jumping up to a comfortable spot. Paint large black eyes on the box—it's entertaining for your guests and it just might get the point across to the dog.

| | | |
|---|---|---|
| H | Health of the Dog | T |
| E | Environment Enrichment | |
| L | Leadership and Training | O |
| M | Management Procedures | |
| Y | Yield Compromise | O |
| E | Eliminate the Trigger | |
| S | Systematic Desensitization | L |
| T | Take Away the Reward | B |
| R | Remove the Trigger | |
| A | Acclimate | O |
| I | Improve the Association | |
| N | Not Much Nasty Stuff | X |

# NEUTERING YOUR MALE DOG

Routine neutering is a simple procedure causing only minimal discomfort. It is typically performed at about six months of age and consists of complete surgical removal of the testicles. It allows our pets to be healthier, happier, and calmer.

## Benefits

Male dogs are far less likely to roam once they have been neutered, and they are less aggressive toward other dogs. This makes them less likely to get wounded in a dog fight, get chased off by angry homeowners when roaming the neighborhood, or be hit by a car (80% of all dogs hit by cars are males that have not been neutered). Fewer injuries means fewer veterinary bills.

Male dogs commonly develop the habit of urine marking (lifting their leg on everything they encounter). Neutering helps control urine marking. Other destructive behaviors are also reduced.

Neutered dogs tend to be more responsive to their owners. They devote much less time and energy toward proving themselves, defending territory, and breeding. Their anxiety levels due to sexual frustration are greatly reduced.

Each year millions of unwanted dogs are euthanized at animal shelters. We must all take responsibility for this tragedy. We must not allow the birth of any more accidental puppies. Neutering dogs prevents the tragedy of unwanted births.

Many medical benefits also arise from neutering. For example, neutered dogs cannot get testicular cancer, and their risk of prostate cancer is dramatically reduced. Other diseases of the prostate are also minimized. Perineal hernias are much less likely to occur in neutered dogs.

## Summary of Benefits

- Less roaming
- Less aggression, without the loss of "watchdog" abilities
- Fewer injuries, fewer veterinary bills
- Reduced chance of developing cancer and other diseases, fewer veterinary bills
- Control of urine marking
- A more responsive pet

# SPAYING YOUR FEMALE DOG

Spaying involves complete surgical removal of the uterus and ovaries. It is typically performed at about six months. It allows our pets to be healthier, happier, and calmer.

## Benefits

Once spayed, females no longer go into heat. Thus there will be no messy blood spotting around the house, no romantic males prowling your yard, and no unexpected pregnancies.

One of the greatest benefits of spaying is the huge reduction in breast cancer. Breast cancer is the leading form of cancer in unspayed females. That number can be reduced by a whopping 99% just by spaying your dog.

Cancer of the uterus or ovaries does not occur in spayed females. Also eliminated are ovarian cysts and uterine infections. Most vaginal infections will be prevented.

Since she is no longer subject to her biological urges, a spayed female is generally calmer and more responsive to her human family. She is less likely to roam in search of a mate or to get into fights, both of which can be dangerous and costly in terms of veterinary bills. And YOU get to avoid trying to confine her against her will.

Unplanned pregnancies are very common in females that have not been spayed. Unplanned pregnancies lead to unplanned expenses (such as extra feed bills, possible C-sections, and health care costs for the puppies), and disrupted routines (cleaning up after puppies, feeding puppies, finding homes for puppies, etc.) Each year millions of unwanted dogs are euthanized at animal shelters. We must all take responsibility for this tragedy. We must not allow the birth of any more accidental puppies. Spaying dogs prevents the tragedy of unwanted births.

## Summary of Benefits

- Less roaming, fewer injuries, fewer veterinary bills
- Less aggression without the loss of "watchdog" abilities
- Reduced chance of developing cancer and other diseases, fewer veterinary bills
- No heat cycles
- No unwanted pregnancies
- A calmer, more responsive pet

# CLICK!

## CLICKER BASICS

*This information should sound familiar! It's just like the "YES"/Treat exercise.*

Associate the click with a reward. The click has the power of predicting a food reward. Here's how. Hold five pieces of food in your hand. Click and give a piece of food to your dog. The food immediately follows the click. Your dog can be doing ANYTHING that's neutral, acceptable, or good behavior. It's best not to click if your dog happens to be doing something you consider unacceptable such as jumping on you or mouthing your hand. If you reward any one behavior consistently, you're going to get that behavior! Do this exercise five times a day.

**IMPORTANT:** CLICK followed immediately by food should occur at random time intervals. Example:

| | |
|---|---|
| CLICK/TREAT | Wait 5 seconds before you click and treat again |
| CLICK/TREAT | Wait 15 seconds before you click and treat again |
| CLICK/TREAT | Wait 2 seconds before you click and treat again |
| CLICK/TREAT | Wait 10 seconds before you click and treat again |
| CLICK/TREAT | That's five repetitions! You're done for now! |

**IMPORTANT:** You and/or your dog should be doing something different each time you CLICK/TREAT. Just wait, something will change. If the dog doesn't change, **YOU** can change! Example:

| | |
|---|---|
| Dog walks across floor: | CLICK/TREAT Wait 15 seconds |
| Dog looks at you: | CLICK/TREAT Wait 2 seconds |
| Dog lies down: | CLICK/TREAT Wait 5 seconds |
| Dog still down, you turn | CLICK/TREAT Wait 8 seconds |
| Dog stands | CLICK/TREAT That's five repetitions! You're done for now! |

You are not training your dog to *DO* anything. You are simply building power (value) into the clicker by immediately following the click with a delectable treat. You will find that you have your dog's complete attention after just a few reps. We're not working on attention particularly, but that's a nice side benefit.

The "Click" is a promise that food will follow. This is the first step to a very powerful tool in operant conditioning called a conditioned reinforcer. Food is the primary reinforcer and the click is the secondary or conditioned reinforcer. It's also referred to as a bridge, a promise, a reward marker, and an "acoustical arrow" to point to the exact behavior you want to reward. In beginners class we used the word "Yes" instead of a click. For now, do not use your clicker for any other exercise unless you discuss it with an instructor. We can now proceed to all sorts of fun stuff!

---

A reminder about food selection: Save some of your dog's daily allotment for CLICKER TRAINING. If you prefer, use a soft, tiny yummy treat instead. (Food rule: non-dog food should be less than 10% of your dog's daily caloric intake! Also consider allergies or other sensitivities when feeding non-dog food.)

---

### OPTIONAL: A TIMING EXERCISE TO DO . . . WITHOUT YOUR DOG!

Drop a book on the floor. See if you can click, just as the bang occurs.
Toss a tennis ball into the air. See if you can click at the highest point of the toss.
Watch a TV weather report. See if you can click to coincide with the reporter touching the map.

CONTACT US IF YOU NEED HELP   info@legacycanine.com   360-683-1522

# CLICKS & STICKS

## HOW TO START TARGET STICK TRAINING WITH A CLICKER

Now that your dog is clicker savvy, let's teach him to touch his nose to the tip of a target stick. Borrow or buy a Legacy Click-N-Stick from a staff member. The clicker is permanently attached to a telescoping stick with a safety tip on the end. This combination is much easier to use than a separate clicker and target stick. Remember the saying we had in basic class, *Control the Head, Control the Dog*. The clicker stick is a new application of that principle, plus it gives us more range to do lots of neat, new stuff! Talk to us if your dog is afraid of sticks!

Your dog now realizes the click marks a good behavior that's worth repeating. It also predicts a reward. To get him to touch the stick, we'll use the principle of Shaping by rewarding successive approximations to nose-on-stick behavior. The first goal:

1. Spot sees stick (cue)
2. Spot moves to touch her nose to tip of stick (desired behavior)
3. Spot hears click and gets reward immediately (good consequence!)

Hold the partially opened stick close to your side or a little behind you, thumb on the clicker. Choose a criterion that is a small or preliminary step toward putting the nose on the tip of the stick. Present the stick about 18 inches away from your dog's nose. Do not put the stick on the dogs nose. Do not chase the dog with the stick. We want the dog to learn to do the work. Most dogs are curious and will at least glance at the stick or stretch to sniff it. A small stretch toward the stick is rewardable—even a glance is okay at first. Mentally count to three. If your dog totally ignores the stick, don't click, don't treat—take the stick back out of sight. This is called *limited hold*. It means you will present the cue (the stick) for only three seconds. During those three seconds you are willing to pay the dog for attention to the stick. When the time is up, your offer ends—until the next presentation. This helps the dog to be speedy and attentive. If your dog ignored the stick, take it back after three seconds, and at the next rep, tap it on the floor once. This might cause the dog to look at it. If so, click and treat. Once your dog knows the stick will pay off, it's just a matter of your dog figuring out what she has to do with the stick to make you pay her.

You will do five reps of this shaping exercise, then put your stick away and try again later. Little by little, you will reward better and better touches or attempts to touch the stick. Your dog should learn quickly if you train about five sessions of five reps each day. You can train more, depending on your dog's enthusiasm. Stop training while the dog is still keen and hungry!

In class we will work on:

| | |
|---|---|
| **Random Reinforcement** | .play the lottery |
| **Differential Reinforcement** | .reward only speedy, distinct tip touches |
| **Fluency** | .touch no matter what the situation |
| **Adding a different cue** | .the word "Touch" |
| **Generalizing the touch** | .touch objects other than the stick |

# "FETCH!"

Some of the games and activities we play at Legacy involve retrieving. Would you like to teach your dog to fetch? Here are a couple of methods involving your clicker.

## SHAPING A RETRIEVE

Select a toy or container that's large enough so the dog can't swallow it but small enough to fit comfortably in his mouth. We will use this to hold a food treat. An article that is clear but unbreakable has the advantage of teasing your dog—he can see the food, but needs your cooperation to get it out of the container. A small, plastic food storage container or a clear plastic zippered coin purse works well. If you are worried about transferring the retrieving skill to a competition dumbbell, use a toothbrush travel case or purchase a short length of clear aquarium tubing. You can seal the ends with tape that pulls off and reseals easily to get the food treat in and out.

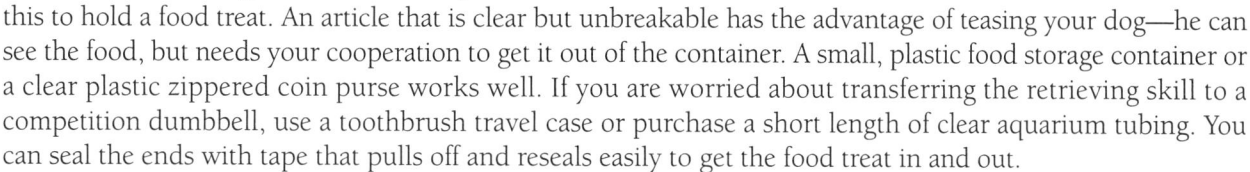

Your dog already realizes the click marks a good behavior that's worth repeating. The click says "a reward is coming." Reward successive approximations to the retrieve. The first goal:

1. Your dog sees the article
2. Your dog looks at or moves to touch his nose to the article
3. Your dog hears the click, then you get the reward out of the article for him

Choose a criterion that is a small or preliminary step toward putting his nose or mouth on the article. A small stretch is rewardable—even a glance is okay at first. Let him see you put the treat in the article, then hold the article close to your side or a little behind you. Present the article about 18 inches away from your dog's nose. Mentally count to three. If your dog totally ignores article, don't click, don't treat—take the article back out of sight. Do not keep the article there longer hoping the dog will do something. Do NOT put the article ON the dog's nose. We want the dog to learn to do the work. Most dogs are curious and will at least glance at the article or perhaps stretch to sniff it. Do not chase the dog around with the article. He lost his chance—for now. This is called limited hold. It means you will present the retrieve article for only three seconds. During those three seconds you are willing to pay the dog for attention to the article. When the time is up, your offer ends—until the next presentation. This helps the dog to be speedy and attentive. If your dog ignored the article, take it back after three seconds, and at the next rep, tap it on the floor once. This might cause the dog to look at it. If so, click and treat. Once your dog knows the article will pay off, it's just a matter of your dog figuring out what he has to do to get you and your opposable thumbs to get the food out for her. Retrieve is a cooperative event.

You will do five reps of this shaping exercise, then put your article away and try again later. (Little by little, you will reward better and better tries.) Your dog should learn quickly if you train up to about five sessions of five reps each a day. You can train more, depending on your dog's enthusiasm. Stop training while the dog is still keen and hungry!

You'll notice we are doing "dead" retrieves. The retrieve will be more reliable if the dog is motivated without the fun of the chase. When the chase is added, your dog will be a retrieve addict.

In class we will work on:

- **Raising the criteria.** A look, smell, or nudge is not good enough now! We want a grab or a grab and hold, or a hold and come! **Work at each step until about 80% reliability.** Perfect is not better in shaping. We don't want him to get "stuck" at one level. He might be so pleased with his reward he won't try anything different.
- **Generalizing the retrieve to any article.**

- **Random reinforcement.** Teach your dog to play the lottery early in the game—Two-fers, Three-fers—before you open the container for him.
- **Remote rewards.** Move the treat from the article to your pocket. Next, keep the food reward somewhere else: the window sill beside you, the table behind you.
- **Differential reinforcement.** If he is not speedy or plays with the article, no reward. This is just "selective" random rewarding. You don't pay for sloppy work.
- **Fluency.** Your dog has to pick up and return the article to you—no matter what distractions his environment throws his way.
- **Adding a cue.** Once he's doing the retrieve reliably, we will precede the event with the label you want to use—"Fetch" or "Get it" are common cues.
- **Generalizing the retrieve to any article.**

## BACKWARD-CHAINED RETRIEVE

Backward chaining refers to the fact that you start at the finish of the behavior and then teach the preceding steps. It's pretty much the opposite of the shaped retrieve mentioned above.

Use a dumbbell or any object. A wooden dowel works well. (Ask a Legacy staff for one the correct size for your dog.) While your dog is sitting, slip the dowel into his mouth. He'll probably open right up since we are always putting good things into his mouth! If he clenches his mouth, just brush his front teeth up and down in a gentle tooth-brushing type action. You can usually slip it in that way. If he gives it right back to you, **SUCCESS!** That's the end link of the fetch behavior! Click and treat. Don't say anything when putting the dowel in the dog's mouth or when you take it from him. No "Fetch" or "Please"—just silence! Do this until it becomes easy and fun for the dog. Like teaching all new behaviors at Legacy, three to five repetitions, three to five times (sessions) a day is good. Shoot for 5/5 reps, 4/5 sessions before you go on.

Next, put the dowel in the dog's mouth and right away (before he has a chance to spit it back!) say, "Give." Click and treat when the dowel is on the way out. Do this until it's smooth and fun for you both.

Next, wait a second before saying "Give." If the dog holds the dowel, say "Give," and click and treat when the dog spits out the dowel. If the dog doesn't wait for your cue, try again but let gravity help you. Keep his head tipped back with eye contact and a little nudge or steady cradle under his chin. This is the big step! Repeat until your dog will hold the dowel reliably without your help.

Gradually extend the time of the hold about one second each time. Work up to five seconds by ping-ponging the seconds back and forth between one and five. When this is smooth, easy and fun, add the word "Fetch." Immediately hold the dowel in front of his nose, only inches away. If he puts his mouth on it or even leans his head slightly toward the dowel, say, "Give," then click and treat. Gradually ask for more until the dog is rewarded for consistently making contact with the dowel. When the dog begins to reach for the dowel with an open mouth, you are halfway home! **Work at each step until about 80% reliability.**

Now you want the dog to close his mouth on the dowel. He will probably do that, but if you need gravity to help you, that's fine. Watch carefully and click and treat as soon as he bites down. Repeat until he will reliably bite down on the offered dowel.

Next, rather than in front of the dog's nose, offer the dowel slightly to one side, or higher or lower than normal. You know what's next: Click and treat. Can your dog take a step to grab the dowel? Milestone!

The sequence now: "Take" (dog does so, you remove your hand for a second, put hand back). Click and treat as you get the dowel back.

Gradually change the presentation until the dowel is lying on the floor. If you have trouble, try putting it on a box or step first and keep your fingers on it to present a familiar picture to your dog. Gradually take your hand away.

Your dog is doing well when you can have him stay while you place the dowel out of his reach for him to retrieve, or he will run after it if you throw it out of reach. Both skills are important. A "dead" dowel and one to run after should both be fun.

**GOOD JOB! YOU'RE ON YOUR WAY!**

# SCENT DISCRIMINATION

Teach your dog scent discrimination by the refrigerator door method. Using only his sense of smell, your dog picks the vanilla scented item from three identical items.

### TEN REASONS TO DO THIS EXERCISE:

1. You don't have to go outside to exercise your dog.
2. It wears the dog out mentally.
3. Most dogs like their noses close to refrigerators.
4. It's a natural behavior for your dog.
5. You don't have to get out of your chair to do this.
6. It enhances the bond between you and your dog.
7. You can impress your friends and neighbors
8. The dog does not have to be corrected for wrong behavior.
9. The more stuff you teach your dog, the more he can learn.
10. It's fun!

**YOU NEED:** Three magnets of the same shape (Legacy bone magnets are good)
A bottle of vanilla extract, the kind used for baking
Q-tips
A clicker (Review the clicker basics sheet)
Prepare lots of tiny, soft treats

Mark one bone so you can tell it from the others, or use bones of three different colors—we're teaching scent, not color, however.

---

Plan on three to five sessions a day, five repetitions per session.
Move on to the next step when your dog can perform accurately 80% of the time.
Don't go for 100%. It's better to move through steps quickly so he doesn't get "stuck."
Roughly, that's about five out of five repetitions, four out of five sessions.

---

❶ Select one color. With a Q-Tip dab a tiny spot of vanilla extract on only the middle of the magnet, thin enough so it will dry quickly. When dry, wave the magnet in front of the dog, get his attention, put the magnet on the refrigerator door. If the dog touches it with his nose, click and treat. If he only looks at it, it's okay to click and treat a look. Three to five repetitions! Don't overdo it!

❷ Do this three to five sessions per day at whatever level you are getting—looking at, moving toward, or touching. Take the magnet off the refrigerator and put it back, each time putting it in a slightly different place to make sure the dog is touching the magnet and not just the refrigerator. Be careful to handle the edges of the magnet, not the middle where the vanilla is. You only have to refresh the vanilla once a day.

❸ If you are starting with looking at the bone, wait for the dog to move his head toward the magnet before clicking, still removing and placing the magnet each time. Do three to five sessions a day, three to five repetitions per session.

❹ Now wait for the dog to touch the magnet (or to move closer, if he was more than a foot away). Repeat. Three to five sessions a day, three to five repetitions per session, until your dog is 80% correct! Be sure you are removing and replacing the magnet each time.

❺ Turn the dog away from the refrigerator or hide his eyes while you place the vanilla magnet. Encourage him to get it. If he does not move, take the magnet away and stand with your back to the refrigerator for three to five seconds. Turn around and put the scented magnet on the refrigerator. Click and treat when the dog touches it.

❻ Next, pick up an unscented magnet with clean fingers that don't smell like vanilla, and put it on the refrigerator. Then get the vanilla one and also place it on the refrigerator, far away from the clean one. Click and treat if the dog touches the correct (vanilla) magnet.

### IF SHE TOUCHES THE WRONG (CLEAN) MAGNET:

For the first couple of times:
Ignore her if she touches the wrong one, but then:

Pick up and place the vanilla magnet again to draw her attention to it.

After three to four "mistakes" of touching the wrong magnet, remove the vanilla magnet. Say and do nothing. Let her touch the wrong magnet as much as she wants. Remain passive. Don't click/treat.

Repeat Step 6, keeping the same distance between the magnets but varying where you put the scented one in relation to the unscented one, until she touches the correct one 80% of the time.

❼ You can add the cue "vanilla" before you turn your dog to the refrigerator. Vary the position of the vanilla magnet each time until your dog can find it anywhere on the door 80% of the time.

❽ With clean hands, add another unscented magnet, trying to keep the three magnets the same distance apart and varying the position of the vanilla magnet. Say your cue before you turn the dog to face the refrigerator each time.

❾ Keep adding magnets and switching the positions around. It's awesome. Call us for more magnets!

❿ **Invite the neighbors over! They'll think you have the smartest dog in town!**

# FOUR ON THE FLOOR—"STAND"

If you want to teach your dog something new and practical, try Stand. Stand is best started after Sit and Down are well established. Start with five pieces of food. With a food "magnet" on the nose, lure your dog into four on the floor. For large dogs, you might have to take a few steps forward with your lure. Some dogs will simply get up to follow you when you walk forward. Stop when all four feet are still. Keep the dog still by focusing on you. "YES!"/Treat. 3–5 repetitions, 3–5 times a day. Remember, no cues, it's just another luring game at first. Go at your own speed! When you are able to lure a four on the floor, feet still, for three seconds, 80% of the time, move on!

**NOW NAME THE STAND**—Add a hand signal cue. The dog may have considered your luring hand as a signal anyway. Again, one of the problems with using the word *Stay* is the dog focusing on the word *Stay* instead of Sit or Down or Stand. Teach Stand separately from Sit and Down as too many stationary positions taught at the same time or in the same place can be a bit confusing. For example, I teach Stand several weeks after Sit and Down are looking good. It's also good to move the dog to a slightly different location in the room between doing Sits and Downs, although this is not absolutely necessary. Help your dog stay by controlling her head with the lure or leash and, if need be, controlling the rear by placing your hand and arm in front of her hind legs. To teach her exactly what Stand means, don't use the word unless she is perfectly still. Pay four on the floor behavior with "YES!"/Treat! Go at your own speed! When your dog is able to stand on cue and stay still for three to five seconds, 80% of the time, move on!

**MAINTAIN THE STAND / RELEASE THE STAND**—Keep the Stand-Stay short and successful. Stand within inches of the dog. Ping-pong between various short durations. Introduce the stay and release cues. Don't allow her to move until she's released. (Same sequences as Sit and Down.)

**ALTERNATIVE METHOD—*The Pop Up Stand.*** Your dog is sitting. Instead of luring her forward having her step into a stand, the lure will be used in the opposite direction. Take the lure from in front of the nose quickly into the dog's chest, between her front legs. Some dogs will pop up backwards to reach the lure. This way has the advantage of keeping your dog more or less in the same place without forward movement. It makes for a very quick stand stay, if it works. Some dogs are great at this and some dogs just don't get it at all!

**AN ADVANTAGE—*Use a Step.*** For dogs that tend to move their feet a little, place your dog on a step or other safe, elevated platform. Your dog will have to think about it before creeping forward on the Stand.

> **GOAL FOR STAND**—*This is extra homework, so set your own goal. A reasonable goal is:*
> Dog allows owner to help her into a Stand. Owner is within reaching distance of the dog. Once standing, dog is able to stand four on the floor without additional help or cues. Dog can stay still 30 seconds without moving. Minor distractions. Dog should allow her body to be touched gently during the Stand and Stay.

**PRACTICAL APPLICATIONS FOR STAND—*Walks in the Rain.*** On wet days you may want to ask your dog to Stand instead of Sit when you need to stop on your walks. It keeps her rear dry! Stand puts her in a convenient position to wipe muddy feet too! Grooming—You can brush twice as much in half the time if she'll stand still! Pinpoint times when she's very still and cooperative to put in a "YES!"/Treat and release. Will you use the Stand cue at the veterinarian? Think about it—Do you want your dog to stand happily on cue and then have a bad experience?

# The Decathlon Event

Divide dogs into two or more groups, about three or four dogs per group. Each dog must participate in at least two events. Make up the events to reflect the goals of your class. The contestants will know the ten main categories of events as outlined below. The team members get together and decide which dog is best at which events. Only at the time each event begins will the contestants know EXACTLY how the event will be run. Some examples are listed below. The same exercises are done for all groups. Do this for fun and training, coaching the people to get the most out of their dogs. Scoring is optional. Determine how your students feel about competition. Three volunteer judges are recruited from the spectators. The judges hold up one to ten fingers for each dog's performance, similar to the type of scoring at Olympic events.

Here are some ideas for exercises:

**Sit:** Owner puts a bag on his own head. Asks the dog to Sit
Owner lies face down on the floor, no eye contact with dog, asks for a Sit
Dog is lying down ten feet away, owner asks for a Sit.

**Come:** Fastest from line to line, use a stopwatch
Owner calls while sitting in a chair, back to dog
Dog is held on leash, owner goes out of sight

**Distance Control:** Owner stands on a start line:
Sends dog to a carpet square, dog stays in any position for five seconds
Sends dog around a cone and back
Dog left on a Stand, on a line 10 feet away, must lie with most of body behind line

**Leash:** *Figure 8.* Owner holds leash in same hand as a spoon which contains an egg
Owner is blindfolded, friend guides dog and owner through a course without bumping
Trace a letter written on the floor—go for precision

**Fetch:** Several toys, all tied together
A ball from a bucket of water
A package of potato chips

**Stand:** Hurricane—dog stands for 10 seconds with a fan blowing on his rear
Dog stands and stays while wearing a sun visor
Dog stands with a cookie on floor under his belly

**Obstacle:** Go over a very low jump, owner at least six feet away
Dog walks backward between two tables laid on end to form a chute
Dog walks through poles lying flat on the floor without touching them

**Down:** Roll dog on back, legs up, stay for count of 10
Ball rolls by
Must keep head on floor during Down

**Dancing:** Must work three compulsory moves into a dance
Music is known in advance, practice is allowed, dance for one minute
Make it up as you go along—surprise music.

**Trick:** Owner's Choice!

*GAMES Decathlon.doc*

# IF YOU WANT TO SCORE THE DECATHLON:

|   |   |   |   |   | TEAM ... | TEAM ... |
|---|---|---|---|---|---|---|
| 1 | Sit | Response Time | # of Cues | Attitude |   |   |
| 2 | Come | Response Time | # of Cues | Attitude |   |   |
| 3 | Distance Control | Response Time | # of Cues | Attitude |   |   |
| 4 | Leash | Response Time | # of Cues | Attitude |   |   |
| 5 | Fetch | Response Time | # of Cues | Attitude |   |   |
| 6 | Stand | Response Time | # of Cues | Attitude |   |   |
| 7 | Obstacle | Response Time | # of Cues | Attitude |   |   |
| 8 | Down | Response Time | # of Cues | Attitude |   |   |
| 9 | Dancing | Response Time | # of Cues | Attitude |   |   |
| 10 | Trick | Response Time | # of Cues | Attitude |   |   |
|   |   |   |   | TOTALS |   |   |

# TRAINING GAMES

## FOR KINDERPUPPY AND PET DOG MANNERS CLASS

### SAFETY FIRST!

If outdoors, don't allow dogs off leash unless in a fenced area. If indoors, beware of slippery floors. Use mats or don't play games that require speed. One game leader should be in charge and keep control. Watch for potentially troublesome interactions between dogs or people and dogs. If you're not sure that all dogs will play well together in exciting situations, don't guess; keep them on leash and play games that limit contact. Alternate active games with passive games, so the participants don't get "worked up" and become reckless.

Keep the playing group small to reduce time standing around waiting for turns. Divide a large class into several groups, one leader in charge of each group. Play different games simultaneously, then switch. Take breaks to relax the people and dogs. When the energy levels get too high and dogs and people too aroused, accidents can occur. At times like that I play relaxation music. It's a cue that everyone must put their dog into a down and do doggy massage to the speed of the music. Not only does it calm everyone down, it prevents competitive people from gaining a "lead" in that game because everyone starts over again when the music stops!

### ONE FOR ALL AND ALL FOR ONE

In a group with mixed skills, everyone can still be involved. Plan games that will be fun, productive, and safe for the participants' skill level and personalities. It's important not to push a dog too far in the name of fun. You can plan a variety of games so everyone is good at something. Prizes are not given because we don't really have winners. A team or class award can be given to share: a package of funny stickers, a small bag of candy, a box of dog biscuits. If you need to divide the class for reasons of space, try not to have one half "compete" against the other. Divide the class randomly and refrain from allowing team captains to "choose up sides." Have you ever been the one chosen last? It's not a good feeling. If there is an uneven number, a volunteer on the short team can run twice.

## IS THE GAME WORTH IT?

*Not if more time is used explaining the game rules than playing the game*
*Not if more time is spent waiting in line for turns than playing the game*
*Not if the instructor can't explain the pet dog skill being practiced via the game*
*Not if feelings are hurt*
*Not if personal space is invaded*
*Not if dogs and people get out of control and reckless*

Following are the standard "compulsory" games listed in the KinderPuppy and Pet Dog Manners lesson plans. I have also listed a few beginner level games that are my favorites. Other games played during each class are the personal preference of the lead instructor. If you need more game ideas, see the resources at the end of this section.

## I SPY (HANDLING, DESENSITIZING)

Divide the participants into pairs. Dogs are standing. Owners take turns naming various places on the other dog's body. Owner has to touch his dog in that place. For example, Jim and Patch are playing with Tom and Champ.

- Tom: I spy Patch's front foot. Jim touches Patch on the front foot.
- Jim: I spy Champ's tail. Tom must touch Champ's tail.
- Tom: I spy a fang! Jim opens Patch's mouth and touches a canine tooth.
- Jim: I spy the inside of Champ's ear. Tom must touch Champ's ear.

Set the timer for one minute or establish a number of repetitions so the activity doesn't drag on. If the game leader sees someone having trouble touching their dog, a brief talk on counter conditioning and systematic desensitization is appropriate.

## TIC TAC TOE (STAYS, COMMUNITY SPIRIT)

Create a large Tic-Tac-Toe grid with each square at least 4–5 feet wide. Squares must be large enough for dogs to lie down in them with room to spare. Know your dogs. Some groups will need larger grids for the game to run smoothly. Teams are selected: "O" and "X". "O's" line up on one side of the grid. For each turn, a team member will go to a square on the grid and place their dog, facing their team, into a down. "X's" are on the opposite side facing the grid. Each member of this team will place their dog's facing their team, into a sit for each of their turns. First team to get a line of three dogs (vertical, horizontal, diagonal) wins. Talk about good citizenship—take care not to disturb other dogs. Dogs that break position lose that turn. That spot then becomes available for the opposing team. Dogs that break position can try again on their next turn if the game isn't over first. At the lower skill level, owners stay in the squares to help their dogs remain in position. For quick identification of the dogs in the grid, each team could wear a colored bandana. For variation, the "X" and "O" teams switch from Sit to Down or Down to Sit and play again.

## STADIUM WAVE (SITS AND DOWNS, THINKING OF TWO THINGS AT ONCE)

Dogs and owners form a row. Dogs are sitting. Owners pretend they are in the Seattle Seahawks stadium. A touchdown was made! When the music plays, the first owner in the row lures or cues her dog into a down and then a sit. That dog coming back up into a Sit is the cue for the next dog's turn. Each dog takes a turn going into a Down and coming up into a Sit, like a wave, until you get to the last dog. Alternately, you could form a circle and keep on going, or form two rows if you are competitive. Assistants should stand by to help and encourage.

## RING AROUND A ROSIE (FAST RESPONSE TO CUE, COMMUNITY SPIRIT)

Mark a perimeter on the floor. Play music. The students walk around in a circle. When the music stops, dogs are placed into a down position. Bonus Bones go to the students who are considerate of the dog in front of and behind them. Body language and personal space comments should be made here. Should the dogs turn away from each other? Figure out the rules—Fast downs? Long downs? Distracted downs?

## SIT/STAY DRESS UP (STAYS, HANDLING)

This is a Sit Stay while a scarf is tied on the dog. Sometimes we use t-shirts. Get a variety of sizes at garage sales. You can do it as a relay. Issue one scarf or t-shirt per team. A timed event makes it more of a challenging Stay exercise because owners tend to hurry.

## ROLL THE DICE (DURATION OF STAYS AND HABITUATION TO NOISES)

Make a large die out of a perfectly square cardboard box (12 to 18 inches is a good size). Draw the customary dots. On two sides write SIT, on two sides write DOWN, on one side write STAND, and on one side write JOKER. The game leader spins and drops the die in front of each dog. Not too close! The dog performs that exercise for that number of seconds. The person getting the JOKER chooses between Sit or Down.

## 1-2-3 GAME (SIT/STAY/RELEASE, GOOD CITIZENSHIP, A PERSONAL BEST GAME)

Play music with a good beat for one minute. When the music begins, owners walk their dogs three steps, being careful to avoid collisions with other students. On the third step the dogs Sit for a limited hold of three seconds. They stay for three seconds, they are clearly and distinctly released, and then dogs and owners walk three more steps and repeat the Sit Stay until the music stops. Assistants stand by to help. Spectators can help. Each spectator is assigned a dog and counts how many Sits that dog performs in a minute. The individual goal for each dog is to play again the next week and manage at least one more sit.

## WORK THE CLOCK (STAYS, DISTRACTIONS)

Each sitting dog represents the middle of a clock. Dog can be sitting, standing, or lying down. Owners go the end of their leash or to half the length of their leash and face their dogs at the 6:00 position. Ask them to go to 9:00, 12:00, and 3:00 in any order. Have fun and give them ten after the hour. Power outage . . . the clock stops for a couple of minutes. Make up your own rules. A good game for teaching dogs they must stay even if eye contact is broken.

## JUNK FOOD (CONTROL AT DINNER TIME)

Set up a table and chair at the end of the room for each owner. At the opposite end of the room is a table or chair with individually wrapped snacks on it for each team. Handler places dog on Down Stay under the chair or table and goes to get a snack, returns to sit at the table, unwraps and eats the snack and throws the paper in a nearby trash container. If the dog breaks the Down Stay, the owner must start again by picking up a snack and repeating the steps. (Owners only have to eat one snack!) First team done wins.

## SIT LOTTERY CARDS (STAYS, DISTRACTIONS)

I learned this one from Ian Dunbar, who has written lots of dog books. Make a deck of cards. Paste each one of these instructions on an index card. Make up your own variation. Students pull a card and need to do the sit exercise by the rules on their card. If time is short, one student can pick a card and all students have to perform the exercise listed on the card.

DOG IS STANDING, INSTRUCTOR HOLDS DOG'S LEASH,
YOU SAY "SIT" FROM SIX FEET AWAY

DOG IS IN THE DOWN POSITION, YOU SAY "SIT"

DOG IS STANDING, YOUR BACK IS TO THE DOG, YOU SAY "SIT"

DOG IS STANDING, INSTRUCTOR RATTLES A BAG,
PLACES IT AT DOG'S FEET, YOU SAY "SIT"

DOG IS STANDING, PLACE BROWN BAG OVER YOUR HEAD, YOU SAY "SIT"

DOG IS STANDING, YOU SAY "A, B, C, D, *SIT*, F, G"

## LEAP FROG (STAYS, DOG-TO-DOG SKILLS, COMMUNITY SPIRIT)

Establish a finish line. The start line should be at least 30 feet away from the finish line. Place markers at even intervals, about four feet apart starting at the start line and ending at the finish line. There should be twice as many markers as the number of dogs playing. The first dog lies down on the first marker. Depending on skill level, owners can stay with their dog. When the first dog down is told "Stay," the next person on the start line walks past (not too close!) the dog and does a Down on the next marker, etc. until all the dogs are on markers. There are markers left! The first dog down gets up and goes to the end of the line. When that dog hears "Stay," the second dog gets up, goes to the end and lies down on the next marker. This goes on until a team member reaches the finish line. (Fun variation: Pretend they are leapfrogging across a river. If a dog breaks, teacher says Shark! Shark! And all must get up and move quickly to the start line (bank of the river) and start over. Beware of too much excitement when the shark comes. This can be fun as a competitive event, for teams, and for an advanced class.

## ANIMAL SQUARES (LOOSE WALKING, STAYS)

You will need at least three or four times as many sheets of poster paper as you have dogs playing the game. Divide the papers evenly into three stacks. On each paper in one stack draw (or use computer clip art) an animal in a sitting position. I use a cat. Another stack is prepared with a different animal lying down. I use a bunny drawing for the down. On the last stack draw yet a different animal standing. I use cows. Mark a perimeter for some loose leash walking. Place half of each animal poster along the walking line. Scatter the other half at random within the circle. When the music plays the owners and dogs walk around the circle. When the music stops, they must progress to the next closest animal square in front of them. If it's a sitting cat, they put their dog on it in a Sit Stay and then leave the dog there and go to the middle, find another sitting cat and stand on it! When all owners and dogs are in position, start the music again and repeat. Variation: Owners, as well as their dogs, have to Sit, Down, or Stand as the card depicts!

## CALL THE COLOR (LOOSE WALKING, STAYS, GOOD CITIZENSHIP)

Dogs and owners do some loose leash walking around the training area while music is playing. Have a means of traffic control, such as lines or obstacles to mark corners. When the music goes off, the game leader calls out a color. The owner finds that color somewhere in the training area, and while touching that color, Sits his dog. (Or Down, if you wish). You can't use a color on your own body or your dog's. For example: Music ends and game leader calls, "Sit by red." Perhaps someone will find the color red in a picture on the wall, or a red purse might be laying on table. Next time: "Down by blue." Perhaps someone will find a blue curtain or blue coat hanging up. Variation: Make up rules suitable for the skill level of your group. You might want to be sure to specify only one person for one item, no colors on other dogs or handlers and no running. Point out that each dog should do his best to make the other dogs in the area successful.

## RED LIGHT, GREEN LIGHT (A FUN WAY TO PRACTICE LIMITED HOLD)

This game requires a fairly large playing area with start and finish lines. An instructor or helper designated "IT" turns her face to the finish line, back to the dogs.

The dogs and owners line up on the opposite line or wall, facing "ITS" back. When "IT" says "Green Light!" the line of dogs walks toward the finish line while "IT" counts to three. At three , "IT" calls out "Red Light" and a position such as Down or Sit, waits three seconds and turns. Dogs not in the position when 'IT' turns around must leave the floor. Repeat procedure but call a different position.

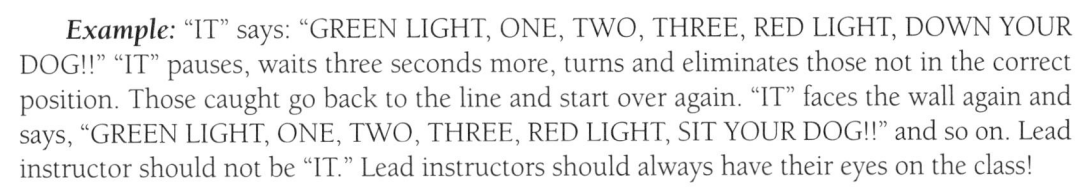

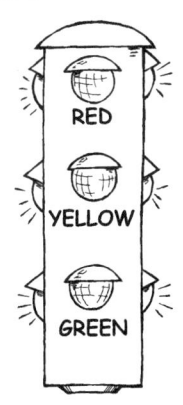

*Example:* "IT" says: "GREEN LIGHT, ONE, TWO, THREE, RED LIGHT, DOWN YOUR DOG!!" "IT" pauses, waits three seconds more, turns and eliminates those not in the correct position. Those caught go back to the line and start over again. "IT" faces the wall again and says, "GREEN LIGHT, ONE, TWO, THREE, RED LIGHT, SIT YOUR DOG!!" and so on. Lead instructor should not be "IT." Lead instructors should always have their eyes on the class!

## SPELLING GAME (STAYS, DISTRACTIONS, COMMUNITY SPIRIT)

Make two or three teams with at least two dogs in a team. These teams have a planning and practice session in secret. When we all reconvene, each team takes a turn spelling a word using their bodies and their dog's bodies. Teams can choose to spell the word standing or lying down on the floor or a combination. The other teams have to guess the word. Point out that each dog has a comfort zone and the owner should make sure their part of the word is a good place for their dog. Team work! Consideration of others!

## OLYMPIC SYMBOL GAME

This is a fun way to train the basics. Mark a starting line and finish line about 30 feet apart. In the middle of the space, arrange five hula hoops like the Olympic rings (but not overlapping). We make two stations, so you will need ten hula hoops and one class assistant to help with this game. A different class exercise will take place in each ring. Use the goals for your class to plan the exercises. Demonstrate the game ahead of time to the class. Once the game begins, the instructor, or class assistant, accompanies the student and explains what exercise takes place in each ring. If the dog has trouble, the owner is coached how to help the dog.

*Sample Exercises for Each Ring:* Loose leash walking or heeling to the first ring, dog into ring, dog is praised and patted by student while instructor counts to three. Second ring, dog Sits for a count of three. Third ring, dog Downs for a count of three. Fourth ring, "four-on-the-floor" (similar to Stand) for a count of three. Since we don't teach "Stand" in Pet Dog Manners class, this is presented as a challenge to the students. They have the luring skills to succeed—praise their success at working out the problem. The fifth and last ring is a Sit-Stay. The student goes to the finish line (or end of leash) and calls the dog. The instructor counts to three while the student keeps the dog's attention focused with praise and rewards.

GAMES PUP&PDM.doc *Coaching People to Train Their Dogs* © Terry Ryan 2005

# ACTIVITIES MENU FOR THE LAST MEETING OF CLASS

Here are some games and activities I especially enjoy saving for the last class party:

## USE IT OR LOSE IT (Application of Basics)

We prepare for this a couple of weeks ahead of time. I'll have a deck of index cards with basic exercises written on them. For example: Sit, Down, Come, Heel. Each student pulls a card. They then have to make up a real life exercise that practices this basic. They present it to us the last night of class as an activity. They can talk with any instructor to help plan or they can just surprise us on the night. However an instructor will help present the activity, making sure everything is safe and appropriate for the group. Just in case anyone is shy about asking for help throw out some ideas:

| | |
|---|---|
| **Sit:** | Dog sits calmly while owner places shirt on dog. |
| **Down:** | Dog does a Down and stays while owner takes shoes off and puts them back on |
| **Come:** | Dog is called, but suddenly toy squirrel appears |
| **Heel:** | Dog needs to walk nicely even though a ball is bouncing nearby |
| **Handling:** | Owner must wipe all four of the dog's feet with a towel |
| **Attention:** | Oops, some dog biscuits were spilled |

## HOMEMADE OBSTACLE COURSE (Instructor-directed Confidence Building)

At least two weeks ahead of time, tell the students they can participate in planning an obstacle course. Each is to bring an obstacle and, with the help of an instructor, present the obstacle safely as a confidence building experience. The students might need some help thinking of what to bring. Give them lots of ideas and bring a couple yourself. If someone forgets to bring an obstacle, bring out yours and work together with the student.

### IDEAS:

| | |
|---|---|
| Two bricks and a ten-inch plank: | Dog does a balance beam walk (2 inches off the ground) |
| Hula hoop: | Dog needs to back through the hoop |
| Big plastic garbage bag (empty): | Tape it to the floor, dog needs to walk over it |
| Blanket over a pole: | Dog is called through the "blind" to owner |
| Three large appliance boxes: | Owner hides under one; Dog finds owner |
| Dog-sized cardboard boxes: | Make a short tunnel to call dogs through |

Dogs that seem a bit worried at first, if given a chance to work it out, seem to have overcome their apprehension after the first successful trial. Do give such dogs an immediate second turn.

## DISTRACTION COURSE (Instructor-directed Confidence Building)

Much the same as the obstacle course, students bring something novel to class with them. The lead instructor organizes those things into a supervised walking course, turning it into a lesson on various ways to keep the dog's attention, instinctive drift, anything that comes up.

Some distractions students have brought in the past include: Grass from the neighborhood scent post, a radio-operated bunny, a kitty litter box complete with . . . , an open bait pouch, a CD of wolves howling, and a vacuum cleaner—turned on.

## GOOD CITIZEN EXERCISES (Introduction to the Test)

Cut out the descriptions of the tests. Place each test on one index card. Have the students pick a card. They perform just that one exercise.

## IMPERSONATIONS (Fun, Handling)

Announce this ahead of time. Class members take turns guessing who/what the dog is impersonating. Offer to help any student that needs an idea.

Some impersonations from past classes:

| | |
|---|---|
| *Eggplant* | Black lab sitting with a wide green collar and green pointed hat |
| *Book ends* | Two dogs sitting up, back to back against some books |
| *Elephant* | English cocker's ears held out, sock on her nose |
| *Movie star* | Dog with docked tail sunglasses on his rear, tail is his nose |
| *Domino* | Black dog wearing paper plates does a down stay |

*Impersonation: Son of the Beach*
Art drawn by Carol Byrnes

## LATERAL THINKING GAMES (Confidence Building in Owners)

I always spend a few minutes during the last class to show students how good they've become at problem solving. I remind them not to set unnecessary limitations and laud them for their creativity.

### Godzilla Strikes Again

Bring in a collection of ten, narrow cardboard boxes of varying heights, 10" to 20". Whiskey boxes and cereal boxes are a good size. Wrap them in plain paper if you have time. With a non-toxic marker, draw windows on the boxes to make them look like office buildings. With tape or chalk, mark out the city limits of Tokyo—a square about 20 feet × 20 feet. Erect the buildings within the city limits. The object is for owners to take turns getting their dogs to impersonate the naughty lizard and flatten Tokyo—just like in the movies. All boxes must be knocked over or taken out of the boundary. Owners may not step inside of the Tokyo city limits (the boundary lines). Ask for volunteers. Each volunteer owner and dog has 60 seconds to try to knock over or out as many buildings as possible. But the instructor keeps changing the rules. For example, if the first dog knocked over a box because his owner tossed food on top of it, the rule for the next dog is NO FOOD and don't step in the city limits. If that dog's owner gets him to retrieve a box to get it out of the boundary, the next dog has the rules NO FOOD and NO RETRIEVING and don't step in the city limits. Keep it up! You'll run out of volunteers as it becomes more difficult to be creative while tackling the problem within the existing rules. Allow people that just have ideas, but don't want to demonstrate with their dog, to participate also by simply explaining their tactic.

### Four on the Floor

Put a piece of masking tape down on the floor about 4 feet long and 2 inches wide. Tell the owners that the task is to "get all four feet on the tape." Each owner will have a different idea of what these instructions mean. The rules are much the same as the Godzilla exercise. Change the rules after each attempt. Dog lies down on his side with all four feet touching the tape. Good! Next time dog cannot lie down and to "get all four feet on the tape." Next participant rips the tape in half and places them in a more dog friendly conformation. Good! Next time, no downs, don't rip the tape in half, and to "get all four feet on the tape," etc.

### Ten Chances

The start and finish lines are about 20 feet apart. The dog stays on one line, his human on the other. The owner is able to use exactly ten different cues (that's 10 words and/or signals). Each cue must produce a perceivable behavior! Following the requests of the owner, the dog must finish within reaching distance of the owner. A typical sequence might go like this: Dog is standing on the start line, owner says (1) Down, (2) Roll Over (3) Come, (4) Sit, (5) Stand, (6) Spin, (7) Stay, (8) Speak, (9) Sit Up, and (10) Touch. You might give people a few minutes to think about this before they try. There are quite a few good strategies! (I learned about this game from Lonnie Olson!)

## Out of Ideas?

You can find more ideas in two of Legacy's booklets: *Games People Play to Train Their Dogs* and *Life Beyond Block Heeling*.

# DO IN CLASS, WEEK 2 (DOGS' DEBUT)...

- **ESCORT TO CHAIRS FROM PARKING LOT**—Check collar fit

- **FIRST 10–15 MINUTES:** Play relaxation music
   1. Give Focusing Toy, ask permission and check owner preference first
   2. Walk around chair / muscle massage / Lavender?

- **TAKE ROLL**—"What do you like best about your dog?"
  Talk about Trick—Offer help after class
  Answer questions about L.E.A.D. Program

- **DEMO:** Students Hold Leads, Instructors Do Work:
  Reward Spontaneous Sits—Leave Rude Dogs—Try Again

## ✻ START REVIEW ✻

**"YES"/TREAT**
   Five treats in hand, "YES!," followed immediately by food, do five times

**SIT HAPPENS! STEPS 1 & 2**
   Warm-up: lure dog's head up and down/back and forth, "YES!"/Treat
   Food magnet sit, lure moves up and back between ears.
   "YES!"/Treat when dog's bottom makes contact with floor
   Don't say "Sit" yet!

**EYE CONTACT—STEPS 1 & 2**
   Get your dog focused on a toy
   Use the toy to lure eye contact up to your face
   Say dog's name—cheerfully
   Play with your dog and/or praise him 3–5 seconds (no food)

## ✻ END REVIEW ✻

- **GAMES**    I Spy (with own dog—partners)

- **L.E.A.D.**    Any questions?

*more . . .*

# Do In Class, Week 2

## ❋ START NEW EXERCISE STEPS ❋

**EYE CONTACT—STEP 3**
   Distraction free area.
   No lure! Keep still, say your dog's name cheerfully
   When dog makes eye contact
   Praise or play with dog for 3–5 seconds (no "YES!", no food)

**SIT—STEP 3**
   Keep still (no lure yet!) Say dog's name. Say "Sit"
   NOW use the lure if needed
   When Sit happens, "YES!"/Treat

**COME—STEPS 1, 2, 3**
   Gotcha exercise
   Food bowl come—find other opportunities as well
   Surprise, on leash—engage dog for 3–5 seconds

**LEASH WORK – LET'S GO**
   Demo & Practice "Let's Go" Concept
   Let's Go is a separate exercise

**LEASH WORK—HEELING STEPS 1, 2, 3**
   Curb or lure your dog into a heel position, "Sit"—"YES!"/Treat
   Dog will eventually learn to sit automatically when you stop.
   Step, step, "Sit"—"YES!"/Treat
   If dog is luring well, use the word "Heel" as dog steps out.
   Change directions, pivot, still only a step or two at a time.

## ❋ END OF NEW EXERCISES ❋

♦ **Questions from Students?**

♦ **Comments from Assistants?**

♦ **PLAY GOODBYE MUSIC**

# Do In Class, Week 3

♦ **ESCORT TO CHAIRS FROM PARKING LOT**

♦ **START MUSIC**

## \* START REVIEW \*

**EYE CONTACT—STEP 3**
   Distraction-free area.
   No lure! Keep still, say your dog's name cheerfully
   When dog makes eye contact, praise and play for 3–5 seconds

**SIT—STEP 3**
   Keep still (no lure yet!). Say dog's name. Say "Sit"
   NOW use the lure if needed
   When Sit happens, "YES!"/Treat

**COME—STEPS 1, 2, 3**
   Gotcha exercise review
   Individually: Surprise, move backward—engage dog for 3–5 seconds

**LEASH WORK—LET'S GO**
   How is "Let's Go" exercise going? Gentle Leader® anyone?

**LEASH WORK—HEELING—STEPS 1, 2, 3**
   Curb or lure your dog into a heel position sit—"YES!"/Treat
   Dog will eventually learn to sit automatically when you stop.
   Step, step, sit—"YES!"/Treat
   If dog is luring well, use the word "Heel" as you step out.
   Change directions, pivot, only a step or two at a time.

## \* END REVIEW \*

♦ **GAMES** — Spin Dice Challenge Game: How would you help your dog stay for the number of seconds indicated on the dice cube?

♦ **TAKE ROLL** — "What's Your Dog's Favorite Food Treat?"

♦ **TRICK** — Need Help?

♦ **L.E.A.D.** — Brags / Questions

♦ **LET'S GO**

♦ **PERSONAL BEST CHALLENGE**

*more . . .*

# Do In Class, Week 3

## ✳ START NEW EXERCISE STEPS ✳

**EYE CONTACT—STEP 4**
Distraction
Name. OK to go back to using a toy lure temporarily.
When eye contact (with or without a lure) praise and play for 3–5 seconds.

**SIT AND DOWN EXERCISES—IMPORTANT**
*Teach use of Verbal Cue "Stay"*
*Teach use of Verbal Release Cue*

**SIT—STEP 4**
Start using Stay and Release cues, omit "YES!"/Treat
Say dog's name, say "Sit," say "Stay," help stay for a few seconds, massage or treat
Demonstrate examples of Four D's, increase reinforcement rate
    "Stay," wait 3–10 seconds (don't leave dog), reward, release
    "Stay," take one step away, immediately return, reward, release
    "Work the Clock"

**LEASH WORK & COME—TWO STATIONS**
Leash work—Trace easy alphabet letters or a Figure 8
Treat while walking instead of sitting—two-fers, three-fers one-fers, etc.
Come practice—in chute-Posture? Hand signal? Different Cue/New Cue?

**DOWN—STEPS 1–4**
Lured Down, Macaroni Down, Alternative?
Start using Stay and Release cues, omit "YES!"/Treat
Say dog's name, say "Down," say "Stay," help stay for a few seconds, massage or treat
Demonstrate examples of Four D's, increase reinforcement rate
    "Stay," wait 3–10 seconds (don't leave dog), release
    "Stay," take one step away, immediately return, release
    "Work the Clock"

## ✳ END OF NEW EXERCISES ✳

♦ **Personal best challenges!**

♦ **L.E.A.D. Program**

♦ **Questions from Students?**

♦ **Comments from Assistants?**

♦ **PLAY GOODBYE MUSIC**

# DO IN CLASS, WEEK 4

♦ **START MUSIC**

## ❋ START REVIEW ❋

**EYE CONTACT—STEP 4**
   Distractions! Name. (OK to go back to using a toy lure temporarily.)
   When eye contact (with or without a lure) praise and play for 3–5 seconds.

**SIT—STEP 4**
   Start using Stay and Release cues, omit "YES!"/Treat
   Say dog's name, say "Sit," say "Stay," help stay for a few seconds, massage or treat
   Demonstrate examples of Four D's, increase reinforcement rate
      "Stay," wait 3–10 seconds (don't leave dog), release
      "Stay," take one step away, immediately return, release
      "Work the Clock," Tic Tac Toe or instructors choice

**COME—STEP 4**
   Conduct two chute stations
      a. no distraction
      b. distraction

**LEASH WORK—HEEL—STEP 4**
   **With Sits Two Stations**
   Half class does Sit Stay one end of room
   Other half class Heels toward them, turn at cone in middle go back to place
   Variable reinforcement schedule—2-fers, 3-fers, 1-fers
   Reward walking, alternate with reward sitting

**DOWN—STEPS 1–4**
   Lured Down, Macaroni Down, Alternative?
   Start using Stay and Release cues, omit "YES!"/Treat
   Say dog's name, say "Down," say "Stay," help stay for a few seconds, massage or treat
   Demonstrate examples of Four D's, increase reinforcement rate
      "Stay," wait 3–10 seconds (don't leave dog), release
      "Stay," take one step away, immediately return, release
      "Work the Clock"

## ❋ END REVIEW ❋

♦ **GAMES: 1-2-3-Sit/Release/Praise for 3—Take Their Counts (1 min)**
♦ **TAKE ROLL—"Tell us what trick you are working on"**
♦ **Encourage students to try Leader of the Pack Figure 8 Challenge**
♦ **L.E.A.D. Program Questions, Reports, Brags?**
♦ **LET'S GO**
♦ **PERSONAL BEST CHALLENGE**

**more . . .**

# Do In Class, Week 4

## ✳ START NEW EXERCISE STEPS ✳

**EYE CONTACT—STEP 5**
 Instructor has a potato chip bag on a leash as distraction.
 Owner waits. No luring. Dog must decide to check in.
 Even if the dog is late, eye contact should be enthusiastically rewarded with praise and play.

**SIT—STEP 5—DO AS A DRILL:**
 Give the cue "Sit"—no luring—immediate reward.
 Reward and release at varying durations.
 Say "Stay." Use release word. "YES!" is phased out, but you can still give a food reward at random before the release.
 Dog doesn't Sit? Jump-start. WORK THE CLOCK

**COME—STEP 5**
 Continue to add challenges at home
 Coin in arm pit game: Instructor holds leash, owner goes three feet
 Owner still has coins? Owner reached for dog?

**LEASH WORK—HEEL—STEP 5**
 Chair-to-chair walk to music, dog sits at each chair
 Vary rewards, sometimes treat, sometimes praise, sometimes toy

**DOWN—STEP 5**
 Say "Down" once—no luring—immediate reward.
 Reward and release at varying durations
 Say "Down," say "Stay." Dog doesn't go down? Jump-start
 Give a food reward at random before the release. Use release word.
 WORK THE CLOCK

## ✳ END OF NEW EXERCISES ✳

◆ **Remind of two personal best activities**

◆ **Questions from Students?**

◆ **Pass out evaluations, exchange for a bonus bone**

◆ **PLAY GOODBYE MUSIC**

# DO IN CLASS, WEEK 5

♦ **START MUSIC**

## ✻ START REVIEW ✻

**EYE CONTACT—STEP 5**
   Owner uses own toy—hold at arms length or place on floor as distraction. Wait. No luring. Dog initiates check in.
   Even if the dog is late, eye contact should be enthusiastically rewarded with praise and play.

**SIT—DO STEP 5**
   Give the cue "Sit" once—no luring—immediate reward.
   Dog doesn't sit? Jump-start as described in the handout.
   Next reward and release at varying durations.
   Four D drills and games—instructors choice
   Say "Stay." Use release word. "Yes" is phased out, but you can still give a food reward at random before the release.

**LEASH WORK—HEEL—STEP 5**
   Half practice leash work, half practice come
   Leash work—trace difficult letters or Figure 8
   Vary reward, sometimes treat, sometimes praise, sometimes toy

**"COME"—STEP 5**
   Come—practice in chute with distractions in path

**DOWN—STEP 5**
   Say "Down" once—no luring—immediate reward.
   Dog doesn't go down? Jump-start
   Reward and Release at varying durations.
   Four D drills and games—Stadium Wave, instructors choice
   Say "Stay." Give a food reward at random before the release
   Use release word. ("Yes" is phased out)

## ✻ END REVIEW ✻

♦ **TAKE ROLL**   "What's Your Dog's Best Class Exercise?"
                  "Who has a Personal Best Report"
                  Talk about Leader of the Pack Figure 8 Challenge

♦ **GAMES**       a. Sit Lottery Game Cards
                  b. 1-2-3 Game

♦ **LET'S GO**

♦ **L.E.A.D.**

♦ **TRICK**

♦ **COLLECT MID-COURSE EVALUATIONS; EXCHANGE FOR BONUS BONES**          more . . .

# DO IN CLASS, WEEK 5

## ✱ START NEW EXERCISE STEPS ✱

**EYE CONTACT—STEP 6**
Dog makes eye contact, ignoring distractions.
Random Reward: 2-fers, 1-fer, 3-fers, etc.
Vary type of reward: toy, games, food

**OLYMPIC SYMBOL GAME.** First, luring ok. Second time, only 3 pieces of food:

### SIT—STEP 6
Sit Lottery: 1-fers, 2-fers, 3-fers.
Say "Sit"—no luring, don't repeat the word.
Remember stay and release cue.
Lose the food! Randomize rewards!

### DOWN—STEP 6
Down Lottery: 1-fers, 2-fers, 3-fers.
Say "Down"—no luring, don't repeat the word.
Remember stay and release cue.
Lose the food! Randomize rewards! Down lottery

**LEASH WORK AND COME—STEP 6**

### LEASH WORK
Random, remote, delayed rewards
   *Trace letters or Figure 8*

### COME
Encourage owners to choose options from Come list
Remember to change locations, and use different distractions
Practice in chute, instructor holds dog's collar, distracts dog

***IF TIME LEFT:***

**COME CHUTES—Delayed, Remote Rewards**

   *alternating stations with*

**HEELING—Sit at three cones, food or toy on shelf at end.**

## ✱ END OF NEW EXERCISES ✱

♦ **Questions from Students?**

♦ **Comments from Assistants?**
   **Evaluation Forms to Hand In for Bonus Bone?**

♦ **Figure 8 Leader of the Pack challenge?**

# DO IN CLASS, WEEK 6

◆ **START MUSIC**

## ✱ START REVIEW ✱

**EYE CONTACT—STEP 6**
   Dog makes eye contact, ignoring distractions.
   Random Reward: 2-fers, 1-fer, 3-fers, etc.
      Instructor distracts three times, dog is rewarded for contact once

**SIT—STEP 6**
   Say "Sit"—no luring, don't repeat the word.
   Remember stay and release cue.
   Lose the food! Randomize rewards!

**COME—STEP 6**
   Remind Come Menu. Be safe, use your leash.
      Come Chutes, owner hides at end

   *Alternating stations with:*

**LEASH WORK—STEP 6**
   Back and forth between cones
   One piece of food, instructor says "now"

**DOWN—STEP 6**
   Down Lottery: 1-fers, 2-fers, 3-fers
   Say "Down"—no luring, don't repeat the word.
   Remember stay and release cue.
      Do as a group, food and toys should be out of sight

## ✱ END REVIEW ✱

◆ **GAMES**         Compulsory: Musical Chairs
                    Restrained, Timed Recalls

◆ **TAKE ROLL**     "Brag—anything at all good this week"

◆ **Remind to stay after for Figure 8 Challenge**

◆ **Any reports on personal best?**

◆ **LET'S GO**

◆ **L.E.A.D.**

*more . . .*

# Do In Class, Week 6

## ✵ START NEW EXERCISE STEPS ✵

**EYE CONTACT—STEP 7**
  Remind class—random, delayed rewards, examples

**SITS AND DOWNS—STEP 7**
  Say cue—no luring, don't repeat the word.
  Remember stay and release cue.
  Remote and randomized rewards!

**COME—STEP 7**
  Outdoors in the run

  *Alternating with:*

**LEASH WORK—STEP 7**
  Tracing 2–3 Letters, with distractions

**RED LIGHT, GREEN LIGHT GAME OR INSTRUCTOR'S CHOICE FOR SITS AND DOWNS**
  If time permits

## ✵ END OF NEW EXERCISES ✵

♦ **Questions from Students?**

♦ **Comments from Assistants?**

♦ **Remember Bonus Bones Next Week!**

♦ **Who's staying for the Figure 8 Leader of the Pack challenge?**

♦ **Special announcements about next week's activities**

♦ **PLAY GOODBYE MUSIC**

# Do In Class, Week 7

## * START REVIEW *

**EYE CONTACT**
**SIT**
**DOWN**
**COME**
**LEASH WORK**

All of these exercises should now have random, delayed, and remote rewards.

## * END REVIEW *

- **FUN AND GAMES**
  - Show Off Tricks
  - Lateral Thinking Games for Humans
  - Last chance: Leader of the Pack Figure 8 Challenge
  - Continuing Education Announcements

- **GAMES, PLANNED INTERACTIVE EVENTS:**
  _____
  _____
  _____
  _____
  _____
  _____

- **BONUS BONE DRAWING**
- **CERTIFICATES**
- **GROUP PHOTO**
- **REFRESHMENTS**

# Class Challenges and "Bonus Bones"

## Challenges

Traditionally, dog training classes in many parts of the world involved a competitive event as the last class of the course. Dogs were evaluated, scored, and placed. Those that did not make the grade, failed the course and were asked to repeat. Originally I followed this practice with my own classes. Over the years I found that most of the people coming to my training classes were not interested in tests. In fact, in the "old days" of my classes many students would have perfect attendance up until the end, but be absent for the very last class, the test. On the other hand, I had students that seemed to be more successful at reaching the class goals if they had the pressure of a pass or fail environment.

**CLASS CHALLENGE:** As a compromise I now use class challenges as an optional pass or fail event for those interested. Two examples of challenges are explained in the Pet Dog Manners Lesson Plans. In Week Four I present "The Personal Best Walkabout Challenge" as an option and in Week Five students receive "The Leader of the Pack Challenge." Students have until the end of the course to do the challenge. The challenge always takes place AFTER class so as not to take time away from anyone else in class, especially those not wanting to participate. In our classes, we have a short break time between back-to-back classes. This is a good time for an assistant instructor to conduct the challenge. Teams passing the challenge might receive a special recognition or a gift. Perhaps they will receive a "certificate" form used to put their name into a drawing for a grand prize to be drawn at the end of the entire course. The task I choose is something within the reach of all members of the class, but some might have to work a little harder at it than others. Good luck is always beneficial as well. The "It's Just Not Our Lucky Day" aspect can relieve the competitive pressure even more. The challenge can work in one of several different ways. What follows are the schemes I have used in my own classes most recently:

---

### WEEK 3 CHALLENGE: SIT

(Dog Sits within Three Seconds of One Cue. Stays for a Count of Ten)

**LEGACY** Canine Behavior & Training

Successfully Completed by: _____

---

INSTRUCT BonusBones&Challenges.doc    *Coaching People to Train Their Dogs* © Terry Ryan 2005    365

**CHALLENGE OF THE WEEK:** This idea can be announced the week before so people can practice if they want to or you can surprise them. When the challenge of the week is over, there is no more opportunity to take that particular challenge. Next week there will be a different challenge. Take a look at your goals for the week and an exercise that reflects one of the goals. Clearly define the judging rules. Perhaps they win a prize outright or a token to go into a grand drawing. You can make mini certificates for the drawing on your computer. I usually do 4 or 5 to a page to save paper. A sample is shown below.

---

### WEEK 6 CHALLENGE: Come-When-Called

(Dog comes immediately to owner when called past instructor with distraction.)

**LEGACY**
Canine Behavior & Training

*Successfully Completed by:* _____

---

# BONUS BONES

I got the bonus bone idea from being a parent aid when our children were in elementary school. If the kids were good, they'd get a "green slip." Every Friday the teacher would put out a variety of gifts and the children could go shopping with their green slips.

Over the years I have cut bone shaped slips of paper out of colored card stock to give to someone that deserves "an event marker." I would decorate them in various themes with little stickers. In the early years, I'd get my kids to cut out bonus bones for me. When they grew up I did it myself. It was a favorite airplane pastime until scissors were no longer permitted on aircraft. It was a sure way to get the guy next to me NOT to talk to me.

I give a bone in class for something good that happens. For example, when a person volunteers to demonstrate or when a person gives another classmate a plastic bag. Students write their names on the back of the bones and put them into a dog dish. At the end of the course, we pull names out, lottery style, and those folks get a prize.

I got tired of cutting out bones so I began to recycle them by drawing a line through the names. It's fun for a student to see a bone with a name written in Japanese! One person got a bone again—the same one he had earned a couple of years before! Once a seminar student found a very well-known "name" in dog training on the bone she received. She decided she would rather just keep the bone as a souvenir and the heck with the lottery!

I've also made magnets in the shape of a bone. It has the Legacy logo on it and the advice "Catch Them In The Act of Doing Something Good." When I give these as rewards, people simply keep them and hopefully put them on their refrigerator door.

## TWO-FER TOKENS

Susan Garrett gave me the idea of "Two-fers." When someone does a good thing in class and deserves a bone, he gets a "two-fer" token. There is room for two names on the token. The first recipient has to catch a classmate in the act of doing something good. Reward him with the 2-fer token. When the paper has two names on it, it is placed into the dog bowl and BOTH students receive a prize—for doing something appropriate themselves and for recognizing and rewarding good in others!

## CLASS DOOR PRIZES

We have fun giving away gifts. Here are some of the themes we have used in the past:

### GO FISHING
Instead of the bonus bone-shaped token, I have found small notepads in the shape of tropical fish. Stock up on these the next time you go to Hawaii. Put prizes in blue lunch sacks and draw fish or paste colorful fish postcards on the bags and set them out on some sand along with some shells. Those lucky at the end of the day drawing get to go fishing, but have no idea what's in the bag.

### PICK A FLOWER
I have notepads with daisies on them. If I cut the pages in half, it's just right for a bonus bone token. I'll get plain brown lunch sacks (garden dirt color) and paste on flowers from old Better Homes and Gardens magazines or just draw some on. End of the day lottery: Go pick a flower.

### ADOPT A DOG
We doggy people have all kinds of doggy paper. Surely you can come up with something to use as dog-oriented tokens. Use those instead of the traditional bonus bone shapes. The bags are decorated with dogs from old dog magazines.

### LEADER OF THE PACK
Download some line art of wolves, print them out, and paste them on brown bags. Since I have a black and white printer, I dab the eyes with a yellow marking pen. I have notepads in the shape of paw prints. Those slips of paper serve as the reward tokens. Winner go adopt a wolf.

### TRIVIA QUESTIONS FOR A PRIZE
What famous actor "won" Lassie in a poker game? (John Wayne—for 24 hours). What is the name of the first woman to have won the Iditarod sled dog race in Alaska? (Libby Riddles—Susan Butcher won several times, but was not the first).

### TRULY RANDOM REWARDS
Cut up a copy of the class roster, pick a name . . . that's the random reward winner. Before you get the chairs out of the closet, paste stickers on the bottoms of some of them . . . random reward winner. Variety shops have cute little paper punches in the shape of dogs, bones, and paw prints. Before you hand out the homework, punch a dog print in a couple of them, mix them up . . . random reward winner.

# THE CHINESE WISDOM PUZZLE

This is a helpful game for instructors.

The directions for playing are in Chapter 6.

Photocopy the puzzle on heavy cover stock or card stock paper.

Cut the pieces out very carefully, so the shapes remain true.

Your puzzle will have five triangles, one square, and one parallelogram.

This template is set up so that you can get two puzzles from one sheet of paper.

# "P.R.E.D.I.C.T.O.R."
## An Acronym Aid for Instructional Formatting

*Class Training Sequence for:* _____

|  | Week 1 | Week 2 | Week 3 | Week 4 | Week 5 | Week 6 | Week 7 | Week 8 |
|---|---|---|---|---|---|---|---|---|
| **P**REPARE |  |  |  |  |  |  |  |  |
| **R**EVIEW |  |  |  |  |  |  |  |  |
| **E**XPLAIN |  |  |  |  |  |  |  |  |
| **D**EMONSTRATE |  |  |  |  |  |  |  |  |
| **I**NSTRUCT |  |  |  |  |  |  |  |  |
| **C**OACH |  |  |  |  |  |  |  |  |
| **T**RAIN AT HOME |  |  |  |  |  |  |  |  |
| **O**BSERVE |  |  |  |  |  |  |  |  |
| **R**EVISE |  |  |  |  |  |  |  |  |

INSTRUCT PREDICTOR.doc     *Coaching People to Train Their Dogs* © Terry Ryan 2005

**LEGACY PUPPY HEADSTART MENU. INSTRUCTORS: SELECT FROM ALL SEVEN PAGES.**

# 1. FAMILY RELATIONSHIPS WITH THE PUPPY

- **GOTCHA (TO PREVENT KEEP AWAY)**
  Owner very close to pup, reach out, grab collar, treat, let go.

- **HANDS AND EMPTY BOWL EXERCISES**
  Owner: Puts food into empty bowl on floor . . . Picks up a bowl, puts food in, puts it down for pup . . . Keeps hands on bowl while pup eats . . . Holds bowl while pup eats. Puts more food into the bowl as pup is eating.

- **ATTENTION: NAME, EYE CONTACT, REWARD**
  Owner teases pup with a squeaky toy. When pup is focused owner draws toy up to face to lure eye contact. Contact, name, praise, play to keep pup engaged at least three seconds.

- **PUPPY PICK UP AND PUT DOWN IF HE'S STILL**
  Owner picks up pup with full body support. Pause, hold feet an inch from surface. Put pup down if he's still. Wiggling puppies are easy to drop.

- **PROGRESSIVE MUSICAL CRATES**
  Several different crate types. When relaxation music starts, owner puts pup into a crate, gives treat, and a 30-second massage. Music goes off, change crates, repeat.

- **RUB THOSE GUMS**
  Owners are given a square of gauze dampened with water. Gentle gum massage, notice new teeth, healthy color of gums.

- **GIVE TOYS BACK NICELY—FUN STARTS WITH RELEASE**
  Owner makes the toy "die" by holding it motionless against body. Says nothing. Pup will go through extinction burst and eventually release. Owner resumes playing tug after release. Or: Trade toy with food, but then give the toy back, too.

- **TAKE FOOD FROM HAND GENTLY**
  Owner feeds only very small pieces, so pup always has to make contact with fingers. Don't release food until gentle. Or: Owner places food into the bowl of a metal spoon, covering food with thumb. Pup learns to be careful and gentle.

- **CALL BETWEEN FAMILY MEMBERS**
  Each member has a bag of treats and a toy. Taking turns, one owner gets pup interested in the bag and toy while backing away from the pup. That owner cheers the pup on, sucking him in like a vacuum cleaner. Don't say "Come" unless pup is obviously on a dead run. Pup arrives, say "Yes," give food, and play with toy for five seconds. Grab collar next time.

**LEGACY PUPPY HEADSTART MENU. INSTRUCTORS: SELECT FROM ALL SEVEN PAGES.**

## 2. CARE AND HANDLING OF THE PUPPY

☐ **CHECK COLLARS**
Owners check: Too loose? Too tight?

☐ **PLAY DOCTOR**
Owner puts pup on table, touches pup with an "instrument," praises, gives treat, takes off, ignores. Back on table, "instruments," owner and instructor treat, praise, owner takes pup off table, pup is ignored. Next: instructor in white coat touches pup with instrument.

☐ **DRESS UP**
Give each owner appropriate size T-shirt for pup. Put it on, take it off.

☐ **I SPY (INSTRUCTOR CALLS OUT PUPPY BODY PARTS)**
Owners touch that part, instructor helps with desensitizing jumpy pups.

☐ **BRUSH PUP ON GROOMING TABLE—PEANUT BUTTER THERAPY**
Touch pup with a soft brush, immediately apply a tiny smear of peanut butter at nose level on arm of table's noose. No noose? Push table against a washable wall.

☐ **PUPPY MASSAGE**
Play relaxation music. Coach owners to gently push the skin in a circular motion over large muscles (neck, shoulder, thigh). If pup goes down, belly rub too.

☐ **GOOD VIBRATIONS (ELECTRIC HAIR DRYER)**
Let pup investigate (unplugged, on floor). Sprinkle food on it. If ok, next time plug it in with air directed away from approaching pup. See if the pup is still willing to investigate. If OK, owner holds pup and touches her with handle of dryer—no air.

☐ **COUNT TOES, RESTRAIN LEGS, HEAR SOUND OF A TOE NAIL CLIPPER**
Owner holds pup, gently manipulates each paw. If pup pulls back, go with the pull, not against it until pup settles. Instructor approaches settled pup with clipper and matchstick. Clip stick, give pup a treat. (Pick up the pieces of wood!)

☐ **WIPE FEET WITH A DRY WASH CLOTH**
Owner starts with hind feet. If pup struggles or mouths the cloth, hold it still on her foot. Don't take it away from foot until she becomes calm. Put peanut butter on a toy as a distraction.

☐ **A DRY BATH!**
Put one inch of water into half of divided sink. Owner puts puppy in the dry half. Wash pup's face with warm, damp cloth. Make noise with water. Open shampoo and let pup sniff it.

☐ **FOOD-LURE MAGNET (BODY FOLLOWS NOSE!)**
Owner holds a piece of food right on pup's nose. It will act as a "magnet." Lure pup's head up and down. Now have him say "No" by luring his nose left and right. Say "YES!" and give the treat. Try a couple more magnetic moves, say "YES!" and give the food.

**LEGACY PUPPY HEADSTART MENU. INSTRUCTORS: SELECT FROM ALL SEVEN PAGES.**

# 3. GOOD HOUSE AND TOILET MANNERS

- **POTTY BREAK—PRACTICE CUE**
  Class goes out, on leash, to fenced area for potty. Coach owners through steps to put potty on cue. Help clean up.

- **STADIUM WAVE: FOOD-LURE MAGNET FOR A SIT AND DOWN**
  Individual coaching, then form wave, then add football music.

- **THE SIT-STAY FOR CLEAN-UP CHALLENGE**
  Give owner a poop bag. Put a poop-sized object on ground; owner picks it up with bag. Next time pup must sit and stay (lure for stay can be used) while owner holds leash with one hand and picks up "poop" with the other. Didn't work? Try again.

- **TIGHT LEASH? STOP WALKING**
  Owner puts something of interest on the floor and carries puppy away from it. Put pup down and progress toward object only if leash is not tight. No cues, just stop and go.

- **WHERE'S THE PUPPY?**
  Owners take turns putting the puppy in various crates. Door closes and blanket goes over the crate. Lots of verbal praise while the puppy "hides quietly" for five seconds. Off with blanket, owner is quiet, takes pup out and ignores for several seconds.

- **THE SIT–STAY LEASH SNAP CHALLENGE**
  Loan extra leash. Spin a die. That's the number of seconds pup stays. Owners lure and maintains it by keeping the pup's head up. Next spin help pup sit still while leash is snapped on and off.

- **Q & A ON TOILET TRAINING**
  Discuss handout and offer to schedule a few minutes to discuss progress individually.

- **SIT-STAY WHILE DOOR OPENS**
  Lure a sit in front of closed restroom door. Pup stays while you open the door. If the dog gets up, close the door. Try again.

- **GOOD TOY / BAD TOY GAME**
  Place a shoe and three dog toys on the floor. Owner brings the pup to the pile. If pup investigates a legal toy, praise and play with him. If he investigates the shoe, ignore him. You can make the shoe yukky by spraying with a taste deterrent.

LEGACY PUPPY HEADSTART MENU. INSTRUCTORS: SELECT FROM ALL SEVEN PAGES.

# 4. INTERACTIONS WITH OTHER PEOPLE

☐ **GIVE PUP TO INSTRUCTOR**
Owner GIVES pup to an instructor (rather than instructor TAKES pup). Instructor holds pup for a few seconds. Give back when pup is relaxed. Safety: Don't dangle leash. Repeat.

☐ **PUPPY EXCHANGE**
Families sit on the floor and exchange puppies with each other. Instructor supervises interactions.

☐ **EVERYONE LAUGH LOUDLY AT A JOKE**
Tell a joke instructing everyone to laugh even if it's not funny. Low-key laughing at first produces a treat for the pup. If all goes well get noisier.

☐ **MEET A BABYDOLL**
Carry the doll to each pup for a sniff. Next round doll makes "eye contact" with pup.

☐ **HANDS AND BOWLS**
Repeat the bowl exercise listed under *#1 Family Relationships*. Instructor handles the bowl and food instead of owner.

☐ **CANES, WALKER, WHEELCHAIRS, CRUTCHES**
Allow pup to come up and visit equipment. Instructor moves around room a little with aid of equipment.

☐ **GOTCHA**
Owners did this under *#1 Family Relationships*. Instructors do it this time.

☐ **ROLE PLAY INTERACTIONS**
Instructors demonstrate low impact body postures for interacting with puppies: Low, sideways, no eye contact, extend hand just a little, holding it an inch above the floor. Let the pup decide if he wants to make contact or not.

☐ **KIDS AND CANINES**
When children are present, coach and supervise (one-on-one) appropriate interactions with their own pup and other pups. Give parents the *Kids and Canines* handout.

☐ **COSTUME BOX**
Have everyone choose a hat, beard, or mask from the box. Puppies watch people trying on some weird stuff.

**LEGACY PUPPY HEADSTART MENU. INSTRUCTORS: SELECT FROM ALL SEVEN PAGES.**

# 5. INTERACTIONS WITH OTHER DOGS

- **MIRROR**
  Let pup see herself in the wall mirror.

- **INVESTIGATE TOY DOG**
  Show pups several toys using good body language. (Allow pup to sniff nose and anal area, then toy does the same.)

- **BARKING CD**
  Play the Legacy SOUNDS GOOD Barking CD on low. Owners engage their puppies with play and food to keep the pups happy to prevent them from joining in with the barking.

- **AGILITY CLASS OBSERVATION**
  Or flyball or freestyle. Do a quick demo with advanced dogs or invite pups to a practice to observe fast (and perhaps noisy!) adult dogs having a good time.

- **INVESTIGATE TOY DOG**
  Show pup several toy dogs. Manipulate toy dogs so they have good body language. Allow pup to sniff toy dog. Toy dog sniffs pup.

- **MEET AN ADULT STAFF DOG**
  An approved staff dog on leash visits with each puppy individually to help determine pup's suitability for a puppy play session.

- **PING-PONG PLAY GROUP**
  Two or four puppies selected for compatibility play together for 1–2 minutes. In turn, instructor selects one to be "sucked" out of group to owner: Owner comes in and touches pup and engages him with a toy. Owner immediately runs backward outside of the ring of activity, waving the toy and cheering the pup in. Avoid saying "Come" unless pup is unquestionably committed. Say "Yes" when he arrives, interact for at least 3–5 seconds, and take pup back to go play again. Coach others on sidelines to turn away if pup comes to them. **Caution:** Play groups can go badly. Don't allow bullying.

- **SHARING FOOD**
  Divide puppies and owners into small groups. Everyone takes turns giving treats to puppies. Do quickly so pups can't worry if their turn is coming or not.

- **SHARING SPACE**
  Two at a time, pups sit in a cardboard box and share this small space nicely for a few seconds. Pups can acknowledge each other, but keep the pups focus on the owners.

LEGACY PUPPY HEADSTART MENU. INSTRUCTORS: SELECT FROM ALL SEVEN PAGES.

# 6. NEW EXPERIENCES: OBSTACLES, SURFACES, SMELLS, ETC.

- [ ] **CAVALETTI**
  Have people and pups walk around the PVC caveletti "spokes" to gain body coordination and awareness.

- [ ] **PEEL AN ORANGE**
  . . . or open a bottle of vanilla or peppermint extract, let the pup sniff it.

- [ ] **WALK THROUGH LADDER**
  Put a ladder down flat on the floor. Let the puppy investigate and then coax him to walk through it. If he hesitates, put him between rungs and let him walk out.

- [ ] **WAGON RIDE**
  Sit pup in the wagon, owner on one side, instructor on the other, and roll it a few inches.

- [ ] **OVEN GRATES**
  Get pup to walk over grates or put him in the middle of the grate and let him walk out of it.

- [ ] **BATHROOM SCALE**
  Pup watches owner get on, then it's his turn.

- [ ] **SHORT TUNNEL OR CARDBOARD BOX TUNNEL**
  Instructor holds pup while owner goes to other end and calls pup through tunnel.

- [ ] **JUMP**
  Put a four-inch board across a door opening, Mom steps over and then entices pup to join her.

- [ ] **SMELLY MOP**
  Pour cleaning agent on a mop. Let pups sniff and see the mop move.

- [ ] **SKATEBOARD RIDING**
  Let pups see it roll. Turn it over and spin the wheels. Get pup to stand on it, wheels up so it can't roll. Turn it over and see if pup will put two feet on it and move it a little.

- [ ] **LARGE PLASTIC GARBAGE BAG TAPED TO FLOOR**
  Encourage pup to walk over it and sit on it.

- [ ] **UP AND DOWN STEPS**
  Owner goes up steps with puppy. If pup balks, put him on bottom step and let him step off.

- [ ] **SMALL HULA HOOP**
  Instructor holds it while owner gets pup to walk through.

- [ ] **WOBBLE BOARD**
  Encourage pups one at a time to step on wobble board and make it move, for balance and confidence building.

**LEGACY PUPPY HEADSTART MENU. INSTRUCTORS: SELECT FROM ALL SEVEN PAGES.**

# 7. NEW EXPERIENCES: SIGHTS, SOUNDS, TOUCH, MOTION, ETC.

- ❏ **EXPLORE VARIOUS WIND-UP TOYS**
  Take turns visiting 3–4 moving wind-up toys in separate areas of the room.

- ❏ **BACKGROUND MUSIC**
  Instrumentals, march, opera, rap . . . fireworks, cars racing . . . Play during class . . .

- ❏ **OWNERS CHOOSE A HAND PUPPET FROM THE BOX**
  Owners let pup smell it, see it, and then pet pup with puppet and play with him.

- ❏ **CLICKER**
  Instructor clicks, puppy gets food from family members.

- ❏ **BIG BALLS**
  Instructor kicks a soccer ball or rolls a giant beach ball. Be sure ball doesn't hit the dog!

- ❏ **DOORBELL, BUZZER, CHIME, HONK, KNOCK**
  Instructor operates, owners focus dog, keeping them calm and quiet.

- ❏ **TOY ACCORDION, VIOLIN, DRUM, ETC.**
  Each owner selects one. Introduce slowly before instructor conducts the orchestra.

- ❏ **SHUFFLE A DECK of CARDS**
  At a distance and then up close so puppies can investigate.

- ❏ **PUT YOUR HEAD IN DIFFERENT BOXES FOR A TREAT**
  Big enough so pup won't get stuck. She dips head in to get a treat off the bottom of box.

- ❏ **UMBRELLAS**
  At first folded, then open. If puppy is brave, slowly open an umbrella as pup watches.

- ❏ **FLEXI-LEAD**
  Experience walking on a noisy retractable leash.

- ❏ **DROPPED ITEMS**
  Drop a bag of empty cans or a book, being sure not to frighten the puppy.

- ❏ **INSTRUCTOR RIDES BY ON SKATEBOARD**
  Not too close!

- ❏ **CLEANING MACHINE**
  Operate the machine on the other side of the training room.

# RANDOM WORD LIST

| | | | | | |
|---|---|---|---|---|---|
| 1 | BIRD | 2 | COLOR | 3 | WATER |
| 4 | TABLE | 5 | JET | 6 | COW |
| 7 | PEN | 8 | MOTOR | 9 | SILVER |
| 10 | TREE | 11 | RING | 12 | DIRT |
| 13 | PAPER | 14 | RUN | 15 | LETTER |
| 16 | DISH | 17 | PARK | 18 | WOOL |
| 19 | SHIRT | 20 | RIBBON | 21 | NAIL |
| 22 | WOOD | 23 | LEAF | 24 | PLATE |
| 25 | SAND | 26 | WALL | 27 | FLOWER |
| 28 | CARROT | 29 | WALLET | 30 | IRON |
| 31 | BRUSH | 32 | TIE | 33 | APPLE |
| 34 | FLOOR | 35 | ROOF | 36 | ORANGE |
| 37 | FISH | 38 | SPOON | 39 | MOOSE |
| 40 | HAMMER | 41 | MAN | 42 | TEENAGER |
| 43 | TV | 44 | GRASS | 45 | HOT |
| 46 | ISLAND | 47 | ROSE | 48 | STAR |
| 49 | GIVE | 50 | CUP | 51 | JUMP |
| 52 | OIL | 53 | DRIVE | 54 | MONEY |
| 55 | WATER | 56 | STIR | 57 | MONKEY |
| 58 | JUICE | 59 | PLANE | 60 | BABY |

# Six Hats: Lateral Thinking for Dog Training

## WHITE HAT
FACTS OBTAINED, NEEDED
NEUTRAL, OBJECTIVE

## RED HAT
EMOTIONS, HUNCHES
IMPRESSIONS, OPINION

## BLACK HAT
LOGICAL-NEGATIVE
STUCK ON USUAL WAY
CRITICAL, PESSIMISTIC

## YELLOW HAT
LOGICAL-POSITIVE
FOCUS ON BENEFITS
BRIGHT, SPECULATIVE, OPTIMISTIC

## GREEN HAT
CREATIVE, CHANGE
NEW ALTERNATIVES

## BLUE HAT
DEFINE & SUMMARIZE
PLAN THE PROGRAM

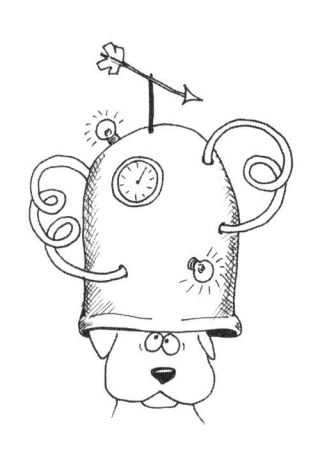

Art and Summary © Terry Ryan, 1996
Six Hats Concept is Dr. Edward de Bono's

# STUDENT PROFILE FORM

**LEGACY** Canine Behavior & Training

---

Office will fill out blanks in THIS box:

**Class** _____     **Attendance:**  1  2  3  4  5  6  7

Shots.........Tuition.........Video.........GL

Handout Follow Up _____    Notes _____

---

Your Name _____    Dog's Name _____

Dog's Breed Type _____    Dog's Age _____    Dog's Sex  M / F

Your Address _____    Zip _____

Your Phone—Day _____    Night _____    E-mail _____

Your Vet's Name _____    Has your dog been neutered? Y / N    When? _____

Does your dog have physical limitations/medical problems?  Y / N    What? _____

Is the dog on medication now?  Y / N    What? _____

Do YOU have a physical limitation we should allow for in class or homework?  Y / N    What? _____

List other family members including pets _____

Dog was acquired from (circle):   PET SHOP   SHELTER   BREEDER   OTHER _____

Age of dog when acquired _____    How long have you had this dog? _____

Have you attended an obedience class before with any dog?  When/Where: _____

What did you like most about that class? _____

What do you want to accomplish in this class?  1. _____  2. _____  3. _____

Approx. % of time dog is:   Inside ____%   Outside ____%   Without humans ____%   Tied ____%

About how many minutes per day do you: Walk your dog on leash—____ mins.  Play with your dog—____ mins.

Dog can have a focusing toy in class. (Circle flavors permitted)    PEANUT BUTTER    CHEESE    LIVER

(OVER)

---

MISC StudentProfileForm.doc    *Coaching People to Train Their Dogs* © Terry Ryan 2005    385

If you've had previous dogs: What did you **like** about them? _____

What did you **like least** about them? _____

What do you **like best** about THIS dog? _____

What **concerns you most** about your relationship with THIS dog? _____

Rank 5 of your dog's favorite:

| | Food Treats | Toys | Interactions with You |
|---|---|---|---|
| (1) | | | |
| (2) | | | |
| (3) | | | |
| (4) | | | |
| (5) | | | |

What is your dog's regular food? _____

What times are your dog's meals? _____

*Circle anything that applies to your dog:*

| | | | |
|---|---|---|---|
| GROWLS | SHY | FEARFUL | GUARDS FOOD/TOYS |
| PUSHY | BITES | DESTRUCTIVE | WON'T LISTEN TO ME |
| EXCESSIVE ENERGY | DOMINANT | AGGRESSIVE | NOISY |
| TOO ATTACHED TO ME | MOUTHY | NOT GOOD WITH PEOPLE | NOT GOOD WITH DOGS |
| OTHER _____ | OTHER _____ | OTHER _____ | OTHER _____ |

*Briefly explain anything you have circled:*




PLEASE READ AND SIGN THE FOLLOWING

(THIS IS WHERE THE HOLD HARMLESS AGREEMENT AND PHOTO RELEASE STATEMENTS APPEAR. ASK YOUR OWN LAWYER FOR ADVICE)


_____                    _____
Signature                                          Date

# Tape & Towel

We are looking forward to having you in a class! You have indicated that your dog might be a bit apprehensive about the classroom environment. To help your dog be more comfortable with the strange environment, we suggest that you "tape and towel" your pet this week!

## THE TAPE! IT SOUNDS LIKE DOG CLASS!

We have loaned you an audio cassette or CD that was recorded during our Pet Dog Manner's classes. The sounds are typical noises you and your dog will hear in class. Instructors will be encouraging their students, students will be asking questions, there will be some barking, and some dogs will be making noises as if to say "It's my turn!" You will hear squeaky toys, people saying "YES" and folks praising their dogs. Since we play music in class, you will hear that too.

## THE TOWEL! IT SMELLS LIKE DOG CLASS!

The towel or mat we have given you has been sitting on the shelf in our training building for a while. Even though it is clean, it smells like class! Well, at least your dog will be able to smell it. A dogs' sense of smell is more acute than ours. For example, if your dog could talk, he'd be able to tell you which neighbor walked by your sidewalk yesterday!

## THE HOMEWORK! IT'S EASY!

Play the audio cassette or CD for your dog at a low volume during a time he or she is calm anyway. Before bed or during a meal are examples. Don't make a big issue of it, just turn it on low and go about your business. Your dog will probably orient toward and then ignore the sound. That's good. He hears it and considers it a "ho-hum" sound. Turn it up a bit, or play it in a different room, or play it in the car if your dog enjoys going for car rides.

Place the towel under his water bowl as a placemat or even in his bed. He'll probably sniff it over and eventually decide it's just a part of his environment. That's also good. Your dog will have a head start being familiar with class via two different senses.

# PUPPY
# FLOWER
# BUTTERFLY

# STAND STILL, LIKE A POST

# PLEASE DON'T BOTHER ME WHEN I'M CHEWING

# Index

**A**

Adenovirus vaccination, 88
Aggressive behaviors
    agonistic reaction and, 42–43
    alpha roll-over technique and, 28–29
    biting, 42, 44–45, 47–48
    classroom management and, 46–47, 187
    critical zone issues and, 34–35
    defensive threats/aggression, 43–44
    dominance assertion, 45
    fear-motivated aggression, 44–45
    neutering/spaying and, 24
    offensive threats/aggression, 43
    pack-facilitated aggression, 46
    pain-related aggression, 45
    possessive aggression, 45
    predatory behavior and, 46
    protective aggression, 45
    redirected aggression, 46
    territorial aggression, 45
    triggers/rationale for, 44–46
    *See also* Emotional health; Remodeling behaviors
Aging
    chronic pain, 96
    cognitive dysfunction syndrome, 95
    malaise, 96
Agonistic behaviors, 41
    aggression threats/aggression, 42–43
    anxiety, 90, 96
    appeasement, 41
    avoidance, 41
    conflicted threat/aggression and, 44
    defensive threat/aggression and, 43–44
    offensive threat/aggression and, 43
    submission, 41–42
    triggers/rationale for, 44–46
Allergic reactions, 90
Alpha roll-over technique, 27–29

American Animal Hospital Association Vaccine Guidelines, 89
American Board of Veterinary Behaviorists, 98
American Humane Association, 10
American Sign Language (ASL), 185
American Veterinary Medical Association, 98
American Veterinary Society of Animal Behavior, 98
Anemia, 90
Animal-Assisted Activities (AAA), 5
Animal-Assisted Therapy (AAT), 5
Animal Behavior Enterprises (ABE), 55
Animal Behavior Society, 98
Animal Fanciers School, 9
Animal shelters, 88
Anthropomorphism, 14, 31
Anxiety. *See* Agonistic behaviors; Fear responses; Stress behaviors
Appeasement behaviors, 30, 41
Association of Pet Dog Trainers (APDT), 10, 11, 97
Aversives. *See* Punishment
Avoidance behaviors, 41, 56

**B**

Bailey, Bob, 64, 67
Barking, 29–30, 107
Behavior education, 97, 98
Behavior issues, 88
    aging effects and, 95–96
    bite response, 90
    emotional condition and, 96, 98
    medical conditions and, 93–95, 98
    medication effects, 95
    psychotropic medications and, 96–97, 98
    thyroid, role of, 95
    *See also* Medical conditions; Training
Behavioral disorders. *See* Emotional health; Remodeling behaviors
Behavioral traits
    drive-based training, 21–22

Index 395

Behavioral traits *(continued)*
    fixed action patterns, 20
    food acquisition sequence, 19
    instinctive drift principle/Breland effect, 21–22
    neoteny and, 17
    ontogenetic behaviors, 20
    phylogenetic behaviors, 19
    predatory behavior, 18
    temperament, nature/nurture synergism and, 20–21
    *See also* Biology of learning; Language of dogs; Learning theory; Social hierarchy; Stress behaviors
Behavior analysis, 72
    backward chaining, 77
    behavior acquisition and, 73
    catching behaviors, 75
    chaining behaviors, 76–77
    luring/fading lures and, 74
    physical modeling, 73
    shaping behavior, 75–76
    target training, 74–75
    *See also* Cueing behaviors; Learning theory; Remodeling behaviors; Stress behaviors
Behavior training. *See* Behavior analysis; Dog training; Instructors; Remodeling behaviors
Belyaev, Dmitry, 16, 17
Biological factors
    ancestral lineage, 14–15
    fear reactions, 37
    neoteny, morphology/behavior and, 17
    *See also* Behavioral traits; Biology of learning
Biology of learning
    brain-behavior relationship, 24
    critical windows of learning and, 22–23
    engrams/muscle memory, 24–25
    limbic system/cerebral cortex, coordination of, 25–26
    opposition reflex, 26, 158
    puberty/hormones and, 23–24
    reticular activation system, 25
    vomeronasal organ and, 32
Bite response, 90
Biting
    classification of, 47–48
    fear-biting, 44–45
    management of, 47
    threats of, 42

Body language. *See* Language of dogs
Booster vaccinations, 88, 89
Booth, Sheila, 21
Bordatella vaccination, 89
Brain function. *See* Biology of learning
Breeders
    schooling opportunities and, 87–88
    socialization process and, 87
    *See also* Training
Breeding
    purposeful domestication, 16–17
    scent of receptivity, 30
Breland effect, 21
Business management, 112
    advertising planning, 118–119
    business expense classification, 117
    business plan, 113–114
    business set-up, 112
    ethics/professional limitations, 115
    fee structures, 116
    first-contact information, 120
    food handling regulations, 114–115
    instructor attributes and, 130–133
    insurance, 115–116
    legal matters, 114–115, 118
    payment plans, 116–117
    record keeping needs, 116, 127
    refund policy, 117
    registration procedures, 120
    safety issues, 117–118
    staff compensation, 117
    training site specifics, 121–126
Bustad, Dr. Leo K., 4

## C

Calming signals, 39–41
Canine Good Citizen Association, 8, 9
Certification
    pet dog trainer certification, 10
    visitation handlers and, 5
Certification Council for Pet Dog Trainers (CCPDT), 97
Certification of trainers, 97–98
Certified Applied Animal Behaviorists (CAAB), 98
Certified Pet Dog Trainers (CPDT), 97
Chinese wisdom puzzle, 174–177
Chronic pain, 96
Classical conditioning, 55–56
    counter conditioning, 232

disadvantage of, 56
emotional response, 56–57
extinction and, 62–63
Class organization, 182
   acting out, offensive/defensive behaviors, 184
   associate instructors and, 188–190
   blind/deaf dogs and, 185–186
   continuing education classes, 206–210
   disabled dogs and, 184–186
   dog fights, prevention methods, 187
   dog participants, 183–187
   fearful dogs, 183–184
   female dogs in estrus, 186
   homework assignment format, 205
   human participants, 183
   individual exercises, instructional formatting and, 199–202
   KinderPuppy class, 198
   last class options, 213–214
   moving exercises, traffic control and, 203–205
   orientation class and, 191–194
   Pet Dog Manners class, 198–199
   puppy classes, 196–199
   Puppy HeadStart classes, 197–198
   safe-refuge site and, 185
   single household, two handlers/two dogs and, 187
   special event planning, 211–213
   stationary exercises, traffic control and, 202–203
   training methods, selection considerations, 195
   *See also* Remodeling behaviors
Clever Hans, 30–31, 185
Cognitive dysfunction syndrome (CDS), 95
Collars. *See* Training equipment
Communication. *See* Demonstration methods; Instructors; Language of dogs; Visual aids
Companion Animal Partnership Program (CAP), 4
Compulsion method, 9
Conditioning. *See* Classical conditioning; Learning theory; Operant conditioning
Conflict resolution. *See* Agonistic behaviors
Congenital abnormalities, 94
Continuing education classes, 206–210
Coppinger, Dr. Raymond, 19, 21, 23, 29
Coppinger, Lorna, 23
Coyotes, 15
Critical zone issues, 34–35

Cueing behaviors, 78
   cue introduction, 78–79
   environmental cues and, 79
   overshadowing/blocking, salience and, 79–80
   stimuli packages and, 79
   stimulus control, discrimination/generalization and, 80–81
   superstitious behavior/coincidental learning, 81–82
Curriculum development
   elementary classroom, 4
   pet classes, community needs and, 6
   *See also* Class organization; Remodeling behaviors
Cushing's disease, 95

## D

Deaf Dog Education Action Fund, 185–186
Death, 4, 147–149
De Bono, Edward, 150
Defensive behaviors, 19, 21, 43–44, 45, 184
The Delta Society, 4, 5, 10, 11, 149, 223
Demonstration methods, 154
   dog-based demonstrations, 154–156
   opposition reflex principle and, 158
   owner-based demonstrations, 157–158
   prop-based demonstrations, 156–157
   puppets/toys and, 156
   test/punish vs. lure/reward and, 158–159
   training game/interactive exercise, 159–160
D.I.N.G.O. (Dog Instructors' Network of Great Opportunity), 10, 11
Disabilities. *See* Class organization; Delta Society; Therapeutic animal partnerships
Disabled handlers, 166–167
Disease prevention, 88
   disease incidence, 88
   environmental hygiene and, 90
   infectious diseases, 88–89, 90
   kennel cough complex, 89, 90
   parasites, 89–90
   spaying/neutering procedures and, 93
   vaccination programs, 88–89
   *See also* Medical conditions; Veterinary care
Displacement behavior, 38
Distemper vaccination, 88, 89
Dog appeasing pheromones (DAP), 30
Dog Instructors' Network of Great Opportunity (D.I.N.G.O.), 10, 11

Dogs, 14
    ancestral lineage of, 14–15
    cognition in, 17
    early humans, contact with, 15–16
    humans, comparison with, 14
    neoteny in, 17, 18
    selective breeding and, 16–17, 18
    social hierarchy and, 26–29
    temperament, nature/nurture synergism and, 20–21
    wolf-dog hybrids, 18
    wolf-human symbiosis, 16
    wolves, comparison with, 17–18
    See also Behavioral traits; Biology of learning
Dog training, 6–7
    approaches to, 7–8
    community needs and, 6
    compulsion method, 9
    drive-based programs, 21–22
    evolution of, 9
    music and, 124, 168–169
    phylogenetic behaviors and, 19
    reward-based method, 7, 8
    societal impact of, 6–7
    standards for, 10
    wolf-dog hybrids and, 18
    See also Biology of learning; Class organization; Instructors; Language of dogs; Learning theory; Training equipment; Training site
Domestication process, 15
    cognitive processes and, 17
    dispersed wolves, symbiosis and, 16
    early humans and, 15–16
    neoteny and, 17
    proto-dogs, natural selection and, 16
    selective breeding and, 16–17, 18
    taming process and, 18
Dominance hierarchy, 26–29, 45
Drive-based training, 21–22
Dunbar, Dr. Ian, 47–48

## E

Educational programs, 4, 5
    global developments in, 8, 9, 10
    national instructor organizations, 10
    on-line courses, 10
    See also Class organization; Dog training; Human students; Instructors
Electronic training devices, 107, 108

Emergency preparedness, 90
Emotional issues, 96, 98
Environmental factors
    behaviorists, ethological perspective and, 97
    environmental hygiene, 90
    fecal soiling, clean-up of, 90
    kennel cough complex and, 89, 90
    novel stimuli, 87
    social experiences, 87
    See also Disease prevention
Epilepsy, 94
Estep, Dr. Dan, 22
Ethological studies, 17, 20
Euthanasia, 4
Extinction, 62–63
    extinction burst, 63
    negative punishment and, 64
    reward removal, 229–230
    spontaneous recovery and, 63–64

## F

Fear responses, 19, 23, 26, 37, 90, 96
    classroom situation and, 183–184
    conditioned emotional response and, 56–57
    fear-biting, 44–45
    submissive gestures, 41–42
    See also Stress behaviors
First aid, 90
    are you prepared, 118
    blind dogs and, 186
    Good Samaritan Statute, 118
    See also Veterinary care
Fleas, 90
Flight response, 18, 34
Food acquisition behaviors, 18, 19, 21, 46

## G

Gastrointestinal parasites, 89
Gentle Leader head collar, 101–103
Gentle Leader Easy Walk harness, 104
Goodmann, Pat, 21, 28–29
Good Samaritan Statute, 118
Gray wolves, 15
Grief experience, 4, 147–149

## H

Hackles, 33, 43
Hazard avoidance behaviors, 19, 23
H.E.L.M. methodology, 225–226

Health care. *See* Disease prevention; Medical conditions; Veterinary care
Hearing, 29–30
Heartworms, 89
Hepatic encephalopathy, 94
Hepatitis vaccination, 89
Hierarchies, 26–29
Hines, Linda, 4, 5
Homework assignments, 205
Hookworms, 89
Hormonal influences, 23–24, 30, 186
Housetraining, 94, 95
Human-animal bond, 3
    global interest in, 6, 9
    instructor responsibility and, 3–4
    supportive programs for, 4–5
    *See also* Dog training
Humane training standards, 10
Human health care, 4, 5
Human students
    absence from class and, 170–171
    children, accommodations for, 164–166
    disabilities and, 166–167
    left/right brain paradigm and, 140–142
    personality differences and, 149
    problem behaviors of, 146–147
    Six Thinking Hats method and, 150–153
    verbal communication, roadblocks to, 135–140
    *See also* Instructors
Hybrids, 18
Hydrocephalus, 93–94
Hypoglycemia, 94–95
Hypothyroidism, 95

## I

Impulse control, 37
Infectious canine tracheobronchitis, 89, 90
Infectious diseases, 88–89, 90
Instinctive drift principle, 21–22
Instructors, 130
    active student participation, 163–167
    auditory learning and, 134–135
    change, experience of, 173–174
    children, accommodations for, 164–166
    Chinese wisdom puzzle, teaching skills and, 174–177
    comprehension cross-checks, 138
    cross-over instructors, 9
    demonstration methods, 154–159

    disabled handlers, 166–167
    evaluation formats, 171–172
    human-animal bond and, 3–4
    impartiality and, 169–170
    international developments and, 8, 9, 10
    learning styles and, 133, 140–142
    listening skills and, 143–145
    music for communication and, 124, 168–169
    name memory and, 169
    national organizations for, 10
    positive attributes of, 130–133
    positive vs. negative instructions, 143, 145
    private lessons, 172–173
    Six Thinking Hats method and, 150–153
    student absence and, 170–171
    telephone instruction, 137–138
    training game/interactive exercise, 159–160
    training instructors, 177, 188–190
    verbal communication, roadblocks to, 135–140
    visual aids, 161–163
    *See also* Class organization; Dog training; Human students
International Association of Animal Behavior Consultants (IAABC), 97
International Association of Human-Animal Interaction Organizations (IAHAIO), 6, 11
International training opportunities, 8, 9, 10
Internet resources:
    professional/certifying organizations, 97–98

## J

Jacobson's organ, 32
Japanese Animal Hospital Association, 9

## K

Kennel cough complex, 89, 90
KinderPuppy class, 198
Klinghammer, Dr. Erich, 17, 18, 21, 27–28

## L

Language of dogs, 29
    agonistic behaviors, 41–46
    anthropomorphizing and, 31
    baseline posture, 33
    bow posture, 33
    critical zones, personal space and, 34–35
    curving behavior, 33
    defensive threat/aggression, 43–44
    ear positions, 31

Language of dogs (continued)
    escape-intention actions, 39
    eye contact, 31–32
    facial elements, 32
    holistic approach to, 31
    offensive threat/aggression, 43
    raised hackles, 33
    sight, 30–31
    smells, 30, 32
    sounds, 29–30
    stress behaviors, 35–41
    tail wag, 32
    *See also* Aggressive behaviors
Lateral thinking styles, 150–153
Law of Effect, 57
Law of Parsimony, 218–219
Learning theory, 54–55
    antecedent-behavior-consequence relationship and, 58
    classical conditioning, 55–57
    cueing behaviors, 78–82
    extinction and, 62–64
    Law of Effect and, 57
    operant conditioning, 21, 57, 58–61
    reinforcement-punishment interactions, 58–61
    *See also* Behavior analysis; Biology of learning; Human students; Reinforcement; Remodeling behaviors; Social hierarchy
Leptospirosis vaccination, 89
Limbic response, 25–26, 46
Lindsay, Steven, 23
Lorenz, Konrad, 15, 20
Lyme's disease vaccination, 89

## M

Malaise, 96
McCort, Ken, 28
McCulloch, Michael, 5
Medical conditions, 93, 98
    aging issues, 95–96
    breed-related health concerns, 91, 94, 95
    congenital abnormalities, 94
    Cushing's disease, 95
    diabetes, 95
    epilepsy/psychomotor seizures, 94
    hepatic encephalopathy, 94
    hormonal diseases, 95
    hydrocephalus, 93–94
    hypoglycemia, 94–95
    hypothyroidism, 95
    insulin-secreting tumors, 95
    involuntary voiding, 94
    metabolic disorders, 94–95
    portosystemic shunt and, 94
    *See also* Disease prevention; Training; Veterinary care
Metabolic disorders, 94–95
Modeling, 6–7, 73
Morphological traits, 17
Music messaging, 124, 168–169

## N

National Association of Dog Obedience Instructors (NADOI), 10, 11, 97, 196
Nature/nurture synergism, 20–21
Neoteny, 17, 18
Neutering, 24
    procedure, 91, 93
North American Wildlife Park Foundation, 17
Novel stimuli, 87
Nursing home visitation, 4

## O

Offensive behaviors, 43, 184
O'Heare, James, 25
Operant conditioning, 21, 57
    antecedent-behavior-consequence relationship and, 58
    counter conditioning, 232
    extinction and, 62–63
    reinforcement-punishment interactions, 58–61
Opposition reflex, 26, 158
Orientation class, 191–192
    materials notebook and, 193
    schedule format decisions and, 193–194
    topics in, 192–193
    *See also* Class organization
Owner education. *See* Class organization; Human students; Instructors
Owners
    disease prevention and, 88, 89, 95
    handling errors, 93
    medical problems, diagnosis/treatment of, 96
    *See also* Puppies; Training

## P

Pack-facilitated aggression, 46
Pain, 96

Pain-related aggression, 45
Parasites, 89
    allergic skin reactions and, 90
    anemia and, 90
    external parasites, 90
    gastrointestinal parasites, 89
    heartworms, 89
    hypoglycemia and, 95
Parent Effectiveness Training (PET), 132, 143–145
Partnership in Equine Therapy and Education (PETE), 4
Parvovirus vaccination, 88, 89, 90
Pavlov, Ivan Petrovich, 55
People-Pet Partnership (PPP), 4
Personal space issues, 34–35
Pet Dog Manners (PDM), 198–199
Pet Education Partnership Program (PEP), 4
Pet-facilitated therapy, 5
Pet Loss, 4, 147–149
Pet Loss Partnership (PLP), 4
PetsMart, 9
Pheromones, 30
Physical modeling, 73
Piloerection, 33, 43
Portosystemic shunts, 94
Positive reinforcement, 7, 8, 57
Possessive aggression, 45
Postural behaviors. *See* Language of dogs
Predatory behavior, 18, 46
Premack principle, 77
Prescription pets, 4, 5
Preventive health programs. *See* Disease prevention; Veterinary care
Prison Pet Partnership (PPP), 4
Private lessons, 172–173
Professional organizations, 97–98
Protective aggression, 45
Proto-dogs, 16
Psychotropic medications, 95, 96–97, 98
Punishment, 57, 59
    extinction and, 64
    negative punishment, 61
    positive punishment, 60
    remodeling behaviors and, 224
Puppies, 87
    behavior problems and, 88
    class participation for, 87–88
    environmental hygiene and, 90
    infectious diseases among, 88–89
    maternal antibodies and, 88, 89
    socialization of, 87, 88
    spaying/neutering procedures and, 91, 93
    vaccinations for, 88–89
    windows of opportunity and, 87
    *See also* Disease prevention; Medical conditions; Socialization process; Training
Puppy HeadStart, 197–198

## Q
Quinn, Sister Pauline, 4

## R
Rabies vaccination, 89
Raised hackles, 33, 43
Reinforcement, 57, 58–59
    clicker training, 71, 72
    continuous schedule of, 68
    criteria selection and, 66–67
    desirable/undesirable outcomes and, 61, 67
    differential reinforcement, 69
    food as reinforcer, 65, 78
    jackpot principle and, 70
    limited hold reinforcement, 69
    negative reinforcement, 60–61
    positive reinforcement, 61
    Premack principle and, 77
    primary reinforcer in, 65–70
    random reinforcement, 68–69
    rate of, 67
    schedules of, 68–70
    secondary reinforcers, 70–72
    timing of reinforcer, 66
    value of, 67
    variable schedules of, 68–70
    word reinforcers, 71–72
    *See also* Behavior analysis; Learning theory; Remodeling behaviors
Remodeling behaviors, 218
    creative problem-solving and, 219
    documentation and, 219–220
    goal-setting and, 222–223
    harm principle and, 218
    H.E.L.M. methodology, 225–226
    instructional format, build-a-house metaphor and, 221
    Law of Parsimony and, 218–219
    punishment/aversives and, 224
    simplicity, rule of, 219

Remodeling behaviors *(continued)*
    training programs, dimensions in, 225
    Y.E.S. T.R.A.I.N. tools for, 227–233
    *See also* Behavior analysis
Reproductive behaviors, 19, 21
Reward-based method, 7, 8
    criteria selection in, 66
    incompatible behaviors and, 230
    no-reward marker and, 64, 229–230
    permanent criteria and, 67
    rewards, selection of, 106–107
    temporary criteria and, 66–67
    *See also* Reinforcement; Remodeling behaviors
Roundworms, 89
Rugaas, Turid, 39

## S

Scent signals, 30
Schooling. *See* Training
Schwartz, Dr. Stefanie, 24
Seizure activity, 94, 95
Shaping skills, 75–76, 159–160
Shelters, 88
Six Thinking Hats method, 150
    black hat style, 151
    blue hat style, 153
    green hat style, 152–153
    red hat style, 151
    white hat style, 150
    yellow hat style, 152
Skin lesions, 90
Skinner, Dr. Burrhus Friedrich, 21, 55, 57, 133
Smell, 30, 32
Social conflict. *See* Agonistic behaviors
Social experiences, 87
Social hierarchy, 26–27
    alpha roll-over technique and, 27–29
    dominant/subordinate ranking and, 27
Socialization process, 87
    infections during, 88
    restrictions on, 87–88
    schooling for, 87–88
    *See also* Training
Spaying, 24, 91, 93
Standards for training, 10
Stress behaviors, 26, 35–36
    ambivalence, 38
    calming signals and, 39–41
    displacement behavior, 38
    escape-intention actions and, 39
    excitable/reactive behavior, 37
    fearful behavior, 37
    impulse control and, 37
    interpretation/intervention and, 38–39
    signs of stress, 36
    *See also* Agonistic behaviors; Remodeling behaviors
Submission, 41–42

## T

Tail wag, 32
Taming process, 18
    *See also* Dogs; Domestication process
Tapeworms, 90
Target training, 74–75
Teacher Effectiveness Training (TET), 143–145
Teaching. *See* Dog training; Human students; Instructors
Temperament
    nature/nurture synergism and, 20–21
    *See also* Biology of learning
Territorial aggression, 45
Therapeutic animal partnerships, 4, 5
Thigmotaxis, 26
Thorndike, Edward, 57
Threats. *See* Aggressive behaviors; Agonistic behaviors; Stress behaviors
Ticks, 90
Tinbergen, Nikolaas, 20, 39
Training, 87–88
    aging, issues of, 95–96
    certification/professional organizations, 97–98
    chronic pain and, 96
    emotional issues and, 96
    environmental hygiene and, 90
    first aid/emergencies and, 90
    food rewards and, 91
    housetraining, 94, 95
    inappropriate behaviors, 88
    infections during, 88, 90
    medical conditions, behavioral outcomes and, 93–95, 96
    medication effects and, 95

psychotropic medications and, 96–97, 98
veterinarians, partnerships with, 96, 97
windows of opportunity, 87
See also Behavior issues; Biology of learning; Class organization; Dog training; Instructors; Learning theory; Remodeling behaviors; Socialization process; Veterinary care

Training equipment, 183
belt-type collar, 100
body harness, 105
break-away safety collar, 104
choke-chain collar, 105
collar types, 100–105
crate training, 107
electronic fencing systems, 108
electronic training devices, 107
equipment policy, 99
Gentle Leader head collar, 101–103
Gentle Leader Easy Walk harness, 104
leashes, 105–106
limited-slip collar, 100
long line, 106
pinch collar, 105
retractable leash, 106
rewards, selection of, 106–107
training leash, 106

Training site, 183
acoustic qualities and, 124
flooring and, 123
furnishings for, 124–125
public address system and, 142
restroom availability, 122
selection criteria, 121
signage and, 123
size considerations, 122
supplies for, 125–126
trash receptacles and, 123
wait/stash area, 126
water sources and, 122

## V

Vaccination programs, 87, 88
booster shots, 88, 89
complete series, importance of, 89
core vaccinations, 88, 89
guidelines for, 89
infectious diseases and, 88–89, 90
non-core vaccinations, 89
See also Disease prevention; Veterinary care

Veterinary care
aging issues, 95–96
anticonvulsant therapy, 94
behavior education and, 97, 98
body condition guidelines, 91, 92
breed-related health concerns, 91, 94, 95
emergency protocols, instruction on, 90
feeding schedules, manipulation of, 91
first aid, 90, 118
hepatic dysfunction, 94
medical conditions, behavioral outcomes and, 93–95
medication effects, 95
obesity problems, 91
physical examinations, 87, 91, 96
psychotropic medications, 95, 96–97, 98
spaying/neutering procedures, 91, 93
trainers, partnerships with, 96, 97
vaccination programs, 87, 88–89
wellness programs, 87–88, 91
See also Breeders; Disease prevention; Medical conditions; Puppies

Violence
training programs and, 6–7
See also Aggressive behaviors

Vision, 30–31

Visiting pet program, 4, 5

Visual aids
bulletin boards, 162
handouts, 162–163
motivational messages, 161
post-its/plastic write-erase sheets, 162
slides/PowerPoint/overhead projectors, 161
spontaneous white board visuals, 161–162
videos, 160–161
See also Demonstration methods

Vomeronasal organ, 32

## W

Wellness. See Disease prevention; Medical conditions; Veterinary care

Wisdom puzzle, 174–177

Wolf Park, 17, 18, 27

Wolves, 15
dispersing wolves, symbiosis and, 16
dogs, comparison with, 17–18

Wolves *(continued)*
    dog-wolf hybrids, 18
    ethological studies of, 17
    neoteny and, 17, 18
    proto-dogs, natural selection and, 16
    *See also* Social hierarchy

## Y

Y.E.S. T.R.A.I.N. tools, 227
    acclimation/habituation, 231
    eliminating triggers, 228
    improving association/counter conditioning, 231–232
    nasty stuff, minimization of, 232–233
    rewards, incompatible behaviors and, 230
    systematic desensitization, 228–229
    taking rewards away/extinction, 229–230
    yielding selectively, 227

## Z

Zimen, Erik, 27
Zink, Dr. Christine, 24

# About the Author

Terry Ryan's enduring area of interest is in pet dogs and their people. A busy national and international workshop presenter herself, Terry also hosts camps and seminars taught by well-known dog experts from around the world. Her business, Legacy Canine Behavior and Training, Inc., founded in 1975, conducts a wide variety of community pet dog classes.

From 1981 until 1994, Terry was the program coordinator for Leo Bustad, then dean of the Washington State University's College of Veterinary Medicine and founder of the People-Pet Partnership, an organization active in the human-animal bond. She has maintained membership and held various offices in local, national, and international organizations including past president and board member of the National Association of Dog Obedience Instructors. She is a charter member of the Association of Pet Dog Trainers and a CPDT (certified pet dog trainer). A class instructor since 1968, Terry specializes in using motivational exercises presented as games. Terry was a committee chairperson for the research and writing of *Professional Standards for Dog Trainers, Effective, Humane Principles* (Delta Society, 2001).

Starting in 1990, Terry has been spending several months each year in Japan teaching a national dog training class instructor program for the Japanese Animal Hospital Association. She also is a director of and teaches several times a year at the Animal Fanciers School in Tochigi, Japan—a residential training complex where instructors are trained and classes are taught. Terry helped create and often conducts the Japanese Canine Good Citizen testing and passport program that allows entry of qualified dogs into participating national hotels and restaurants.

From 1994 until 1998 Terry taught yearly ten-day instructors' courses for the Animal Welfare League in Australia. Terry is on the advisory board of the Institute of Ethology at the North American Wildlife Foundation at Wolf Park and for many years taught workshops there. Terry was one of the first members of the Delta Society, working on a variety of human-animal bond projects and was a Delta Pet Partners Instructor and Animal Evaluator from 1993 until 1996. Her early work with dogs included search and rescue, animal assisted activities, and a bit of service dog training. She has been training and exhibiting her own dogs in obedience, conformation, and tracking since 1966. Terry became an obedience trial judge in 1984 and is currently on emeritus status. She was a regular contributor to the training column of the *American Kennel Club Gazette* from 1995 until 2002. She is the author of a variety of publications and articles on the human-animal bond, behavior, training, and dogs in general. Her works have been published in several foreign languages as well. Most recently Terry has produced a series of desensitization CD's entitled "Sounds Good." She wrote *Leadership Education for Anyone with a Dog,* 2001, *The Bark Stops Here,* 2000, *Games People Play . . . To Train Their Dogs,* 1994, and *Life Beyond Block Heeling,* 1996, all published by LegacyCanine. In 1998 Howell, New York, published her hardcover book, *The Toolbox for Remodeling Your Problem Dog.*

In addition to offering a variety of pet dog training classes and activities at their training center in Sequim, Terry and her staff also conduct DogSense and The Instructors Course. Participants in these courses often train rats, chickens, and dogs. LegacyCanine and its branch in Asia, LegacyJapan, is continually developing materials, products, and programs to help pet dog trainers and class instructors.

Proud parents of a daughter and a son, Terry, husband Bill and their dog Brody, live on the Olympic Peninsula in Washington State.